TAFSEER OF JUZ AMMA

SURAHS An-Naba, An-Naziat, Abasa, At-Takwir,
Al-Intifar, Al-Mutaffifin, Al-Inshiqaq,
Surah Al-Burooj, Surah At-Tariq, Surah Al-Ala,
Surah AL Ghashiya, Surah Al- Fajir,Surah Al-Balad, Ash-Shams, Al-Lail, Ad-Dhuha, Al-Inshirah, At-Tin, Al-Alaq, Al-Qadr, Al-Bayyina, Al-Zalzala, Al-Adiyat, Al Qariah, At-Takathur,Al-Humaza, Al-Fil, Quraish, Al-Maun, Al-Kauther, Al-Kafiroon,An-Nasr, Al-Masadd, Al-Ikhlas, Al-Falaq, An-Nas

SERENA HUSAIN YATES

Copyright © *Serena Husain Yates*, 2025

All Rights Reserved

This book is subject to the condition that no part of this book is to be reproduced, transmitted in any form or means; electronic or mechanical, stored in a retrieval system, photocopied, recorded, scanned, or otherwise. Any of these actions require the proper written permission of the author.

Table of Contents

SURAH NABA	12
SURAH NAZIYAT	42
SURAH ABASA	68
SURAH AT-TAKWIR	90
SURAH AL-INFITAR	109
SURAH AL-MUTAFFIFIN	125
SURAH AL-MUTAFFIFIN	126
SURAH INSHIQAQ	148
SURAH AL-BUROOJ	170
SURAH AT-TARIQ	192
SURAH AL-ALA	208
SURAH AL-GHASHIYA	227
SURAH AL-FAJIR	248
SURAH BALAD	272
SURAH ASH-SHAMS	289
SURAH AL-LAIL	312
SURAH DUHA	331
SURAH INSHIRAH	347
SURAH INSHIRAH	348
SURAH TIN	358
SURAH AL-ALAQ	369
SURAH AL-QADR	382
SURAH BAYYINA	391
SURAH AL-ZALZALAH	401
SURAH AL-ADIYAT	411
SURAH AL-QARIAH	422
SURAH AT-TAKATHUR	427
SURAH ASR	438
SURAH AL-HUMAZA	448
SURAH AL-FIL	459
SURAH QURAISH	469
SURAH AL-MAUN	478
SURAH KAUTHAR	487
SURAH AL-KAFIROON	496
SURAH AN-NASR	506
SURAH AL-MASADD	516
SURAH IKLAS	526

SURAH FALAK	536
SURAH AN-NAS	546

A TRIBUTE TO YOUNG MINDS: A DEDICATION TO AARON, MUSA, KEYAAN, JASMINE, EVA AND LEYAH.

I am excited to dedicate this Book to six remarkable young souls—my grandsons, Aaron, Musa and Keyaan, and my granddaughters Jasmine, Eva and Leyah

As they embark on their journey of studying and memorising Juz Amma, their passion for learning and growth fills my heart with pride and hope.

THE GIFT OF KNOWLEDGE

Juz Amma, the 30th part of the Quran, is not just a section of scripture; it is a treasure trove of wisdom and guidance, rich with lessons that can shape character and inspire action. For Aaron, Musa, Keyaan, Jasmine, Eva and Leyah, this study is more than an academic pursuit; it is a foundation for their spiritual growth and moral development. As they delve into the meanings and teachings of the Quran and the Sunnah of Prophet Muhammad (SWS), they are not only learning about their faith but also about compassion, integrity, and the importance of community.

A Journey of Discovery

As I reflect on their journey, I am reminded of my own experiences with learning. The process of understanding scripture is akin to peeling back layers of an onion—each layer revealing deeper meanings and insights. I encourage Aaron, Musa, Keyaan, Jasmine, Eva and Leyah to embrace this journey of Quranic knowledge with open hearts and inquisitive minds. Let each verse spark questions and discussions, allowing their understanding to blossom and grow.

Inspiration in Everyday Life

In dedicating this book to Aaron, Musa, Keyaan, Jasmine, Eva and Leyah, I hope to inspire them to see the beauty of learning in every aspect of life. Knowledge is not confined to textbooks; it is present in our interactions, our experiences, and our environment. As they study Quran, I encourage them to apply the principles they learn to their daily lives to cultivate a sense of empathy and understanding towards others. By embodying the values of patience, kindness, and respect, they can create a positive impact not only in their lives but also in the lives of those around them. Each lesson learned is an opportunity to spread compassion, foster community, and build a brighter future—one thoughtful action at a time.

Aaron, Musa, Keyaan, Jasmine, Eva and Leyah I am so proud of your commitment to learning and growing in your faith.

May Allah bless you all with knowledge, wisdom and deep understanding of his words. Ameen

EXPLANATION OF WHAT THE TERM JUZ MEANS!

In Islam, the term "Juz" (plural: "Ajza") refers to a division of the Quran. The Quran is divided into 30 equal sections, known as Juz, to facilitate its recitation and memorization.

Significance of Juz

1. **Ease of Recitation:** The division allows Muslims to recite the entire Quran over the course of a month, particularly during the month of Ramadan, where it is common to recite one Juz per day.
2. **Memorization:** For those who are memorizing the Quran, the division into Juz makes it more manageable to learn smaller sections at a time.
3. **Structured Study:** The Juz system provides a structured approach to studying the Quran, allowing individuals to focus on specific sections during their study sessions.

The holy Quran consists of 30 juz and Juz amma is the last of them. It starts with Surah Naba and ends with Surah Nas It'.

Juz amma is one of the easiest juz to memorize because it includes several short surahs that are easy to recite during prayer, making it a good choice for memorization for new convertors to Islam and children alike.

Facts About Juz Amma

1. Juz Amma is the 30th and last section of the Quran. It starts with Surah An-Naba' (Chapter 78) and ends with Surah An-Nas (Chapter 114).
2. Juz Amma is relatively shorter in length compared to other sections of the Quran. It consists of 37 surahs (chapters) in total, and most of these surahs are shorter in length.
3. Juz Amma contains several well-known surahs, including Surah Al-Ikhlas (The Sincerity), Surah Al-Falaq (The Daybreak), and Surah An-Nas (Mankind). These surahs are frequently recited in daily prayers.
4. Juz Amma covers various themes and topics, including the oneness of Allah, the Day of Judgment, the consequences of actions, seeking refuge in Allah from evil, and the importance of faith and righteousness.
5. Juz Amma is considered accessible and easy to understand for both children and new learners of the Quran due to its simpler language and shorter surahs. It serves as a great starting point for beginners in their journey of Quranic study and memorization.

Why is it called Juz Amma?

The reason it's called juz amma is that the first surah in this juz (surah Al- Naba) opens 'Amma Yatasaa-aloon (what they're asking about). It's the first verse in this surah and after which this juz is called.

COMMON THEMES OF SURAHS IN JUZ AMMA

Juz Amma, which comprises the last part of the Quran (Surah An-Naba to Surah An-Nas), contains several common themes that are significant in Islamic theology and moral guidance. Below is an in-depth exploration of these themes:

1. **Day of Judgment and Accountability**

Many surahs in Juz Amma lay emphasis on the reality of the Day of Judgment. They describe the resurrection of the dead, the gathering of humanity, and the accountability each individual will face for their deeds.

For example:

- Surah An-Naba (78) discusses the signs of the Day of Resurrection and the consequences for those who disbelieved versus the rewards for the righteous.

- Surah Al-Infitar (82) also highlights the unfolding of events on that day and the registration of people's deeds.

2. **The Signs of Allah in Creation**

Several of the Surahs in this Juz encourage reflection on the natural world as a sign of Allah's existence and power. The descriptions of the heavens, the earth, and various natural phenomena serve to remind believers of Allah's greatness and sovereignty.

3. **Moral and Ethical Guidance**

Juz Amma provides moral teachings and ethical guidance, often focusing on the importance of charity, compassion, justice, and community. The surahs often call for righteous behaviour and warn against wrongdoing.
- Surah Al-Ma'un (107) highlights the importance of prayer and charity, criticizing those who neglect their religious duties and fail to help the needy.

4. **The Nature of Faith and Disbelief**

The contrast between believers and disbelievers is a recurring theme. These Surahs often reflect on the consequences of faith versus disbelief, illustrating the rewards for the faithful and the punishments for the disbelievers.

5. **Divine Mercy and Forgiveness**

These Surahs highlight Allah's mercy and the potential for forgiveness for those who repent sincerely. This theme reassures believers that no matter what their past sins are, they can always turn back to Allah and seek His forgiveness.

6. **The Importance of Prayer and Worship**

These surahs stress the significance of maintaining regular prayer (Salah) and worship as central components of a believer's life. This theme reinforces the idea that prayer is a direct link between the believer and Allah.

- Surah Al-Ma'un (107) again serves as a pertinent example, where neglecting prayers and helping the needy is criticized, highlighting the integral nature of worship in Islam.

7. Social Justice and Care for the Vulnerable

Juz Amma frequently addresses social justice issues, advocating for the rights of the poor, orphans, and those in need. This theme encourages a sense of community responsibility and compassion towards others.
- Surah Al-Balad (90) discusses the trials of life and emphasizes the importance of aiding the less fortunate as a means to attain righteousness.

8. Prophethood and Revelation

The role of prophets as messengers of Allah and the significance of divine revelation are recurring themes. These surahs often reaffirm the truth of the messages brought by the prophets and the consequences of accepting or rejecting them.

- Surah Al-Nazi'at (79) discusses the stories of past prophets and the consequences faced by those who denied their messages.

9. The Duality of Life and the Hereafter

This theme highlights the contrast between the temporary nature of worldly existence and the everlasting nature of the Hereafter. It serves to remind believers that life on earth is fleeting and that true success lies in preparation for the life to come.

Key points include:

- Temporal vs. Eternal: Many of these surahs emphasize that worldly pleasures, achievements, and material possessions are temporary and shall eventually fade away. In contrast, the rewards of the Hereafter, which include Paradise, are eternal and far more valuable. For instance, Surah Al-Naba (78) contrasts the fleeting joys of this life with the everlasting bliss of Paradise.

- Consequences of Actions: The surahs often remind believers that their actions in this life directly impact their fate in the Hereafter. Good deeds are met with rewards, while sinful actions lead to punishment. This serves as a call to live a life of righteousness, as highlighted in Surah Al-Infitar (82), where it speaks about the recording of deeds and the accountability of individuals.

- Encouragement to Prepare: Believers are encouraged to be mindful of their actions and to prepare for the Day of Judgment. This preparation involves performing good deeds, seeking forgiveness, and engaging in acts of worship. Surah Al-Mutaffifin (83) warns against dishonesty and injustice in business dealings, emphasizing that such actions can lead to severe consequences in the Hereafter.

- Reflection on Human Existence: The surahs prompt reflection on the purpose of life and the inevitability of death. They encourage believers to consider their mortality and the transience of life, thus motivating them to focus on what truly matters—faith and good deeds.

Overall, the duality of life and the Hereafter serves as a profound reminder for believers about the significance of their choices and actions in this temporary world. It encourages a balanced perspective, urging individuals to engage with the world responsibly while keeping their ultimate goal in mind: the attainment of success in the Hereafter.

Key Takeaways:

1. Prioritization of the Hereafter: Believers are reminded to prioritize their spiritual and moral responsibilities over the fleeting pleasures of this world. This perspective encourages a life of purpose and intention.
2. Encouragement of Good Deeds: The focus on good deeds is paramount, as acts of kindness, justice, and worship are viewed as investments for the Hereafter. The surahs inspire believers to engage in positive actions that will yield rewards in the afterlife.
3. Awareness of Accountability: The constant reminder of accountability reinforces the idea that individuals are responsible for their choices. This awareness cultivates a sense of moral responsibility and encourages ethical behaviour.
4. Hope and Fear Balance: The duality of life and the Hereafter also creates a balance between hope in Allah's mercy and fear of His justice. This balance is essential for maintaining a sincere and devoted approach to faith.
5. By emphasizing the duality of life, the surahs in Juz Amma guide believers to navigate life's challenges with a clear understanding of their ultimate purpose and the importance of their actions in shaping their eternal destiny. This theme resonates throughout the Quran, serving as a foundational aspect of Islamic belief and practice.

TAFSEER OF JUZ AMMA

SURAHS, An-Naziat, Abasa, At-Takwir, Al-Intifar, Al-Mutaffifin, Al-Inshiqaq, Surah Al-Burooj, Surah At-Tariq, Surah Al-Ala, Surah AL Ghashiya, Surah Al- Fajir,Surah Al-Balad, Ash-Shams, Al-Lail, Ad-Dhuha, Al-Inshirah, At-Tin, Al-Alaq, Al-Qadr, Al-Bayyina, Al-Zalzala, Al-Adiyat, Al Qariah, At-Takathur,Al-Humaza, Al-Fil, Quraish, Al-Maun, Al-Kauther, Al-Kafiroon,An-Nasr, Al-Masadd, Al-Ikhlas, Al-Falaq, An-Nas

SURAH NABA

Bismillahi ar-Rahmani ar-Raheem

TAFSEER OF SURAH NABA – 78ᵀᴴ CHAPTER OF QURAN

Why was Surah Naba revealed?

Surah An-Naba, also known as "The Tidings" or "The Announcement," is the 78th chapter of the Holy Quran. Revealed in Mecca, this surah holds profound spiritual, moral, and practical significance for Muslims, addressing the themes of resurrection, the Hereafter, and the signs of Allah's creation.

The verses of this surah are a powerful reminder of the transient nature of worldly life and the certainty of the Hereafter, encouraging believers to lead lives of righteousness and accountability. This surah offers a wealth of insights and lessons that guide and inspire the faithful in their spiritual journey.

The surah's literary style is notable for its compelling imagery and rhythmic cadence, making it particularly impactful when recited. Its eloquence and clarity has a profound effect on listeners, stirring their hearts and minds towards greater faith and contemplation.

Historical Context

Surah An-Naba is a Makki surah, revealed during the early years of the Prophet's (SAW) mission in Mecca. This period was marked by intense opposition and hostility towards the Prophet SAW as he endeavoured to convey the message of Islam to a largely pagan society entrenched in idolatry and traditional beliefs. The surah was revealed to address the scepticism and denial of the Meccan disbelievers, who often ridiculed the concept of the resurrection and the Hereafter.

In the face of such adversities, Surah An-Naba served as a compelling divine revelation that aimed to affirm the reality of the Day of Resurrection. T

he disbelievers questioned the plausibility of being resurrected after death, often mocking the idea as absurd. Surah An-Naba responds to these doubts with a powerful narrative that emphasizes the certainty of the Hereafter. It begins by posing a rhetorical question about the "great news" that people are disputing, then proceeds to describe the signs of Allah's creation as evidence of His power to resurrect.

The surah's vivid descriptions of the Day of Judgment—where the earth and mountains will tremble, the heavens will split open, and the dead will be resurrected for divine accountability—serve as a stark warning to the disbelievers and a reassurance to the believers. By illustrating the dramatic and unavoidable nature of this event, Surah An-Naba reinforces the necessity of preparing for the Hereafter through faith and righteous deeds.

> *"Indeed, the Day of Judgement is an appointed time –, The Day the Horn is blown and you will come forth in multitudes, And the heaven is opened and will become gateways, And the mountains are removed and will be [but] a mirage."*

Surah An-Naba, verses 78:17 – 78:20

Moreover, this surah is significant for its role in providing solace and strength to the early Muslim community, who faced persecution and hardship. The promise of divine justice and the eventual triumph of truth over falsehood helped sustain the believers' faith and resilience. Surah An-Naba thus played a crucial role in fortifying the early Muslims' spiritual resolve and conviction during one of the most challenging periods of the Islamic mission.

Key Themes and Virtues

1. **Grandeur of Allah's Creation:** The surah paints a vivid picture of Allah's creation, from the mountains to the earth, highlighting the meticulous design and purpose behind each element. This deepens our appreciation for the natural world and reinforces our belief in a meticulous Creator, fostering a sense of gratitude and awe.
2. **Reminder of the Day of Resurrection:** The surah details the events of the Day of Resurrection, emphasizing the temporary nature of life and the ultimate reality awaiting every soul. This serves as a crucial reminder for believers to live a life of purpose and accountability.
3. **Moral and Ethical Guidance:** The surah outlines the consequences for both the righteous and wrongdoers, serving as a moral compass. Believers are guided towards righteousness and away from error, ensuring their decisions align with divine guidance.
4. **Meditation and Reflection:** The verses of Surah An-Naba offer rich material for deep reflection. Whether contemplating the intricacies of creation or the vastness of the universe, the surah encourages introspection, leading to personal growth and a deeper connection with one's surroundings.
5. **Gratitude:** Surah An-Naba cultivates gratitude through its verses by reminding us of the bounties bestowed by Allah SWT, specifically through natural phenomena like rain. He said: ***"And sent down, from the rain clouds, pouring water, That We may bring forth thereby grain and vegetation, And gardens of entwined growth."*** These verses prompt reflection on the essential resources provided for human survival, fostering a sense of thankfulness for the continuous and generous gifts of nourishment and natural beauty, ultimately deepening our appreciation and gratitude towards Allah SWT

Lessons from Surah An-Naba

1. **Affirmation of the Hereafter:** A central theme of the surah is the affirmation of the Day of Resurrection. The Quran confirms that there will indeed be a Day of Judgment when every individual will be recompensed for their deeds.
2. **Signs of Allah's Creation:** The surah draws attention to various signs in the universe as evidence of Allah's power and wisdom. This includes the mountains, earth, human creation, and natural phenomena, urging individuals to reflect on the greatness of the Creator.
3. **Detailed Description of the Hereafter:** The surah provides vivid descriptions of the Day of Resurrection, emphasizing the transient nature of this world and the eternal reality of the Hereafter.
4. **Consequences of One's Actions:** It highlights that individuals will face consequences for their actions in the Hereafter. The righteous will be rewarded with eternal bliss, while wrongdoers will face punishment, serving as ethical guidance for believers.
5. **Importance of Belief:** The surah underscores the importance of belief in the unseen, especially the Hereafter. It challenges those who mock the concept of resurrection to reflect on the signs of Allah's creation as evidence of His power.

Conclusion

Surah An-Naba serves as a profound reminder of the reality of the Hereafter, urging believers to live a life of accountability and purpose. It reinforces the importance of reflecting on the signs of Allah's creation and maintaining a strong ethical framework. The surah's detailed depiction of the Day of Resurrection serves as a moral guide, encouraging believers to strive for righteousness and avoid sinful behaviour.

Moreover, the regular recitation of Surah An-Naba is believed to bring divine rewards, protection, and spiritual enrichment, fostering a closer connection with Allah and strengthening one's faith.

In conclusion, Surah An-Naba is a cornerstone of Islamic teaching, offering valuable lessons and virtues that guide believers towards a life of faith, purpose, and accountability. By reflecting on its verses and incorporating its teachings into daily life, Muslims can deepen their spiritual journey and strengthen their connection with the Divine.

Verse 1

Amma Yatasaa-aloon

Concerning what are they disputing?

Verses 2

Anin-nabaa-il 'azeem –

Concerning the Great News

Surah Naba opens with the question:

"Amma yatasaa'aloon"?

"About what are they asking one another?"

This question is then followed by a clarification:

"About the great news - over which they disagree." (Verse 2)

This "great news" refers to the concept of the Day of Resurrection and the Hereafter, which the disbelievers dispute and deny.

The fate of the righteous and the disbelievers is portrayed through intense imagery, highlighting both reward and punishment.

The surah emphasizes a certainty.

What is this certainty?

It is the Day of Judgement. It is not a myth, but a reality that is bound to happen.

Who are these disbelievers and what are they disputing and denying?

These are the people of Quraysh at the time of the Prophet (SAWS). They were in deep denial about the resurrection and mocked the concept of being resurrected after death.

Verse 3

Allazi hum feehi mukh talifoon –

"About which they cannot agree".

The above verse do not name the event but describes it to enhance the feeling of wonder and amazement at such people. The dispute was between those who believed in resurrection and those who denied it, but the questions were raised by the latter only.

The surah does not provide any more details about the event in question. It simply describes it as great before adding an implicit threat which is much more frightening than a direct answer.

Verses 4 & 5

Thumma kallaa sa y'alamoon.

Alam naj'alil arda mihaa da

"No indeed, they shall certainly know! Again, no indeed, they shall certainly know!" (Verses 4-5)

The phrase, 'no indeed,' is used here as the nearest possible rendering of the Arabic term, kalla, which denotes strong shunning. The whole sentence is repeated to add force to the threat implied.

The surah then puts aside, apparently, that great event which is at the centre of controversy, only to pick it up later on. We are then taken on a quick round of the universe in verses 6 to 16 in which we see a multitude of scenes, creatures and phenomena. Contemplation of which strongly shakes any human heart.

Summary of verses 6 to 16

In the collection of verses 6 to 16 we traverse the vast universe, observing a great multitude of scenes and phenomena, which are sketched out with great economy of words.

These verses point to a supreme being with the power to create and recreate. Therefore, it raises the question: why would anyone with a sound mind reject the notion of the Day of Resurrection?

Verse 6

Alam naj'alil arda mihaa da –

"Have We not made the earth as a bed?"

This verse uses the imagery of a bed to illustrate the earth's function as a comfortable and secure place for humans to live. The earth's surface is relatively flat and provides a stable platform for human activity.

Verse 7

Wal jibaala au taada –

"And the mountains as pegs?"

Here the role of mountains in stabilizing the earth is highlighted. Just as pegs hold a tent in place, the mountains are seen as anchors that prevent the earth from excessive shaking or movement. Modern scientific understanding also suggests that mountains play a role in the earth's geological structure and stability.

Verse 8

Wa khalaq naakum azwaaja –

"And We have created you in pairs?"

This verse is referring to the creation of men and women. It mentions "Pairing". This pairing is essential for procreation and the continuation of the human species.

Verse 9

Waja'alna naumakum subata

"And made your sleep for rest".

Here the divine provision of sleep as a means of rest and recuperation is addressed.

When we sleep the body produces the natural tranquilizer melatonin.

Melatonin is a hormone that helps regulate the sleep-wake cycle, and its production is linked to the daily rhythm of light and darkness. As darkness falls, melatonin levels rise, signalling the body that it's time to sleep

Verse 10

Waja'alnal laila libasa

"And made the night as a cover".

The night is described here as a covering, providing darkness and a sense of security. This verse is explaining that the night, with its darkness, serves as a covering or a garment for the world, providing rest and tranquillity. It's a time for humans and animals to find repose, creating peace and order in the world.

The darkness of the night is compared to clothing, suggesting it envelops the world and its inhabitants, providing a sense of comfort and protection.

This in turn induces sleepiness and cessation of activity, allowing for physical and mental rest. This imposition of sleep on humans and animals during the night contributes to the peace and tranquillity of the world.

Verse 11

Waja'alnan nahara ma 'aasha

"And made the day for livelihood. The day is designated for work and earning one's living".

Here we learn that Allah has designed the day to be a time for human activity and earning a living. It's a period for work, seeking provision, and pursuing one's livelihood.

This verse is often pairs with verse 10 which describes the night as a covering or a time for rest. Together, these two verses highlight the complementary nature of day and night, each with its distinct purpose in the human experience. This point to the divine wisdom in structuring time to allow for both work and rest. The day provides the opportunity for effort and productivity, while the night offers a time for recuperation and rejuvenation.

This verse serves as a great reminder of Allah's mercy and provision. By making the day a time for livelihood, Allah has facilitated human survival and well-being.

Verse 12

Wa banaina fauqakum sab 'an shi daada

"And built above you seven strong ˹heavens˺".

This verse discusses the creation of the seven heavens and the sun, emphasizing their strength and structure.

The "seven strong (heavens)" refer to the vast, elevated, and perfectly structured celestial spheres above us. These heavens are adorned with stars, both fixed and moving, showcasing Allah's power and precision.

The verse highlights Allah's creation as a sign of His power and wisdom. The creation of the heavens and the sun serves as a testament to Allah's ability to create and sustain the universe.

Verse 13

Waja'alna siraajaw wah haaja

"And have appointed a dazzling lamp".

The "shining lamp" is understood to be the sun, a powerful and radiant source of light that illuminates the entire world.

The term "siraajan wahhaajan" is used to describe the sun, translating to "a burning lamp" or "a radiant torch". This signals the sun's function as a powerful source of light and heat.

This verse is one of many in Surah An-Naba that points to the wonders of creation and the divine power and mercy of Allah. The sun's creation and its role in sustaining life are presented as clear signs for those who reflect on them.

The sun has multiple benefits. It provides light for us to see, heat to warm the earth, and energy for plants to grow, which in turn support all other life forms. It is a key component in the water cycle, influencing rainfall and climate patterns.

The verse also connects the earthly blessings of the sun with the Day of Judgment, hinting at the greater rewards or punishments that await in the Hereafter. The mention of the sun's light and heat can be seen as a reminder of the potential for both blessings and torment in the afterlife.

Verse 14

Wa anzalna minal m'usiraati maa-an thaj-jaaja

"And have sent down from the rainy clouds abundant Water".

This verse is demonstrating Allah's action and control over the natural phenomenon of rain. The rain is not just falling from the sky in general, but specifically from the clouds, which are described as "mu'sirat" (meaning clouds laden with water).

The term "thajjajan" describes the rain as heavy and abundant, indicating a generous provision from Allah.

All of this showcase Allah's mercy and provision for creation, as rain is vital for sustaining life, providing sustenance, and maintaining ecological balance.

This verse is also linked to the concept of resurrection. Just as Allah brings life to the earth through rain, He is also capable of resurrecting the dead on the Day of Judgment.

All are reminders of Allah's power and control over the natural world, highlighting the almighty's ability to create and manage all aspects of existence.

Verse 15

Linukh rija bihee habbaw wana baata

"Thereby to produce grain and plant".

The rain is shown to be essential for the growth of crops and vegetation. This indicates the diverse types of food and plant life that are produced as a result of the rain, providing sustenance for humans and animals. Again here we see Allah's mercy and provision for creation.

Verse 16

Wa jan naatin alfafa

"And gardens of interwoven paths".

This verse discusses the creation of gardens, specifically "jannatin allafa," which translates to "gardens of interwoven growth" or "thickly growing gardens". It is where trees and plants grow together in abundance and in close proximity, creating a dense, interwoven pattern.

The creation of these gardens, with their diverse fruits, fragrances, and textures, is presented as a sign of Allah's power and ability to create anything He wills.

This verse is closely linked to the concept of the Hereafter, as it demonstrates Allah's capacity to create and recreate, suggesting that the destruction of this world will be followed by a new, magnificent creation.

The verse also implies that the creation of this world, with its diverse and interconnected elements, is not without purpose. It points to a larger plan, including a Day of Judgment where individuals will be held accountable for their actions.

The verse highlights the abundance of plant life, with different fruits, colours, tastes, and smells, even within a single piece of land, further emphasizing Allah's power and artistry

Summary of Verses: 17-20

"Indeed, the Day of Judgment is an Appointed Time Creation is not without purpose".

The Creator, who has accurately measured human life and carefully provided perfect harmony between it and the universe, will not let people just live and die in vain. Reason cannot accept that those who do good and the evildoers should both end in dust. The rightly-guided and the straying folk, the just and the tyrants cannot all share the same fate. There must be a day when everything is judged and evaluated. The day is appointed by Allah subhanahu wa ta'ala,

"Indeed, the Day of Judgment is an appointed time," [78: 17]. It is a day when upheaval overtakes the universe and destroys its systems, "the Day the Horn is blown and you will come forth in multitudes," [78: 18]. The 'Trumpet' is a kind of horn of which we know nothing except its name and that it will be blown. We need not waste our time trying to discover how, for such discovery will not strengthen our faith. Allah subhanahu wa ta'ala has revealed to us what we need to know of the secrets of the universe so that we may not waste our energy in the futile pursuit of useless knowledge. We can imagine, however, a blast on a Trumpet which people answer by arriving in droves.

We can visualize the scene whereby all the generations of mankind rise up, walking in their multitudes, from all directions, to attend the great reckoning. We can imagine the fearful sight of people rising from their graves and the great, huge, endless crowd they form. We can feel the horror of the day, people's helplessness and fear. "And the heaven is opened and will become gateways," [78: 19] heaven, the mighty heaven, is opened up so that it becomes gates for the angels to descend. "And the mountains are removed and will be [but] a mirage," [78: 20] it is, as described elsewhere in the Qur'an - "And you will see the mountains and think them solid, but they shall pass away as the passing away of the clouds," [27: 88]. He also says, "And the mountain will be like carded wool," [101: 5]

The firmly dug-in pegs, i.e. the mountains, are made to move away. They are hammered, scattered, turned into dust, blown by the wind, as other Qur'anic ayaat describe. Hence, they become non-existent, like a mirage which has no reality. Or, probably, different rays are reflected against them after they have been turned into dust and they look like a mirage. All in all, horror is apparent in the upheaval which envelops the universe as well as in men's resurrection after the Trumpet is blown. Such is the Day of Decision carefully and wisely fixed.

Verse 17

Inna yaumal-fasli kana meeqaata

Verily the Day of Sorting out is a thing appointed,

This verse presents the Day of Judgement as "an appointed time" or "a fixed time." It underscores that this moment is not random but rather a specific occasion ordained by Allah. This verse lays the groundwork for the following passages that elaborate on the events of that day.

Verse 18

Yauma yun fakhu fis-soori fataa' toona afwaaja

"The Day the Trumpet will be blown and you will come forth in crowds"

This verse introduces the pivotal moment of the Day of Judgement—the blowing of the trumpet, which heralds the resurrection of the deceased.

Israfil is the angel tasked with blowing of the trumpet. It will be blown twice.

Some accounts state that Israfil has been waiting since the beginning of creation, with his gaze fixed on the throne, ready to start the process.

This initial blast of the trumpet will cause everyone in the heavens and earth to die, except for those Allah specifically chooses to exempt, according to the Quran.

After a period of time, the trumpet will be blown again. This time, everyone will be resurrected and will stand before Allah, looking on.

Verse 19

Wa futiha tis samaa-u fakaanat abwaaba

"The sky will be ˹split˺ open, becoming ˹many˺ gates".

The verse uses the phrase- "wa futiḥati as-samā'u fa kānat abwābā", which translates to "and the sky will be split open, becoming gates".

This depicts a dramatic event where the sky, normally a solid-seeming barrier, is fractured and transformed into multiple openings or pathways. This highlights the extraordinary nature of the Day of Judgment and the power of Allah to transform reality.

The "gates" symbolize a transition, a passage from one realm to another. In this context, it signifies the transition from the earthly life to the afterlife, specifically the Day of Judgment.

So what does this mean for the disbelievers?

For disbelievers, this verse serves as a reminder of the certainty of the afterlife and the need to prepare for it. It underscores the significance of the Day of Judgment as a crucial moment in human existence and those who come unprepared will live in the hell-fire for eternity.

Verse 20

Wa suyyi raatil jibaalu fa kaanat saraaba

"And the mountains will be blown away, becoming ˹like˺ a mirage".

The verse is teaching us the immense power of Allah on the Day of Judgment and the insignificance of even the most solid and imposing creations of the world in the face of His power. It serves as a reminder of the transient nature of this world and the certainty of the afterlife. The mountains, which are seen as symbols of strength and permanence, will be reduced to nothingness, highlighting the magnitude of the Day of Judgment.

The destruction of the mountains on the Day of Judgment symbolizes the complete annihilation of the material world and the beginning of the afterlife. It signifies the end of the current order and the beginning of a new one.

Summary of verses 21 to 36

Ayaat 21-36 - Reward and Reckoning.

The Surah takes another step, beyond Resurrection, to describe the fate of the tyrant unbelievers and also that of the righteous. It begins with the former group who raise doubts about the fateful tiding, "Indeed, Hell has been lying in wait for the transgressors, a place of return, in which they will remain for ages [unending]," [78: 21-23].

Hell has been created so that it may watch the tyrants and transgressors and await their arrival. They find it well prepared to receive them, as if they are returning to their natural home after having sojourned on earth a while. It is a home in which they stay endlessly. But they taste "neither coolness nor any drink." [78: 24] The next ayah provides an exception to this, but the exception is even worse: "except scalding water and [foul] purulence," [78: 25]. Their throats and stomachs burn as they drink the scalding water. The Qur'an comments that this is 'a fitting recompense'. It is in keeping with what they have done in their lives. For they thought they would never return to Allah subhanahu wa ta'ala,

"Indeed, they were not expecting an account. And denied Our ayaat with [emphatic] denial." [78: 27-28].

Their denial, as the Arabic text suggests, is strongly emphatic and stubbornly upheld. But Allah subhanahu wa ta'ala keeps a meticulous record which does not leave out anything they do or say, "But all things We have enumerated in writing," [78: 29]. Then follows a reproach coupled with the tiding that they can hope for no change in their condition and no abatement of its intensity, "So taste [the penalty], and never will We increase you except in torment." [78: 30]

We then have the corresponding scene of the righteous in complete bliss, "Indeed, for the righteous is attainment," [78: 31]. If hell is a vigilant watch guard which the tyrants cannot escape, the righteous, the Allah-fearing will end in a place of security. What a place it is: "gardens and grapevines." [78: 32] The vine tree is specifically mentioned because it is well known to the addressees. The Allah-fearing will also have companions who are described here as high-bosomed and of equal age. They also drink from a cup overflowing with refreshing beverage. These luxuries are given a physical description so that we may better appreciate them. There they shall hear no idle talk, nor any falsehood. It is a pure life there, free of the idle chatting and falsehood which give rise to controversy. The reality is known to everyone, which means that there is no room for futile argument. Then follows the Qur'anic comment, "reward from your Lord," [78: 36].

Verse 21

Inna jahan nama kaanat mirsaada

"Indeed, Hell has been lying in wait":

This part of the verse describes Hell as a place of ambush, suggesting it is a trap for those who deny Allah and the Hereafter.

Hell is the ultimate destination for those who have rebelled against Allah and His commands.

The term "ambush" (mirṣād) is used metaphorically to convey the idea that Hell is not something the disbelievers expect or prepare for, but rather a sudden and unavoidable consequence of their actions.

Verse 22

Lit taa gheena ma aaba

The Arabic word "ṭāghīn", translated as "transgressors," refers to those who have exceeded the limits in disobedience to Allah. This includes those who engage in rebellion, exceed the bounds of faith, or commit acts of disobedience.

The word "mābā", translated as "place of return" or "resort," indicates that Hell is the final destination for those who have transgressed. It highlights that they will have no escape from the consequences of their actions.

Will Muslims also experience the hellfire?

In Islam, the majority belief is that while Muslims may face punishment in hell for their sins, they will not remain there eternally. Muslims believe that those who die as believers in Allah and his messengers, even if they have committed sins, will eventually be admitted to paradise (Jannah), though they may first experience a period of purification in hell (Jahannam).

What about the non-believers:

The Quran and Islamic teachings indicate that those who die as non-believers (those who reject Allah and his messengers) will remain in hell eternally.

The verse serves as a warning to those who are inclined towards transgression, emphasizing that their actions have consequences and that Hell is the ultimate outcome for those who choose to defy Allah.

It highlights the importance of faith and righteous deeds as a means to avoid the punishment of Hell.

Verse 23

Laa bitheena feehaa ahqaaba

"They will dwell therein for ages".

This translates to "abiding therein for ages".

The word **Ahqab** refers to a very long period of time, often interpreted as a duration of time that has no end.

So this verse is underscoring that the punishment for those who reject Allah and the Hereafter will have a prolonged and seemingly endless stay in Hell.

Verse 24

Laa ya zooqoona feeha bar daw walaa sharaaba

"They will not taste therein [any] coolness or any drink, except boiling water and pus."

This verse describes the punishment awaiting the wicked in Hell. It highlights that they will not experience any relief or refreshment, only intense heat and foul substances.

This indicates a complete lack of comfort, refreshment, or anything pleasant to consume. The absence of coolness emphasizes the intense heat of Hell.

The purpose of this verse, along with others in Surah An-Naba, aims to warn wrongdoers about the severe consequences of their actions and to emphasize the reality of the Hereafter.

Verse 25

Illa hamee maw-wa ghas saaqa

"Save a boiling fluid and a fluid, dark, murky, intensely cold"

Here, we understand what awaits the disbelievers in the hell fire.

It describes the punishment in Hell, stating that the disbelievers will not experience coolness or refreshing drinks, but only boiling water and pus. It highlights the severity of their suffering and the stark contrast to the blessings promised to the righteous.

Verse 26

Jazaa-aw wi faaqa

"A fitting recompense (for them)".

Verse 26 is telling us that the punishment in hell is a direct consequence of the disbelievers' actions and choices they made in this life.

The term "fitting recompense" signifies that the punishment will be proportionate to their deeds, reflecting divine justice. Hence, assuring that no one will be wronged or treated unfairly.

It also acts as a reminder of the accountability that awaits everyone on the Day of Judgment, urging people to prepare for it.

Verse 27

Innahum kaanu laa yarjoona hisaaba

"Indeed, they were not expecting an account."

Verse 27 serves as a warning against the dangers of denying the Day of Judgment and the importance of preparing for it by living a life of faith and righteous deeds.

The disbelievers never believed they would be brought before Allah for a reckoning. They lived as if their actions had no consequences beyond this world, and made no effort to prepare for this day.

Verse 28

Wa kazzabu bi aayaa tina kizzaba

"But they (impudently) treated Our Signs as false".

These are the ones who reject the signs of Allah swt.

Those who reject the signs of Allah swt, the Almighty says that they are spiritually deaf, dumb and blind.

These terms are used metaphorically to describe those who reject faith or truth, rather than referring to literal physical disabilities.

We learn in the previous verses of Surah Naba that the consequences of rejecting faith and guidance is the eternal stay in the hellfire.

Verse 29

Wa kulla shai-in ahsai naahu kitaa ba

"And We have everything recorded precisely."

This verse is telling us that every deed, big or small, good or bad, is meticulously recorded by angels, and ultimately judged by Allah on the Day of Judgment.

Islam tells us that there are two angels, Kiraman Katibin, assigned to every person.

One angel is believed to be positioned on the right shoulder, recording good deeds, while the other is on the left shoulder, recording bad deeds.

The Quran mentions these angels in Surah Al-Infitar (82:10-12) as "keepers, noble and recording".

These records will become available on Judgement Day and will determine whether we gain or deny entry to Jannah. (Heaven)

While some traditions associate the names Raqib and Atid with these angels, the Quran refers to them by their function, not by specific names.

It's important to note that while these angels record actions, it is ultimately Allah's mercy and forgiveness that determines a person's fate.

Verse 30

Fa zooqoo falan-nazee dakum ill-laa azaaba

"So taste ye (the fruits of your deeds); for no increase shall We grant you, except in Punishment."

Verse 30, conveys a stern warning to those who reject the truth and deny the Day of Judgment.

And what is this warning?

Their torment will be intensified in the Hellfire, with no reprieve or reduction in their punishment. This is the ultimate consequence of rejecting divine guidance.

The verse serves as a stark reminder that denying the truth and rejecting Allah's signs will lead to severe and escalating punishment in the Hereafter.

The verse also reinforces the concept that there will be a Day of Judgment and individuals will be held accountable for their actions and beliefs.

So, we must self-reflect on the consequences of our actions and prepare ourselves for that inevitable day.

Summary of Verses 31 to Verse 36

These verses are promising rewards for those who live righteous lives, highlighting the importance of belief and the requirement to follow the commands of Allah swt.

There is a promise of rewards!

And what will this reward be?

Jannah!!!

The Holy Quran describes Jannah as "Gardens of Pleasure" prepared for the righteous believers to dwell in for eternity. It contains "all that the souls could desire, all that the eyes could delight in …" (43:71). Whoever attains Jannah has attained the "Supreme Success" (9:89).

The people of Jannah will be in the presence of Allah and will receive His good pleasure:

"Allah has promised to Believers, men and women, gardens under which rivers flow, to dwell therein, and beautiful mansions in gardens of everlasting bliss. But the greatest bliss is the good pleasure of Allah: that is the supreme felicity" (9:72).

The greatest spiritual pleasure in paradise will be to see Allah:

"For those who have done good is the best reward and even more (i.e. having the honour of glancing at the Countenance of Allah)" (10:26).

The phrase "even more" means to see Allah, as the Prophet (PBUH) explained in this Hadith:

"When the people of Paradise enter Paradise, Allah will say, 'Do you want anything more?' They will say, 'Have You not brightened our faces, admitted us to Paradise and saved us from Hell?' Then the veil will be lifted and they will not have seen anything more dear to them than looking upon their Lord, may He be glorified and exalted. This is what is meant by 'even more.'" Then He (PBUH) recited the verse:

"For those who have done good is the best reward and even more (i.e. having the honor of glancing at the Countenance of Allah)"[Yoonus 10:26] (Sahih Muslim)

The people of Jannah will also receive the honour of being in the company of the elite servants of Allah:

"All who obey Allah and the Messenger, then they will be in the company of those on whom Allah has bestowed His Grace, of the Prophets, the steadfast affirmers of truth, the martyrs, and the righteous. And how excellent these companions are! (4:69)

Jannah is as wide as the heavens and the earth (3:133). The people of Jannah will live in beautiful mansions (9:72) amidst gardens with flowing streams (2:25). Jannah contains springs (15:45), dense shrubbery (80:30), deepening shade (4:57), and bunches of fruit hanging low within reach (76:14).

The people of Jannah will have abundant food and drink (38:51). They will eat fruits, meats, and whatever is desired (52:22). They will drink from rivers of pure water, milk, wine and honey (47:15). The wine of paradise will be "crystal-white, delicious to those who drink, free from intoxication…" (37:46-47)

The people of Jannah will wear bracelets of gold and pearl and green garments of fine silk and brocade. They will recline on adorned couches (18:31) and raised thrones, and the weather will always be mild (76:13).

The people of paradise will always be healthy and will never feel fatigue (15:48).

The people of Jannah will enjoy the companionship of pure spouses (2:25). People will enter Jannah with their righteous family members (13:23).

Angels will wish peace upon the inhabitants of Jannah (13:24).

The people of Jannah will feel no resentment in their hearts. They will feel like brothers and sisters to one another (15:47).

The people of Jannah will never wish to leave Jannah (18:108). They will never hear any ill speech; only greetings of peace (19:62).

May Allah make us the people of Jannatul Firdaus, Ameen!

Verse 31

Inna lil mutta qeena mafaaza

"Verily for the Righteous there will be a fulfilment of (the heart's) desires"

This verse is telling us that those who are mindful of Allah and strive to live righteously will achieve success and salvation. **Taqwa (Allah-consciousness):**

The core concept here is "taqwa," which refers to a state of being mindful of Allah, fearing His displeasure, and striving to do what is right. In turn, their righteous actions in this life will lead to a favourable outcome in the Hereafter.

The Arabic word "mafaza" signifies a place of success, triumph, or achievement. It implies not just a physical place of comfort but also a state of spiritual and eternal well-being.

This verse encourages reflection on one's own state of faith and actions, urging believers to strive for righteousness and prepare for the Day of Judgment.

Verse 32

Hadaa-iqa wa a'anaa ba

Gardens enclosed, and grapevines

Verse 32 describes a key aspect of Paradise for the righteous: "Gardens and vineyards."

The verse specifically mentions "gardens and vineyards," which are often used in Islamic texts to symbolize paradise and its blessings. These images evoke a sense of peace, tranquillity, and abundance, representing the material and spiritual delights awaiting the righteous.

This verse is part of a larger section in Surah An-Naba that contrasts the rewards of the righteous with the punishments of the wicked. The preceding verses describe the torment of Hellfire, while verses following verse 32 describe other blessings of Paradise, such as "well-matched, full-breasted maidens" and "a cup of pure wine".

While the verse focuses on physical blessings like gardens and vineyards, it is important to remember that these are symbolic representations of the spiritual and emotional contentment that will be experienced in Paradise. The verse points to the ultimate success, which is a state of complete satisfaction and closeness to Allah.

The verse also serves as a reminder of the Day of Judgment, where deeds will be weighed and rewarded accordingly. It encourages believers to strive for righteousness and prepare for the afterlife.

Verse 33
Wa kaawa 'iba at raaba

"And voluptuous women of equal age"

Here the companions in paradise are described as "Kawa'ib", meaning youthful maidens of equal age, "atraba". These words signify the beauty and youthfulness of the women who will be in paradise, and also their harmonious nature with their husbands. This depiction emphasizes the blessings and rewards awaiting the righteous in the afterlife.

This verse, in its entirety, paints a picture of a blissful and harmonious paradise, where the righteous will enjoy the company of beautiful, youthful, and well-matched companions. It serves as a reminder of the rewards that await those who strive for righteousness in this life.

Verse 34
Wa ka'san di haaqa

"And a cup full (to the brim)"

"And a cup": This refers to a vessel, traditionally associated with drinking.

"overflowing" (or "full to the brim" or "brimming"): This signifies that the cup is not just filled, but constantly replenished, suggesting an unending source of pleasure and enjoyment.

The imagery of an overflowing cup emphasizes the abundance and purity of the blessings in paradise. It's not just a limited quantity, but an endless supply of what is good and desirable.

Ultimately, the verse points to the grace and generosity of Allah, who provides these blessings as a reward for those who strive for righteousness.

Verse 35
Laa yasma'oona fiha lagh waw walaa kizzaba

"No vanity shall they hear therein, nor Untruth": -

This verse is telling us that a key aspect of Paradise will be the absence of idle talk and falsehood.

The resident of paradise will not be subjected to frivolous or deceptive speech. It highlights the contrast between the worldly life, often filled with vain talk and lies, and the blissful state of the Hereafter, where such negativity will be absent.

Hence, we learn of the absence of lies and deception in Paradise. The world is often marred by dishonesty, betrayal, and the spreading of false information. Paradise, on the other hand, will be a place of truth and genuine interactions, where believers will not be subjected to lies or false accusations.

This verse is a source of hope and encouragement for believers. It assures them that their efforts to avoid vain talk and falsehood in this world will be rewarded in the Hereafter, where they will experience a life of peace, truth, and genuine interaction.

Verse 36

Jazaa-am mir-rabbika ataa-an hisaaba

"Recompense from thy Lord, a gift, (amply) sufficient",

Verse 36 speaks of the reward for the righteous as a "gift from your Lord, a sufficient giving". It is telling us that Allah will grant them more than they deserve, highlighting His generosity and mercy. This verse contrasts with the fate of the disbelievers, who will receive only punishment as recompense.

The verse uses the word "ʿaṭāʾan", which translates to "gift" or "giving," stressing that the blessings of Paradise are a bestowal from Allah's grace, not solely earned through deeds.

The word "ḥisāba" means "sufficient" or "abundant." Some scholars interpret it to mean that the reward will be more than enough to satisfy the righteous, highlighting Allah's boundless generosity.

This verse serves as a stark contrast to the description of Hellfire in the preceding verses, where the disbelievers are given "a fitting recompense" for their actions.

The promise of such a generous gift is a powerful motivator for striving to be among the righteous and fearing Allah (taqwa).

The verse reminds believers of Allah's immense kindness and His ability to give far more than what is expected or deserved.

Summary verses 37 to Verse 40

Man will Wish He was Dust.

The Surah closes with the final scene of the Day when all this happens. It is a scene in which we see the angel Jibreel ʿalayhi salaam and all the angels standing in ranks before Allah subhanahu wa taʿala, their Most Merciful Lord. They stand in awe of Him; no one dares utter a word without prior permission from Him. The recompense given to the righteous and to the tyrant transgressors is from Allah subhanahu wa taʿala - the Supreme Lord of man, the heavens and earth, this life and the next, who metes out reward for righteousness and punishment for transgression and tyranny. But above all He is the Most Gracious. The reward He assigns to each group is a manifestation of His mercy. Even the torment endured by the transgressors originates from His mercy. For it is indeed part of mercy that evil should be punished and that it should not have the same end as good. The other divine attribute implied here is majesty,

"They possess not from Him [authority for] speech." [78: 37]

In this situation neither man nor angel can speak without permission from the Most Gracious. Whatever is said will be right because He does not permit anyone to speak whom He knows will not be saying what is right. When we think that the angels stand silent in front of Allah subhanahu wa taʿala and dare not speak without His permission, we are bound to feel how the atmosphere is. The Surah therefore delivers a warning to those who have chosen not to hear or see,

"That is the True Day." [78: 39] There is no room left for doubt and controversy. Yet there is time for mending one's erring ways before the fearful watch guard, i.e. hell, becomes a permanent home,

"So he who wills may take to his Lord a [way of] return." [78: 39] "Indeed, We have warned you of a near punishment," meaning it will not be long coming, for man's life is but a short period. The scourge is so fearful that the unbelievers, when faced with it, will send up that great cry expressing the wish that they had never lived,

"On the Day when a man will observe what his hands have put forth and the disbeliever will say, 'Oh, I wish that I were dust!'" [78: 40] This is the cry of one who is in great distress, who feels ashamed for what he has been and what he has done. He feels that it is better not to be, or to be something as worthless as dust, than to witness such a fearful occasion.

Verse 37

Rabbis samaa waati wal ardi wa maa baina humar rahmaani laa yam likoona minhu khitaaba

"(From) the Lord of the heavens and the earth, and all between, (Allah) Most Gracious: None shall have power to argue with Him".

This verse describes Allah as the Lord of all creation and emphasizes His attribute of Ar-Rahman (the Most Compassionate). It also highlights the fact that on the Day of Judgment, no one will have the power to speak to Allah without His permission.

Verse 38

Yauma yaqoo mur roohu wal malaa-ikatu saf-fal laa yatakallamoona ill-laa man azina lahur rahmaanu wa qaala sawaaba

"The Day that the Spirit and the angels will stand forth in ranks, none shall speak except any who is permitted by (Allah) Most Gracious, and He will say what is right"

This verse describes the scene on the Day of Judgment when the angels will stand in rows, and only those permitted by Allah, the Most Merciful, will be allowed to speak.

The verse paints a vivid picture of the Day of Judgment, where the angels, including the Angel Gabriel (often referred to as the "Spirit" in interpretations), will stand in rows, forming a solemn and majestic scene.

A key element in this verse is the restriction on speech. No one will be permitted to speak without the express permission of Allah, the Most Merciful.

Even when permission is granted, the speech allowed will be only that which is true and just.

This verse underscores the profound power and authority of Allah, accentuating that He is the ultimate judge and that no one can act independently on that Day. It also highlights the accountability of all humans, as they will be presented with their deeds and judged accordingly. This serves as a strong reminder for believers to strive for righteousness and to prepare for the Hereafter.

The mention of "Ar-Rahman" (the Most Merciful) in the verse also points to Allah's attribute of mercy, reminding believers that while there will be judgment, there is also hope for those who strive to please Him.

Verse 39

Zaalikal yaumul haqqu faman shaa-at ta khaaza ill-laa rabbihi ma-aaba

"That Day will be the sure Reality: Therefore, whoso will, let him take a (straight) return to his Lord"!

Verse 39 explicitly states that the Day of Judgment is "the True Day", underscoring its undeniable reality serving as a warning to those who deny or doubt it.

The verse then urges those who wish to return to their Lord to do so through obedience and good deeds.

By urging individuals to return to their Lord, it implies that they will be held responsible for their actions in this life.

The phrase "whoever wills" highlights the freedom of choice individuals have in this life. They can choose to prepare for the afterlife by seeking Allah's pleasure or face the consequences of their choices on the Day of Judgment.

In essence, the verse calls for self-reflection, encourages believers to strengthen their faith and righteous actions, and serves as a reminder of the importance of preparing for the inevitable Day of Judgment.

Verse 40

In naa anzar naakum azaaban qareebaiy-yauma yan zurul marr-u maa qaddamat yadaahu wa ya qoolul-kaafiru yaa lai tanee kuntu turaaba

Verily, We have warned you of a Penalty near, the Day when man will see (the deeds) which his hands have sent forth, and the Unbeliever will say, "Woe unto me! Would that I were (mere) dust!"

Verse 40 serves as a powerful conclusion to the surah, which focuses on the Day of Judgment and the consequences of one's actions. The verse is a stark reminder of the accountability that awaits all of humanity on that day.

The verse begins by warning of an "imminent punishment," re-inforcing the nearness of the Day of Judgment and the consequences that await.

It describes the moment when a person will see the consequences of their deeds, both good and bad, as presented before them.

The disbeliever's exclamation,

"Would that I were dust!" encapsulates the depth of their despair and regret. They wish they had never been resurrected or even created, as they face the harsh reality of their choices.

The verse also mentions that even animals will be judged and their disputes resolved, with the hornless taking their right from the horned. After justice is served, Allah will command them to turn to dust. This is when the disbeliever wishes he was dust instead of facing the accountability of his actions.

Reflections and Lessons from Surah Naba

Sura Naba serves as a powerful reminder of the importance of faith and righteous actions in this life, as the consequences in the Hereafter are severe. It highlights the futility of denying the truth and the ultimate regret that will befall those who reject Allah's message. The surah encourages reflection on one's deeds and the choices one makes, as every action has a consequence.

It also emphasizes the justice of Allah, who will judge all of creation with fairness and equity.

MAY ALLAH SWT GRANT US JANNATUL FIRDOUS. AMEEN!

Surah An-Naba - Surah 78

Questions

These questions and answers can help students understand the key concepts and messages of Surah An-Naba.

1. What is the main theme of Surah An-Naba?
2. What are the people questioning in the opening verses of Surah An-Naba?
3. How does Surah An-Naba describe the Day of Judgment?
4. List some of the creations mentioned in Surah An-Naba that are signs of Allah's power.
5. What is the fate of the disbelievers as described in the Surah?
6. What reward is promised to the righteous in Surah An-Naba?
7. In Surah An-Naba, how is the contrast between the lives of the believers and the disbelievers portrayed?
8. How does Surah An-Naba describe the resurrection of the dead?
9. What is the significance of the mountains as mentioned in the Surah?
10. How does the Surah emphasize the importance of the message being conveyed?

Answers

1. Main Theme: The main theme of Surah An-Naba is the Day of Judgment, emphasizing resurrection, accountability, and the contrasting destinies of the believers and disbelievers.

2. Questioning: The people are questioning about the "Great News" or "An-Naba," which refers to the Day of Judgment and resurrection.

3. Day of Judgment: Surah An-Naba describes the Day of Judgment as an event of immense upheaval where the earth and mountains crumble, and everyone is held accountable for their deeds.

4. Signs of Allah's Power: The Surah mentions the earth as a resting place, mountains as pegs, human creation in pairs, sleep as a rest, the night as a covering, and the day for livelihood as signs of Allah's power.

5. Fate of Disbelievers: The disbelievers are warned of severe punishment in Hell, described as a blazing fire with no relief.

6. Reward for the Righteous: The righteous are promised gardens and vineyards, and companions of equal age, along with cups full of drink in Paradise.

7. Contrast in Lives: The Surah contrasts the fate of the disbelievers facing torment with the eternal bliss and rewards for the believers in Paradise.

8. Resurrection of the Dead: The Surah describes the resurrection as a certainty where all the dead will be brought back to life for judgment.

9. Significance of Mountains: Mountains are described as pegs to indicate stability and balance in the creation, highlighting Allah's precision in creation.

10. Emphasis on the Message: The Surah emphasizes the importance of the message by warning of the severe consequences of ignoring it and the certainty of the events described.

Multiple Choice Questions

These questions and answers can help students review and solidify their understanding of Surah An-Naba.

1. What is the primary subject of Surah An-Naba?

    - A) The story of Prophet Moses
    - B) The Day of Judgment
    - C) The creation of the universe
    - D) The life of Prophet Muhammad

2. In the opening verses of Surah An-Naba, what are people questioning?

    - A) The prophethood of Muhammad
    - B) The authenticity of the Quran
    - C) The "Great News" concerning the resurrection
    - D) The rules of inheritance

3. Which of the following is NOT mentioned in Surah An-Naba as a sign of Allah's power?

    - A) The sun as a radiant lamp
    - B) The moon's phases
    - C) The mountains as pegs
    - D) The creation of human beings in pairs

4. According to Surah An-Naba, what will happen to the earth and mountains on the Day of Judgment?

    - A) They will remain unchanged
    - B) They will collapse and be scattered
    - C) They will transform into gold
    - D) They will rise to the heavens

5. What punishment is described for the disbelievers in Surah An-Naba?

    - A) Eternal sleep
    - B) Burning in a blazing fire
    - C) Being turned to dust
    - D) Wandering in confusion

6. What reward is promised to the righteous in Surah An-Naba?

    - A) Gold and silver
    - B) Gardens and vineyards
    - C) Palaces in the sky
    - D) Endless wealth

7. How does Surah An-Naba depict the resurrection of the dead?

   - A) As a myth

   - B) As an uncertain event

   - C) As a definite and inevitable occurrence

   - D) As a metaphorical concept

8. What is the significance of the mountains mentioned in the Surah?

   - A) They symbolize obstacles

   - B) They represent eternal life
   - C) They serve as stabilizers or pegs for the earth

   - D) They are a source of wealth

9. How does the Surah characterize the message it conveys?

   - A) As a tale of the past

   - B) As a warning and a certainty

   - C) As a fictional story

   - D) As a historical account

10. What is the contrast between the lives of believers and disbelievers in Surah An-Naba?

    - A) Both live in harmony

    - B) Disbelievers face torment while believers enjoy eternal bliss

    - C) Both are promised paradise

    - D) Disbelievers are rewarded, and believers are punished

Answers

1. *Answer: B)* The Day of Judgment
2. *Answer: C)* The "Great News" concerning the resurrection
3. *Answer: B)* The moon's phases
4. *Answer: B)* They will collapse and be scattered
5. *Answer: B)* Burning in a blazing fire
6. *Answer: B)* Gardens and vineyards
7. *Answer: C)* As a definite and inevitable occurrence
8. *Answer: C)* They serve as stabilizers or pegs for the earth
9. *Answer: B)* As a warning and a certainty
10. *Answer: B)* Disbelievers face torment while believers enjoy eternal bliss

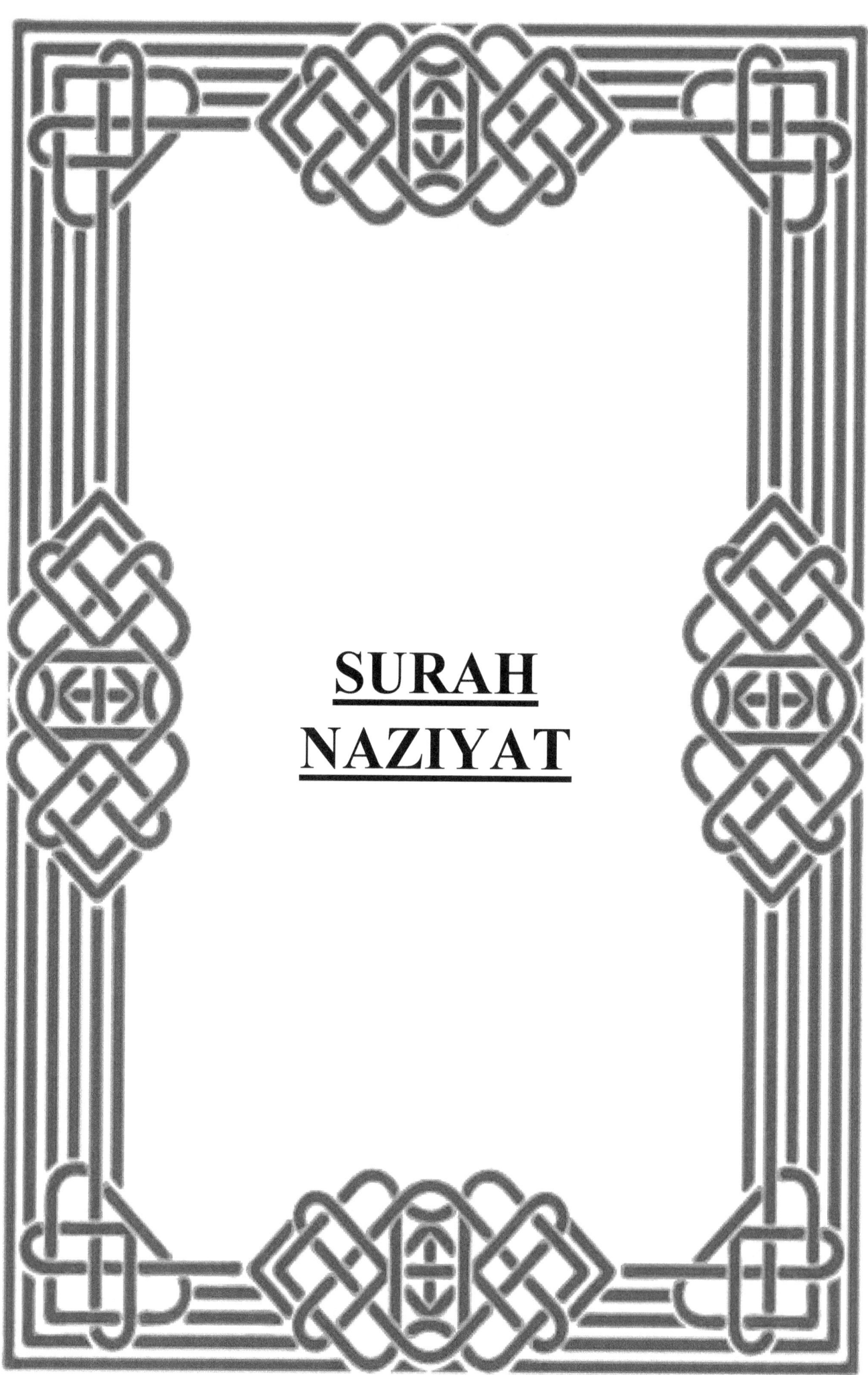

SURAH NAZIYAT

Bismillahi ar-Rahmani ar-Raheem

TAFSEER OF SURAH AN NAZIAT

Surah An-Nazi'at (Chapter 79 of the Quran)

Surah An-Nazi'at (Chapter 79 of the Quran) is believed to have been revealed in Mecca and primarily addresses themes related to the Day of Judgment, resurrection, and the fate of disbelievers and believers. The surah is named after the word "Nazia'at," which refers to the angels who pull out the souls of the deceased.

The context of the revelation is important, as it was a time when the Prophet Muhammad (SWS) faced significant opposition from the Quraysh tribe and other polytheists in Mecca. The surah serves to remind the disbelievers of the inevitable reality of resurrection and accountability in the Hereafter. It emphasizes the signs of Allah's power in creation and the consequences of denying His message.

The surah also contrasts the fate of the disbelievers, who will face severe punishment, with that of the believers, who will be rewarded. This duality serves as both a warning and encouragement, urging people to reflect on their beliefs and actions in light of the ultimate truth of existence and the afterlife.

The Key Points

1. Affirmation of the Afterlife: The surah emphasizes the reality of the Day of Judgment and the resurrection of the dead. This was particularly relevant as many of the disbelievers in Mecca questioned the possibility of life after death. The surah serves to reinforce the belief in an afterlife, urging listeners to reflect on their beliefs and actions.
2. Warning to Disbelievers: The surah provides a stern warning to those who deny the message of Islam. It vividly describes the consequences they will face in the Hereafter, serving as a reminder of the seriousness of their choices and the fate that awaits them if they continue in disbelief.
3. Encouragement for Believers: In contrast to the fate of the disbelievers, the surah reassures believers of their reward. It highlights the mercy and justice of Allah, encouraging those who follow the Prophet to remain steadfast in their faith despite the challenges they face.
4. Reflection on Creation: The surah invites reflection on the signs of Allah's creation, including the natural world and human existence. By recognizing these signs, individuals are encouraged to acknowledge Allah's power and the truth of His message.
5. Response to Opposition: The surah addresses the mocking and ridicule faced by the Prophet and his followers. By emphasizing the reality of the Day of Judgment, it serves as a reminder that ultimate justice will be served, regardless of the rejection the Prophet experienced in his lifetime.

In summary, Surah An-Nazi'at was revealed to strengthen the faith of believers, warn disbelievers,

Key themes within the surah:

Oaths and the Certainty of the Hereafter:

- The surah begins with oaths sworn by angels who "pluck out" (An-Naziat) the souls of the wicked and those who "draw out" (An-Nashitat) the souls of the righteous, and by those who hasten to execute Allah's commands.
- These oaths serve to emphasize that the Day of Resurrection and the afterlife are definite events.

- The surah suggests that the same angels who take souls in death can also restore them in the resurrection, and the same divine will that governs the universe can also bring about its end and renewal.

The Power of Allah and the Possibility of Resurrection

- The surah challenges the notion that resurrection is impossible by highlighting Allah's power over creation.
- It reminds people that Allah, who brought them into existence from the earth, can also bring them back from it in the resurrection.
- This is presented as both a demonstration of Allah's power and a demand of His wisdom, which necessitates holding people accountable for their actions in this life.

The Fate of the Deniers

- Verses 28-40 depict the fate of those who deny the Day of Judgment, addressing their fear, terror, and suffering.
- These verses highlight the consequences of rejecting Allah's message and the reality of the afterlife.

The Rewards of the Believers

- Verses 41-46 focus on the rewards and blessings that await those who believe in the Day of Judgment and strive to improve their Hereafter.
- These verses emphasize the importance of faith, righteous actions, and abstaining from disbelief and immoral behaviour.

The Angels of Death

- The terms "Naziat" (those who pluck out) and "Nashitat" (those who draw out) refer to different classes of angels responsible for taking the souls of the dead.

In essence, Surah An-Naziat uses powerful imagery and divine oaths to emphasize the certainty of the Day of Judgment, the power of Allah to bring about resurrection, and the consequences of belief and disbelief in the afterlife. It serves as a reminder to humanity to live their lives in preparation for the accountability that awaits them.

Verse 1

Wan naazi 'aati gharqa

"By those who forcibly extract the soul of the disbeliever."

This verse is part of a series of oaths that introduce the surah. It refers to the angels responsible for taking the souls of individuals at the moment of death, particularly those who do not believe. The phrase "forcibly extract" underscores the intensity and gravity of the moment when a soul is taken, especially for those who have rejected faith.

This verse establishes the surah's tone, which explores themes of resurrection, accountability in the afterlife, and the consequences of one's actions. The imagery invites reflection on the realities of life, death, and what follows, urging listeners to recognize the importance of faith and righteousness.

Verse 2

Wan naa shi taati nashta

"And gently release the soul of the believer."

Here we see a contrast with the first verse. Here we are learning that the angels take the souls of believers with gentleness and mercy.

This gentle release of the souls signifies Allah's mercy towards those who have lived righteously and maintained their faith. It illustrates the overarching theme of the surah regarding the different outcomes in the afterlife for believers and disbelievers, emphasizing the rewards awaiting the faithful. This verse encourages contemplation on life, death, and the significance of one's faith.

Verse 3

Wass saabi-haati sabha

"And glide swiftly in their course."

Reference here is made to the angels involved in taking souls and executing Allah's commands. The statement "glide swiftly in their course" suggests the speed and efficiency with which these angels fulfill their duties, demonstrating their obedience and readiness.

Continuing the theme established in the previous verses, the swift movement of the angels signifies the urgency of their mission, highlighting that the moment of death is significant and that the angels diligently perform their roles.

Verse 4

Fass saabi qaati sabqa

"And manage affairs (of the world)."

Now we are directed to the broader roles of the angels. They are not only responsible for taking the souls of individuals but also have a broader role in managing the affairs of the universe as ordained by Allah. This indicates that the angels have responsibilities beyond just the moment of death; they are involved in the administration and execution of divine commands throughout creation.

The phrase highlights the concept of divine order and governance, illustrating that there is a systematic and organized approach to how the universe operates, which is overseen by the angels. It emphasizes that everything is under Allah's control and that the angels play a crucial part in maintaining this order.

This verse, like the others in the surah, serves to remind believers of the reality of divine accountability and the importance of faith. It encourages a recognition of the unseen forces that operate in the world and the need for humans to align their lives with the guidance provided by Allah.

Verse 5

Fal mu dab-bi raati amra

"The Day the quaking will quake."

Now the focus shifts to an apocalyptic scene, referring to the Day of Judgment. "The Day the quaking will quake" signifies a time of immense upheaval and disturbance, where the earth will tremble and shake in response to the events unfolding during this significant day. It conveys a sense of fear, awe, and the overwhelming nature of the events that will take place.

The quaking of the earth serves as a metaphor for the profound changes that will occur, including the resurrection of all individuals for judgment based on their deeds in this life. It illustrates the reality of accountability and the consequences of one's actions.

This verse serves as a reminder of the transient nature of worldly life and the importance of being prepared for the inevitable reality of the afterlife. It encourages believers to reflect on their lives, their faith, and the significance of their choices, as they will ultimately face the consequences of those actions on that momentous day.

Verse 6

Yawma tarjufur raajifa

"And after it, another quake will follow."

"Another quake" refers to a subsequent event that occurs after the initial quaking mentioned in the previous verse. A second blast will happen and creation will come back to life. The imagery of quaking emphasizes the intensity and significance of this day, indicating that it will be marked by profound changes and upheavals.

The repetition of the concept of quaking serves to underline the seriousness of the situation. It suggests that the Day of Judgment will not only involve an initial disturbance where everything is destroyed but a second occurrence when life is restored. This reinforces the theme of accountability and the reality of resurrection, where individuals will be brought forth for judgment based on their deeds in this life.

Verse 7

Tatba'u har raadifa

Followed by oft-repeated (commotions):

The term "oft-repeated commotions" refers to the significant and tumultuous events that will occur during the end times, particularly the upheaval in the natural order and the signs that will precede the resurrection. These "commotions" can be understood as the catastrophic events that will shake the earth and create a state of chaos, signalling the end of the world as we know it.

The context of this verse emphasizes the inevitability of the Day of Judgment and serves as a reminder of the power of Allah to bring about such dramatic changes. It reflects the seriousness of the events that will unfold, which will affect all of creation and lead to the final reckoning of humans for their deeds.

Verse 8

Quloobuny-yau maaiziw-waaji-fa

"Some hearts that Day will tremble"

Now we are seeing the emotional state of individuals on the Day of Judgment. "Some hearts that Day will tremble" conveys the intense fear and anxiety that people will experience as they face the consequences of their actions in this worldly life. The use of "hearts" symbolizes the innermost feelings and fears of individuals, reflecting their apprehension about their fate.

This verse highlights the gravity of the Day of Judgment, where all individuals will be held accountable for their deeds. The trembling of hearts signifies the uncertainty and worry that many will feel as they await their judgment, knowing that their actions will be scrutinized. It serves as a reminder of the importance of living a life of righteousness, faith, and good deeds in preparation for this inevitable day.

In summary, this verse focuses on the emotional and spiritual realities of the afterlife, encouraging believers to remain mindful of their actions and to seek forgiveness and guidance from Allah. It reinforces the Quranic themes of accountability, the consequences of one's choices, and the need for awareness of the transient nature of worldly life.

Verse 9

Absaa ruhaa khashi'ah

"Their eyes humbled."

The imagery of "eyes humbled" reflects the state of individuals on the Day of Judgment. It signifies a posture of submission, humility, and recognition of the overwhelming reality of their situation. On that day, as people stand before Allah for judgment, they will feel a deep sense of awe and fear, leading them to lower their gaze.

This verse emphasizes the profound impact of the Day of Judgment on human beings, highlighting their vulnerability and the seriousness of the moment. The act of lowering one's eyes is a sign of humility and recognition of one's shortcomings, particularly in the face of divine judgment. It underscores the idea that on that day, all pride and arrogance will be stripped away, and individuals will be confronted with the reality of their actions and the divine authority of Allah.

Hence, this verse serves to remind believers of the importance of humility in their lives, both in their relationship with Allah and in their dealings with others. It encourages reflection on one's actions, the need for repentance, and the significance of preparing for the Day of Accountability.

Verse 10

Ya qoo loona a-inna lamar doo doona fil haafirah

"And yet, some say, 'What! Are we indeed to be restored to our former state –"

Here we see the skepticism and disbelief of some people regarding the concept of resurrection after death. It captures the attitude of those who question the possibility of being brought back to life after they have died and their bodies have decayed. The phrase "to be restored to our former state" emphasizes their doubt about the feasibility of returning to life in the same form they had during their earthly existence.

This verse serves to highlight a common human concern about life after death, addressing the doubts that arise when faced with the concept of resurrection. It sets the stage for the subsequent verses, which affirm Allah's power and ability to resurrect people, regardless of their physical state after death.

Verse 11

Aizaa kunna 'izaa man-nakhirah

"What! - when we shall have become rotten bones?"

In this verse, the speaker (The Prophet Muhammad, Saws) is instructed to respond to the question posed by individuals about resurrection with a clear affirmation of Allah's power. This is a reminder that just as Allah created human beings initially, He is fully capable of resurrecting them after death.

This verse serves to reinforce the belief in resurrection and the omnipotence of Allah. It highlights the connection between the act of creation and the act of resurrection, illustrating that the same divine power that brought humans into existence can also bring them back to life after death.

This verse addresses doubts regarding the possibility of resurrection and emphasizes the importance of faith in Allah's capabilities. It encourages believers to trust Allah's wisdom and power.

Verse 12

Qaalu tilka izan karratun khaasirah

They say: "It would, in that case, be a return with loss!"

This verse reflects the doubt and disbelief of those who question the possibility of resurrection after death. The phrase "return with loss" indicates that these individuals believe that being resurrected after death would not only be impossible but also disadvantageous or futile. They are expressing doubt about the resurrection, viewing it as a loss rather than a gain, as they struggle to comprehend how they could return to life after having turned to dust.

This sentiment is often found among those who reject the idea of the afterlife and the accountability that comes with it. The verse captures the reaction of disbelievers who cannot fathom how resurrection could occur.

Verse 13

Fa inna ma hiya zajratuw-waahida

"Indeed, it will be but one shout":

This refers to the single blast of the horn (Israfil's trumpet) that will initiate the resurrection. It's a powerful, earth-shattering blast that will jolt all of humanity into awareness of the impending Day of Judgment. It signifies the transition from this life to the afterlife. **The verse emphasizes the suddenness and finality of the event**. It highlights that the resurrection will occur with one command, leaving no room for doubt or delay.

Verse 14

Faizaa hum biss saahirah

"And suddenly they will be [alert] upon the earth's surface".

This describes the state of the resurrected individuals, who will be standing on a barren, flat expanse, the earth transformed into a place of judgment. This is the "Sahiarah", the place of awakening. The verse serves as a warning to those who deny the afterlife and the Day of Judgment.

The verse encourages reflection on one's actions in this world, as they will determine one's fate in the Hereafter, and to prioritize their preparation for the Hereafter over the temporary pleasures of this world.

Verse 15

Hal ataaka hadeethu Musaa

"Has the story of Prophet Musa(pbuh) reached you?".

This is an introduction to the narrative of Prophet Musa(pbuh) (peace be upon him) and his encounter with Pharaoh, which is then detailed in the following verses.

The verse is a rhetorical question, meant to draw the listener's attention to the important story of Prophet Musa (pbuh). It serves as a taster to the following verses, which recount the encounter between Prophet Musa(pbuh) and Pharaoh, highlighting the prophet's mission to guide Pharaoh and his people to the truth.

The story highlights Musa(pbuh)'s mission.

Allah instructed Prophet Musa(pbuh) to call Pharaoh towards purification and guidance. However, Pharaoh rejected his message and even denied Allah, ultimately leading to his downfall.

The verse hints at the concept of divine justice, where those who disobey and transgress will face consequences. The destruction of Pharaoh serves as a reminder that Allah is just and will hold individuals accountable for their actions.

Verse 16

Iz nadaahu rabbuhu bil waadil-muqad dasi tuwa

"When his Lord called to him in the sacred valley of Tuwa":

This refers to the story of Prophet Musa (pbuh) being called by his Lord in the sacred valley of Tuwa.

It describes the moment when Allah spoke to Musa in a specific location, a valley which is considered sacred – The Valley of Tuwa.

The verse implicitly calls for fearing Allah's punishment and recognizing the consequences of disobedience.

Pharaoh's story serves as a cautionary tale against pride, transgression, and rejecting divine truth.

Verse 17

Izhab ilaa fir'auna innahu taghaa.

"Go thou to Pharaoh for he has indeed transgressed all bounds:

In this verse, we are learning that Allah instructed Prophet Musa (pbuh) to go to Pharaoh and deliver the message of Tawhid (belief in one Allah) and to free the Israelites from the slavery.

The word **taghaa** [طَغَى] translated here as transgressed is from the root tay-ghayn-ya and it means 'exceed a limit, to transgress, exceed the bound, or deviate'.

Neither tyranny nor transgression should be allowed to take place or be left unchecked. They lead to corruption and to what displeases Allah subhanahu wa ta'ala. Therefore, Allah subhanahu wa ta'ala selected one of His noble servants and tasked him to put an end to them.

Despite Pharaoh's tyrannical behaviour Prophet Musa(pbuh) invited him to islam using kind speech and gentle words.

What we take away from this is quite significant. We learn that when we give Dawah(encourage others to embrace the truth), it is important to be gentle and respectful.

Verse 18

Faqul hal laka ilaa-an tazakka

'Would you [be willing to] purify yourself"

Look at the way the question has been put: would you be willing to purify yourself. When a person is indulged in transgression his heart hardens and he loses his way. So the first question was whether or not the tyrant would like to purify himself of the stains of tyranny and abominable disobedience. Here is an important lesson for any preacher regarding what our goal should be. Our goal should not only be for that the person to listens and follows us but rather we should also genuinely care for their well-being and work on their soul purification.

Verse 19

Wa ahdi yaka ila rabbika fatakh sha

"And that I may guide you to your Lord, so you should fear Him".

This verse continues this invitation highlighting the consequence of disbelief.

In essence, in this verse Allah swt uses the story of Musa and Pharaoh to illustrate the consequences of rejecting Allah's message and the importance of purification, guidance, and fearing Allah.

The verse shows us that even in the face of overwhelming evidence, the choice to purify oneself is ultimately up to the individual. Despite the fact that the prophet came to Pharaoh with so many miracles, he still chose disbelief.

Verse 20

Fa araahul-aayatal kubra.

"Then [Musa (Prophet Musa(pbuh)] showed him the great sign."

This miraculous sign is the transformation of the staff of Prophet Musa into a serpent. This is indeed a Great Sign and a powerful demonstration of Allah's power and a challenge to the magic that Pharaoh's magicians were practicing.

The purpose of showing this sign is to prove the truthfulness of Prophet Musa's message and to warn Pharaoh of the consequences of rejecting Allah's message.

The verse highlights the importance of heeding divine guidance and the consequences of arrogance and disobedience. It also demonstrates the power of Allah and the miracles He bestows upon His prophets.

Verse 21

Fa kazzaba wa asaa

"Then he showed him the great sign, but he denied and disobeyed."

After calling Pharaoh to believe in Allah, Musa showed him the great miracle of his staff turning into a serpent, but Pharaoh rejected the sign and disobeyed the message.

Verse 21 teaches that those who fear Allah will benefit from the warnings, while those who deny and disobey, will face the consequences. This highlights the importance of fearing the Hereafter and the accountability that comes with it.

Verse 22

Thumma adbara yas'aa

"Then he turned his back, and went about striving (against the truth)."

This verse describes Pharaoh turning away and striving against the truth after Prophet Musa (AS) showed him the great sign.

Instead of accepting the truth, Pharaoh rejects it, turning away from the message and actively working against it. This highlights the arrogance and defiance of Pharaoh, who, despite witnessing a clear sign from Allah, chooses to persist in his disbelief and opposition.

This verse serves as a warning against wilful blindness and stubbornness in the face of divine signs.

Verse 23

Fa hashara fanada

"Then he collected (his men) and made a proclamation"

This verse describes Pharaoh's actions after being shown the "great sign."

His heart became hardened and he defied Allah swt. He then called his people together to make a grand announcement. And what was this grand announcement?

He proclaims to be the supreme lord. This act of public declaration was a form of rebellion against Allah and a demonstration of his inflated ego.

This story serves as a reminder that even in the face of clear truth, one can still choose disbelief. Furthermore, it is a cautionary tale against arrogance, pride, and rejecting divine guidance. The verse emphasizes the importance of humility and submitting to the truth, as opposed to arrogance and defiance. It also serves as a reminder of Allah's power and authority, and that those who defy Him will face His wrath.

Verse 24

Faqala ana rabbu kumul-a'laa

"I am your Lord, the Most High".

Pharaoh turned away to mobilize his forces and bring forward his sorcerers for an encounter between magic and the truth. Essentially, Pharaoh was determined not to accept the truth or submit to it. He summoned all his men and made a proclamation to them, **"I am your most exalted lord,"**

Pharaoh, in his arrogance, declares himself the supreme lord, attempting to elevate himself above Allah.

Pharaoh found his people so ignorant, submissive and devoid of faith that he was able to make his insolent, blasphemous declaration, "I am your most exalted lord!" He would never have dared to make it had his nation believed in Allah.

The verse sets the stage for the consequences of Pharaoh's actions, which ultimately lead to his downfall and punishment.

This is a stark reminder of the dangers of pride and the importance of submitting to Allah's will.

Verse 25

Fa-akha zahul laahu nakalal aakhirati wal-oola

Allah seized him "with a punishing example for the Hereafter and the first (life)".

Recounting the death of Firawn, Ibn Kathir said, "The curtain fell on **Pharaoh's** tyranny, and the waves threw his corpse up to the western seashore. The Egyptians saw him and knew that the "Allah" whom they worshipped and obeyed was a mere man who could not keep death away from his own neck."

During his reign, Pharaoh possessed strength, good health, wealth, and power, yet he stubbornly refused to accept the religion and believed in Allah SWT. However, when confronted with the approach of death, the Pharaoh cried out to Allah SWT in horror and fear. He repented but his repentance was not accepted.

This serves as a reminder that if humanity remembers Allah during times of abundance and ease, Allah SWT will, in turn, remember us even in the most sinful humans in times of distress.

Verse 26

Inna fee zaalika la'ibratal limaiy-yaksha

"Indeed in that is a warning for whoever would fear [Allah],"

This verse discusses Pharaoh's punishment by Allah. Allah punished Pharaoh both in this life, with him drowning in the sea, and in the afterlife, with eternal torment.

This is teaching us that Pharaoh's punishment extends beyond his earthly life, encompassing both his worldly demise and his fate in the afterlife.

The verse serves as a warning to those who transgress and reject Allah's message.

Verse 27

A-antum a shaddu khalqan amis samaa-u banaaha.

Allah asks a question in this verse:

"Is it more difficult to create you, or to create the vast and complex heavens?"

The question serves to highlight Allah's power and to challenge the notion that resurrection is impossible. If Allah could create the heavens, then recreating human beings should be even less difficult.

Verse 27 encourages reflection on the grandeur of creation and the power of the Creator. It emphasizes that the same divine power that brought forth the universe can also resurrect the dead.

Verse 28

Raf'a sam kaha fasaw waaha

"On high hath He raised its canopy, and He hath given it order and perfection".

In this verse, Allah challenges the disbelievers who deny the resurrection by pointing to the magnificent creation of the heavens. The verse highlights the vastness and intricate design of the sky, suggesting that if Allah could create such a complex structure, then bringing humans back to life after death is certainly within His power. The verse implies that the disbelievers should reflect on the greatness of Allah's creation and acknowledge His power to recreate life.

This also verse encourages contemplation of Allah's creation as proof of His power and wisdom, and as a reminder of the inevitability of the Day of Judgment.

Verse 29

Wa aghtasha lailaha wa akhraja duhaaha.

"And He darkened its night and brought forth its daylight.

The alternation of night and day is seen as a testament to Allah's perfect design and wisdom. The Quran emphasizes that the night and day, along with the sun and moon, are all part of a divinely ordained system, each with its own specific orbit, working in harmony. This natural phenomenon is considered a sign for those who reflect on the grandeur of creation.

The regular cycle of night and day, with the sun and moon following their respective courses, demonstrates a meticulously planned and harmonious universe.

The Quran encourages contemplation of these natural phenomena, suggesting they hold profound meaning and guidance for those who ponder.

While the Quran speaks of night and day as creations of Allah, scientific understanding reveals that these phenomena are a result of Earth's rotation and its position relative to the sun. However, Islamic texts suggest the underlying cause, even if explained scientifically, is still attributed to divine will and design.

Verse 30

Wal arda b'ada zaalika dahaaha.

"And after that He spread the earth."

The verse emphasize that the Earth's features were not created by chance, but rather by a wise and purposeful design to sustain life.

The spreading of the earth is seen as a key step in making it habitable and a suitable place for humans and animals to live, highlighting Allah's mercy and provision.

Verse 31

Akhraja minha maa-aha wa mar 'aaha.

"And after that He spread the earth."

This verse highlights Allah's power in creating and shaping the earth, specifically mentioning its spreading or flattening after its initial creation. This is presented as a testament to Allah's power and a precursor to the blessings He provides for humanity and their livestock.

Every day, the light of the Sun causes the cycle of night and day to follow each other. After that, Allah spreads the Earth, which is how the sky is formed. He created the Earth after the sky.

From this, we understand that Allah spread out the Earth, making it vast and liveable so that humans can live comfortably. He also separated the Earth from what it was joined with before, specifically from the sky.

From the Earth, water flows for your use, and Allah also created plants and grasses that grow from the Earth, which animals eat. Therefore, water, plants, and animals come from the Earth itself, making the Earth self-sufficient—there's no need to rely on other planets for water or food.

Verse 32

Wal jibala arsaaha

"And the mountains hath He firmly fixed";-

Allah swt has firmly anchored the Earth by placing mountainsto provide stability and support, , much like ships anchored in water.
These mountains also serve as protection.

Verse 33

Mataa'al lakum wali an 'aamikum.

"For use and convenience to you and your cattle".

From the water and the plants, humans and animals both benefit. The verse informs that Allah provides not only for humans but also for their animals, highlighting His boundless mercy and care for all creatures.

Reflecting, we are all dependent on Allah's provisions. Allah is always caring for us. How can we forget Him when He is so constant in His mercy?

Verse 34

Fa-izaa jaaa'atit taaam matul kubraa.

"But when the great catastrophe comes."

This verse refers to the Day of Judgment, specifically the most overwhelming and impactful event, often translated as the "Great Calamity" or "Overwhelming Disaster". It signifies the onset of the Resurrection and the beginning of the reckoning for all humanity.

On this day, every problem and disaster we face in life will seem insignificant. The Day of Judgment will surpass all calamities, and it is ongoing; it will never end and we cannot escape from it. It is a moment when humans will remember what they worked for and what they ran after in life.

Verse 35

Yauma Yata zakkarul insaanu ma sa'aa.

"The Day when man will remember that for which he strove".

Here we are reminded of the accountability of humans on the Day of Judgment, reminding them of their actions and deeds in this world. It highlights the inevitable reckoning where every individual will recall everything they strived for during their earthly existence.

We need to reflect today on what we are striving for—whether what benefits us only in this world or what will also benefit us in the Hereafter. Often, we rush after worldly gains and forget the eternal life. When the Hereafter is brought into view, Hellfire will be exposed and visible for all to see. According to Hadith, Hellfire will be brought in 70,000 reins, each held by 70,000 angels, so that everyone can witness it.

Verse 36

Wa burrizatil-jaheemu limany-yaraa.

"And Hellfire is brought forth for whoever sees."

This verse describes the Day of Judgment, specifically when Hellfire will be made visible to all. It emphasizes the undeniable reality of Hell and the consequences for those who have transgressed and preferred worldly life.

Hellfire will be their refuge because they prioritized temporary pleasures over eternal salvation. Conversely, those who feared standing before their Lord and His judgment and who controlled their desires—who stopped themselves from chasing worldly temptations—are the ones who will succeed.

Desires are very strong—they make people fall when they pursue them. It is when people chase their desires they will stumble and fall into temptation. It's crucial to remember that resisting desires is part of fearing Allah and preparing for the Hereafter.

Verses 37 to verse 40

Fa ammaa man taghaa.

"Then, as for him who transgressed".

Verse 38

Wa aasaral hayaatad dunyaa

"And had preferred the life of this world",

Verse 39

Fa innal jaheema hiyal maawaa.

"The Abode will be Hell-Fire"

Verse 40

Wa ammaa man khaafa maqaama Rabbihee wa nahan nafsa 'anil hawaa

"And for such as had entertained the fear of standing before their Lord´s (tribunal) and had restrained (their) soul from lower desires"

In these verses, Allah describes the people of the Hellfire as those who are arrogant, stubborn, and have rejected the truth.

These are the people who follow their desires. Cravings or desires can become so strong, causing a person to cheat, lie, or do things that are forbidden just to satisfy their desires.

But when can a person control this desire?

The answer is when they fear Allah—their Lord—and understand His greatness and power. If someone respects and fears Allah, they will avoid doing things that go against His commands.

People's lives are divided into two parts: one is their home in Paradise, and the other is what leads to Hell. Following desires can lead us to Hell, while avoiding them can help us reach Paradise. When asked about the Day of Judgment, many try to find out when it will happen, just like asking when a ship will arrive and be anchored. But instead of preparing for it, they spend time questioning and debating.

Verse 41

Fa innal jannata hiyal ma'waa

"Those who feared the position of their Lord"

This refers to individuals who recognize the accountability they will face on the Day of Judgment and strive to live their lives in accordance with Allah's commands, fearing His displeasure.

Verse 42

Yas'aloonaka 'anis saa'ati ayyaana mursaahaa

"They ask you about the Hour: 'When will it be?'". This verse addresses the disbelievers' persistent questioning of Prophet Muhammad about the exact time of the Day of Judgment. They asked this not out of genuine curiosity, but to mock and deny its occurrence.

Allah reminds us that we don't have the knowledge of when the Day will occur—that knowledge is only with Him. Only Allah knows when the Hour will come, and His knowledge is final. We may ask others, but no one can tell us for sure. Our role is to be warned and prepared, especially those who fear the consequences of that day.

Verse 43

Feema anta min zikraahaa

This verse directly addresses the disbelievers who were questioning the Prophet Muhammad (peace be upon him) about the exact time of the Hour (Day of Judgment). It essentially means, "What concern is it of yours? What do you hope to gain by knowing the exact time? You have no knowledge of it, nor any ability to affect it".

Verse 44

"To your Lord is its finality"

It clarifies that the knowledge of the exact time of the Hour is not something that has been revealed to anyone else.

We must not be preoccupied with the timing but we should focus on righteous actions and prepare ourselves for that day.

When the Day of Judgment arrives, people will see it clearly. They will feel as if they haven't lived in this world for long—like the brief time between morning and evening. The world will seem so short, and the life in this world will pass quickly. We find it difficult to control our desires; we fear how we will survive another day, or how we will fast the entire day. But in reality, our worldly life is only a moment—like an afternoon or morning.

This highlights that everything in this life—hardships and pleasures—is temporary. We should prioritize the Hereafter over worldly enjoyments. If we focus only on the pleasures of this world, we forget that they are fleeting. Even our efforts and pursuits here are limited—they will not last forever. So, it's wise to make the right choices now.

Verse 45

Innamaaa anta munziru maiy yakhshaahaa

"You are only a warner for those who fear it".

This verse emphasizes that the Prophet Muhammad's role is to warn those who are apprehensive about the consequences of **their** actions and the Day of Judgment. It highlights that his message is specifically directed towards those who possess a fear of Allah and are mindful of His commands.

Verse 46

Ka annahum Yawma yarawnahaa lam yalbasooo illaa 'ashiyyatan aw duhaahaa

The Day they see it, (It will be) as if they had tarried but a single evening, or (at most till) the following morn!

This verse discusses the Day of Judgement and the perception of time in the afterlife. It states that on the Day when they see the Hour (of Judgement), it will be as if they had only remained (in the world) for an evening or a morning. This verse emphasizes the brevity of worldly life in comparison to the eternity of the Hereafter.

As we near the end of the Surah, Allah reminds us of the results of our actions. There are two ways to live: one is by rebelling against Allah's limits and fulfilling every desire without regard, which leads to a terrible ending. This way of life is based on pleasing ourselves and ignoring what Allah has commanded.

Surah Naziat – Surah 79

Questions

1. What are the main themes of Surah An-Nazi'at?
2. How does Surah An-Nazi'at describe the Day of Judgment?
3. What is the significance of the oaths at the beginning of the surah?
4. How does the surah use the story of Prophet Moses and Pharaoh?
5. What do verses 27-33 say about the creation of the heavens and the earth?
6. How does the surah address the beliefs of the Quraysh tribe regarding the afterlife?
7. What are some notable stylistic features of Surah An-Nazi'at?
8. How do various tafsir (interpretations) explain the meaning of the term "An-Nazi'at"?

Answers

1. Main Themes:
    - The surah emphasizes the resurrection and the afterlife, highlighting the power and authority of Allah. It warns of the consequences of disbelief and arrogance and underscores the inevitability of the Day of Judgment.

2. Description of the Day of Judgment:
    - The surah vividly describes the Day of Judgment with scenes of chaos and upheaval. It portrays the resurrection as a sudden event that will leave people in awe and fear.

3. Significance of the Oaths:
    - The oaths at the beginning of the surah emphasize the certainty and significance of the events being described. They serve to draw attention to the themes of death, resurrection, and divine judgment.

4. Story of Moses and Pharaoh:
    - The surah uses the story of Moses and Pharaoh as an example of Allah's power and the fate of those who are arrogant and deny the truth. It serves as a warning to those who reject the message of the Prophet Muhammad.

5. Creation of Heavens and Earth:
    - Verses 27-33 highlight Allah's power in creating the heavens and the earth, emphasizing the meticulous and purposeful nature of creation, which underscores Allah's ability to resurrect the dead.

6. Addressing Quraysh Beliefs:
    - The surah challenges the skepticism of the Quraysh regarding the afterlife, asserting the certainty of resurrection and divine judgment, and reminding them of past nations that faced consequences for their disbelief.

7. Stylistic Features:
    - The surah is noted for its powerful imagery and rhythmic verses, which create a sense of urgency and intensity. The use of oaths and rhetorical questions enhances its impact.

8. Interpretation of "An-Nazi'at":
    - The term "An-Nazi'at" is often interpreted as referring to the angels who extract the souls at the time of death. Different tafsir provide various perspectives on this, but generally agree on the theme of divine intervention in the process of death and resurrection.

Multiple-Choice Questions Based on Surah An-Nazi'at

1. What is the primary theme of Surah An-Nazi'at?

    - A) Wealth and prosperity

    - B) Resurrection and the afterlife

    - C) Dietary laws

    - D) Marriage and family

2. What event is vividly described in Surah An-Nazi'at?

    - A) The migration to Medina

    - B) The Battle of Badr

    - C) The Day of Judgment

    - D) The creation of Adam

3. What is the significance of the oaths at the beginning of the surah?

    - A) To introduce the rules of fasting

    - B) To highlight the certainty of the events being described

    - C) To provide a list of dietary restrictions

    - D) To narrate the story of creation

4. Which historical figure does the surah mention as an example of arrogance and disbelief?

    - A) King Solomon

    - B) Pharaoh

    - C) Prophet Abraham

    - D) The Queen of Sheba

5. What is described in verses 27 33 of Surah An Nazi'at?

    - A) The laws of inheritance

    - B) The creation of the heavens and the earth

    - C) The story of Noah's Ark

    - D) The rules of prayer

6. How does the surah address the beliefs of the Quraysh tribe regarding the afterlife?

    - A) By confirming their beliefs

    - B) By challenging their skepticism and asserting the certainty of resurrection

    - C) By ignoring their beliefs

    - D) By providing a list of their deities

7. What does the term "An-Nazi'at" most commonly refer to in the context of this surah?

    - A) The stars

    - B) The angels who extract souls

    - C) The mountains

    - D) The righteous believers

8. What style is Surah An-Nazi'at known for?

    - A) Detailed genealogies

    - B) Poetic imagery and rhythmic verses

    - C) Lengthy legal discussions

    - D) Lists of commandments

Answers

1. *Answer:* B) Resurrection and the afterlife

2. *Answer:* C) The Day of Judgment

3. *Answer:* B) To highlight the certainty of the events being described

4. *Answer:* B) Pharaoh

5. *Answer:* B) The creation of the heavens and the earth

6. *Answer:* B) By challenging their skepticism and asserting the certainty of resurrection

7. *Answer:* B) The angels who extract souls

8. *Answer:* B) Poetic imagery and rhythmic verses

Feel free to use these questions for study or discussion purposes! If you need more questions or have any other queries, let me know.

SURAH ABASA

SURAH ABASA

Bismillahi ar-Rahmani ar-Raheem

Verse 1

'Abasa wa tawallaa.

"He frowned and turned away."

This verse is addressing the Prophet Muhammad (peace be upon him) for his reaction towards a blind man named Abdullah Ibn Umm Maktum. The Prophet (PBUH) had turned away and frowned when the man approached him while he was engaged in conversation with some prominent Quraish leaders.

Verse 2

An jaa-ahul 'a-maa

Because there came to him the blind man (interrupting).

This explains why the Prophet Muhammad (peace be upon him) frowned and turned away from the blind man.

Verse 3

Wa maa yudreeka la'allahu yaz zakkaa.

"And what would make you perceive, [O Muhammad], that perhaps he might be purified?"

Verse is a gentle admonition to the Prophet (PBUH) for overlooking the potential for spiritual growth in the blind man. Allah is reminding him that he cannot know for sure who will benefit from guidance and who will not.

The Background story behind these verses

Ibn Umm Maktum, a poor blind man, comes to the Prophet (peace be upon him) at a time when he is busy with a group of the most powerful and influential personalities in Makkah, including 'Utbah and Shaybah, sons of Rabi`ah, Abu Jahl, `Amr ibn Hisham, Umayyah ibn Khalaf, al- Walid ibn al-Mughirah. Also present is al-`Abbas ibn `Abd al-Muttalib, the Prophet's uncle. It is a crucial meeting. The Prophet explains the message of Islam to them and hopes for a favourable response. He feels that the cause of Islam stands to gain much by such a response. Islam is facing a hard time in Makkah. Those very people have been using all their wealth, power and influence to check its advancement, and stop people from accepting it. They have managed to freeze Islam in Makkah and hinder its progress elsewhere. Outside

Makkah, the other tribes have adopted an attitude of wait and see. For they feel this to be their best stand in a society which gives paramount importance to the tribe's attitude. They are aware that against Muhammad, the Prophet of Islam, stand his own kinsmen, who, theoretically speaking, should be his most ardent supporters.

It must be emphasized that when it is said that the Prophet is busy with these people, he has no personal interest in them. He is simply working for Islam. Acceptance of Islam by these influential and powerful people means the removal of all impediments from the path of Islam in Makkah. It also ensures for Islam the freedom to progress in the rest of Arabia.

While this crucial meeting is in progress, a poor man comes and interrupts the Prophet (peace be upon him) saying: **'Messenger of God!** Teach me some verses of what God has taught you.' Although he could sense that the Prophet is busy, he repeats his request several times. The Prophet dislikes this interruption. His face, which remains unseen by the blind man, expresses his aversion. He frowns and looks away from the poor man. Indeed, the Prophet's motive has been his great enthusiasm to win badly needed support for Islam.

However, Allah is gently correcting His Messenger that even such a minor facial expression like a frown was inappropriate in this context.

This incident shows that even the Prophet (peace be upon him), with his perfect character, had moments where he was corrected by Allah for his demeanor—specifically, his facial expression.

From this, we learn two key lessons:

9. Even when dealing with difficult situations or people who offend us, our behaviour should reflect patience and humility—even in our facial expressions and body language.
10. We should invest our energy in those who sincerely seek guidance and value it, rather than chasing after those who show no interest. The Prophet (peace be upon him) focused on those influential personalities, despite their dis-interest.

Verse 4

Aw yazzakkaru fatanfa 'ahuz zikraa

Or that he might receive admonition, and the teaching might profit him?

This verse questions whether the blind man, who had interrupted the Prophet (PBUH) might be receptive to the message and benefit from it. This highlights the importance of not overlooking anyone seeking guidance, regardless of their social status or physical condition.

Here the lesson for us is that Allah's guidance is irrespective of class and colour. We should be more inclined toward teaching those who show their interest in learning matters of religion. The rest, if Allah *subhanahu wa ta'ala* sees any good in them, will follow on their own. We see that in the early days of Islam the weak and the downtrodden formed the majority among the believers. Only a handful of influential people had joined this new religion. Then as word spread and people witnessed the truth themselves social dignitaries such as the 'Umar ibn al-Khattab and 'Uthman ibn Affan *radhiAllahu 'anhum* embraced Islam too and worked their entire life for it.

Verse 5

Fa-anta lahu tasaddaa

"As for the one who regards himself self-sufficient":

This part of the verse describes the individual who believes he has no need for spiritual guidance.

The concept of guidance and misguidance is intertwined with Allah's will and human agency. While Allah guides whomever He wills, this guidance is often contingent upon an individual's willingness to seek and accept it. Those who turn towards Allah, seeking knowledge and striving for righteousness, are more likely to be guided, while those who reject guidance or persist in wrongdoing may find themselves further astray.

If Allah has guided someone to Islam, it means that He knows this person has something within them that not only does He love so much, but knows that it will benefit the Ummah and other people's lives. Those who sincerely seek guidance through prayer, reflection, and righteous actions are more likely to be guided.

And in contrast, those who turn away from guidance, persist in wrongdoing, or actively reject Allah's message may find themselves increasingly distanced from His path.

Verse 6

Fa-anta lahu tasaddaa

"To him dost thou attend"

This verse refers to the Prophet Muhammad (peace be upon him) being reproached for giving more attention to the wealthy and influential individuals who considers themselves self-sufficient than to a blind companion, Ibn Umm Maktum, who was seeking guidance.

This verse highlights the importance of not prioritizing those who are wealthy or self-satisfied over those who are seeking knowledge and guidance, especially the less privileged

Verse 7

Wa ma 'alaika allaa yaz zakka

"And not upon you [is any blame] if he will not be purified."

The prophet is being reminded that it is not his responsibility to ensure the spiritual purification or guidance of every individual. The verse emphasizes that the Prophet's duty is only to convey the message of Islam, and he is not to be blamed if some people choose not to accept it or benefit from it.

Reflecting:

The core message of islam is that while Muslims have a responsibility to convey the message of Islam, it is ultimately Allah who guides individuals to belief.

No one can force belief upon another, and it is Allah's will that determines who is guided and who is not.

Verse 8

Wa amma man jaa-aka yas'a

"But as for him who came to you striving":

This part of the verse emphasizes the positive attitude of the person seeking knowledge. The word "striving" highlights his eagerness and earnestness.

This Surah serves as a reminder to Muslims to prioritize those who seek knowledge and guidance, regardless of their social standing, and to approach all individuals with respect and attention, as the Prophet (PBUH) was instructed to do.

Verse 9

Wahuwa yakhshaa

"While he fears [Allah]"

In the context of the surah, it refers to the blind man who approached the Prophet Muhammad (peace be upon him) seeking guidance, and who is described as someone who fears Allah.

This verse shows us the blind man's state of mind: he is described as someone who yas'a (strives, comes running) and yakhsha (fears) Allah. The fear of Allah, in this context, is not a terrorizing fear, but rather a reverential fear, a deep awareness of Allah's presence and power, which motivates him to seek knowledge and purification.

The surah, through this passage, teaches Muslims about the importance of:

- **Prioritizing those who seek knowledge and fear Allah:**

Even if they are not influential or wealthy, their seeking of guidance should be valued and attended to.

- **Not being distracted by worldly status or appearances:**

The Prophet (PBUH) was gently reminded that his attention should not be solely focused on those who seem important in the eyes of society, but rather on those who are genuinely seeking Allah's guidance.

- **Being sensitive to the needs and concerns of others:**

The surah highlights the importance of being mindful of others, even in seemingly small interactions, and not letting social status or other distractions hinder one's ability to show compassion and offer guidance.

Verse 10

Fa-anta 'anhu talah haa

"From him you are distracted,"

The verse highlights the importance of giving attention to those seeking religious guidance, regardless of their social status or apparent circumstance.

Verse 11

Kalla innaha tazkirah

"No! Indeed, these verses are a reminder."

The preceding verses describe the incident where the Prophet Muhammad (peace be upon him) frowned and turned away from a blind man.

Verse 11, therefore, serves as a reminder that the Quranic verses, including those detailing this incident, are not just stories or historical accounts but are meant to provide guidance and lessons for all believers. They are meant to be a source of reflection and a reminder of the importance of humility, compassion, and equal treatment of all individuals.

Verse 12

Faman shaa a zakarah

"So whoever wills, let him remember it."

The verse essentially means that the message of islam is available for anyone who wishes to benefit from it, and it is up to the individual to seek, choose and be guided by it, as the verse says "So whoever wills, let him remember it," serves as a reminder that the message of the Quran is for everyone, and those who seek guidance will find it.

In other words, religious guidance is available to all, and individuals have the freedom to choose whether or not to accept and benefit from it.

Verse 13

Fi suhufim mukar rama

"(It is) in Books held (greatly) in honour".

This verse refers to the Preserved Tablet.

So what is the Preserved Tablet?

The Preserved Tablet, is also known as al-Lawh al-Mahfuz in Arabic. It is a tablet which has been in existence before the creation of the universe, and has a record of all past, present, and future events. Nothing can be added to, subtracted from, or altered within the Preserved Tablet, as it reflects Allah's perfect knowledge and decree.

While humans cannot access the Preserved Tablet directly, it is believed to be the source from which Allah reveals knowledge to prophets and messengers.

The concept of qadar, or divine destiny, is closely linked to the Preserved Tablet, as it signifies Allah's preordained plan for all creation.

Verse 14

Marfoo'atim mutah hara

Exalted (in dignity), kept pure and holy

This refers to the high status and purity of the scriptures, signifying their divine origin and the sanctity of the information they contain.

It informs us that the angels who are entrusted with conveying the divine message are honourable and righteous beings who carry out their duties with integrity.

The verses emphasize that the Quran, being a divine revelation, is a precious and pure message that should be treated with respect and reverence.

Verse 15

Bi'aidee safara

(Written) by the hands of scribes

"By the hands of scribes, honourable and virtuous,"

This is refering to the angels who are entrusted with recording and conveying divine revelation. These angels are described as noble, righteous, and devoted to their duties. The verse highlights the purity and integrity of the Quranic text, emphasizing that it is transmitted through trustworthy and honourable beings.

Verse 16

Kiraamim bararah

"Noble and dutiful," refers to the angels who record and transmit divine revelations. The verse emphasizes their high status and integrity in carrying out their responsibilities. It also highlights the importance of the Quran, which these angels are entrusted with conveying.

The description emphasizes the angels' incorruptibility and dedication to their duties, suggesting a high moral standard.

In essence, verse 16 of Surah 80 serves as a reminder of the divine origin of the Quran and the integrity of those who transmit it, while subtly rebuking those who disregard its message.

Verse 17
Qutilal-insanu maa akfarah

"Accursed is man, how disbelieving is he!".

This verse is highlighting the ingratitude of man. Despite all the signs the creator has presented, they are still those who still choose to ignore his blessings and dismiss his guidance.

Verse 17 encourages reflection on one's own faith and actions, urging individuals to examine their relationship with Allah and strive for righteousness.

Verse 18 and verse 19
Min aiyyi shai-in Khalaq

"From what substance did He create him?

Min nutfatin khalaqahoo faqaddarah

"From a sperm-drop He created him, and then proportioned him.":

From a sperm-drop He created him and proportioned him," serves as a stark reminder of man's humble beginnings. It emphasizes that Allah created man from a lowly substance, yet fashioned him with a perfect form and proportion. This contrast between origin and form is meant to humble the arrogant and remind them of their dependence on Allah.

The verse also points out the ease with which Allah made the path for man, through various blessings and provisions. However, man often forgets these blessings and turns away from Allah's path.

Verse 20
Thummas sabeela yas-sarah

"Then He made the path easy for him,"

This refers to the ease with which Allah provides the means for humanity to navigate life, including both physical sustenance and the paths of righteousness and wickedness. It highlights the divine facilitation of both the good and the bad ways, emphasizing human free will in choosing between them.

This facilitation also carries a significant responsibility for humans. Since both paths are easily accessible, individuals are accountable for their actions.

In summary, this verse encourages reflection on how one navigates life's challenges and opportunities. It prompts individuals to consider the choices they make and the impact they have on themselves and others.

Verse 21

Thumma amatahu fa-aqbarah

Then He causeth him to die, and provides a grave for him

This verse highlights the completion of a human life cycle, encompassing death and burial. It teaches us that Allah is the one who brings about death and also provides a place of rest in the grave, signifying the end of life and a return to the earth.

- **"and provides a grave for him"**: After death, Allah provides a final resting place, the grave, where the body is laid to rest. This act of providing a grave is seen as a form of honour and respect for the human being, even in death. This verse follows the previous verses that discuss the creation of humans from a sperm drop, the easy path laid out for them, and their subsequent death.

Verse 22

Thumma iza shaa-a ansharah

"Then, when it is His Will, He will raise him up (again)".

This highlights that the timing of resurrection is solely determined by Allah's decree and not by human choice or capacity.

The verse follows the creation and death of man, emphasizing Allah's complete control over all stages of human existence. It follows the verse that states "Then He causes him to die. And puts him into the grave" (80:21), which highlights Allah's power over life and death.

Reminder and Reflection

The verse serves as a reminder of Allah's power and sovereignty, and that humans are accountable to Him. It also emphasizes the insignificance of human life in the face of divine power and the certainty of the afterlife.

Verse 23

Kalla lamma yaqdi maa amarah

"No! But he has not yet fulfilled what He commanded him.

The phrase "No! But he has not yet fulfilled..." highlights that people have not yet done their duties to Allah, suggesting that there is always room for improvement and encouraging action. The part "...what He commanded him." refers to the commandments and responsibilities that Allah has set for everyone, including both natural guidance and laws revealed by Him. The verse shows that humans generally struggle to fully meet their obligations to Allah, despite having guidance. It encourages us to think about Allah's blessings and the importance of working hard to follow His commands. In summary, this verse reminds us of our shortcomings in fulfilling our divine duties and urges us to reflect and strive to do better.

Summary of verses 24 to 32

These verses tell story of food, the provision of which is carefully planned by the hand which created man, Allah swt. Man plays no role in any of its stages. Even the seeds and grains the Almighty casts on the earth are not of his making. The miraculous aspect here lies in the original production of these seeds and grains, which is beyond man's comprehension. Various seeds may be planted on the same piece of land, irrigated by one kind of water; yet each produces its own fruit. It is the hand of the Creator which makes this infinite collection of plants and their fruits, and preserves in the little seed the characteristics of its mother plant so that they may reappear in the plant which issues from it. Man remains ignorant of the secrets of this process. He has no power over it. It is Allah's own production: **"For you and your cattle to delight in."** This delight is, however, for a limited period. There follows something totally different which needs to be carefully considered by man before it actually arrives – The Day of Judgement

Verse 24

Falyanzuril insanu ilaa ta-amih

"Then let man look at his food,"

This verse encourages reflection on the origins and sustenance provided by Allah. It prompts a deeper consideration of how food is created, distributed, and made available for human consumption, highlighting the divine power behind these processes.

The verse serves as a reminder of Allah's grace and provision, urging humans to acknowledge the intricate system the almighty has established to sustain life. It invites contemplation on the various stages involved in bringing food from its source to our tables, emphasizing that these are not coincidental occurrences but rather intentional acts of divine creation and management.

Here's a more detailed breakdown:

"Then let man look at his food":

This phrase directs human attention to the food we consume, encouraging us to move beyond merely eating to a deeper appreciation of its origins.

Reflecting on the process:

The verse calls for reflection on the various stages involved in food production, including the earth, rain, seeds, and the processes that enable growth and nourishment.

Divine Providence:

Ultimately, the verse points to Allah as the ultimate provider and sustainer, emphasizing His role in creating and making food available for humanity.

Verse 25

Anna sabab nalmaa-a sabba

"Then We pour forth water in abundance."

This verse talks about the rain that Allah sends down from the sky. Rain is a vital source of life and sustenance for both humans and animals.

This verse follows earlier verses that discuss the creation of sustenance for humans. It informs the important role that rain plays in providing for our needs.

Additionally, the verse reminds us of Allah's mercy and provision. It encourages us to think about the many blessings we receive from rain and how the earth can produce vegetation because of it.

Then We pour forth water in abundance" relates to the theme of Surah Abasa by focusing on the importance of reflection on Allah's creation and His provision for humanity.

Surah Abasa addresses various aspects of human life, including the significance of divine guidance, the importance of being grateful for Allah's blessings, and the need to recognize our dependence on Him.

1. Reflection on Creation: The verse encourages contemplation of how Allah provides for all living beings through the natural elements, like rain. This ties into Surah Abasa's overall message that urges individuals to recognize the signs of Allah's creation and His role as the sustainer of life.
2. Gratitude for Provision: By highlighting the vital role of rain in agriculture and sustaining life, the verse serves as a reminder to be thankful for Allah's blessings. Surah Abasa emphasizes the importance of acknowledging and appreciating these provisions.
3. Inclusivity of Divine Mercy: The Surah addresses a diverse audience, including those who might be overlooked or marginalized. The mention of rain, a fundamental necessity for life that benefits everyone, reinforces the idea that Allah's mercy extends to all, regardless of their social status.

In essence, the verse contributes to the Surah's theme by urging reflection on Allah's generosity and the need to recognize the blessings that nurture life and promote gratitude towards the Creator.

Verse 26

Thumma sha qaqnal-arda shaqqa.

"And We cleave the earth in fissures,"

This verse describes the splitting of the earth by rain and the growth of plants. It highlights Allah's power to create life and bring forth sustenance from the earth, demonstrating the natural process of vegetation growth after rainfall.

The verse connects the splitting of the earth with the subsequent sprouting of plants and vegetation. It showcases Allah's power to make the earth fertile and bring forth life from seemingly barren ground.

Verse 26 encourages reflection on the natural processes that provide sustenance and prompts gratitude for Allah's blessings.

Verse 27

Fa ambatna feeha habba

"And We have caused grain to grow therein."

This verse like verse 26 is talking about how Allah creates and supports life, focusing on providing food. It shows that the growth of grain is a gift from Allah, highlighting His role in taking care of humans and all living things.

Again this is a reminder of Allah's power and kindness in providing for us. It encourages us to think about the blessings of food and the complex processes that make it possible, pointing to a higher power behind it all.

Additionally, this verse relates to others in the Quran that discuss resurrection and the Day of Judgment, suggesting that the ability to grow grain is evidence of Allah's control over life and death.

Verse 28

Wa 'inabaw-wa qadba

And Grapes and nutritious plants,

Here we learn about how Allah provides food for people. It mentions "grapes and green nutritious plants" as examples. These are important because grapes are a nutritious fruit enjoyed by many, and the fresh plants are also used as food for animals, helping them stay healthy and productive.

The verse shows Allah's care for His creation by giving these necessary resources. It reminds us to think about the blessings and the process of getting food from the earth to our tables.

Verse 29

Wa zaitoonaw wanakh la'

And Olives and Dates

This verse speaks about olive trees and date palms, showing them as part of what Allah supplies for people and livestock. It comes after earlier verses that mention grains, grapes, and greens, highlighting the diversity of food provided by Allah. This verse reminds us of Allah's blessings and His ability to provide for all living things.

Overall, the verse invites people to think about all the types of food Allah gives, showing His power, kindness, and care for His creation. The range of offerings, from grains to fruits to trees, highlights the richness of what Allah provides.

Verse 30

Wa hadaa-iqa ghulba

"And gardens of dense shrubbery":

Verse 30 discusses the provision of sustenance from Allah, specifically mentioning various fruits and vegetation as a means of benefit for both humans and animals. The verse highlights the bounty of God's creation, emphasizing the abundance of food sources like grapes, greens, olives, date palms, and orchards, all provided for the sustenance of mankind and their livestock.

- "And gardens of dense shrubbery":

This refers to the lush, green vegetation that provides food and shelter.

- **"And enclosed orchards, dense with lofty trees":**

Reflecting, this verse serves as a reminder of Allah's generosity, specifically focusing on the provision of food and sustenance for all living beings.

Verse 31

Wa faki hataw-wa abba

And fruits and fodder,

"And fruits (Fakihah) and herbage (Abb)":

This is telling us the wide variety of fruits and fodder for animals, highlighting the diversity of sustenance available.

Verse 32

Mata'al-lakum wa li-an'amikum.

"A provision and benefit for you and your cattle":

This demonstrates the practical purpose of all the mentioned vegetation, which is to provide sustenance and benefit for both humans and animals.

Verses 33 to 37

Faiza jaa-atis saakhah - At length, when there comes the Deafening Noise,

Yauma yafir-rul mar-u min akheeh - And from his mother and his father,

Wa ummihee wa abeeh - And from his mother and his father,

Wa sahi batihee wa baneeh - Wa sahi batihee wa baneeh.

Likul limri-im-minhum yawmaa-izin shaa nuy-yughneeh- Each one of them, that Day, will have enough concern (of his own) to make him indifferent to the others.

These verses paints a vivid picture of the intense fear that will engulf individuals on the Day of Judgment. This day is characterized by the overwhelming events that lead people to abandon even their closest relatives. The gravity of the situation will cause individuals to prioritize their own fate over familial bonds that are often deemed unbreakable in this worldly life.

What would be the reason for the flight depicted in these verses?

One significant reason is the fear and instinct for self-preservation that will compel individuals to focus solely on their own well-being in a situation of unparalleled severity. Additionally, some may choose to distance themselves from their relatives to avoid complicity in their sins or to escape any accountability that may arise from their family members' wrongdoings.

The choice of broad terms such as "brother," "mother," "father," "wife," and "children" indicates that the separation experienced on that day will resonate universally, affecting everyone regardless of their familial ties. This universality highlights the profound nature of the events of the Day of Judgment, serving as a stark reminder that when faced with divine accountability, all human relationships may pale in comparison to the urgency of personal judgment.

Ultimately, this verse contrasts the deep, worldly attachments that individuals cultivate for their families with the radical shift in priorities that will occur on the Day of Judgment. It illustrates the changes in perspective that arise when the stakes are significantly heightened, emphasizing the importance of self-reflection and the need to focus on one's own actions in preparation for the ultimate accountability that lies ahead.

Verses 38 to 42

Wujoo huny-yauma-izim-musfira; -

Some faces that Day will be beaming,

Wa wujoohuy yauma-izin 'alaiha ghabar –

And other faces that Day will be dust-stained,

Tarhaquha qatarah -

Blackness will cover them:

Ulaa-ika humul-kafa ratul-fajarah –

Such will be the Rejecters of Allah, the doers of iniquity.

Verses 38 to 42 of Surah Abasa emphasize the significance of the Day of Resurrection, where every individual's actions and beliefs will come into focus. On this day, what truly matters is how one lived their life, as each person will be held accountable for their deeds.

The verses highlight the condition of the faithful, indicating that those who have embraced righteousness and understood the message of faith will find themselves in a favourable state. This aspect reflects hope for believers, reinforcing the idea that faith and good actions lead to a positive outcome.

Additionally, the inevitability of accountability is a significant theme in these verses, reminding us that every human will confront the reality of their life choices. This serves as a powerful reminder of the transient nature of worldly life and the importance of considering the hereafter.

Lastly, the passages underscores Allah's omniscience, affirming that He is fully aware of all actions and intentions. This knowledge provides the foundation for ultimate judgment, emphasizing the need for individuals to act with integrity and faith in their daily lives. Overall, these verses serve as a compelling reminder of the significance of faith, righteous conduct, and the reality of life after death.

Reflecting on Surah Abasa

The story of the blind man in Surah Abasa serves as a profound lesson in compassion, humility, and the essence of true faith. This narrative revolves around the Prophet Muhammad's interaction with a blind man who approached him seeking guidance and understanding. The Prophet, while preoccupied with a group of influential leaders, initially turned away from the blind man.

This moment reveals an important teaching: the value of every individual, regardless of their social status or physical condition. The narrative emphasizes that true worth lies not in one's societal position but in the sincerity of one's heart and the pursuit of faith. The blind man, despite his disability, displayed a yearning for knowledge and connection with Allah, highlighting that spiritual insight is not limited by physical barriers.

Additionally, the response from Allah in this context shows us that the Prophet's attention should have been directed toward those seeking truth, sincerely, rather than those who were already established in their worldly positions. This reprimand serves as a reminder of the importance of compassion and the responsibility of leaders to prioritize the needs of the underprivileged and the sincere seekers of guidance.

Moreover, the story reinforces the idea that the path to faith and understanding is open to all. It illustrates that, regardless of one's circumstances, every individual has the potential to connect with Allah and seek righteousness. This narrative ultimately calls for a deeper reflection on our attitudes toward others, urging us to recognize the intrinsic value of every soul, fostering empathy, and understanding in our interactions.

In summary, the story of the blind man in Surah Abasa highlights the importance of compassion, the value of sincere seekers of faith, and the need to give attention to those who may be marginalized, offering rich lessons on humility and the true essence of belief.

Personal accountability plays a central role in the context of Surah Abasa, in the verses that discuss the Day of Resurrection. The concept of accountability demonstrates that every individual is responsible for their own actions, decisions, and beliefs.

Firstly, the verses underscore the idea that on the Day of Judgment, each person will stand alone to face the consequences of their deeds. This individual responsibility highlights the importance of living righteously and adhering to the teachings of faith, as one's actions will directly influence their fate in the hereafter.

Moreover, personal accountability serves as a reminder of the transient nature of worldly life. The verses encourage individuals to reflect on their choices and behaviours, understanding that ultimately, they will be judged not by societal standards or the opinions of others, but by their own actions and the purity of their intentions.

Additionally, the assurance of divine knowledge reinforces the importance of personal accountability. Allah is aware of all actions, including those hidden from others, which adds weight to the idea that each person must act with integrity and sincerity. This awareness calls believers to be conscious of their conduct and to strive for goodness in all aspects of life.

In summary, personal accountability in Surah Abasa highlights the individual nature of judgment in the hereafter, urging every person to take responsibility for their actions and emphasizing the significance of faith and righteousness in determining their ultimate outcome.

Surah Abasa, Surah 80

Questions

Questions based on Surah Abasa, which can help in understanding its themes and messages:

These questions can serve as a starting point for a deeper exploration and discussion of Surah Abasa.

1. Context and Revelation:
    - What event led to the revelation of Surah Abasa?
    - Who was the blind man mentioned in the context of the surah's revelation?

2. Themes and Messages:
    - What are the primary themes highlighted in Surah Abasa?
    - How does the surah emphasize the importance of humility?

3. Lessons on Social Interaction:
    - What lesson does Surah Abasa teach regarding how we should treat people, regardless of their social status or physical abilities?
    - How does the surah highlight the value of every individual in the eyes of Allah?

4. Description of the Quran:
    - How does Surah Abasa describe the Quran and its purpose?

5. Day of Judgment:
    - What description does the surah provide about people's reactions on the Day of Judgment?
    - How does the surah depict the state of people who were heedless of guidance?

6. Human Creation:
    - What does Surah Abasa say about the creation and origin of human beings?
    - How does the surah remind humans of their dependence on Allah?

7. Stylistic Features:
    - What are some notable stylistic features of Surah Abasa?

8. Moral and Ethical Implications:
    - What moral and ethical lessons can be drawn from the incident involving the Prophet Muhammad (peace be upon him) and the blind man?

Answers

1. Context and Revelation:
   - Surah Abasa was revealed when the Prophet Muhammad (peace be upon him) frowned upon being interrupted by a blind man, Abdullah ibn Umm Maktum, while he was engaged in conversation with some of the Quraysh leaders.
   - The blind man was Abdullah ibn Umm Maktum.

2. Themes and Messages:
   - The primary themes include humility, the importance of guidance, and the value of every human being.
   - The surah emphasizes humility by showing that everyone deserves respect and attention, regardless of their social standing or physical abilities.

3. Lessons on Social Interaction:
   - Surah Abasa teaches that we should treat all individuals with respect and kindness, irrespective of their social status or physical abilities.
   - It highlights the value of every individual by demonstrating that divine guidance and attention are not limited to the elite but are meant for all.

4. Description of the Quran:
   - Surah Abasa describes the Quran as a reminder and guidance for those who seek it, emphasizing its accessibility and significance for everyone.

5. Day of Judgment:
   - The surah describes people on the Day of Judgment as being preoccupied with their own concerns, worried about their fate.
   - It depicts those who were heedless of guidance as facing the consequences of neglecting the divine message.

6. Human Creation:
   - Surah Abasa reminds humans of their humble origin, being created from a mere drop, and emphasizes their dependence on Allah.
   - It serves as a reminder of the reliance on Allah for sustenance and guidance.

7. Stylistic Features:
   - Notable stylistic features include vivid imagery and concise, impactful language that conveys the message effectively.

8. Moral and Ethical Implications:
   - The incident teaches the moral lesson that one should not judge others based on superficial attributes and that everyone deserves attention and respect. It reinforces the importance of humility and the equal value of all individuals in the eyes of Allah.

Multiple Choice Questions

1. What is the main theme of Surah Abasa?

    - A) Wealth and prosperity

    - B) Humility and the importance of guidance

    - C) Dietary laws

    - D) Warfare and peace

2. What event prompted the revelation of Surah Abasa?

    - A) The Prophet Muhammad's interaction with a wealthy merchant

    - B) The Prophet Muhammad's migration to Medina

    - C) The Prophet Muhammad's interaction with a blind man, Abdullah ibn Umm Maktum

    - D) The Prophet Muhammad's marriage to Khadijah

3. How does Surah Abasa emphasize the value of every individual?

    - A) By highlighting the importance of wealth

    - B) By focusing on the physical appearance of people

    - C) By showing that guidance should be offered to everyone, regardless of social status

    - D) By emphasizing the importance of lineage

4. What does Surah Abasa say about the Quran?

    - A) It is an old and outdated text

    - B) It is a reminder and guidance for those who seek it

    - C) It is only for scholars and the elite

    - D) It is a book of rules and punishments only

5. What lesson can be learned from the incident involving the blind man in the surah?

    - A) Wealth is more important than knowledge

    - B) Social status should determine who receives guidance

    - C) Everyone deserves attention and respect, regardless of their abilities or status

    - D) Physical appearance is crucial in religious matters

6. How does the surah describe the reaction of people on the Day of Judgment?

    - A) Calm and composed

    - B) Joyful and relaxed

    - C) Distraught and worried about their own affairs

    - D) Indifferent and unaware

7. What does the surah say about those who are heedless of guidance?

- A) They will be rewarded

- B) They will face consequences for neglecting the message

- C) They will be ignored by everyone

- D) They will never have another chance for redemption

8. What is a significant stylistic feature of Surah Abasa?

- A) Detailed historical accounts

- B) Vivid imagery and concise, impactful language

- C) Long poetic verses

- D) Philosophical debates

Answers

1. *Answer:* B) Humility and the importance of guidance
2. *Answer:* C) The Prophet Muhammad's interaction with a blind man, Abdullah ibn Umm Maktum
3. *Answer:* C) By showing that guidance should be offered to everyone, regardless of social status
4. *Answer:* B) It is a reminder and guidance for those who seek it
5. *Answer:* C) Everyone deserves attention and respect, regardless of their abilities or status
6. *Answer:* C) Distraught and worried about their own affairs
7. *Answer:* B) They will face consequences for neglecting the message
8. *Answer:* B) Vivid imagery and concise, impactful language

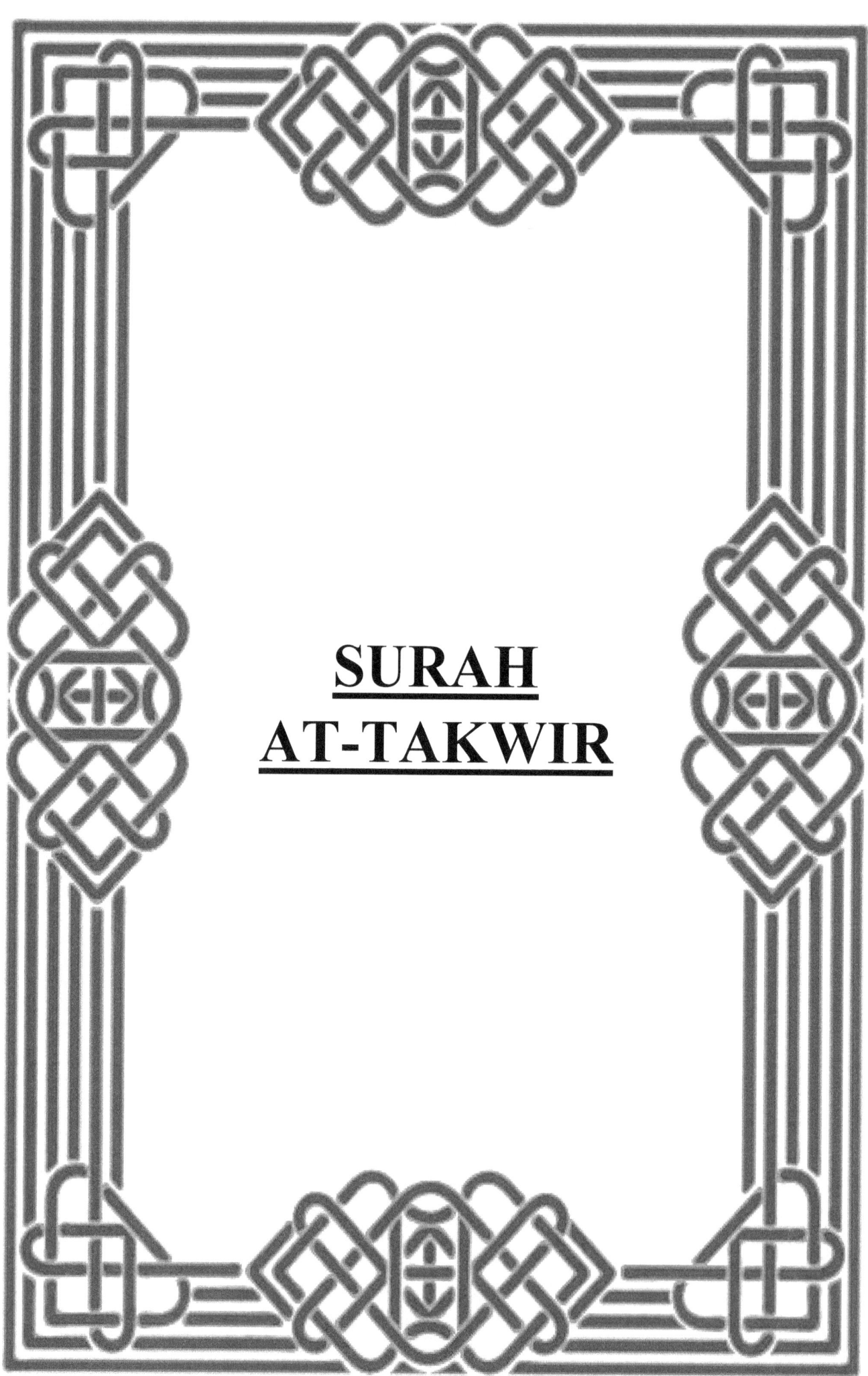

SURAH AT-TAKWIR

SURAH AT-TAKWIR

Bismillahi ar-Rahmani ar-Raheem

Verse 1

Izash shamsu kuwwirat

[When the sun shall be wound round and its light is lost and is overthrown.]

This will happen when the first trumpet will be blown and everything will be destroyed. Prophet Muhammad (peace and blessings of Allah be upon him) said:

"The sun and the moon will be folded up (or joined together or deprived of their lights) on the Day of Resurrection." [Narrated by Al-Bukhari]

Verse 2

Wa izan nujoomun kadarat

[And when the stars shall fall.]

This is another sign of the Hour. Ubayy bin Ka'b, a companion of the Prophet said:

"Six signs will take place before the Day of Judgment. The people will be in their marketplaces when the sun's light will go away. When they are in that situation, the stars will be scattered. When they are in that situation, the mountains will fall down upon the face of the earth, and the earth will move, quake and be in a state of mixed up confusion. So the Jinns will then flee in fright to the humans and the humans will flee to the Jinns. The domestic beasts, birds and wild animals will mix together, and they will surge together in a wave (of chaos). … So they will all go to the sea, and it will be a blazing fire. While they are in that state, the earth will be split with one huge crack that will extend from the lowest, seventh earth to the highest, seventh heaven. So while they are in that state, a wind will come that will kill all of them." [Tafsir Ibn Kathir]

Verse 3

Wa izal jibaalu suyyirat

[And when the mountains shall be made to pass away;]

This means, on that day mountains will not be in their places and will be destroyed; then the earth will be left as a flat, level plain.

Verse 4

Wa izal 'ishaaru 'uttilat

[And when the pregnant she-camels shall be neglected;]

Pregnant she-camels were the most precious assets of people in Arabia during the time of the Prophet. This verse indicates that people will be careless about their precious possessions on the day when everything will be destroyed.

Verse 5

Wa izal wuhooshu hushirat

[And when the wild beasts shall be gathered together.]

This event signifies the end of the world and the start of the afterlife, where even animals will be judged. The verse highlights the overwhelming fear and chaos of that day, where fearful creatures will be brought together, losing their natural instincts and acting in an unnatural way.

Verse 6

Wa izal bihaaru sujjirat

[And when the seas shall become as blazing Fire (or shall overflow]

This verse describes the oceans being set ablaze on the Day of Judgment, stating. This signifies a dramatic shift in the natural order, as the very water, a source of coolness and life, will become a source of intense heat and destruction

Verse 7

Wa izan nufoosu zuwwijat

[And when the souls shall be joined with their bodies (the good with the good and the bad with the bad).]

It has been narrated that every type of souls will be gathered with their peers or mates based on their records.

Verse 8

Wa izal maw'oodatu su'ilat

[And when the female (infant) buried alive (as the pagan Arabs used to do) shall be questioned:]

[For what sin was she killed?]

Pre-Islamic Arabs used to bury infant girls alive due to their hatred to girls. Therefore, on the Day of Judgment, the female infant (buried alive) will be asked what sin she committed that caused her to be murdered. This will be a means of frightening her murderer.

Verse 9

Bi ayyi zambin qutilat

[And when the (written) pages (of good and bad deeds of every person) shall be laid open.]

On the Day of Judgment the righteous people will receive their records in their right hands and the wicked people will receive their records in their left hands.

Verse 10

Wa izas suhufu nushirat

[And when the scrolls are laid open]

This verse describes a scene from the Day of Judgment, specifically when the records of everyone's deeds, both good and bad, are made public. It signifies the opening of the books containing the actions of all humans, allowing each person to see their own record.

Verse 11

Wa izas samaaa'u kushitat

[And when the sky is stripped away]

The "sky" in this context refers to the visible expanse above us, the blue dome that we see. The verse suggests that on the Day of Judgment, this familiar structure will be taken away, revealing what lies beyond it.

This stripping of the sky is part of the horrific events that will unfold on the Day of Judgment, alongside the kindling of Hellfire and the drawing near of Paradise

Verse 12

Wa izal jaheemu su'-'irat

[And when the blazing sky is kindled bright]

In this verse, the imagery of a "blazing sky" evokes a sense of awe and fear, marking a significant event in the context of the Day of Judgment. The term "kindled bright" suggests a dramatic and overwhelming transformation of the sky, illustrating the intensity of the moment when divine signs manifest.

This depiction serves multiple purposes:

1. Sign of Judgment: The blazing sky signifies the extraordinary events that will unfold as the world approaches its end. It indicates that the established order of the universe will be disrupted, emphasizing the seriousness of the Day of Judgment.
2. Awakening Reflection: Such vivid imagery encourages listeners and readers to reflect on their lives and the reality of the afterlife. It serves as a warning that the consequences of one's actions in this life will be made manifest in the hereafter.
3. Divine Power and Control: By portraying the sky in such a dramatic manner, the verse emphasizes Allah's absolute power over creation. It serves as a reminder of His authority and the inevitability of the Day of Judgment, where all will be held accountable.

Verse 13

Wa izal jannatu uzlifat

[And when Paradise is brought near.]

"And when Paradise is brought near," signifies the nearness of Paradise to the believers on the Day of Judgment, contrasting with the blazing Hellfire mentioned in the previous verse. It highlights the rewards awaiting the righteous and emphasizes the reality of the afterlife.

The nearness of Paradise serves as an encouragement for believers to strive for righteousness and to prepare for the Hereafter.

The nearness of Paradise also highlights Allah's mercy and grace, as He will grant His blessings to those who have earned them

Verse 14

Alimat nafsum maaa ahdarat

[Every human being will know what he has prepared for himself.]

This verse signifies that on the Day of Judgment, each individual will become fully aware of their deeds, both good and bad, and will understand the consequences of their actions in this life. It emphasizes the accountability that awaits every person.

These deeds encompasses all actions, thoughts, and intentions.

In essence, verse 14 emphasizes the comprehensive and undeniable nature of accountability on the Day of Judgment. It serves as a reminder for people to reflect on their actions and strive to do good, as they will ultimately have to face the consequences of their choices.

Verse 15

Falaaa uqsimu bil khunnas

[I swear by the retreating stars]

This verse is part of a series of oaths, where Allah swears by certain celestial bodies and natural phenomena to emphasize the gravity of the subject matter to follow, which is the Day of Judgment. The "retreating stars" are interpreted as those that appear and disappear, moving in their orbits, symbolizing the transient nature of worldly existence and the certainty of the afterlife.

Verse 16

Al jawaaril kunnas

[The planets that run their course and disappear]

This describes the planets (or stars) that run their courses and then disappear. It refers to the celestial bodies that appear to move across the sky and then vanish, either from view or from existence, during their orbits. This verse is part of a series of oaths (swearing by certain things) in the beginning of the Surah, emphasizing the power and control of Allah over creation.

Reflecting, this verse is part of a series of oaths that highlight the signs of the Day of Judgment. By swearing by these celestial phenomena, the verse emphasizes the power and control of Allah over the universe and all creation. The disappearance of these celestial bodies serves as a reminder of the temporary nature of this world and the certainty of the Hereafter.

Verse 17

Wallaili izaa 'as'as

[And the night as it darkly falls]

This verse, here again, along with others in the surrounding verses, is part of a series of oaths sworn by Allah, showing the certainty and significance of the events to come, specifically those related to the Day of Judgment. The verse highlights the night as it approaches and covers the world, symbolizing the end of the day and the beginning of darkness.

The night in this context symbolizes the end of an era, the fading of light, and the approach of a time of judgment. It signifies the end of worldly life and the beginning of the afterlife.

Verse 18

Wassubhi izaa tanaffas

[And by the dawn when it breathes]

This verse uses a powerful metaphor to describe the arrival of dawn, likening it to a living being inhaling and exhaling, bringing with it a sense of renewal and new beginnings.

The imagery of the dawn breathing evokes a sense of calmness, peace, and the start of a new day. It's a stark contrast to the darkness of the night, signifying the transition from darkness to light, from dormancy to activity.

Once again, this verse is a series of oaths in Surah At-Takwir, where Allah swears by various aspects of creation to emphasize the importance and truth of the Quran and the Prophet Muhammad's message. The dawn, with its gentle awakening, is presented as a powerful symbol of the divine power and order in the universe.

Verse 19

Innahoo laqawlu rasoolin kareem

[Indeed, the Qur'an is the word of a noble messenger]

This verse establishes that the Quran is not the product of human invention or whims, but rather a divine revelation delivered by a noble messenger, Jibreel (Gabriel).

"of a noble messenger...":

This identifies the intermediary who conveyed the Quran to the Prophet Muhammad (peace be upon him). This messenger is Jibreel (Gabriel), a highly respected angel known for his trustworthiness and close proximity to Allah.

The verse is significant because it:

- **Highlights the Quran's authenticity:** By attributing the Quran to a noble messenger, it underscores the Quran's divine nature and reliability.

- **Affirms the role of Jibreel:** It acknowledges Jibreel's crucial role as the conveyor of divine messages.

- **Reinforces the message of guidance:** It reminds readers that the Quran is a source of guidance and wisdom, sent to humanity through a trusted messenger.

In essence, Surah Takwir, verse 19, is a declaration of the Quran's divine origin and the role of Jibreel as its noble messenger.

Verse 20

Zee quwwatin 'inda zil 'arshi makeen

[Endued with Power, with rank before the Lord of the Throne]

This verse is describing angel Jibril (Gabriel) and is telling us of his great power, high status with Allah, and trustworthiness. It highlights his strength, his elevated position with the Lord of the Throne (Allah), and his reliability in delivering divine messages. This verse emphasizes Gabriel's role as a powerful and trustworthy messenger in conveying divine revelation.

In summary, this verse paints a picture of Gabriel as a powerful, respected, and dependable angel, highlighting his crucial role in the transmission of divine revelation.

Verse 21

Mutaa'in samma ameen

"Obeyed there [in the heavens] and trustworthy."

This verse is continuing to tell us about angel Jibril (Gabriel), highlighting his high status and reliability in delivering divine revelation.

"Obeyed there [in the heavens]":

This part emphasizes Jibril's authority and leadership among the angels. He is obeyed by all the angels in the celestial realm.

"and trustworthy":

This highlights Jibril's integrity and faithfulness in conveying the divine message from Allah to the prophets. He does not alter or tamper with the revelation.

In essence, the verse assures that the Quran, as revealed through Jibril, is a truthful and reliable source of guidance, coming from a messenger who is both powerful and trustworthy.

Verse 22

Wa maa saahibukum bimajnoon

[And your companion is not [at all] mad]

This verse is a direct response to accusations from the disbelievers who claimed the Prophet Muhammad(pbuh) was insane because of the Quranic revelations he was sharing. The verse affirms the Prophet's sanity and the divine nature of his message, emphasizing that he is not possessed by a jinn or mentally unsound.

Verse 23

Wa laqad ra aahu bilufuqil mubeen

[And he has already seen him in the clear horizon]

This is in reference to Prophet Muhammad (peace be upon him) witnessing the angel Gabriel in his true form in the clear horizon. Specifically, the verse clarifies that the Prophet had seen Gabriel on the eastern horizon.

The angel Gabriel appeared to the Prophet in his true form on the eastern horizon.

The verse highlights the authenticity of the Prophet's message and the divine nature of the Quran. It also emphasizes that the Prophet's message is not from Satan, but from Allah through the angel Gabriel.

Verse 24

Wa maa huwa 'alal ghaibi bidaneen

[And he (Muhammad) is not a withholder of the unseen]

This verse clarifies that the Prophet Muhammad (peace be upon him) is not withholding any knowledge of the unseen that has been revealed to him by Allah. He conveys the divine message without alteration or concealment.

..Conveying the Message...

This is highlighting the Prophet's honesty and trustworthiness in conveying the divine message. He doesn't try to manipulate or hide any part of the revelation for personal gain or any other reason.

Verse 25

Wa maa huwa biqawli shaitaanir rajeem

[And it [the Quran] is not the word of an outcast devil]

This verse refutes the claims of some disbelievers who attributed the Quran to Satan or a devil, asserting that it is a divine revelation, not the work of any evil spirit.

It affirms that the Quran is the word of Allah, sent down through the Angel Gabriel to Prophet Muhammad (peace be upon him).

Verse 26

Fa ayna tazhaboon

[So where are you going?]

Here we see a rhetorical question that prompts reflection on one's path and ultimate destination. It addresses humanity directly, urging them to consider where their current actions are leading them. It is a call for self-reflection, urging individuals to assess their choices and ensure they align with Allah's guidance.

Surah Takwir, through this verse, emphasizes the certainty of the Day of Judgment and the responsibility of each individual to prepare for it by living a life guided by faith and good deeds.

Verse 27

In huwa illaa zikrul lil'aalameen

[It is nothing but a reminder to the worlds]

This verse emphasizes that the Quran, revealed through the angel Gabriel, is a message and guidance for all of mankind and jinn (the worlds), not just a specific group or individual. It highlights the universal nature of the Quran's message and its purpose to serve as a reminder and source of guidance for all creation.

It signifies that the Quran is not meant to be a source of confusion or misguidance. Instead, it serves as a clear and concise reminder of Allah's message, His commandments, and the path to righteousness.

The Arabic word "lil'alamin" translates to "to the worlds," encompassing all of creation, including humans and jinn. This emphasizes that the Quran's message is not limited in scope but is intended for all beings who have been given the capacity to understand and act upon it.

The verse implies that the Quran's purpose is to awaken people to their true purpose, to warn them of the consequences of disobedience, and to guide them towards a life of virtue and righteousness.

Verse 28

Liman shaaa'a minkum ai yastaqeem

[For whoever wills among you to take a right course]

This verse emphasizes that the Quran is a reminder for all of humanity, but its guidance is only beneficial for those who actively seek to follow the straight path.

It focuses on the individual's role. It implies that simply hearing or reading the Quran is not enough. One must actively desire and choose to follow the path of righteousness.

This highlights the concept of free will and individual responsibility in accepting guidance. It suggests that Allah has provided the Quran as a means of guidance, but it is up to each person to choose to benefit from it.

The "right course" or "straight way" refers to the path of Islam, which is considered the true and correct way of life leading to success in this world and the hereafter.

Verse 29

Wa maa tashaaa'oona illaaa ai yashaaa 'al laahu Rabbul 'Aalameen

[And you do not will except that Allah wills – Lord of the worlds]

Here we are learning that humans have free will, but their ability to exercise that will is ultimately dependent on Allah's divine will. It highlights the concept that while humans have the capacity to choose, their choices are ultimately guided and enabled by Allah as reflected in the second part of the verse "except that Allah wills," demonstrating that Allah's will is supreme and encompasses all things. It means that even our desires and choices are ultimately under Allah's control and dependent on His permission.

This verse presents a balanced view of free will and divine will. It acknowledges human agency while affirming Allah's absolute sovereignty. It suggests that while humans make choices, their ability to do so is a gift from Allah and is ultimately subject to His will.

BACKGROUND INFORMATION ON SURAH AL-INFITAR

Surah Al-Infitar (The Sky Splitting Open), Chapter 82 of the Quran, is a powerful revelation that vividly describes the events of the Day of Judgment. This early Meccan chapter serves as a stark reminder of the inevitable reality that awaits all of humanity — the complete unravelling of the natural world, the resurrection of all souls, and the final divine reckoning. The Surah can be divided into three key themes: the apocalyptic signs of the Last Day, a warning to humanity for its ingratitude, and the final fate of the righteous and the wicked.

The Shocking Signs of the Final Hour

Allah begins the chapter with a series of dramatic and terrifying scenes meant to awaken human consciousness:

"When the sky splits open, and when the stars fall away, and when the seas burst forth, and when the graves spill out…"

Each of these descriptions paints a picture of utter chaos. The heavens, once a symbol of stability, will be torn apart. The stars, which have guided humanity for ages, will collapse and scatter. The vast seas, so powerful yet contained, will overflow uncontrollably. And finally, the graves will be overturned, bringing forth all of humanity for judgment.

"…then each soul will know what it has sent forth or left behind."

At this moment, every individual will come face to face with their deeds — whether good or evil. There will be no more excuses, no more denial. The reality of every action taken in life will become undeniably clear.

A Question to Humanity

Allah then turns to humanity with a profound and piercing question:

"O humanity, what has emboldened you against your Lord, the Most Generous?"

This verse is a direct challenge to those who ignore Allah's countless blessings and instead persist in wrongdoing. He is Al-Karim — the Most Generous, the one who created, fashioned, and perfected human beings, moulding them in the most beautiful form.

"Who created you, fashioned you, and perfected your design, molding you in whatever form He willed."

Despite all this, many remain heedless of the truth. They reject the coming judgment, ignoring the signs around them and within themselves. But Allah, in His mercy, does not immediately punish. Instead, He gives countless opportunities for people to repent and return to Him.

Yet, rather than being grateful, many continue to deny the truth:

"But no! In fact, you deny the Final Judgment."

The Recording of Every Deed

To reinforce the certainty of accountability, Allah reminds us that nothing we do goes unnoticed:

"While you are certainly observed by vigilant, honorable angels, recording everything. They know whatever you do."

Every word spoken, every action taken, and even the hidden intentions of the heart are meticulously documented by noble angels. Nothing is lost or forgotten — on the Day of Judgment, all will be presented in full detail.

The Destiny of the Righteous and the Wicked

With perfect justice, Allah declares the ultimate fate of every soul:

"Indeed, the virtuous will be in bliss, and the wicked will be in Hell, burning in it on Judgment Day, and they will have no escape from it."

The righteous, those who lived with faith and integrity, will be rewarded with eternal joy and peace. Meanwhile, those who lived in defiance of the truth will face the torment of Hell, from which there will be no refuge.

The Weight of Judgment Day

To emphasise the gravity of this moment, Allah repeats a haunting question:

"What will make you realize what Judgment Day is? Again, what will make you realize what Judgment Day is?"

This repetition is meant to shake the reader, highlighting the sheer magnitude of what is to come. It is a day unlike any other — a day when all illusions of power, status, and wealth will vanish. No one will be able to intercede on behalf of another, nor will anyone be able to escape the consequences of their actions.

"It is the day no soul will be of any benefit to another whatsoever, for all authority on that day belongs to Allah entirely."

On that day, the reality of divine justice will be absolute. All authority, all decision-making, and all power will rest solely with Allah. No human influence, wealth, or lineage will hold any weight — only faith and deeds will determine one's fate.

Final Reflection

Surah Al-Infitar serves as a stark reminder that this life is temporary and that every soul will one day stand before its Creator. It urges us to reflect on our actions, to acknowledge Allah's blessings, and to prepare for the inevitable Day of Judgment.

As believers, we must strive to remain conscious of our deeds, seek forgiveness for our shortcomings, and work towards righteousness, knowing that Allah's justice is perfect and His mercy is vast.

Surah At-Takwir – Surah 81

Questions

1. What are the major signs mentioned in Surah At-Takwir that indicate the coming of the Day of Judgment?
2. How does the surah describe the transformation of the natural world during the Day of Judgment?
3. What is the significance of the imagery of the sun being wrapped up and the stars losing their light?
4. How does Surah At-Takwir emphasize the concept of accountability and the presentation of deeds?
5. What role do the angels play according to the descriptions in Surah At-Takwir?
6. How does the surah address the concept of divine revelation and its authenticity?
7. What message does Surah At-Takwir convey regarding the truthfulness and reliability of the Prophet Muhammad (peace be upon him) as a messenger?
8. How does the surah highlight the contrast between the temporary nature of this world and the permanence of the hereafter?
9. In what ways does Surah At-Takwir challenge the listener to reflect on their own life and actions?
10. hat lessons can be drawn from Surah At-Takwir regarding the power and authority of Allah over the universe?

Answers

1. Surah At-Takwir mentions signs such as the sun being wrapped up, stars losing their light, mountains being set in motion, pregnant camels being neglected, and wild beasts being gathered.

2. The surah describes the natural world as undergoing immense transformation, with cosmic changes that signify the end of the world as we know it.

3. The imagery signifies the end of the natural order and the beginning of the Day of Judgment. It represents the loss of familiar sources of light and guidance, emphasizing the seriousness and magnitude of the event.

4. The surah emphasizes accountability by depicting the Day of Judgment as a time when all deeds will be presented and judged, highlighting the importance of one's actions.

5. Angels in the surah are described as witnesses to human deeds and as beings who convey divine revelation, emphasizing their role in the divine order.

6. The surah affirms the authenticity of divine revelation by describing it as a message delivered by noble and trustworthy angels.

7. The surah reinforces the reliability of Prophet Muhammad (peace be upon him) by stating that he has seen the angel Gabriel in clear view and that he is not insane or misleading.

8. By describing the end of the world and the presentation of deeds, the surah contrasts the fleeting nature of worldly life with the everlasting reality of the hereafter.

9. Surah At-Takwir challenges listeners to reflect on their actions by reminding them of the inevitable Day of Judgment and the presentation of their deeds.

10. The lessons highlight Allah's supreme control over the universe and the certainty of the Day of Judgment, encouraging believers to turn to Allah and prepare for the hereafter.

Multiple-choice questions based on Surah At-Takwir:

1. What does Surah At-Takwir primarily describe?

    - A) The creation of the universe

    - B) The events of the Day of Judgment

    - C) The story of a prophet

    - D) The laws of inheritance

2. Which of the following is mentioned as a sign of the Day of Judgment in Surah At-Takwir?

    - A) The sky being clear

    - B) The sun being wrapped up

    - C) The earth splitting open

    - D) The sea calming down

3. What happens to the stars according to Surah At-Takwir?

    - A) They increase in brightness

    - B) They fall to the earth

    - C) They lose their light

    - D) They become larger

4. How are pregnant camels described in the surah during the Day of Judgment?

    - A) They will be sold

    - B) They will be given special care

    - C) They will be neglected

    - D) They will become more valuable

5. What role do angels play in Surah At-Takwir?

    - A) They fight battles

    - B) They deliver revelation

    - C) They build mountains

    - D) They harvest crops

6. How is the Prophet Muhammad (peace be upon him) described in relation to receiving revelation?

    - A) As confused and misleading

    - B) As having seen the angel clearly

    - C) As having no knowledge of the unseen

    - D) As a king on earth

7. What imagery is used to describe the mountains during the events of the Day of Judgment?

    - A) They become taller

    - B) They turn to dust

    - C) They are set in motion

    - D) They disappear completely

8. What is the main theme conveyed by Surah At-Takwir?

    - A) The mercy of Allah

    - B) The importance of charity

    - C) The certainty of the Day of Judgment and accountability

    - D) The rules of prayer

9. What happens to wild beasts on the Day of Judgment according to Surah At-Takwir?

    - A) They become tame

    - B) They gather together

    - C) They start speaking

    - D) They disappear

10. What is highlighted about the revelation received by Prophet Muhammad (peace be upon him) in Surah At-Takwir?

    - A) It is a new invention

    - B) It is a continuation of old myths

    - C) It is delivered by noble and trustworthy angels

    - D) It is incomplete

Answers

1. *Answer:* B) The events of the Day of Judgment
2. *Answer:* B) The sun being wrapped up
3. *Answer:* C) They lose their light
4. *Answer:* C) They will be neglected
5. *Answer:* B) They deliver revelation
6. *Answer:* B) As having seen the angel clearly
7. *Answer:* C) They are set in motion
8. *Answer:* C) The certainty of the Day of Judgment and accountability
9. *Answer:* B) They gather together
10. *Answer:* C) It is delivered by noble and trustworthy angels

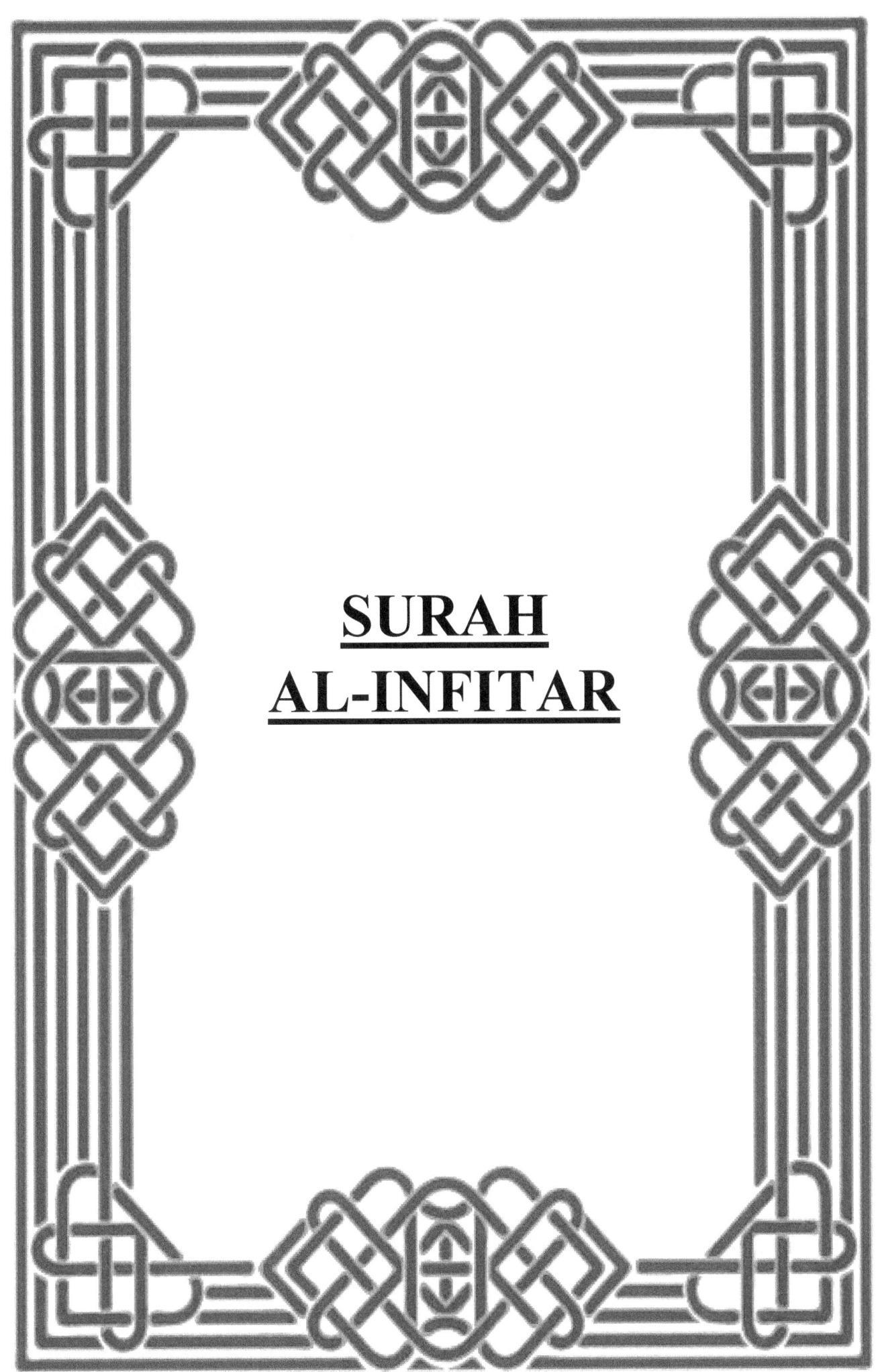

SURAH
AL-INFITAR

SURAH AL-INFITAR

Bismillahi ar-Rahmani ar-Raheem

Verse 1

Izas samaaa'un fatarat

"When the sky has been split apart."

This verse introduces the dramatic opening of the surah, which depicts the terrifying events of the Day of Judgment. The splitting of the sky signifies a complete breakdown of the established cosmic order and serves as a powerful image of the impending end of the world.

This opening sets a tone of awe and terror, highlighting the magnitude of the Day of Judgment. The Arabs, who were familiar with the sky and its beauty, would have found this image particularly impactful.

The verse aims to awaken humanity to the reality of the afterlife and the consequences of their actions. It serves as a warning and a reminder that the current world order will not last forever.

This verse is closely linked to the following verses, which describe the falling of the stars, the overflowing of the seas, and the resurrection of the dead, all occurring as a result of the sky splitting.

Verse 2

Wa izal kawaakibun tasarat

"And when the stars are scattered."

This verse describes a key event of the Day of Judgment, where the stars lose their orderly arrangement and are scattered, signifying the destruction of the universe's established order.

There will be this dramatic scene of the stars falling and scattering.

This scattering contrasts with the current, ordered state of the universe, where stars are held in their constellations and galaxies.

Hence, this verse is a powerful image to convey the magnitude of change and destruction that will occur on the Day of Judgment.

Reflecting

Imagine the stars in the night sky, neatly arranged in their constellations. Now, imagine them falling and scattering like beads from a broken necklace. That's what this verse describes – the stars losing their order and being dispersed, marking the end of the world.

Verse 3

Wa izal bihaaru fujjirat

"And when the seas are erupted"

Here we see a description of the splitting apart and eruption of the seas on the Day of Judgment. It signifies a dramatic and chaotic event where the oceans lose their boundaries and either merge together, explode, or dry up, symbolizing the end of the natural order and the onset of the apocalypse.

There are various interpretation of this occurrence:

Merging: The seas might merge into one vast ocean, obliterating the boundaries between them.

Exploding: The oceans might explode, possibly due to the intense heat or some other unknown force, causing them to lose their form and structure.

Drying Up: Some interpretations suggest that the oceans might dry up completely, signifying the end of water as a fundamental element.

Verse 4

Wa izal qubooru bu'sirat

"And when the graves are overturned...":

This verse describes the scattering of the contents of the graves on the Day of Judgment, signifying the resurrection of the dead. It's a scene of upheaval where the earth yields up its hidden dead, preparing for the final reckoning.

Verse 4 powerfully captures the scene of resurrection: graves will be violently upturned, bodies thrust into the light, paving the way for each soul to confront its deeds. It marks the surge from cosmic upheaval to personal reckoning, emphasizing that on that Day, nothing remains hidden.

Verse 5

Alimat nafsum maa qaddamat wa akhkharat

"Then every soul will know what it has put forth and held back."

This verse indicates that on the Day of Judgment, each individual will be fully aware of all their past actions, both those they did and those they neglected to do. Hence, there can be no denial.

This implies a complete and undeniable understanding of one's deeds, both good and bad.

- **"what it has put forth":**

This refers to the actions, deeds, and intentions that a person has actively done during their lifetime.

- **"and held back":**

This refers to the good deeds a person had the opportunity to do but chose not to, or the bad deeds they could have avoided but didn't.

In essence, the verse highlights the comprehensive nature of accountability on the Day of Judgment. People will not only be held responsible for their overt actions but also for their omissions and shortcomings. It emphasizes the importance of reflection and conscious decision-making in this life, as every action has a consequence.

Verse 6

Yaaa ayyuhal insaaanu maa gharraka bi Rabbikal kareem

"O mankind, what has deceived you concerning your Lord, the Gracious?"

This is a rhetorical question posed to humanity, asking what has deluded them from their Lord, the Generous. It highlights humanity's forgetfulness and negligence towards their Creator, despite the blessings and perfection bestowed upon them. The verse serves as a reminder to reflect on Allah's grace and the bounties He has provided, prompting introspection about one's duties and responsibilities.

The word "deceived" (or "lured," "enticed," "seduced") suggests that humanity has been distracted or led astray from the path of righteousness.

And what are these deceptions!!

- Love for worldly desires and pleasures.
- Neglecting religious duties and obligations.
- Forgetfulness and a lack of consideration for the afterlife.

The verse's purpose is to awaken consciousness. It aims to evoke a sense of guilt and shame in the individual, prompting them to question their loyalty to their Lord.

It encourages introspection and a re-evaluation of one's relationship with Allah.

By reminding humanity of Allah's grace, the verse seeks to inspire gratitude and a return to the path of righteousness.

Verse 7

Allazee khalaqaka fasaw waaka fa'adalak

"Him Who created thee. Fashioned thee in due proportion, and gave thee a just bias"

This verse highlights Allah's perfect creation and proportioning of man. It emphasizes that Allah created humans, then fashioned them perfectly and gave them due proportion. This refers to the physical and physiological symmetry and harmony of the human body, as well as the balanced disposition.

The verse can be broken down as follows:

"He created you". This refers to the initial act of creation.

"then fashioned you perfectly". This signifies the completeness and perfection of the human form.

"then gave you due proportion". This emphasizes the balance and harmony in the human body's construction and the well-balanced disposition granted to humans.

Essentially, the verse is a reminder of Allah's immense power and grace in creating humans in the most perfect form, with all limbs and organs well-placed and functioning in harmony. It also highlights the unique balance given to humans, despite their complex nature.

Verse 8

Feee ayye sooratim maa shaaa'a rakkabak

Verse 8, asks humanity,

"In whatever form He willed has He assembled you?".

This verse follows the previous verses that highlight Allah's creation and shaping of humans, emphasizing His perfect design and artistry. It questions what could make humans forget or disregard their Creator, despite His numerous blessings and the miraculous formation of their being.

Hence, the verse poses a rhetorical question, prompting reflection on Allah's creative power and the human condition. It references Allah's act of bringing humans into existence, shaping them, and giving them a balanced and well-proportioned form.

The phrase "in whatever form He willed" highlights Allah's absolute authority and freedom in choosing the form for each individual, emphasizing the uniqueness and diversity of human beings.

In essence, verse 8, challenges humanity to acknowledge Allah's sovereignty, recognize His blessings, and reflect on their own existence and purpose.

Verse 9

Kalla bal tukazziboona bid deen

"No! But you deny the Recompense (of the Hereafter)?"

This verse directly confronts those who disbelieve in the Day of Judgment and the accountability that comes with it. It points out that despite clear signs and warnings, people often choose to deny the existence of a final reckoning.

The verse implies that this denial is a form of self-deception. People may be deluded into thinking that their actions have no consequences beyond this world, leading them to a life of heedlessness and disregard for moral and religious obligations.

We also learn here the importance of recognizing that every individual will be held accountable for their deeds on the Day of Judgment. This accountability is a fundamental aspect of divine justice and wisdom.

By denying the Day of Judgment, individuals may fall into a state of heedlessness, engaging in actions that displease Allah without fear of consequence. This denial is a major obstacle to true faith and righteous living.

The verse serves as a powerful reminder for humans to reflect on their beliefs and actions. It urges them to acknowledge the reality of the Day of Judgment and to live their lives in accordance with Allah's will.

Verse 10

Wa inna 'alaikum lahaa fizeen

"And indeed, [appointed] over you are keepers."

This is refering to the angels who are assigned to record the deeds of humans, both good and bad. It highlights the concept of divine accountability and emphasizes that every action is being observed and documented.

- **"And indeed, [appointed] over you are...":**

This part of the verse establishes the presence of beings who are specifically assigned to oversee and record human actions.

- **"...keepers":**

The Arabic word used here, "kiraman katibeen," translates to "noble scribes" or "honorable recorders." These are the angels who act as guardians and keepers of records for each individual.

The verse implies that every action, no matter how small or insignificant it may seem, is being carefully observed and recorded. This should serve as a reminder for humans to be mindful of their behaviour.

The concept of keepers also implies that there will be consequences for both good and bad deeds. The records kept by these angels will be presented on the Day of Judgment, and individuals will be rewarded or punished accordingly.

Verse 11

Kiraaman kaatibeen

Kind and honourable,- Writing down (your deeds):

Refers to the angels who are recording the deeds of humanity. These angels are described as "honourable scribes" or "noble writers" who meticulously document everything humans do.

The verse emphasizes that these angels are responsible for recording all actions, both good and bad, of every individual. This record-keeping serves as a testament to their actions on the Day of Judgment.

Here we are reminded that every action, no matter how small or insignificant it may seem, is being observed and recorded. It encourages reflection and accountability for one's actions, as there will be consequences for them on the Day of Judgment.

Verse 12

Ya'lamoona ma taf'aloon

"They know whatever you do."

This verse is telling us that that these angels who are recording are aware of everything a person does. It highlights the comprehensive and precise nature of their record-keeping, as they are not only aware of actions but also the underlying motives.

Since they have complete knowledge of all human actions including the intentions, nothing will be overlooked or missed.

Verse 13

Innal abraara lafee na'eem

"Indeed, the righteous will be in bliss."

"Indeed, the righteous...":

This refers to those who were pious and performed good deeds in their lives, following Allah's commandments and abstaining from what He prohibited.

"...will be in bliss":

This signifies that the righteous will be granted eternal happiness and comfort in Paradise, a place of ultimate reward and pleasure.

The verse highlights a core concept in Islam: that righteous actions are rewarded by Allah with eternal bliss in the afterlife. It contrasts with the following verse, which describes the fate of the wicked.

Verse 14

Wa innal fujjaara lafee Jaheem

"And the Wicked - they will be in the Fire",

This verse highlights the fate of those who are considered wicked or disbelievers. It serves as a warning to those who reject faith and commit evil deeds, indicating that their ultimate end will be in Hellfire. This message is part of the broader theme in Surah Al-Infitar, which contrasts the destinies of the righteous and the wicked, emphasizing accountability and the consequences of one's actions on the Day of Judgment.

Verse 15

Yaslawnahaa Yawmad Deen

"They will [enter to] burn therein on the Day of Recompense."

This verse describes the fate of the wicked on the Day of Judgment, specifically that they will enter Hellfire and experience its burning torment. It emphasizes the certainty and permanence of their punishment, as they will not be able to escape or be absent from it.

"They will [enter to] burn therein":

This refers to the wicked entering the Hellfire, a place of intense suffering and punishment.

"on the Day of Recompense":

This clarifies that this punishment will occur on the Day of Judgment, the day when all souls will be judged and recompensed for their deeds.

"And they will not be absent therefrom":

This highlights the permanence of their punishment, emphasizing that they will not be able to escape or be absent from Hellfire for even a short period.

Further Information!

Do you know that Muslims who have not repented for their sins will also experience the hellfire?

For sinful believers who have faith but have committed major sins, the prevailing view is that they may enter Hell temporarily as a form of purification, but they will ultimately be admitted to Paradise due to their faith and Allah's mercy.

Verse 16

Wa maa hum 'anhaa bighaaa 'ibeen

"They will [enter to] burn therein on the Day of Recompense."

"They will [enter to] burn therein":

This refers to the wicked entering the Hellfire, a place of intense suffering and punishment.

"on the Day of Recompense":

This clarifies that this punishment will occur on the Day of Judgment, the day when all souls will be judged and recompensed for their deeds.

"And they will not be absent therefrom":

This highlights the permanence of their punishment, emphasizing that they will not be able to escape or be absent from Hellfire for even a short period.

In essence, this verse serves as a warning to those who disbelieve and disobey Allah, highlighting the severe consequences they will face in the afterlife. It is paired with verse 14, which states, "And indeed, the wicked will be in Hellfire," further emphasizing the contrasting fates of the righteous and the wicked.

Verse 17

Wa maaa adraaka maa Yawmud Deen

"And what can make you know what the Day of Recompense is?"

This rhetorical question emphasizes the immense and incomprehensible nature of the Day of Judgment, highlighting that it is beyond human understanding.

The question is not meant to seek information, but rather to highlight the immense and awe-inspiring nature of this event.

It acknowledges that humans, limited in their earthly understanding, cannot fully grasp the reality of the Day of Judgment.

It contrasts the fleeting nature of worldly concerns with the eternal consequences of the Day of Judgment.

Purpose of Repetition:

The repetition of the question in the subsequent verse further emphasizes the profound importance and incomprehensibility of the Day of Judgment.

Verse 18

Summa maaa adraaka maa Yawmud Deen

"Then, what will make you know what the Day of Recompense is?"

The verse repeats the question, "What will make you know what the Day of Recompense is?" This repetition is a literary device used to emphasize the profound nature of the Day of Judgment and its significance.

The question serves to magnify the importance and gravity of the Day of Judgment, indicating that it is a momentous occasion that demands serious contemplation.

The verse encourages reflection on the Day of Judgment and its implications, prompting individuals to consider the consequences of their actions and strive to live a righteous life.

Verse 19

Yawma laa tamliku nafsul linafsin shai'anw walamru yawma'izil lillaah

"It is the Day when no soul will possess for another soul [power to do] a thing...":

This verse demonstrates the absolute helplessness of every individual on the Day of Judgment. No one will be able to help another, regardless of their relationship or status in this world.

"...and the command, that Day, is [entirely] with Allah.":

This part clarifies that Allah alone will have absolute authority and control on that day. There will be no one to intercede or intervene except by His permission.

This verse serves as a reminder of the certainty of the Day of Judgment and the individual's responsibility to prepare for it. It underscores the fact that on that day, everyone will stand alone before Allah, and no one can rely on anyone else for salvation.

REFLECTING ON SURAH AL-INFITAR OFFERS SEVERAL IMPORTANT LESSONS AND THEMES:

11. Awareness of the Day of Judgment: The surah vividly describes cosmic events that will occur at the end of the world, reminding believers of the inevitable Day of Judgment. This serves to awaken consciousness about the transient nature of this life and the certainty of accountability in the hereafter.
12. Accountability: It emphasizes that everyone will be held accountable for their actions. Each person will see the results of what they have done, whether good or bad. This encourages individuals to live righteously and be mindful of their deeds.
13. Divine Justice: The surah assures that divine justice will prevail. The righteous will be rewarded with pleasure, while the wicked will face consequences for their actions. This reinforces the belief in Allah's just nature and the moral order of the universe.
14. Human Negligence: The surah addresses human tendencies to be heedless or negligent of their duties towards Allah and their own spiritual well-being. It serves as a reminder to stay conscious of one's relationship with Allah and the spiritual obligations one has.
15. Allah's Knowledge: It highlights that Allah is fully aware of all actions and thoughts. This awareness should instill a sense of humility and encourage sincere worship and ethical behaviour.
16. Reflection on Creation: The surah invites reflection on the natural world and cosmic phenomena as signs of Allah's power and wisdom, encouraging believers to see the divine in the world around them.

Overall, Surah Al-Infitar urges believers to reflect on their lives, remain conscious of their actions, and prepare for the afterlife by adhering to the guidance provided by Allah.

SURAH AL-INFITAR – SURAH 82

Questions

1. What are the main themes presented in Surah Al-Infitar?
2. How does Surah Al-Infitar describe the events of the Day of Judgment?
3. What is the significance of the imagery used in the initial verses of Surah Al-Infitar, such as the sky being cleft asunder and the stars scattering?
4. How does the surah address the concept of human accountability and the recording of deeds?
5. What lessons can be drawn from the mention of the "honorable scribes" (angels) in the surah?
6. How does Surah Al-Infitar highlight the contrast between the righteous and the wicked?
7. What warnings and reminders does this surah provide to those who deny the Day of Judgment?
8. How does the surah emphasize the power and authority of Allah over all creation?
9. In what ways does Surah Al-Infitar encourage self-reflection and introspection regarding one's actions and beliefs?
10. How can the messages in Surah Al-Infitar be applied to contemporary life and personal development?

These questions can serve as a guide for studying and understanding the spiritual and moral teachings of Surah Al-Infitar.

Answers

1. What are the main themes presented in Surah Al-Infitar?
   - The main themes include the events of the Day of Judgment, the inevitable transformation of the natural world, human accountability, the recording of deeds by angels, and the ultimate fate of the righteous and the wicked.

2. How does Surah Al-Infitar describe the events of the Day of Judgment?
   - The surah describes vivid cosmic changes, such as the sky being split, stars scattering, seas bursting forth, and graves being overturned, symbolizing the upheaval and transformation that will precede the Day of Judgment.

3. What is the significance of the imagery used in the initial verses of Surah Al-Infitar, such as the sky being cleft asunder and the stars scattering?
   - This imagery conveys the magnitude and inevitability of the cosmic events that will occur, highlighting the transient nature of the current world and the certainty of the afterlife.

4. How does the surah address the concept of human accountability and the recording of deeds?
   - The surah emphasizes that every person's deeds are meticulously recorded by "honorable scribes," underscoring the idea that individuals will be held accountable for their actions on the Day of Judgment.

5. What lessons can be drawn from the mention of the "honorable scribes" (angels) in the surah?
   - The presence of these scribes serves as a reminder that every action is observed and recorded, encouraging individuals to lead righteous lives and be mindful of their deeds.

6. How does Surah Al-Infitar highlight the contrast between the righteous and the wicked?
   - The surah contrasts the fate of the righteous, who will be in eternal bliss, with that of the wicked, who will face punishment, emphasizing the moral consequences of one's actions.

7. What warnings and reminders does this surah provide to those who deny the Day of Judgment?
   - The surah warns of the dire consequences for those who deny the reality of the afterlife, urging them to reflect on the signs of creation and the certainty of divine justice.

8. How does the surah emphasize the power and authority of Allah over all creation?
   - By describing the cataclysmic events of the Day of Judgment and the precise recording of deeds, the surah underscores Allah's supreme control and authority over the universe and human destiny.

9. In what ways does Surah Al-Infitar encourage self-reflection and introspection regarding one's actions and beliefs?
   - The vivid descriptions of the afterlife and the reminder of accountability serve to prompt self-reflection, encouraging individuals to assess their actions, intentions, and beliefs in light of their eventual judgment.

10. How can the messages in Surah Al-Infitar be applied to contemporary life and personal development?
    - The surah's emphasis on accountability, moral integrity, and the transient nature of worldly life can inspire individuals to prioritize ethical behavior, spiritual growth, and mindfulness of the afterlife in their daily lives.

These answers provide insights into the themes and lessons of Surah Al-Infitar, encouraging deeper contemplation and application of its teachings.

Multiple-choice questions on Surah Al-Infitar, each followed by its correct answer

1. What does Surah Al-Infitar primarily describe?

    - a) The stories of past prophets

    - b) The events of creation

    - c) The events of the Day of Judgment

    - d) Laws of inheritance

2. Which of the following events is mentioned in Surah Al-Infitar as a sign of the Day of Judgment?

    - a) Mountains turning to dust

    - b) The sky being cleft asunder

    - c) Rivers running dry

    - d) The Earth splitting open

3. Who are the "honorable scribes" mentioned in the surah?

    - a) The prophets

    - b) The righteous believers

    - c) Angels who record deeds

    - d) Wise scholars

4. What will happen to the seas on the Day of Judgment, according to Surah Al-Infitar?

    - a) They will dry up

    - b) They will become poisonous

    - c) They will burst forth

    - d) They will freeze

5. How are human deeds recorded, as mentioned in the surah?

    - a) By prophets

    - b) By written scrolls

    - c) By angels

    - d) By the stars

6. What is the fate of the righteous as described in Surah Al-Infitar?

    - a) They will be given wealth

    - b) They will be in eternal bliss

    - c) They will be forgotten

    - d) They will be reincarnated

7. What does Surah Al-Infitar say about those who deny the Day of Judgment?

    - a) They will be granted forgiveness

    - b) They will be shown mercy

    - c) They will face punishment

    - d) They will be given more time

8. What does the surah emphasize about Allah's power?

    - a) Allah's power is limited to the heavens

    - b) Allah's power is absolute and comprehensive

    - c) Allah's power is shared with humans

    - d) Allah's power only affects the afterlife

These questions and answers serve as a tool to test and reinforce understanding of the key concepts and themes within Surah Al-Infitar.

Answers

2. *Answer:* c) The events of the Day of Judgment
3. *Answer:* b) The sky being cleft asunder
4. *Answer:* c) Angels who record deeds
5. *Answer:* c) They will burst forth
6. *Answer:* c) By angels
7. *Answer:* b) They will be in eternal bliss
8. *Answer:* c) They will face punishment
9. *Answer:* b) Allah's power is absolute and comprehensive

SURAH AL-MUTAFFIFIN

SURAH AL-MUTAFFIFIN

Bismillahi ar-Rahmani ar-Raheem

Verse 1

Wailul lil mutaffifeen

"Woe to the defrauders"

This verse introduces the central theme of the surah: condemnation of those who cheat in weights and measures. The word "mutaffifin" refers to those who give short measure or weight, and the phrase "Woe to them" is a strong warning of divine punishment.

The Mutaffifin:

This term is derived from "tatfif," which means to give less than what is due, especially in weights and measures. It implies dishonesty and unfairness in transactions.

While the verse directly addresses cheating in weights and measures, the concept extends to any form of dishonesty where someone is deprived of their due rights, whether through tangible or intangible means.

The verse emphasizes the importance of honesty and fairness in all transactions and dealings, highlighting that such cheating is a serious offense that will be accounted for on the Day of Judgment.

Verses 2 & 3

Allazeena izak taaloo 'alan naasi yastawfoon

"Those who, when they have to receive by measure from men, exact full measure"

Wa izaa kaaloohum aw wazanoohum yukhsiroon

"But when they have to give by measure or weight to men, give less than due".

These two verses refer to those who, when taking a measure from others, take it in full, meaning they take more than their due. This verse describes the dishonest traders who cheat people by giving less when measuring or weighing for others, while demanding their full measure when buying.

The two verses together highlight the hypocrisy of these people. While they are strict in taking their due, they are careless and dishonest when giving to others, often short changing them in weight or measure.

This dishonest practice is condemned by the Quran, as it harms others and undermines societal trust. It emphasizes that such behaviour is rooted in a lack of belief in the Day of Judgment, where everyone will be held accountable for their actions.

The verse is not just about literal measurement and weight, but also about fairness and honesty in all dealings. It highlights the importance of giving others their due in all aspects of life.

Verse 4

Alaa yazunnu ulaaa'ika annahum mab'oosoon

"Do they not think that they will be resurrected?"

The verse addresses the mindset of those who cheat in weights and measures. It questions whether they truly believe they will be resurrected for a great Day. The verse highlights the deceptive nature of their actions, emphasizing that they are not exempt from accountability on the Day of Judgment.

This is a direct challenge to their complacency and disregard for the consequences of their actions.

Verse 5

Li Yawmin 'Azeem

"On a Mighty Day"

The "great Day" refers to the Day of Judgment, a central concept in Islam where all humans will be held accountable for their deeds.

The verse emphasizes that on this Day, all people will stand before the Lord of the worlds, implying that no one can escape the judgment of Allah for their actions, including cheating in business.

This verse connects to the preceding verses (1-3) which describe the act of defrauding in weights and measures. It highlights the core message of the surah: the importance of honesty and integrity in all dealings and the accountability for dishonest practices.

The verse serves as a warning to those who engage in fraudulent activities, reminding them of the ultimate accountability before Allah on the Day of Judgment. It encourages reflection on the consequences of their actions and discourages them from prioritizing worldly gains over spiritual well-being.

Verse 6

Yawma yaqoomun naasu li Rabbil 'aalameen

"The Day when mankind will stand before the Lord of the Worlds."

This verse implies that on this momentous day, all people will be resurrected and gathered before Allah, the sole Ruler and Judge of all creation. It highlights the accountability of all individuals before Allah on the Day of Resurrection.

The verse serves as a warning to those who are cheating and defrauding others (as described in the previous verses). It reminds them that they will ultimately have to answer for their actions before Allah, the Lord of all. This verse emphasizes that Allah is the one who will judge everyone's action.

Verse 7

Kallaaa inna kitaabal fujjaari lafee Sijjeen

"No! Indeed, the record of the wicked is in Sijjin".

This verse indicates that the deeds of the wicked are meticulously recorded in a book or register called Sijjin.

The wicked are not free from accountability for their actions. Their deeds are recorded, and they will face the consequences in Sijjin, a place of punishment. This serves as a warning to those who indulge in evil and a reminder of the ultimate justice of Allah.

Verse 8

Wa maa adraaka maa Sijjeen

"And what can make you know what Sijjin is?"

Sijjin is described as a low place of torment where the records of the wicked are kept. The verse emphasizes that the actions of those who cheat and defraud others will be meticulously recorded in Sijjin.

The verse serves as a stern warning against dishonesty and cheating, particularly in matters of trade and commerce. It emphasizes that such actions are not hidden from Allah and will be accounted for.

The mention of Sijjin underscores the idea that every action, good or bad, has consequences and that individuals will be held accountable for their deeds in the afterlife.

Verse 9

Kitaabum marqoom

"Kitaabum" describes the record of the wicked as a "Sijjin," a book inscribed and sealed. It signifies that their deeds and destinies are already determined and recorded, with no possibility of alteration or escape.

Sijjin is the place where the records of the wicked are kept. It is a term associated with confinement and punishment, indicating that their fate is sealed and they are destined for Hell.

This verse highlights the accountability of the wicked and the finality of their judgment. It serves as a warning that their actions have consequences and that their destinies are already set in Sijjin, the register of the condemned.

Verse 10

Wailuny yawma'izil lil mukazzibeen

"Woe unto the deniers that Day!"

The verse specifically targets those who deny the concept of the afterlife, including resurrection, divine judgment, and the rewards or punishments associated with one's actions.

Verse 11

Allazeena yukazziboona bi yawmid deen

"Those who deny the Day of Judgment."

Again this verse is addressing the deniers of the Day of Judgement.

Here it the focusing on the dishonesty and deception of those in business and trade. This surah highlights the importance of fairness and honesty in all dealings, advising that those who cheat others will face divine judgment.

By denying the Day of Judgment, individuals disregard the concept of accountability and the consequences of their actions. They fail to recognize that their dishonesty and cheating in this life will have repercussions in the Hereafter.

The verse serves as a warning to those who are disbelieving and encourages them to reconsider their stance, as the Day of Judgment is a reality that cannot be denied.

Verse 12

Wa maa yukazzibu biheee illaa kullu mu'tadin aseem

"And none deny it except every sinful transgressor,"

This verse is clarifying the deniers of the Day of Judgment. It identifies only those who persistently violate Allah's commandments.

We learn from this that the denial of the Day of Judgment is a serious transgression associated with a pattern of sinful behaviour and a disregard for God's commands and the rights of others

Verse 13

Izaa tutlaa'alaihi aayaatunaa qaala asaateerul awwaleen

"When Our verses are recited to him, he says, 'Fables of the ancients!'".

This verse describes the attitude of those who deny the revelations of Allah. They dismiss the verses of the Quran as mere stories from the past, rather than divine guidance.

- **"When Our verses are recited to him...":**

This refers to the recitation of the Quranic verses, which contain warnings, commandments, and stories about the consequences of actions in this life and the Hereafter.

- **"he says, 'Fables of the ancients!'":**

The individual, upon hearing the divine verses, rejects them as "fables of the ancients" (asāṭīr al-awwalīn). This indicates a disbelief in the divine origin of the Quran and a dismissal of its message.

This verse highlights the arrogance and stubbornness of those who refuse to accept the truth, even when presented with clear evidence and guidance.

The rejection of divine verses is a serious offense, leading to a hardened heart and a lack of faith, which can ultimately result in punishment in the Hereafter.

This verse contrasts with the believers who accept the Quran as divine guidance and strive to live by its teachings.

Verse 14

Kallaa bal raana 'alaa quloobihim maa kaanoo yaksiboon

"Nay, but on their hearts is the stain of what they used to do.".

This verse explains that the hearts of those who disbelieve have been tainted and hardened by their persistent sins. It suggests that their rejection of faith is not due to a lack of evidence, but rather a spiritual impurity that has clouded their judgment and prevented them from recognizing the truth.

- **"on their hearts is the stain..."**:

This refers to a metaphorical "rust" or "stain" on the hearts of the disbelievers, caused by their accumulation of sins.

- **"what they used to do"**:

This highlights that the spiritual damage to their hearts is a consequence of their actions and choices, specifically their sins and disobedience.

The verse suggests that continuous wrongdoing can have a detrimental effect on one's spiritual well-being. The "stain" or "rust" on the heart can be interpreted as a hardening of the heart, making it less receptive to guidance and truth. This can lead to a state where even clear evidence of the truth is rejected or misunderstood.

The hardening of the heart in this life can be seen as a precursor to the spiritual consequences faced in the afterlife. The verse also serves as a warning to believers to be mindful of their actions and to seek repentance for their sins to prevent their hearts from being corrupted.

Verse 15

Kallaaa innahum 'ar Rabbihim yawma'izil lamah jooboon

"Nay! Indeed, from their Lord, that Day, they will be veiled."

Here we are learning that on the Day of Judgment, the wicked will be prevented from seeing Allah. Some Quranic scholars say that this is a punishment for their denial of Allah and their misdeeds in this world. It is contrasted with the believers, who will be granted the blessing of seeing Allah on that day.

The verse also highlights the psychological impact of being veiled from Allah, suggesting it will be a source of pain and regret for the wicked.

Verse 16

Summa innahum lasaa lul Jaheem

"Then indeed, they will [enter and] burn in Hellfire."

Verse 16 is a direct consequence of the previous verse, which describes the disbelievers being veiled from seeing Allah on the Day of Judgment. This veiling is a form of punishment, and verse 16 elaborates on the physical punishment they will face.

The verse explicitly states that they will "enter the fire of Hell" (Jahannam). This signifies their permanent residence in the Hellfire, as a consequence of their actions in this life.

The phrase "burning flame of Hell" demonstrate the intense and excruciating nature of the fire that they will endure. This is not a temporary suffering, but a prolonged and painful experience.

This verse also highlights the reason for their punishment, which is their denial of the truth and their rejection of the Day of Judgment. They mocked the believers and denied the reality of the afterlife.

The verse implicitly contrasts the fate of the disbelievers with the believers, who will be granted access to Paradise and see their Lord. This contrast shows us the ultimate consequences of choosing between good and evil.

In essence, verse 16 serves as a warning and a reminder of the severe punishment that awaits those who deny Allah and the Day of Judgment, emphasizing the eternal nature of their suffering in the Hellfire.

Verse 17

Summa yuqaalu haazal lazee kuntum bihee tukazziboon

"Then it will be said, 'This is what you used to deny'",

This serves as a stark reminder of the consequences of rejecting the truth and denying the Day of Judgment. It highlights the accountability that awaits those who were heedless and disbelieved in the Hereafter. The verse emphasizes that the disbelievers will be confronted with the reality of what they denied, which is the Day of Resurrection and the consequences of their actions in this life.

The verse directly addresses the disbelievers who, despite being warned about the Hereafter, chose to reject the idea of accountability and divine judgment.

Verse 18

Kallaaa inna kitaabal abraari lafee'Illiyyeen

"No! Indeed, the record of the righteous is in 'Illiyyun."

Here we see a contrast of the fate of the righteous and the wicked on the Day of Judgment. It signifies that the good deeds of the righteous are recorded in a place of high honour and esteem, called 'Illiyyun.

This refers to the book or register where the deeds of the righteous are recorded.

'Illiyyun is a place of high honour and elevation, often interpreted as a place in the heavens where the records of the righteous are kept. Some interpretations place it in the seventh heaven, beneath the Divine Throne, or consider it a symbolic representation of the high status of the righteous.

In contrast to the righteous, the wicked are described as having their records in a low and degraded place called "Sijjin" in the following verses (83:7-9).

The verse highlights the ultimate justice and reward for the righteous, emphasizing that their good deeds are not lost or overlooked but are preserved in a place of honour and will be acknowledged on the Day of Judgment.

Verse 19

Wa maaa adraaka maa 'Illiyyoon

This verse is describing the righteous as being "on thrones, looking" at the blessings of Paradise. This implies a state of tranquillity and contemplation, enjoying the bounties of Allah while gazing upon them, possibly also including a view of their Lord. The verse emphasizes the contrast between the righteous and the wicked, who are veiled from seeing their Lord on the Day of Judgment.

This the righteous are in a state of comfort and majesty, seated on elevated platforms.

They will be admiring the vast and beautiful realm of Paradise that Allah has bestowed upon them.

The verse highlights the difference between the two groups, with the righteous enjoying Allah's favour and the wicked being veiled from Him.

Verse 20
Kitaabum marqoom

"Written record"

This record is "witnessed by those nearest [to Allah]". It signifies a book or register where the deeds of the righteous are meticulously documented and acknowledged by Allah and those close to Him.

These records will be placed in the highest heavens where the souls of the righteous and their deeds are preserved.

This verse assures the righteous that their good deeds are not forgotten or overlooked. They are documented in a place of honour and witnessed by those closest to Allah, signifying their ultimate reward and recognition in the Hereafter.

Verse 21
Yashhadu hul muqarra boon

To which bear witness those Nearest (to Allah).

Verse 21, discusses the record of the righteous (al-abrar) which is witnessed by those brought near to Allah. It signifies that the deeds of the pious are so exceptional that they are observed and recognized by the most honoured angels in the presence of Allah.

The verse refers to "Illiyyin," which is described as a place or register of the righteous, where their deeds are recorded.

This verse highlights the high esteem in which the righteous are held, as their actions are witnessed by those in the highest proximity to Allah. It emphasizes the divine recognition of their good deeds and their elevated status.

Verse 22
Innal abraara lafee Na'eem

"Indeed, the righteous will be in pleasure,"

This signifies that those who lead righteous lives, characterized by piety and good deeds, will be granted eternal happiness and delight in the afterlife. This verse contrasts with the fate of the wicked, highlighting the reward for those who adhered to Allah's guidance and abstained from wrongdoing.

The indication here is that the righteous will experience a state of eternal bliss and joy in the Hereafter. This pleasure encompasses not just physical comfort, but also a deep spiritual contentment and satisfaction.

This verse is often understood in the context of the preceding verses of Surah Al-Mutaffifin, which describe the fate of those who cheat in weights and measures. The verse emphasizes the stark contrast between the reward for righteousness and the punishment for wickedness.

The verse serves as a promise from Allah to those who strive for righteousness, assuring them of His mercy and the ultimate reward of eternal pleasure.

Verse 23

Alal araaa'iki yanzuroon

"On Thrones (of Dignity) will they command a sight (of all things)"

Here we see the righteous in Paradise reclining on adorned couches, observing. It is showing us their blissful state and the beautiful surroundings they are immersed in, highlighting the rewards awaiting the pious in the afterlife.

"On Thrones (of Dignity)"

This refers to the luxurious, elevated seats in Paradise, often depicted as bejewelled or elaborately decorated.

- **"command a sight (of all things)"**

The righteous are not merely resting, but actively observing the blessings and wonders around them, including the divine bounty and the beautiful sights.

This verse emphasizes the comfort, beauty, and active engagement that the righteous experience in the afterlife, showcasing the rewards of their piety and good deeds.

Verse 24

Ta'rifu fee wujoohihim nadratan na'eem

"You will recognize in their faces the radiance of pleasure,"

This verse describes the radiant and joyful appearance of the righteous in Paradise. It signifies the visible manifestation of divine favour and the blissful state they experience, making it evident to others who see them. The verse highlights the contrast between the righteous and the wicked, emphasizing the rewards awaiting the former and the punishment awaiting the latter on the Day of Judgment.

"You will recognize in their faces...":

This part of the verse indicates that the joy and bliss experienced by the righteous will be so profound that it will be easily discernible on their faces.

"...the radiance of pleasure":

This phrase describes the visible manifestation of their joy. "Radiance" (nadrah) suggests a bright, radiant, and fresh appearance, while "pleasure" (na'im) refers to the blessings and comforts they enjoy in Paradise.

The verse emphasizes the contrasting fates of the righteous and the wicked. While the righteous will be radiant with happiness, the wicked will be in a state of torment and despair, as depicted in other verses of the surah.

The verse indicates that the blessings of Paradise are not merely abstract but are visibly manifested on the faces of the righteous, making their blessed state clear to others.

The radiance of pleasure on their faces is a sign of Allah's favour and pleasure with them, showcasing their closeness to their Lord.

Verse 25

Yusqawna mir raheeqim makhtoom

"they will be given to drink from sealed, pure wine".

This wine is described as being of the highest quality, and its seal is made of musk. This is a special pure wine. This purity and sealing suggest a high quality and a special, protected nature, not found in worldly wines.

The sealing can be interpreted in two ways:

The container is sealed: The wine is kept in vessels that are sealed, possibly with musk, indicating its preciousness and purity.

The taste is sealed: When the wine is drunk, its final effect and lingering taste will be like musk, a delightful fragrance and flavor.

Verse 26

Khitaamuhoo misk; wa fee zaalika falyatanaafasil Mutanaafisoon

"The seal thereof will be Musk: And for this let those aspire, who have aspirations"

This verse encourages believers to strive for the blessings of Paradise, teaching us that the ultimate reward, like a drink with the fragrance of musk, is worth intense competition among those who aspire to it. The verse highlights the contrast between worldly pursuits, often marked by selfishness and loss for others, and the spiritual competition for Paradise, where striving for one's own success can also benefit others.

Here's a more detailed explanation:

"whose seal is musk":

This refers to the "Tasnim," a pure drink from the highest Paradise, which is described as having the fragrance of musk.

"and for this let those aspire, who have aspirations"

This part of the verse encourages believers to actively strive for the blessings of Paradise, using the word "tanafasa," which implies a competitive spirit, but in a positive and spiritual sense.

Unlike worldly competitions where one person's success often means another's loss, the competition for Paradise is inclusive. It's about striving to be among the best, and helping others do the same.

The verse contrasts the fleeting nature of worldly pursuits with the eternal rewards of Paradise. It suggests that believers should focus their efforts on achieving the ultimate success in the Hereafter, rather than being preoccupied with temporary gains.

The verse serves as a powerful motivator, urging believers to aspire to the highest levels of Paradise and to compete with each other in good deeds and righteousness to attain it.

Verse 27

Wa mizaajuhoo min Tasneem

"With it will be (given) a mixture of Tasnim"

This a special drink in Paradise called Tasneem, which is a source of great pleasure and is mixed with the drinks of the righteous. This verse highlights the superior status of those brought near to Allah (muqarraboon), who will drink from Tasneem directly, while others will have it mixed in their drinks.

The righteous will also drink from a fountain called Tasneem.

In essence, verse 27 emphasizes the divine favour bestowed upon the righteous in Paradise, with Tasneem being a key element of their blissful experience.

Verse 28

Ainaiy yashrabu bihal muqarraboon

"A spring, from (the waters) whereof drink those Nearest to Allah".

This is describing a special spring in paradise called "Tasnim," which is exclusively for those closest to Allah (the muqarraboon). This verse highlights the high status and blessings reserved for the righteous in the afterlife, contrasting it with the punishment faced by those who defraud others.

The verse follows the previous verses that condemn the practice of shortchanging others in weights and measures, highlighting the contrasting fates of the righteous and the wicked.

Many scholars, like Ibn Masud and Ibn Abbas, interpret this as a special drink for the closest to Allah, while others say it's a drink that will be mixed with the drinks of the companions of the right hand (the other righteous individuals).

The verse reinforces the Quranic theme of accountability and the just recompense for actions in this life.

Verse 29

Innal lazeena ajramoo kaanoo minal lazeena aamanoo yadhakoon

"Indeed those who commit crimes, used to laugh at those who believed"

This describes how the wicked in the worldly life would mock and deride the believers, often exchanging scornful glances and making jokes at their expense. The verse highlights the contrast between the believers' eventual triumph and the criminals' mockery in the afterlife.

"Indeed, those who committed crimes...":

This refers to the disbelievers and wrongdoers who indulged in sinful activities and rejected faith.

"...used to laugh at those who believed.":

This indicates the scorn and mockery that the criminals directed towards the believers in the worldly life. They would make fun of the believers' faith, their practices, and their perceived "weakness" or "foolishness".

This verse emphasizes the theme of the ultimate reversal of fortunes between the believers and the disbelievers on the Day of Judgment, where the tables will be turned and those who mocked will face divine judgment.

In summary, verse 29 highlights the arrogance and mockery of those who reject faith and the eventual divine justice that will befall them on the Day of Judgment, contrasting it with the believers' future triumph and honour.

Verse 30

Wa izaa marroo bihim yataghaamazoon

"And when they passed by them, they would exchange derisive glances"

Allah describes how the wicked used to mock the believers during their life in this world. They would pass by the believers and exchange derisive glances, winking at each other in mockery. This behaviour was part of their general attitude of disdain and ridicule towards those who followed the path of righteousness.

Mockery and Derision:

The wicked would not only laugh at the believers (as mentioned in the previous verse) but would also engage in non-verbal mockery. They would wink at each other as they passed by the believers, signalling their contempt and disdain.

Attitude of the Wicked:

This action highlights the arrogant and condescending attitude of the wicked towards the believers. They saw themselves as superior and considered the believers to be misguided.

The verse also serves as a prelude to the reversal of this situation in the Hereafter. While the wicked mock the believers in this world, the believers will be the ones in positions of honour and will look down upon the wicked in the Hereafter.

Hence, the believers are depicted as being patient and steadfast in their faith despite the mockery and ridicule they face. They are encouraged to look forward to the reward they will receive in the Hereafter.

Verse 31

Wa izan qalabooo ilaaa ahlihimun qalaboo fakiheen

"And when they returned to their people, they returned jesting".

This means that after scoffing at and ridiculing the believers, the wicked would return to their families pleased with themselves, perhaps boasting about their actions.

Verse 32

Wa izaa ra awhum qaalooo inna haaa'ulaaa'i ladaaal loon

"And when they saw them, they would say, 'Indeed, those are truly lost.'"

This verse describes the disbelievers' perception of the believers. They see the believers' faith and adherence to Allah's commands as foolishness and a sign of being lost or misguided.

They are so consumed by their own wrongdoing that they cannot recognize the truth and instead mock those who strive for righteousness.

The irony lies in the fact that the disbelievers, who are engaged in deceit and transgression, are the ones who are truly lost, yet they accuse the believers of being astray.

The verse serves to warn believers against the dangers of pride and the importance of recognizing the truth, even when it comes from those who are seemingly weak or marginalized in the eyes of the world.

Verse 33

Wa maaa ursiloo 'alaihim haafizeen

"But they were not sent as watchers over them."

This verse is a rebuke to those who mock and criticize the believers. It highlights that the mockers were not appointed as guardians or overseers of the believers, and therefore have no right to judge or condemn them.

"But they were not sent...":

This phrase emphasizes that the disbelievers who mock the believers were not given any authority or responsibility to monitor or judge their actions or beliefs.

"...as watchers over them":

This further clarifies that the disbelievers were not assigned the role of guardians or overseers, implying they have no right to dictate or criticize the believers.

It also serves as a comfort to believers to not be discouraged by the mockery of others, as those who mock are not in a position to judge them.

The verse also reminds everyone that each person is ultimately accountable to Allah, not to the judgments of others.

Verse 34

Fal yawmal lazeena aamanoo minal kuffaari yadhakoon

"So today, the believers will laugh at the disbelievers".

Verse 34 signifies a reversal of this situation in the afterlife. It indicates that on the Day of Judgment, the believers will be in a position of honour and authority, observing the disbelievers facing their due punishment.

The laughter of the believers is not malicious or vindictive, but rather a consequence of their vindication and the disbelievers' realization of their folly and misguidance.

This verse highlights the concept of divine justice, where those who mocked and persecuted the believers will, in turn, be mocked and punished.

It offers solace and encouragement to believers who may be facing ridicule and adversity in this life, assuring them that their patience and faith will be rewarded.

Verse 35

Alal araaa'iki yanzuroon

"On adorned couches, observing"

This refers to the believers being seated on thrones or couches in Paradise, looking down upon the scene below, which includes the disbelievers facing their judgment.

In this life, the disbelievers used to mock and laugh at the believers. This verse shows the reversal of that situation, with the believers now enjoying a superior position while observing the disbelievers' plight.

The verse also implies that the disbelievers will be paid back for their actions. This is further emphasized in the verse (83:36) which asks "Have not the disbelievers been paid back for what they used to do?"

Verse 36

Hal suwwibal kuffaaru maa kaanoo yaf'aloon

"Have the disbelievers not been rewarded for what they used to do?"

This verse is a rhetorical question, depicting that the disbelievers will be held accountable for their actions in the Hereafter, specifically their mockery and belittlement of the believers. It highlights the contrast between the believers' joy and the disbelievers' punishment in the Hereafter, where the tables are turned.

The verse highlights the concept of divine justice, where those who wronged others will be recompensed for their actions in the Hereafter.

Lessons that can be learned from Surah Mutaffifin (Chapter 83):

1. **Honesty and Fair Trade: ** The Surah emphasizes the importance of being truthful in measurements and transactions, highlighting that cheating others is condemned.
2. **Accountability: ** It reminds believers that everyone will be held accountable for their deeds, especially in business dealings and honesty.
3. **The Consequences of Dishonesty: ** The Surah warns against dishonest behaviour, which can lead to spiritual and social ruin.
4. **The Reality of the Hereafter: ** It encourages believers to be conscious of the Day of Judgment and the rewards or punishments awaiting them based on their actions.
5. **Integrity in Daily Life: ** Upholding honesty and integrity is a core lesson, impacting individual character and community well-being.

SUMMARY OF SURAH AL-MUTAFFIFIN

Surah Al-Mutaffifin, the 83rd chapter of the Quran, focuses on the themes of honesty in dealings, the Day of Judgment, and the contrasting fates of the righteous and the wicked. It strongly condemns those who cheat in weights and measures, highlighting the consequences in the afterlife. The surah also contrasts the mockery of believers by the disbelievers in this life with the triumph of believers and the humiliation of disbelievers on the Day of Judgment.

Key Themes and Topics:

- **Warning against dishonesty:**

The surah begins with a stern warning against those who cheat in weights and measures, emphasizing that this is a grave sin and a form of injustice.

- **The Record of Deeds:**

It introduces the concept of "Sijjin" (a record of the wicked) and "Illiyyun" (a record of the righteous), highlighting that every action is meticulously recorded by angels.

- **The Day of Judgment:**

The surah vividly depicts the events of the Day of Judgment, emphasizing the rewards for the righteous and the punishment for the wicked.

- **Contrast between Believers and Disbelievers:**

The surah contrasts the believers' humility and the disbelievers' arrogance in this life, and the reversal of these roles on the Day of Judgment.

- **Rewards of the Righteous:**

It describes the blissful state of the righteous in Paradise, emphasizing their closeness to Allah and the delights they will experience.

Specific verses and their interpretations:

- **Verses 1-6:**

These verses address the issue of giving less than due in weights and measures, highlighting the severity of this act.

- **Verses 7-17:**

These verses discuss the record of the wicked, "Sijjin," and their denial of the Day of Judgment.

- **Verses 18-28:**

These verses describe the record of the righteous, "Illiyyun," and the rewards they will receive in Paradise.

- **Verses 29-36:**

These verses depict the mockery of believers by disbelievers in this life and the subsequent humiliation of disbelievers on the Day of Judgment.

SURAH MUTAFFIFIN- SURAH 83

Questions

1. What is the main theme of Surah Al-Mutaffifin?
2. Who are the "Mutaffifin" referred to in this Surah?
3. What is the consequence mentioned in the Surah for those who engage in fraudulent activities?
4. How does Surah Al-Mutaffifin describe the fate of the righteous?
5. What does the Surah say about the Day of Judgment?
6. How are the records of the wicked described in Surah Al-Mutaffifin?
7. What is the significance of "Illiyin" in this Surah?
8. What is the attitude of the disbelievers towards the believers as mentioned in the Surah?
9. According to Surah Al-Mutaffifin, what is the ultimate reward for the righteous?
10. How does the Surah depict the concept of accountability in the hereafter?

Answers

1. The main theme of Surah Al-Mutaffifin is the condemnation of fraudulent practices and the moral and ethical responsibilities in business and trade. It emphasizes honesty and fairness.

2. The "Mutaffifin" are those who cheat in trade by giving less than due when they measure or weigh for others, while taking in full when they measure or weigh for themselves.

3. The consequence for those who engage in fraudulent activities is a severe punishment and disgrace on the Day of Judgment.

4. The Surah describes the fate of the righteous as being honored in a state of bliss, with their records in Illiyin, a high and noble registry.

5. The Surah emphasizes the certainty and importance of the Day of Judgment, where everyone will be held accountable for their deeds.

6. The records of the wicked are described as being in "Sijjin," a register that signifies their lowly and disgraceful status.

7. "Illiyin" is significant as it represents the exalted register where the deeds of the righteous are recorded, signifying honor and high status.

8. The Surah mentions that disbelievers mock and laugh at the believers, considering them misguided, but on the Day of Judgment, the roles will be reversed.

9. The ultimate reward for the righteous, according to Surah Al-Mutaffifin, is eternal bliss, satisfaction, and being in the presence of Allah, witnessing His pleasure.

10. Surah Al-Mutaffifin depicts the concept of accountability by illustrating that every action is recorded and will be judged, highlighting the importance of integrity and righteousness.

These questions and answers provide a structured way to understand the key themes and messages of Surah Al-Mutaffifin.

Multiple Choice Questions

1. What does the term "Mutaffifin" refer to in Surah Al-Mutaffifin?

    a) Those who are charitable

    b) Those who cheat in trade

    c) Those who pray regularly

    d) Those who fast during Ramadan

2. In Surah Al-Mutaffifin, what is the fate of those who engage in fraudulent activities?

    a) They will be forgiven

    b) They will receive a severe punishment

    c) They will be honoured

    d) They will be wealthy

3. How does Surah Al-Mutaffifin describe the records of the wicked?

    a) In a book of light

    b) In a high place

    c) In "Sijjin"

    d) In "Illiyin"

4. What is the significance of "Illiyin" in this Surah?

    a) It represents the lowly status of the wicked

    b) It is a place of torment

    c) It is where the deeds of the righteous are recorded

    d) It is a river in paradise

5. According to Surah Al-Mutaffifin, how do disbelievers treat believers?

    a) They honor them

    b) They ignore them

    c) They mock and laugh at them

    d) They follow them

6. What does Surah Al-Mutaffifin say about the Day of Judgment?

    a) It is uncertain

    b) It is a day of rest

    c) It is a day of accountability and justice

    d) It is a day like any other

7. What reward is promised to the righteous in Surah Al-Mutaffifin?

   a) Wealth and power

   b) Eternal bliss and honor

   c) A long life on earth

   d) Authority over others

8. How does the Surah depict the concept of accountability in the hereafter?

   a) It is based on wealth

   b) It is based on social status

   c) Every action is recorded and will be judged

   d) Only major deeds are considered

Answers

1. *Answer:* b) Those who cheat in trade
2. *Answer:* b) They will receive a severe punishment
3. *Answer:* c) In "Sijjin"
4. *Answer:* c) It is where the deeds of the righteous are recorded
5. *Answer:* c) They mock and laugh at them
6. *Answer:* c) It is a day of accountability and justice
7. *Answer:* b) Eternal bliss and honor
8. *Answer:* c) Every action is recorded and will be judged

These questions and answers can help in understanding the key messages and themes of Surah Al-Mutaffifin in a multiple-choice format.

SURAH INSHIQAQ

SURAH INSHIQAQ

Bismillahi ar-Rahmani ar-Raheem

Verse 1

Izas samaaa'un shaqqat

"When the sky has been split apart".

This verse is telling us of the splitting of the heavens(sky) on the Day of Judgment, marking the end of the world as we know it. It indicates a complete and irreversible separation, a point of no return.

This verse signifies the finality of the event, with no possibility of the sky returning to its normal state.

The subsequent verses mention the sky "listening to and obeying its Lord," indicating that even the sky and earth will submit to Allah's command on that day.

This verse sets the stage for the events of the Day of Judgement, including the resurrection of the dead and the reckoning of deeds.

Verse 2

Wa azinat li Rabbihaa wa huqqat

"And hearkens to (the Command of) its Lord, and it must needs (do so)".

This verse describes the earth's response to Allah's command on the Day of Judgment, signifying that it will obey and submit to His will.

The verse highlights the absolute obedience and submission of the earth to Allah on the Day of Judgment.

It indicates that everything in creation, including the earth, is subject to Allah's will and command.

The earth's response also indicates the fulfillment of its duty and purpose as created by Allah.

This verse can be seen as a contrast to some humans who may not listen to or obey Allah's commands.

In essence, verse 2 of Surah Al-Inshiqaq emphasizes the earth's complete submission to Allah's will on the Day of Judgment, highlighting the divine decree and the fulfillment of its purpose as created by Allah.

Verse 3

Wa izal ardu muddat

"And when the earth is stretched forth".

This verse refers to the Day of Judgment, when the earth will be flattened and expanded, creating a vast plain to accommodate all of humanity for their reckoning.

The stretching of the earth is one of the major events associated with the Day of Judgment, as described in the Quran and Hadith.

The mountains, valleys, and other uneven features of the earth will be levelled out.

Verse 4

Wa alqat maa feehaa wa takhallat

"And it casts out what is within it and becomes empty."

Here we are learning of the earth's state on the Day of Resurrection, when it will expel all that is buried within it, becoming completely empty.

The earth will be convulsed and will throw out all the dead bodies and everything else that was buried within it, including treasures and other hidden things.

Then the earth will be completely emptied, leaving no trace of anything that was previously inside it.

Hence, this verse emphasizes the complete and utter transformation of the earth on the Day of Judgment, leaving nothing concealed, then preparing for the final reckoning.

Verse 5

Wa azinat li Rabbihaa wa huqqat

"And has listened to its Lord, and it was obligated [to do so]."

This verse follows the description of the sky splitting and the earth being stretched out, as mentioned in the previous verses. It highlights the absolute obedience and submission of the sky and earth to Allah's command. The verse emphasizes that the sky and earth, despite not being endowed with intellect like humans, respond to Allah's command with complete obedience and without hesitation.

The verse suggests that all creation, including the heavens and the earth, are inherently obedient to their Creator.

It underscores the natural and necessary response of creation to Allah's decree.

In essence, verse 5 of Surah Al-Inshiqaq illustrates the perfect order and harmony in the universe, where all creation, including the inanimate objects, submits to the will and command of Allah, its Creator.

Verse 6

Yaaa ayyuhal insaanu innaka kaadihun ilaa Rabbika kad han famulaaqee

"O mankind, indeed you are striving [hard] toward your Lord, [but] you will meet Him."

"O mankind, indeed you are striving [hard]..."

This part of the verse addresses all of humanity, acknowledging their inherent drive and exertion in life. Whether they are conscious of it or not, they are constantly moving towards their ultimate destination, which is Allah.

- **"...toward your Lord..."**

This phrase emphasizes that the direction of this striving is towards Allah. It implies that all actions, both good and bad, are ultimately leading back to Him.

- **"...[but] you will meet Him."**

This part signifies the inevitability of death and the meeting with Allah on the Day of Judgment. It serves as a reminder that every individual will be held accountable for their deeds.

In summary, the verse conveys the message that life is a journey towards Allah, and every individual will eventually face the consequences of their actions before Him. It encourages reflection on one's actions and striving for righteousness in preparation for this inevitable meeting.

Verse 7

Fa ammaa man ootiya kitaabahoo biyameenih

"Then as for him who is given his record in his right hand,"

This signifies the fate of the righteous individuals on the Day of Judgment. They will be given their record of deeds in their right hand, an indication of their acceptance and success in the afterlife. This is followed by an easy reckoning, where their good deeds will be acknowledged and their minor transgressions overlooked. They will then return to their families joyfully.

This means that the reckoning for these individuals will be light and straightforward. They will not be subjected to intense interrogation or scrutiny regarding their sins. Their good deeds will outweigh their bad deeds, and they will be forgiven.

- **"and shall return to his people joyfully":**

This describes the happiness and contentment that these individuals will experience as they return to their families in Paradise. They will be reunited with their loved ones and experience eternal bliss.

Verse 8

Fasawfa yuhaasab hisaabany yaseeraa

"Then he will be judged with an easy reckoning."

The verse highlights that those who receive their book of deeds in their right hand will be granted an easy and merciful judgment. This means their sins will be overlooked and their good deeds will be multiplied, resulting in a favourable outcome on the Day of Judgment.

Those who are given their record in their right hand will be granted paradise and eternal happiness.

The verse contrasts with the fate of those who receive their record behind their backs, who will face a severe and difficult reckoning.

Verse 9

Wa yanqalibu ilaaa ahlihee masrooraa

"And he will return to his people in happiness,"

This indicates that the person who receives their record of deeds in their right hand on the Day of Judgment will return to his family in Paradise, rejoicing and delighted with the blessings Allah has bestowed upon him. This joyous reunion is a reward for his good deeds and faith in this life.

So, this verse highlights the ultimate reward for the righteous: eternal happiness with their families in Paradise, a consequence of their faith and good actions in this life.

Verse 10

Wa ammaa man ootiya kitaabahoo waraaa'a zahrih

"But as for him who is given his record behind his back,"

This verse is referring to those who will receive their record of deeds behind their backs. Henceforth, in a manner that signifies their doom and despair. This is in contrast to those who receive their record in their right hand, indicating a favourable outcome.

Behind the Back:

This imagery signifies a state of disgrace and rejection. It suggests that the person will be ashamed of their record and try to hide it, or that Allah will present it in a way that humiliates them.

Contrast with Right Hand:

The verse highlights the stark difference between the believers who receive their record in their right hand with joy and those who receive it behind their back with despair.

Receiving the record behind the back is associated with a severe reckoning and entry into Hellfire, as mentioned in other verses of the Surah.

This fate is attributed to those who disbelieved in Allah, denied the Hereafter, and did not heed the warnings of the Quran.

The person receiving their record behind their back is described as calling out for destruction, highlighting their hopelessness and regret.

In conclusion, verse 10 paints a picture of profound despair and punishment for those who rejected faith and accountability in the worldly life, as opposed to those who embraced faith and good deeds.

Verse 11

Fasawfa yad'oo thubooraa

"Soon will he cry for perdition"

Refers to the state of a person who, upon receiving their record of deeds in the Hereafter from behind their back, will realize the gravity of their actions and consequences, leading them to intensely desire death or annihilation as a release from the impending punishment.

Those who receive their record of deeds in their left hand (or from behind their back) are depicted as disbelievers or those who have not lived righteously, signifying a negative outcome in the afterlife.

The verse highlights the profound despair and regret experienced by such individuals. The phrase "cry for perdition" (or "will call for destruction") signifies their intense desire to be annihilated or destroyed, as they face the consequences of their actions.

This is in stark contrast to those who receive their record in their right hand, who are shown to be joyful and content in the Hereafter.

The verse serves as a warning about the importance of preparing for the Hereafter and the consequences of neglecting one's responsibilities and accountability to Allah.

Verse 12

Wa yaslaa Sa'ir

Allah describes the fate of those who are given their record of deeds in their left hand behind their backs. They will "enter the blazing fire" and "taste its burning". This verse highlights the consequences of rejecting faith and engaging in evil actions, emphasizing the severity of the punishment in the afterlife.

The Blazing Fire (Sa'ir):

The term "Sa'ir" refers to a blazing fire, the Hellfire, which is a place of torment and punishment for those who disobey Allah.

- **Taste its Burning:**

This phrase emphasizes the intense and painful experience of the fire, indicating that the punishment will be both severe and prolonged.

- **Warning and Reminder:**

This verse serves as a warning to those who might be tempted to engage in evil actions, reminding them of the dire consequences that await them in the afterlife if they persist in their wrongdoing.

The verse is a stark reminder of the importance of righteous conduct and faith, as well as the consequences of choosing a path of disbelief and disobedience.

Verse 13

Innahoo kaana feee ahlihee masrooraa

"Indeed, he had been among his people in joy."

This verse describes a person who lived a life of pleasure and heedlessness, oblivious to the afterlife and the reckoning that awaits him. The verse highlights the contrast between his worldly joy and the impending consequences of his actions.

Worldly Joy:

The verse points to a person who was content and happy in his worldly life, indulging in pleasures and unaware of the Hereafter.

Neglect of the Hereafter:

He was heedless of the fact that he would eventually return to Allah and face judgment for his deeds.

This verse highlights the stark contrast between his past joy and his future misery, emphasizing the consequences of neglecting the Hereafter.

His previous joy and lack of preparation for the Hereafter are presented as the reasons for his despair and suffering in the afterlife.

While describing a specific individual, the verse serves as a warning and reminder to all humans about the importance of preparing for the Day of Judgment.

Verse 13 of Surah Al-Inshiqaq serves as a cautionary tale, urging individuals to reflect on their lives, prepare for the Hereafter, and not be consumed by worldly pleasures to the point of neglecting their spiritual well-being.

Verse 14

Innahoo zanna an lany yahoor

"Truly, did he think that he would not have to return (to Us)!"

This verse critiques the disbeliever's arrogance and denial of accountability in the afterlife. It highlights their false belief that they would not be resurrected and judged by Allah. The verse emphasizes that despite their denial, they will indeed be returned to Allah for judgment.

"Truly, did he think...":

This phrase indicates a sense of disbelief and astonishment at the disbeliever's flawed reasoning.

"...that he would not have to return (to Us)":

This refers to the disbeliever's assumption that they would not be resurrected and held accountable for their actions in the Hereafter.

The verse is a stern warning to those who reject the concept of an afterlife and divine judgment. It highlights the consequences of such denial, emphasizing that everyone will eventually face Allah.

The purpose of this verse, and the surah as a whole, is to remind people of the inevitability of death and the importance of preparing for the afterlife by living a righteous life.

Verse 15

Balaaa inna Rabbahoo kaana bihee baseeraa

"Nay, but his Lord was ever watchful of him."

This verse emphasizes that despite a person's potential denial of accountability in the afterlife, Allah is constantly aware of their actions and will hold them accountable. It serves as a reminder that actions in this life have consequences in the hereafter.

"Nay, but his Lord was ever watchful of him":

This part of the verse highlights that Allah is aware of everything a person does, even if they try to deny or forget about it.

- **Implications**:

This awareness implies that every action, big or small, is recorded and will be brought to account on the Day of Judgment.

The verse shows the importance of being mindful of one's actions and the consequences they will have in the afterlife. It encourages reflection on the nature of accountability and the certainty of divine judgment.

Verse 16

Falaaa uqsimu bishshafaq

"But nay! I call to witness the sunset's fleeting afterglow,"

This is a powerful oath by Allah, swearing by the red afterglow that follows sunset. This verse, combined with the following verse mentioning "and by the night and what it envelops" (verse 17), signifies a transition from light to darkness, emphasizing the cyclical nature of existence and the certainty of the Day of Judgement.

"But nay! I call to witness...":

This emphatic statement introduces a series of oaths, emphasizing the importance of what is being sworn by.

"the sunset's fleeting afterglow":

This refers to the reddish or yellowish light that lingers in the sky after the sun has set. The Arabic word "shafaq" can also refer to the twilight glow, further highlighting the transition between day and night.

The afterglow, though beautiful, is transient and disappears quickly. This imagery serves to remind humans of the fleeting nature of worldly life and the certainty of the hereafter.

Verse 17

Wallaili wa maa wasaq

"the night and what it envelops"

Allah swears by the night and what it envelops, signifying the vastness and power of His creation and the inevitability of His decree. The verse demonstrates the night's encompassing nature, symbolizing the darkness, mystery, and transition into the unknown that it brings. This oath, along with others in the surah, points to the gradual and inevitable progression of life, death, and the Day of Judgment.

The Night as a Metaphor:

The night, with its darkness and ability to envelop everything, serves as a powerful metaphor for the unknown and the inevitable changes that occur in life, particularly the transition from life to death and the subsequent resurrection.

The surah, including this verse, highlights the theme of gradual progression towards an inevitable end. Just as the night follows the day and the moon goes through phases, so too does life move towards its conclusion.

By swearing by the night and its enveloping darkness, Allah emphasizes His power and control over the universe and all its phenomena. This is a reminder that He is the one who brings about these changes and that He is in control of all things.

The oath serves as a prelude to the subsequent verses, which discuss the Day of Judgment and the accountability of all individuals before Allah. It highlights the certainty of the Hereafter and the need for humans to reflect on their actions.

While the primary interpretation focuses on the night as a symbol of the unknown and the Day of Judgment, some scholars have also interpreted it to refer to the secrets and treasures hidden within the earth, which will be revealed on the Day of Resurrection.

Verse 18

Walqamari izat tasaq

"And the Moon in her fullness"

Allah swears by the moon when it is full, emphasizing its completeness and luminosity. This oath highlights the concept of progression and stages, mirroring the human experience of life's journey from birth to death. The verse also suggests that just as the moon goes through phases, humans also experience different stages in their lives.

The oath by the full moon is connected to the previous verses (16-17) that mention the twilight and the night, which also represent stages and transitions. The moon's phases, from new moon to full moon, symbolize the idea of gradual change and development.

This concept of stages is extended to human life, where individuals go through different phases from birth to death. The verse, in conjunction with the previous ones, emphasizes that life is not static, but rather a journey with distinct stages.

The verse carries a message of hope, as the full moon provides light and guidance, similar to how faith and belief can illuminate the path for believers, even amidst the darkness of life's challenges.

Verse 19

Latarkabunna tabaqan 'an tabaq

"you will surely travel from stage to stage".

This signifies the various stages of life that humans experience, from birth to death, and then the stages of the afterlife: the intermediary state (Barzakh), resurrection, and judgment. The verse emphasizes the continuous and gradual change that occurs in the universe, and that humans will inevitably pass through these predetermined stages.

"Latarkabunna":

This is a strong affirmation, emphasizing the certainty of the journey through different stages.

"tabaq"

This phrase literally means "stage upon stage" or "state after state".

The verse alludes to the various phases of life and the afterlife.

Some commentaries specifically mention:

- **Life's Stages:** From infancy to youth, old age, and finally, death.
- **Afterlife Stages:** The intermediary state (Barzakh), the Day of Resurrection, the gathering of all humanity, the reckoning, and the final reward or punishment.

The verse highlights the transient nature of life and the inevitability of facing the consequences of one's actions in the afterlife. It also serves as a reminder of the continuous change and transformation happening in the universe, urging reflection on the ultimate destination.

The verse is part of a series of oaths that Allah swears by, including the twilight, the night, and the full moon, to emphasize the continuous cycle of change and transformation in the universe and the certainty of the afterlife.

Verse 20

Famaa lahum laa yu'minoon

"So what is the matter with them, that they believe not?",

This is a rhetorical question expressing Allah's astonishment at the disbelievers' persistent refusal to believe, despite the clear signs and evidence presented to them. The verse highlights the disbelievers' denial and lack of submission, even when the Quran is recited to them.

"So what is the matter with them...":

This phrase indicates Allah's wonder at the disbelievers' stubbornness.

"...that they believe not?":

This part of the verse points to the disbelievers' failure to accept the truth of Allah's message, despite the abundant signs and evidence surrounding them.

The verse focuses on the presence of numerous signs and proofs pointing to the truth of Allah's message, making the disbelievers' lack of faith even more perplexing.

The verse is followed by verses that highlight the believers who accept the truth and perform righteous deeds, contrasting them with the disbelievers and foreshadowing their respective fates.

Verse 21

Wa izaa quri'a 'alaihimul Quraanu laa yasjudoon (make sajda)

"And when the Qur´an is read to them, they fall not prostrate",

This refers to the lack of submission and belief among those who disbelieve, even when the Quran is recited to them. They do not bow down in humility and acceptance of the divine message. The verse highlights their arrogance and rejection of the truth, despite the clear guidance and profound impact the Quran should have.

"They fall not prostrate":

This phrase, according to many tafsir scholars, signifies more than just the physical act of prostration (sajda). It represents a lack of humility, submission, and acceptance of the Quran's message. The word "sajda" in this context encompasses bowing down in reverence and obedience to Allah.

The verse points to the arrogance and stubbornness of the disbelievers who reject the truth of the Quran despite its clarity and the divine nature of its message.

The verse serves as a warning to those who reject the Quran, highlighting the dire consequences of their actions. It emphasizes that true believers should be moved by the Quran's message and respond with humility and submission.

While the verse uses the word "sajda", it is not interpreted as a command to prostrate every time the Quran is recited. Rather, it uses the term to signify the general concept of submission and humility that the Quran should inspire.

Verse 22

Balil lazeena kafaroo yukazziboon

"But on the contrary, the disbelievers reject (it),"

The verse highlights the stubborn denial of the disbelievers towards the Quran and the truth it conveys. It shows their rejection of the message despite its clarity and the clear signs presented to them.

"But on the contrary":

This phrase (in Arabic, "bal") indicates a shift in focus, emphasizing the disbelievers' active denial rather than a passive acceptance.

"the disbelievers reject (it)":

This refers to the disbelievers' active rejection of the Quran and the message of Islam. They deny the truth revealed in the Quran, even when it is presented clearly to them.

The verse implies that the disbelievers are not merely confused or uncertain, but rather they actively deny the truth they are presented with. This rejection is a conscious choice they make, despite the evidence and guidance offered.

The verse serves as a warning to those who disbelieve, highlighting the consequences of their rejection. It emphasizes that their denial is a choice they make, with clear repercussions in the afterlife

Verse 23

Wallaahu a'lamu bimaa yoo'oon

"But Allah has full knowledge of what they secrete (in their breasts)."

This means that Allah is fully aware of all the thoughts, intentions, and secrets that people conceal within their hearts and minds, even those they try to hide from others. The verse stresses Allah's omniscience and that nothing is hidden from Him.

"But Allah has full knowledge..."

This signifies Allah's complete and perfect awareness of everything, including the hidden aspects of human beings.

"...of what they secrete (in their breasts)"

This refers to the innermost thoughts, intentions, and secrets that individuals keep hidden within their hearts and minds. This could include disbelief, malice, hostility to the truth, evil intentions, and other hidden aspects of their character.

Verse 24

Fabashshirhum bi'azaabin aleem

"So announce to them a Penalty Grievous,"

This is a stern warning to the disbelievers. While the word "bashshir" typically means to give good news, in this context, it is used ironically to announce a painful and severe punishment. This verse emphasizes the dire consequences of rejecting the truth and highlights the severity of the punishment awaiting those who deny Allah's message.

The irony of "bashshir":

The verse uses the word "bashshir", which usually signifies conveying good news, but in this case, it is used sarcastically to foreshadow the terrible punishment awaiting the disbelievers.

"A'dhaabun Aleem"

This phrase translates to "a painful or grievous punishment." It signifies a severe and agonizing torment that will befall the rejecters of faith.

This verse serves as a warning to those who are heedless of Allah's signs and warnings, emphasizing the consequences of their disbelief and rebellion.

Verse 25

Illal lazeena aamanoo wa 'amilus saalihaati lahum ajrun ghairu mamnoon

"Except for those who believe and do righteous deeds, for them is a reward that will never fail."

This verse highlights that while the Day of Judgment will be a time of reckoning, there is hope for those who believe in Allah and live righteously. Their reward in the afterlife will be continuous and unending.

- **"Except for those who believe...":**

This part emphasizes that faith in Allah is a prerequisite for attaining this reward. It signifies a belief in the Oneness of Allah, His messengers, and the Day of Judgment.

"...and do righteous deeds":

This signifies actions that align with Islamic teachings, fulfilling obligations to Allah and fellow humans. It includes acts of worship, kindness, and justice.

"...for them is a reward that will never fail":

This assures that the reward for believers who act righteously will be everlasting and complete. It will not be diminished or interrupted.

Key aspects of the verse:

- **Conditionality**:

The verse establishes a condition for receiving the unending reward – belief and righteous actions.

- **Promise of Paradise**:

The reward is often understood as Paradise, a place of eternal bliss and divine favour.

- **Emphasis on action**:

While belief is essential, the verse also stresses the importance of good deeds as a manifestation of that belief.

In conclusion, this verse serves as a reminder of the importance of both faith and action in Islam and offers a hopeful prospect for believers who strive to live according to Allah's guidance

LESSONS TO BE LEARNT FROM SURAH INSHIIQAQ

Surah Al-Inshiqaq, the 84th chapter of the Quran, offers several lessons and reflections for believers.

Here are some of the key themes and lessons that can be drawn from this Surah:

1. The Inevitability of the Day of Judgment: The Surah begins with vivid imagery depicting the end of the world, emphasizing the certainty of the Day of Judgment. This reminder serves to encourage believers to live with an awareness of accountability for their actions.
2. The Reality of Human Life: Verses in the Surah highlight that life is a journey of toil and struggle. This reflects the idea that challenges and hardships are inherent parts of human existence, and one should persevere through them with patience and faith.
3. The Record of Deeds: The Surah describes how every person's deeds will be presented to them, with the righteous receiving their record in their right hand as a sign of success, and the wrongdoers receiving it behind their back. This underscores the importance of leading a life of righteousness and obedience to Allah's commands.
4. The Ultimate Return to Allah: The Surah reinforces the concept that all creation will ultimately return to Allah. This serves as a reminder for believers to focus on their spiritual journey and relationship with Allah, rather than being solely caught up in worldly pursuits.
5. The Contrast Between Believers and Disbelievers: The text contrasts the outcomes for those who believe and do good deeds with those who reject faith. This dichotomy is intended to motivate individuals to strive for a life of faith and good conduct.
6. Signs of Allah's Power and Creation: The Surah draws attention to the natural phenomena as signs of Allah's power and the truth of the message. Reflecting on these signs is encouraged to deepen faith and recognition of Allah's greatness.
7. Encouragement to Reflect and Prepare: Overall, the Surah serves as an encouragement to reflect on one's life and prepare for the hereafter, reminding believers that their efforts in this life will determine their fate in the next.

By contemplating these lessons, individuals are encouraged to strengthen their faith, consistently engage in self-reflection, and pursue a path of righteousness and accountability.

This Surah was revealed in Makkah when Muslims were facing a lot of trouble. The people who didn't believe in Islam were trying very hard to make the new Muslims change their minds.

Theme and Subject Matter

The main message of this Surah is to tell those who were being mean to Muslims that their actions would lead to bad results. It also comforts the Muslims, assuring them that if they stay strong and don't give up, Allah will reward them and take care of those who hurt them.

To explain this, the Surah tells a story about people long ago who threw believers into big fires because they wouldn't stop believing in Allah. This story teaches us some lessons. First, the people who hurt others for their beliefs will face Allah's anger, just like the leaders in Makkah at that time. Second, the believers back then were brave and chose to stay true to their faith, even if it was hard. Today's believers should do the same. Third, Allah is very powerful and sees everything. He will make sure that those who do wrong are punished and those who do good will go to a wonderful place called Paradise.

The Surah also warns those who are mean: "Allah is very strong. If you think you are powerful, remember the people long ago who were stronger, but still faced Allah's punishment. You can't escape from Allah's power, and the messages in the Qur'an will always be true and can't be changed."

SUMMARY OF SURAH INSHIQAQ
(SURAH 84)

This chapter is called "Inshiqaq," which means "splitting apart." It talks about how, on the Day of Judgment, the sky will break open and everything will change.

This Surah was revealed early in Makkah. It explains that people were refusing to believe and that there would be a day when everyone has to stand before Allah and explain what they did in their lives.

The main idea of this chapter is about the Day of Resurrection, when everyone will come back to life and stand before Allah.

It says that on that day, the sky will split open, the earth will turn flat and empty, and all the dead bodies will come out of the ground. This will happen because it is Allah's command, and everything in the skies and on the earth must obey Him.

The chapter also tells us that, whether people realize it or not, everyone is moving towards that day. When the time comes, people will be divided into two groups. One group will be given their records in their right hand and will be happy because they will be forgiven. The other group will get their records behind their backs and will be sad because they will be punished forever in Hell.

Some people thought they would never have to face Allah, but they were wrong. Allah always watched what they did, and everyone will have to answer for their actions.

Finally, the chapter warns those who don't believe in the Qur'an that they will face a very serious punishment. But it also gives good news to those who believe and do good deeds: they will be rewarded with endless happiness and blessings from Allah.

Al-Inshiqaq-Surah 84

Questions

1. What is the main theme of Surah Al-Inshiqaq?
2. How does Surah Al-Inshiqaq describe the event of the sky splitting?
3. What will happen to the earth on the Day of Judgment according to Surah Al-Inshiqaq?
4. What is the significance of the phrase "O man, you are laboring toward your Lord with [great] exertion" in this Surah?
5. How are the records of people's deeds presented on the Day of Judgment in Surah Al-Inshiqaq?
6. What is the fate of those who receive their record in their right hand?
7. What is described as the consequence for those who receive their record behind their back?
8. How does Surah Al-Inshiqaq emphasize the certainty of the resurrection?
9. What is the role of the moon, the night, and the dawn mentioned in this Surah?
10. How does Surah Al-Inshiqaq portray the human condition in relation to the afterlife?

Answers

1. The main theme of Surah Al-Inshiqaq is the inevitability of the Day of Judgment, the resurrection, and the presentation of the deeds of individuals.

2. Surah Al-Inshiqaq describes the sky splitting open when it is commanded by its Lord, indicating a cosmic transformation on the Day of Judgment.

3. On the Day of Judgment, the earth will be stretched out and will reveal its burdens, meaning everything hidden will be exposed.

4. The phrase highlights the continuous effort and struggle of human life, emphasizing that every person is moving towards meeting their Lord, where they will be accountable for their actions.

5. On the Day of Judgment, people's deeds will be presented in a record, which will be given either in their right hand or behind their back, indicating their fate.

6. Those who receive their record in their right hand will have an easy reckoning and will return joyfully to their family.

7. Those who receive their record behind their back will call for destruction and enter a blazing fire, indicating punishment.

8. Surah Al-Inshiqaq emphasizes the certainty of the resurrection by describing the cosmic events and the transformation of the world, affirming the truth of the hereafter.

9. The moon, the night, and the dawn are mentioned to illustrate the natural phenomena that testify to the power of Allah and the certainty of the resurrection.

10. The Surah portrays the human condition as one of continuous effort and struggle, reminding individuals of their ultimate return to their Lord and the accountability that follows.

These questions and answers provide a structured way to understand the key themes and messages of Surah Al-Inshiqaq.

Multiple Choice Questions

1. What event is described at the beginning of Surah Al-Inshiqaq?

    a) The creation of the universe

    b) The splitting of the sky

    c) The battle of Badr

    d) The migration to Medina

2. According to Surah Al-Inshiqaq, what will happen to the earth on the Day of Judgment?

    a) It will be destroyed completely

    b) It will be stretched out and reveal its burdens

    c) It will become a paradise

    d) It will be submerged in water

3. In Surah Al-Inshiqaq, what does the phrase "O man, you are laboring toward your Lord with [great] exertion" signify?

    a) The physical labor of mankind

    b) The spiritual journey towards Allah and accountability

    c) The importance of earning wealth

    d) The duty of daily prayers

4. How are the records of people's deeds presented on the Day of Judgment in Surah Al-Inshiqaq?

    a) As an oral report

    b) In a sealed letter

    c) Given in their right hand or behind their back

    d) Through a dream

5. What is the fate of those who receive their record in their right hand, according to Surah Al-Inshiqaq?

    a) They will be punished severely

    b) They will receive a difficult reckoning

    c) They will have an easy reckoning and be joyful

    d) They will be sent back to Earth

6. What consequence is described for those who receive their record behind their back in Surah Al-Inshiqaq?

    a) They will enter a blazing fire

    b) They will receive forgiveness

    c) They will be granted wealth

    d) They will be given another chance

7. How does Surah Al-Inshiqaq emphasize the certainty of the resurrection?

    a) By describing historical events

    b) By highlighting natural phenomena like the moon and dawn

    c) By quoting previous prophets

    d) By providing scientific evidence

8. What natural elements are mentioned in Surah Al-Inshiqaq to signify the power of Allah?

    a) Mountains and rivers

    b) Stars and planets

    c) The moon, the night, and the dawn

    d) Trees and animals

Answers

1. *Answer:* b) The splitting of the sky
2. *Answer:* b) It will be stretched out and reveal its burdens
3. *Answer:* b) The spiritual journey towards Allah and accountability
4. *Answer:* c) Given in their right hand or behind their back
5. *Answer:* c) They will have an easy reckoning and be joyful
6. *Answer:* a) They will enter a blazing fire
7. *Answer:* b) By highlighting natural phenomena like the moon and dawn
8. *Answer:* c) The moon, the night, and the dawn

These questions and answers can help in understanding the key messages and themes of Surah Al-Inshiqaq in a multiple-choice format.

SURAH AL-BUROOJ

SURAH AL-BUROOJ

Bismillahi ar-Rahmani ar-Raheem

Verse 1

Wassamaaa'i zaatil burooj

"By the sky, (displaying) the Zodiac Signs"

This verse talks about the beautiful night sky and its special star patterns, called constellations. These patterns include the zodiac signs and show how powerful and wise Allah is.

Al-Buruj

This word, translated as "Zodiac Signs" or "constellations," refers to the groupings of stars that form recognizable patterns in the night sky.

Oath:

The verse uses "By the sky" as an oath, similar to how people swear by things of great importance. In this case, it draws attention to the vastness and intricate design of the heavens as a sign of Allah's power.

Significance of the Zodiac:

The zodiac signs are not just random arrangements of stars. They have been used for centuries in astronomy and astrology to mark the sun's path through the year and are seen as a symbol of the divine order and precision in creation.

Connection to Oppression:

The surah then shifts to discuss the story of the people of the ditch, who were persecuted for their faith. The oath by the sky with its constellations serves as a reminder that even in the face of oppression, Allah's creation continues in its perfect order, and He is aware of everything that happens.

Lessons for the Believer:

The verse and the surah as a whole encourage believers to reflect on the signs of Allah in the universe, find strength in His power, and remain steadfast in their faith even during times of difficulty.

Verse 2

Wal yawmil maw'ood

"By the promised Day"

This refers to the Day of Judgment. This verse is part of an oath, highlighting the significance of this day as a time of reckoning and divine justice. The verse highlights that the Day of Judgment is a certain and inevitable event, a promise from Allah that will undoubtedly come to pass.

The Day of Judgment:

The "promised Day" is the Day of Resurrection, a time when all of creation will be gathered for judgment.

Significance of the Oath:

Allah takes an oath by this day, signifying its importance and the certainty of its occurrence.

Purpose of the Day:

On this day, Allah will judge all of humanity, rewarding the righteous and punishing the wicked.

Connection to the Story:

This verse is connected to the story of the People of the Trench, as it introduces the concept of divine justice and retribution that will befall the oppressors on the Day of Judgment.

Verse 3

Wa shaahidinw wa mashhood

"By the witness and the witnessed,"

This verse discusses the oaths sworn by Allah, signifying the importance of those who witness and those who are witnessed, particularly in relation to the Day of Judgment.

"By the witness":

This refers to those who will witness the events of the Day of Judgment, including people, angels, and perhaps even prophets. The word "witness" can also imply those who are present and can testify to the truth.

"And the witnessed":

This refers to the Day of Judgment itself, with its terrifying scenes and ultimate reckoning. It can also refer to the deeds of people, both good and bad, which will be presented as evidence.

- **Multiple Interpretations:**

While the core meaning is about witnessing and being witnessed on the Day of Judgment, some scholars offer specific interpretations, such as:

- **Friday and Arafah:** Some narrations suggest the "witness" refers to Friday, and the "witnessed" to the Day of Arafah, highlighting the significance of these days.
- **Believers and their actions:** Others connect the witness to the prophets, and the witnessed to their communities, or to believers who will be presented with their deeds.
- **Emphasis on Divine Justice:**

The oaths emphasize the certainty of the Day of Judgment and the accountability of all people for their actions. It highlights the power and knowledge of Allah, who witnesses everything and will judge justly.

- **Connection to the Previous Verse:**

The verse follows the oath about the "heaven with its constellations", suggesting a link between the celestial realm and the events of the Day of Judgment. The verse also connects to the following verses about the believers being thrown into the pit of fire, as a reminder of the consequences of rejecting faith.

Verse 4

Qutila as haabul ukhdood

"Woe to the makers of the pit (of fire)"

This is about the story of the "People of the Ditch," a group of believers who were persecuted and burned alive for their faith. The verse condemns the oppressors who dug the ditch and set it ablaze, highlighting their cruelty and the believers' steadfastness. It also serves as a warning of the severe punishment awaiting those who persecute believers and do not repent.

- **The Ditch:**

The "pit of fire" refers to a large trench dug by the persecutors, filled with burning fuel to create a fiery furnace.

- **The Oppressors:**

These were tyrannical rulers who forced their subjects to renounce their faith, and those who refused were thrown into the pit.

- **The Believers:**

The victims were devout followers of Allah who chose to die for their faith rather than abandon it.

- **The Punishment:**

The verse condemns the oppressors and promises a severe punishment in Hell for their actions, emphasizing that their cruelty will not go unpunished.

- **Repentance:**

The verse also highlights that those who repent of their persecution will be forgiven, demonstrating Allah's mercy and forgiveness.

- **Witness:**

The verse also notes that Allah is a witness to this event, highlighting His knowledge and power.

In essence, the verse serves as a reminder of Allah's justice, the consequences of oppression, and the reward for steadfastness in faith.

Verse 5

Annaari zaatil waqood

"Fire supplied (abundantly) with fuel"

This describes the fiery pit where the disbelievers are said to have thrown the believers. The fuel-rich fire emphasizes the intensity and severity of the torment the believers faced, highlighting the oppressors' cruelty. It serves as a stark contrast to the believers' faith and a warning to those who persecute them.

- **The Context:**

Surah Al-Burooj recounts the story of the "people of the ditch," who persecuted believers by throwing them into a ditch filled with fire.

- **"Fire supplied (abundantly) with fuel":**

This phrase describes the pit as a furnace, emphasizing the intensity and abundance of the fire. The fuel-rich nature of the fire suggests a raging inferno, highlighting the severity of the punishment.

- **Symbolic Meaning:**

The fiery pit serves as a symbol of the oppressors' cruelty and the believers' steadfastness in faith. Despite the horrific torture, the believers did not renounce their faith, showcasing their devotion and resilience.

- **Contrast with the Believers:**

The verse contrasts the believers' ordeal with the promise of Paradise and Allah's mercy. It emphasizes that while the disbelievers will face the torment of Hell, the believers will be rewarded for their faith and patience.

- **Warning to the Oppressors:**

The verse also serves as a warning to those who persecute the believers, reminding them of the severe consequences of their actions in the afterlife.

Verse 6

"Behold! they sat over against the (fire)",

This is telling us about the oppressors who burned believers in a ditch, watching and delighting in their suffering. This verse highlights the cruelty and callousness of the persecutors, who took pleasure in the torment of those who believed in Allah.

The verse is part of the larger narrative of the "People of the Ditch" (Ashab al-Ukhdud), a story found in Surah Al-Buruj.

- **The Oppressors:**

The verse focuses on the oppressors who, out of their hatred for the believers, devised a cruel punishment.

- **The Ditch and the Fire:**

They dug a ditch, filled it with fire, and forced believers into it, watching as they were burned alive.

- **Their Delight:**

The verse emphasizes that they "sat over against the (fire)", meaning they positioned themselves to witness the believers' agony, finding satisfaction in their pain.

- **Significance:**

This act of watching the believers' suffering is presented as a testament to the oppressors' cruelty and their rejection of Allah's guidance.

In summary, verse 6 of Surah Al-Buruj paints a vivid picture of the oppressors' wickedness, emphasizing their sadistic pleasure in the suffering of those who believed in Allah.

Verse 7

Wa hum 'alaa maa yaf'aloona bilmu 'mineena shuhood

"And they witnessed (all) that they were doing against the Believers,"

This refers to the oppressors who burned the believers in fiery ditches. They were not only the perpetrators of the cruelty but also witnesses to their own actions, actively observing the suffering they inflicted. This verse highlights the severity of their crime and tells us that they were fully aware of their wrongdoing.

- **Awareness and Accountability:**

The tafsir suggests that their witnessing implies they were fully aware of the injustice and suffering they were causing, making them accountable for their actions.

- **Severity of the Crime:**

This detail underscores the severity of their actions, as they were not only cruel but also took pleasure in watching the believers' torment.

- **Contrast with Divine Mercy:**

The verse can also be contrasted with the divine mercy offered to those who repent, as the oppressors are condemned for their lack of repentance and continued cruelty,

Verse 8

Wa maa naqamoo minhum illaaa aiyu'minoo billaahil 'azeezil Hameed

"And they ill-treated them for no other reason than that they believed in Allah, Exalted in Power, Worthy of all Praise"

This verse explains that the companions of the ditch (the believers) were punished solely because they believed in Allah, the Almighty and Praiseworthy. They were persecuted and tormented for their faith, with no other justifiable reason for the oppressors' actions. This highlights the central theme of the surah: the conflict between faith and disbelief, and the ultimate triumph of faith despite persecution.

- **Context:**

Surah Al-Buruj narrates the story of the people of the ditch (ashab al-ukhdud), who were believers thrown into fiery pits by their oppressors for refusing to renounce their faith.

- **Reason for Persecution:**

The verse emphasizes that the only reason the believers were targeted was their belief in Allah, the Exalted in Power and Worthy of all Praise.

- **Divine Attributes:**

The names "Al-Azeez" (the Almighty) and "Al-Hameed" (the Praiseworthy) highlight Allah's attributes of power and worthiness of praise, emphasizing that He is the one who ultimately judges and rewards.

- **Triumph of Faith:**

The surah contrasts the fate of the believers, who are promised gardens and rivers in Paradise, with the fate of the oppressors, who are threatened with the fire of Hell, according to tafsir websites.

- **Lesson for Muslims:**

The story of the people of the ditch serves as a reminder to believers to remain steadfast in their faith, even in the face of persecution, and to trust in Allah's ultimate justice and reward.

Verse 9

Allazee lahoo mulkus samaawaati wal ard; wallaahu 'alaa kulli shai 'in Shaheed

"Him to Whom belongs the dominion of the heavens and the earth! And Allah is Witness to all things".

This emphasizes Allah's absolute sovereignty and comprehensive knowledge. It highlights that Allah is the ultimate owner and ruler of the universe, and nothing escapes His observation. This verse serves as a reminder of Allah's power and that He is aware of everything that happens, both seen and unseen.

- **"Him to Whom belongs the dominion of the heavens and the earth!":**

This part of the verse declares Allah's absolute ownership and authority over all creation. It means that Allah is the sole creator, sustainer, and disposer of all affairs in the universe. The heavens and the earth, with all that they contain, are under His absolute control. This declaration is a powerful statement of Allah's greatness and majesty.

- **"And Allah is Witness to all things.":**

This is telling us of Allah's all-encompassing knowledge and awareness. It means that Allah is aware of everything that happens in the heavens and the earth, nothing is hidden from Him. This includes both the physical and the spiritual realms, the actions of individuals, and the intentions of their hearts. This knowledge is not just passive observation, but active witnessing, meaning He is aware of everything in detail.

- **Connection to the Previous Verses:**

This verse is connected to the previous verses that describe the story of the people of the ditch, who were persecuted for their faith. It reminds the believers that despite the oppression they face, Allah is ultimately in control and aware of their suffering. It is a source of comfort and strength for the oppressed and a warning to the oppressors.

- **Implications of the Verse:**

The verse has significant implications for both believers and disbelievers. For believers, it is a source of hope and reassurance, as it reminds them that Allah is aware of their struggles and will ultimately bring about justice. For disbelievers, it is a warning that their actions are not hidden from Allah and that they will be held accountable for their deeds.

Verse 10

Innal lazeena fatanul mu'mineena wal mu'minaati summa lam yatooboo falahum 'azaabu Jahannama wa lahum 'azaabul hareeq

"Those who persecute (or draw into temptation) the Believers, men and women, and do not turn in repentance, will have the Penalty of Hell: They will have the Penalty of the Burning Fire".

This is describing the severe punishment awaiting those who persecute believers, both men and women, and fail to repent. It highlights that such individuals will face the torment of Hell and the burning fire, emphasizing the consequences of their actions and the importance of repentance.

"Those who persecute the believing men and women":

This part of the verse refers to those who inflict harm, suffering, or temptation upon believers, both male and female.

"and then do not repent":

This highlights that even after committing such actions, if the perpetrators do not turn to Allah in repentance and seek forgiveness, they will face the consequences.

"will have the penalty of Hell":

This indicates the ultimate destination for those who persist in their persecution and do not repent is Hellfire.

"They will have the penalty of the burning fire":

This further emphasizes the severity of the punishment, specifying the burning fire as a form of torment in Hell.

Verse 11

Innal lazeena aamanoo wa 'amilus saalihaati lahum Jannaatun tajree min tahtihal anhaar; zaalikal fawzul kabeer

"For those who believe and do righteous deeds, will be Gardens; beneath which rivers flow: That is the great Salvation, (the fulfilment of all desires)"

This verse is telling us the rewards for believers who perform righteous deeds. It states that they will be granted Gardens beneath which rivers flow, and this is described as the "great salvation" and the "fulfillment of all desires".

"Surely those who believe and do righteous deeds...":

This refers to individuals who have faith in Allah and act according to His guidance.

"...will be Gardens beneath which rivers flow":

This depicts the paradise that awaits them, characterized by lush gardens with flowing rivers.

"...That is the great Salvation, (the fulfilment of all desires)":

This highlights the ultimate success and fulfillment that believers will experience in paradise.

The verse emphasizes the connection between faith, righteous actions, and the ultimate reward in the afterlife.

Verse 12

Inna batsha Rabbika lashadeed

"Truly strong is the Grip (and Power) of thy Lord".

This verse is demonstrating the immense and severe power of Allah's retribution against those who oppress others, specifically referencing the believers thrown into the pit of fire. It highlights that Allah's power to punish is absolute and inescapable.

"Truly strong is the Grip (and Power) of thy Lord":

This translates to the idea that Allah's punishment is severe and inescapable for those who transgress His commands and oppress others.

The verse serves as a warning to oppressors and a source of comfort to the oppressed, assuring them that Allah's justice will prevail. It emphasizes that Allah's power is not to be trifled with and that those who defy Him will face severe consequences.

Verse 13

Innahoo Huwa yubdi'u wa yu'eed

"It is He Who creates from the very beginning, and He can restore (life)"

"Indeed, it is He who originates [creation] and repeats."

This translates to the idea that Allah is the one who brings everything into existence for the first time and will also bring it back to life again. It emphasizes Allah's power over creation and resurrection.

"Indeed, it is He who originates [creation]":

This part highlights Allah's role as the sole creator of everything, bringing it into existence from nothing.

- **"and repeats"**:

This part shows Allah's power to recreate and restore life after death, specifically referring to the Day of Judgment.

Verse 14
Wa Huwal Ghafoorul Wadood

"And He is the Oft-Forgiving, Full of Loving-Kindness." This verse highlights Allah's attributes of forgiveness and love towards His creation.

Explanation:

- **Oft-Forgiving (Al-Ghafoor):**

This refers to Allah's attribute of frequently and extensively forgiving the sins of those who seek His forgiveness. It emphasizes that Allah is ready to pardon and overlook the shortcomings of His servants when they turn to Him with sincerity.

- **Full of Loving-Kindness (Al-Wadud):**

This signifies Allah's attribute of being loving and affectionate towards His believers. It highlights His deep love and care for those who obey Him and turn to Him in faith.

Reflecting, this verse reminds believers that Allah is both forgiving and loving, encouraging them to seek His forgiveness and to strive to live a life that is pleasing to Him.

Verse 15
Zul 'Arshil Majeed

"Owner of the Throne, the Glorious".

This verse emphasizes Allah's supreme power and grandeur, highlighting His ownership of the magnificent Throne and His inherent glory.

- **Dhu Al-'Arsh:**

This part of the verse signifies Allah's ownership and dominion over the 'Arsh, which is often interpreted as the Throne, a magnificent creation above all others.

- **Al-Majid:**

This adjective describes Allah as "The Majestic" or "The Glorious," showing His inherent greatness, splendour, and perfection.

The verse, therefore, declares Allah as the Lord of the Throne, the ultimate sovereign and ruler of the universe, and as the possessor of unparalleled glory and majesty. It serves as a reminder of Allah's supreme power and inspires awe and reverence in believers.

- **Connection to other verses:**

This verse follows Allah's description as "The Oft-Forgiving, the Loving" (Al-Ghafoor, Al-Wadud) in the preceding verse, indicating a balance of divine attributes: both mercy and power. It also precedes the declaration "Fa'aalun limaa yureed" (He does what He wills), further highlighting Allah's absolute authority.

Finally, verse 15 of Surah Al-Buruj presents a powerful image of Allah as the Majestic Lord of the Throne, reminding believers of His supreme power and glory.

Verse 16

Fa' 'aalul limaa yureed

"Doer of whatever He intends"

This signifies that Allah's actions are not constrained or prevented by anything. Whatever He decides to do, He accomplishes without hindrance or opposition, showcasing His absolute power and will.

- **"Fa'aalun"** : This word indicates an action that is done repeatedly and effectively. It emphasizes the constant and powerful nature of Allah's actions.
- **"Lima"**: This means "for what" or "that which."
- **"Yureed"**: This means "He intends" or "He wills."

Therefore, the verse highlights Allah's complete power and sovereignty. He is not subject to the limitations or obstacles that mortals face. When He intends something, He brings it into existence without any resistance.

Some interpretations also emphasize that this verse is a response to those who deny the power of Allah and His ability to carry out His will. It serves as a reminder that Allah's power is absolute, and His actions are guided by wisdom and justice, even if they are not immediately apparent to humans.

Verse 17

Hal ataaka hadeesul junood

"Has the story reached you of the forces?"

This is refering to the powerful armies of the past who opposed Allah and His messengers, specifically mentioning Pharaoh and Thamud. The verse serves as a reminder of Allah's power and His punishment of those who disbelieve and oppress others. It prompts reflection on the consequences of rejecting faith and resisting divine guidance.

The verse introduces the topic of past nations who were destroyed by Allah for their disbelief and oppression. The mention of Pharaoh and Thamud are examples of this. The verse then contrasts this with the story of the believers in the ditch, highlighting Allah's mercy and protection of those who believe. The verse also emphasizes that despite the disbelievers' denial and defiance, Allah encompasses them from all sides, indicating their inability to escape His power and knowledge.

Verse 18

Fir'awna wa Samood

"Of Pharaoh and Thamud?"

This verse serves as a reminder of Allah's power and the consequences of rejecting His messengers. It refers to the mighty armies of Pharaoh and the Thamud, who were destroyed by Allah for their arrogance and defiance of His prophets. The verse prompts reflection on the fate of these powerful nations, highlighting the severe punishment that awaits those who persist in disbelief and rebellion against Allah.

- **Pharaoh:**

A tyrannical ruler who claimed divinity and oppressed the Israelites.

- **Thamud:**

A people known for their sophisticated stone-carving skills, who were also destroyed for their arrogance and rejection of the Prophet Saleh.

The mention of Pharaoh and Thamud serves as a warning to the disbelievers of the Prophet Muhammad's time, and indeed for all time, that Allah's punishment is severe and inescapable for those who persist in their disbelief.

The verse also reminds that the disbelievers, despite their power and defiance, are encompassed by Allah's knowledge and power. They cannot escape His grasp or His judgment.

The surah then emphasizes the divine nature of the Quran, highlighting its truth and authority as a source of guidance.

Verse 19

Balil lazeena kafaroo fee takzeeb

"And yet the Unbelievers (persist) in rejecting (the Truth)!",

This demonstrates the persistent state of disbelief among those who reject Allah's message. It highlights their denial and rebellion, emphasizing that Allah encompasses them, meaning He has complete power and knowledge over them. This verse serves as a reminder of the consequences of rejecting faith and the encompassing knowledge of Allah.

The verse prompts reflection on the nature of faith and disbelief, reminding believers to be steadfast in their belief and to be mindful of Allah's power and knowledge.

Verse 20

Wallaahu minw waraaa'ihim muheet

"But Allah doth encompass them from behind!"

This signifies that despite the disbelievers' apparent control and security, Allah encompasses them and has complete power over them. It highlights that Allah's knowledge and power surround them completely, and their actions cannot escape His grasp. This verse serves as a warning against pride and heedlessness, reminding that worldly power is insignificant compared to Allah's might.

Verse 21

Bal huwa Quraanum Majeed

"Nay, this is a Glorious Qur'an,"

This verse is telling us that the Quran is a noble and magnificent scripture, emphasizing its divine origin and exalted status. It is a statement that highlights the Quran's greatness and its importance as a source of guidance.

Here's a more detailed tafseer:

- **"Nay, but this is a Glorious Qur'an"**

The verse begins with "bal" (بَلْ), which is a particle of strong affirmation and rebuttal, indicating a shift in focus from the previous statements, likely about the disbelievers and their actions. It serves to correct any misconceptions or doubts and to firmly establish the Quran's true nature. The word "majîd" (مَجِيدٌ) translates to "glorious," "noble," or "magnificent." This adjective describes the Quran's exalted status and its inherent nobility, emphasizing its divine origin and profound impact.

- **Emphasis on the Quran's Grandeur:**

This verse emphasizes the Quran's unique and unparalleled status as a divine revelation, highlighting its literary and spiritual grandeur. It is not just any book; it is a source of guidance, wisdom, and truth, worthy of reverence and respect.

- **Contrast with the Disbelievers' Actions:**

The verse can be seen as a contrast to the actions of the disbelievers, who reject the Quran and its message. While they may mock and ridicule the believers and the Quran, this verse asserts the Quran's true glory and magnificence, underscoring its enduring and powerful nature.

Verse 22

Fee Lawhim Mahfooz

"Inscribed) in a Tablet Preserved!",

This is telling us that the Quran being written in a "Preserved Tablet" (Lauh al-Mahfuz), which is a divine record of all that has been and will be. This verse shows the Quran's unchangeable and protected nature, safeguarding it from any alteration or corruption.

Lauh al-Mahfuz (The Preserved Tablet):

This tablet is a heavenly record where Allah has inscribed everything that has been, is, and will be.

- **Guarded and Protected:**

The verse highlights that the Quran is not only inscribed in this tablet but is also guarded from any changes or corruption.

- **Unchangeable and Imperishable:**

The Quran's content is fixed and cannot be altered, ensuring its authenticity and guidance for humanity.

- **Significance:**

This verse serves as a reminder of the Quran's divine origin and its importance as a source of truth and guidance.

- **Connection to Other Verses:**

Some scholars link this verse to the previous verses about the people of the ditch (Ashab al-Ukhdud) and the fire, suggesting that the preserved tablet also contains the knowledge of the ultimate reward and punishment.

- **Connection to "Umm al-Kitab":**

Some interpretations relate the Preserved Tablet to the term "Mother of all Books" (Umm al-Kitab) found in other parts of the Quran.

Essentially, this verse assures believers that the Quran is a divine and protected text, free from any human alteration, and that it holds the key to understanding Allah's will and the ultimate outcome of all things.

LESSONS LEARNT FROM SURAH AL BUROOJ

Lessons from Surah Al-Burooj (The Constellations):

1. Patience and Trust in Allah: The story of the believers who endured persecution teaches us to remain patient and trust in Allah's justice during hardships.
2. The Power of Faith and Perseverance: Despite facing severe trials, such as being thrown into a blazing ditch, the unwavering faith of those believers highlights the importance of steadfastness.
3. Allah's Justice and Sovereignty: The tale of the people who were burnt alive in the ditch illustrates that Allah is All-Powerful, and those who oppress others will ultimately face accountability and punishment from Him.
4. Standing for Truth and Justice: The story encourages us to defend righteousness and stand against injustice, even if it comes with great personal risks.
5. The Significance of Reliance on Allah: Turning to Allah in times of adversity and trusting His plan is a key lesson derived from these stories.
6. Reward for Patience and Faith: The believers' patience in the face of extreme hardship was ultimately rewarded by Allah with His mercy and paradise.
7. Reminder of the Consequences of Disbelief: The story of the people who were burnt in the ditch serves as a warning that denying Allah and oppressing others has severe consequences, but Allah's justice prevails.

GETTING TO KNOW SURAH TARIQ- SURAH 86

This Surah was revealed in Makkah at a time when the disbelievers were trying hard to prevent people from believing in Islam and the message of Prophet Muhammad (peace be upon him). They used many tricks to try to prevent the message from spreading.

The Surah revolves around two themes:

After death we have to face our creator and the second subject matter is that despite the disbelievers' efforts, they will never succeed.

It begins by talking about the stars in the sky. The stars show us that everything in the universe needs someone to take care of it. Then, it asks us to think about how we were created. We started as tiny drops of sperm and grew into people. The Allah who created us in this way has the power to bring us back to life after death. When that happens, everyone will have to answer for what they did in their lives. No one will be able to escape from the consequences of their actions, and no one can help them then.

Finally, it explains that just as rain falling and plants growing are serious tasks, the messages in the Quran are real and cannot be changed. The people who do not believe think they can stop the Quran with their tricks, but Allah has a plan too. His plan will make their tricks useless.

The message ends with a kind message for the Prophet Muhammad (peace be upon him). It says: "Be patient for a little while. Let the disbelievers do what they want. Soon, they will see whether they can stop the Quran or if the Quran will prove stronger than all their tricks."

AL-BUROOJ-SURAH 85

Questions

1. What does the term "Al-Burooj" refer to in the context of this Surah?
2. What is the main theme of Surah Al-Burooj?
3. Who are the "companions of the trench" mentioned in the Surah?
4. What was the fate of the "companions of the trench"?
5. How does Surah Al-Burooj describe the believers who were persecuted?
6. What does the Surah say about Allah's response to the persecution of believers?
7. How is Allah's power and authority emphasized in Surah Al-Burooj?
8. What is the significance of the oath by the sky containing great stars?
9. What message does Surah Al-Burooj convey about the ultimate outcome for the disbelievers and oppressors?
10. How does Surah Al-Burooj provide comfort and reassurance to the believers?

Answers

1. The term "Al-Burooj" refers to the great constellations or stars in the sky, highlighting the majesty and order of the universe.

2. The main theme of Surah Al-Burooj is the persecution of believers, the steadfastness of faith, and the ultimate justice of Allah against the oppressors.

3. The "companions of the trench" are a group of people who were responsible for persecuting and killing believers by casting them into trenches of fire.

4. The fate of the "companions of the trench" is condemnation and punishment for their actions against the believers.

5. Surah Al-Burooj describes the believers who were persecuted as steadfast in their faith, enduring great suffering for the sake of their belief in Allah.

6. The Surah emphasizes that Allah is aware of the persecution and assures that the oppressors will be held accountable and punished.

7. Allah's power and authority are emphasized through the mention of the creation of the heavens and the earth, as well as His ability to enact justice.

8. The oath by the sky containing great stars signifies the grandeur and precision of Allah's creation, serving as a reminder of His power and the certainty of His promises.

9. Surah Al-Burooj conveys that the ultimate outcome for the disbelievers and oppressors is punishment and disgrace, while the believers will be rewarded with paradise.

10. The Surah provides comfort and reassurance to the believers by affirming that their suffering is known to Allah and that they will ultimately be victorious and rewarded in the hereafter.

These questions and answers help capture the key themes and messages of Surah Al-Burooj.

Multiple Choice Questions

1. What does the term "Al-Burooj" refer to in Surah Al-Burooj?

    a) The mountains

    b) The gardens of paradise

    c) The constellations or great stars in the sky

    d) The rivers of heaven

2. Who are the "companions of the trench" mentioned in the Surah?

    a) A group of angels

    b) A people who persecuted and killed believers by casting them into trenches of fire

    c) The people of Makkah

    d) The companions of the Prophet Muhammad (PBUH)

3. What fate does Surah Al-Burooj describe for the "companions of the trench"?

    a) They are forgiven for their actions

    b) They are praised for their bravery

    c) They are condemned and punished

    d) They are rewarded with wealth

4. How are the persecuted believers described in Surah Al-Burooj?

    a) As having weak faith

    b) As steadfast and enduring in their faith

    c) As being victorious in battle

    d) As being wealthy and powerful

5. What does Surah Al-Burooj say about Allah's response to the persecution of believers?

    a) Allah is unaware of their suffering

    b) Allah forgives the oppressors immediately

    c) Allah is aware and will hold the oppressors accountable

    d) Allah sends immediate punishment to the oppressors

6. How is Allah's power and authority emphasized in Surah Al-Burooj?

    a) Through the mention of historical battles

    b) Through the creation of the heavens and the earth

    c) Through the wealth of believers

    d) Through the stories of the prophets

7. What is the significance of the oath by the sky containing great stars in Surah Al-Burooj?

    a) It symbolizes the fleeting nature of life

    b) It emphasizes the majesty and precision of Allah's creation

    c) It represents the wealth of the believers

    d) It signifies the power of the oppressors

8. What ultimate outcome does Surah Al-Burooj convey for the disbelievers and oppressors?

    a) They will be honored and praised

    b) They will escape punishment

    c) They will face punishment and disgrace

    d) They will be given another chance

9. How does Surah Al-Burooj provide comfort to the believers?

    a) By promising them wealth and power in this life

    b) By affirming that their suffering is known to Allah and they will be rewarded in the hereafter

    c) By ensuring immediate victory over their enemies

    d) By predicting a life free of trials

Answers

1. *Answer:* c) The constellations or great stars in the sky
2. *Answer:* b) A people who persecuted and killed believers by casting them into trenches of fire
3. *Answer:* c) They are condemned and punished
4. *Answer:* b) As steadfast and enduring in their faith
5. *Answer:* c) Allah is aware and will hold the oppressors accountable
6. *Answer:* b) Through the creation of the heavens and the earth
7. *Answer:* b) It emphasizes the majesty and precision of Allah's creation
8. *Answer:* c) They will face punishment and disgrace
9. *Answer:* b) By affirming that their suffering is known to Allah and they will be rewarded in the hereafter

These questions and answers can help in understanding the key messages and themes of Surah Al-Burooj in a multiple-choice format.

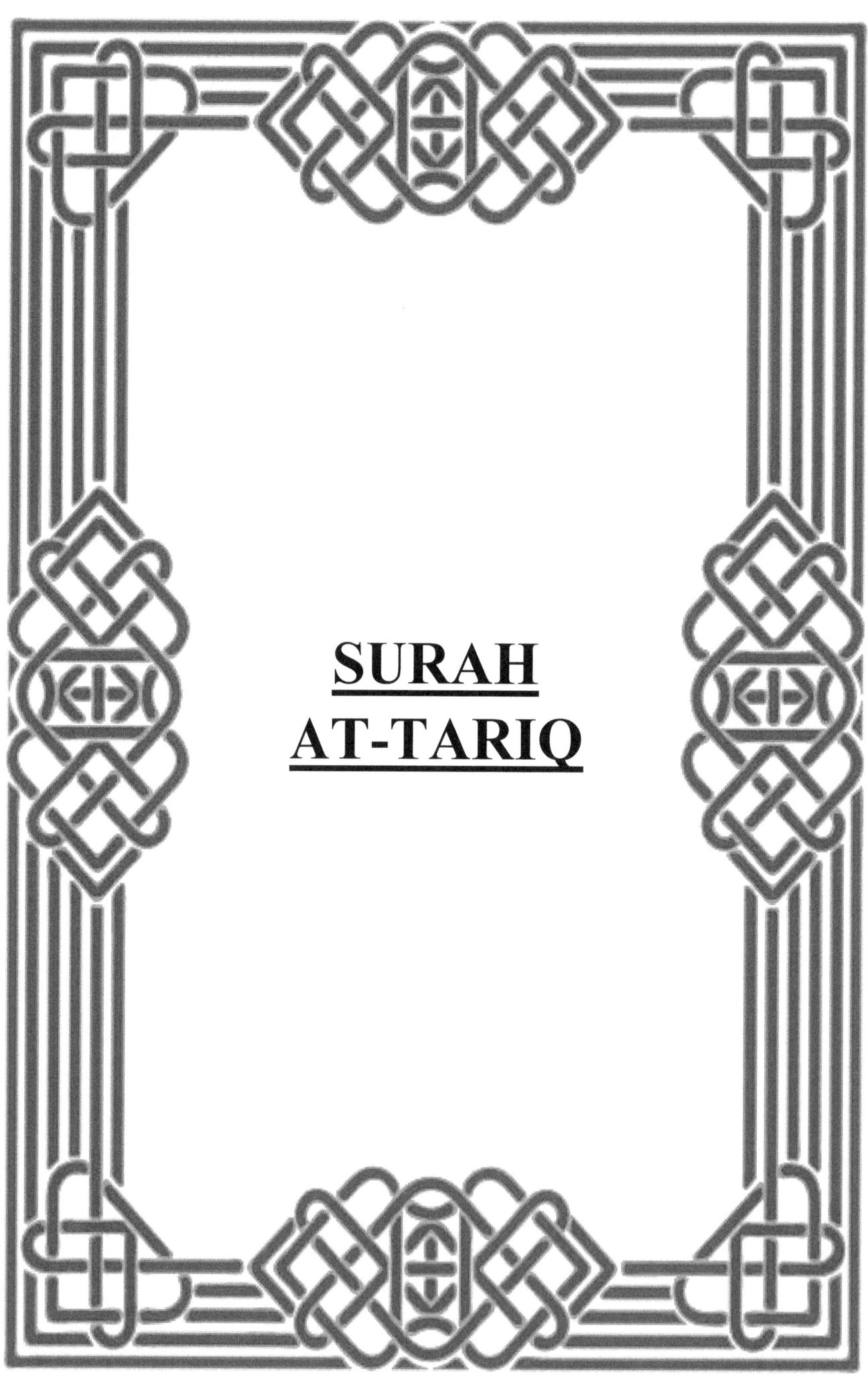

SURAH AT-TARIQ

SURAH AT- TARIQ

Bismillahi ar-Rahmani ar-Raheem

Verse 1

Wassamaaa'i wattaariq

"By the sky and the night visitor".

The verse begins with an oath, swearing by the sky and by "At-Tariq". At-Tariq is generally interpreted as a reference to a bright, piercing star that appears at night. Some scholars also interpret it as someone who comes at night, knocking at the door, and highlighting the unexpected nature of such an arrival.

"By the sky" (wal-sama'i):

The sky is a vast and impressive phenomenon, serving as a witness to the power and grandeur of Allah.

"And the night visitor" (wat-tariq):

This refers to the bright, piercing star that appears at night. The term "tariq" (طارق) literally means "the knocker" or "the night visitor". It is derived from the verb "taraqa" (طرق), which means to strike or knock.

- **Symbolism:**

The oath by the sky and the night visitor is a way to draw attention to the wonders of creation and to prepare the listener for a deeper message. The star, with its piercing light, can symbolize truth, guidance, or the revelation of Allah's signs.

- **Significance of Oaths:**

In the Quran, oaths are used to emphasize the importance of the message that follows. By swearing by the sky and the star, Allah is drawing attention to the power and wisdom evident in the creation and preparing the listener for the subsequent verses which discuss the Day of Judgment and the accountability of mankind.

Verse 2

Wa maaa adraaka mattaariq

"And what will explain to thee what the Night-Visitant is?",

This is a rhetorical question that emphasizes the significance of the "Night-Visitant" (At-Tariq). The verse highlights that this phenomenon is not easily understood, prompting a deeper inquiry into its nature. The subsequent verse reveals that At-Tariq is the "piercing star" (An-Najmu-Thaqib), emphasizing its brightness and ability to penetrate the darkness.

Verse 3

Annajmus saaqib

"the Star of piercing brightness" (an-najmu ath-thaqib)

This refers to a celestial body that is bright and penetrates through the darkness. While some interpretations suggest it refers to a specific star like Saturn or the Pleiades, the more common understanding is that it's a general reference to any bright star that shines powerfully at night, splitting the darkness with its light.

Verse 4

In kullu nafsil lammaa 'alaihaa hafiz

"There is no soul but has a protector over it,"

This is informing us that Allah has assigned a guardian or watcher to every human soul. This protector's role is to observe and record the actions of the individual, emphasizing accountability and the eventual reckoning before Allah. It highlights that no one is ever truly alone, as they are constantly under the observation of this divine guardian.

Hence, no one can escape this divine observation, even in the deepest secrecy, as the guardian has access to all hidden aspects of a person's life.

The verse serves as a constant reminder that one's actions have consequences and that they should be mindful of their choices and behaviour

Verse 5

Fal yanzuril insaanu mimma khuliq

"Now let man but think from what he is created"

This verse is calling on humans to contemplate their origin and consider the miraculous nature of their creation. It prompts reflection on how humans are formed from a "drop emitted, proceeding from between the backbone and the ribs," emphasizing the incredible process of human development and the power of the Creator. This reflection serves as a reminder of Allah's ability to recreate humans for the Day of Judgment.

The verse is not just a scientific statement about human anatomy, but a call to contemplate the intricate process of creation and the power of the Creator.

The verse is closely linked to the belief in the resurrection. By understanding how humans are created from a humble drop, one can grasp the possibility of being recreated by Allah for the Day of Judgment.

Verse 6

Khuliqa mim maaa'in daafiq

"He is created from a spurting fluid".

Classical commentators like Ibn Kathir and others explain that this verse refers to the sperm, which is the origin of human creation. The verse points to the insignificant beginning of human existence, advising that even from this small, ejected fluid, Allah creates a complete human being.

The verse serves to remind people of their humble origin and to encourage reflection on the power of Allah, who can create life from seemingly insignificant beginnings. It also connects to the subsequent verses about the return to Allah on the Day of Judgment.

Verse 7

Yakhruju mim bainissulbi wat taraaa'ib

"Proceeding from between the backbone and the ribs"

This verse has been interpreted by scholars to refer to the ejection of semen, which is produced by both men and women, and plays a crucial role in procreation. The verse emphasizes the miraculous nature of human creation, highlighting Allah's power in bringing life into existence from seemingly simple elements.

Scholars like Ibn Abbas have explained that the "sulb" (backbone) refers to the man's backbone, and the "tara'ib" (ribs) refers to the woman's chest area, highlighting that the seminal fluid comes from both the man's and woman's contribution.

The verse is not meant to be a precise anatomical description, but rather a testament to Allah's creative power. It points out that even from this seemingly ordinary fluid, a complex human being is formed.

Verse 8

Innahoo 'alaa raj'ihee laqaadir

"Surely (Allah) is able to bring him back (to life)"!

In this verse, Allah emphasizes His power to resurrect humans after death, drawing a parallel between the initial creation from a "gushing fluid" and the potential for a second creation through resurrection.

The verse argues that if Allah has the power to create man from this humble origin, He certainly has the power to bring him back to life after death.

This verse highlights the idea that the creation of man, with all its complexity and intricate design, is a testament to Allah's power and wisdom. If He can bring about such a complex creation, then recreating it through resurrection is not beyond His ability.

This verse serves as a reminder of the Day of Judgment, where all secrets will be revealed and examined. It underscores the accountability of humans for their actions and the ultimate authority of Allah.

The verse emphasizes Allah's power, the reality of resurrection, and the Day of Judgment, urging reflection on the purpose of life and accountability for one's actions.

Verse 9

Yawma tublas saraaa'ir

"On the Day when secrets will be tested" or "On the Day when the hidden things will be examined".

This verse signifies that on the Day of Judgment, all the hidden thoughts, beliefs, intentions, and actions of individuals will be revealed and judged.

The term "saraaa'ir" (plural of sarīrah) refers to the hidden aspects of a person's inner self, including their thoughts, beliefs, intentions, and secret deeds.

The word "tubla" means to be examined, tested, or scrutinized. On this day, these hidden aspects will be brought to light and assessed.

This verse highlights that individuals will not only be held accountable for their outward actions but also for their inner intentions and thoughts. According to Islamic teachings, everything will be revealed.

Islamic scholars explain that this could include examining a person's faith, the sincerity of their prayers, the true nature of their fasting, or the hidden motives behind their actions.

The verse also suggests that on this day, individuals will have no power or support to conceal their secrets or escape the consequences of their actions.

Verse 10

Famaa lahoo min quwwatinw wa laa naasir

"Then man will have no power or any helper."

In Tafseer, this verse is understood to mean that on the Day of Judgment, individuals will have no power to defend themselves from Allah's judgment, nor will anyone be able to assist them in escaping His punishment.

This signifies that no other person, angel, or entity can intervene on their behalf or offer any form of assistance to escape Allah's judgment.

This verse is a continuation of the previous verses that discuss the creation of man from a drop of fluid and Allah's power to recreate him. The verse emphasizes that the same God who created man is capable of resurrecting him for judgment, and on that day, man will be completely vulnerable and accountable for his deeds.

This verse highlights the ultimate accountability of each individual before Allah and the absence of any means of escape or assistance on that day.

Verse 11

Wassamaaa'i zaatir raj'

"By the sky which returns (rain)," focuses on the cyclical nature of rain and its connection to the Day of Judgment. It emphasizes that the return of rain is a sign of Allah's power and a reminder of the resurrection of the dead.

This cyclical nature of rain serves as a powerful symbol. Just as the sky brings forth rain repeatedly, Allah has the power to bring about the Day of Judgment and resurrect all of humanity.

The rain cycle is a reminder that life and death are part of a larger divine plan, and that the resurrection is a certainty.

The verse highlights Allah's power and ability to create and recreate, emphasizing His control over the universe and the ultimate accountability of all beings on the Day of Judgment.

The verse also serves as a warning to those who deny the Hereafter, suggesting that they will be held accountable for their actions just as surely as rain returns to the earth.

In essence, verse 11 of Surah At-Tariq uses the returning rain as a powerful symbol to remind humanity of the Day of Judgment and the ultimate power of Allah.

Verse 12

Wal ardi zaatis sad'

And by the earth when it opens out for the gushing of springs and spouting of vegetation."

This verse is an oath where Allah swears by the earth's natural processes—specifically, how it opens up to release springs and allows vegetation to grow.

It highlights the incredible signs of Allah's creation in nature, demonstrating His power and control over the universe.

The earth opening to release water and produce plants is a sign of Allah's mercy and sustenance for all living beings.

It also serves as a reminder of Allah's ability to bring about resurrection, as similar natural processes are signs of life and rebirth.

These signs in nature are meant to encourage humans to recognize Allah's sovereignty and to trust in His ability to resurrect and judge humanity.

Verse 13

Innahoo laqawlun fasl

"Behold this is the Word that distinguishes (Good from Evil)"

Here, the Quran is described as a decisive word (or "a decisive statement") that separates truth from falsehood. This verse emphasizes the Quran's role as a definitive guide, distinguishing between right and wrong, and establishing clear boundaries between good and evil. It highlights the Quran's importance as a source of divine guidance and a standard for judgment.

The verse contrasts the Quran's decisive nature with the schemes of those who reject the truth. It emphasizes that while disbelievers may plot against the message of the Quran, Allah is also planning, and the Quran will ultimately prevail.

Verse 14

Wa maa huwa bil hazl

"And it is not a thing for amusement."

This verse emphasizes that the Quran is not to be taken lightly or considered mere entertainment. It is a serious and decisive message from Allah, containing truth and guidance for humanity.

The verse directly refutes the notion that the Quran is a form of frivolous amusement or jest.

It highlights the Quran's divine origin and its significance as a source of truth and guidance for all mankind.

The verse is often interpreted in the context of the disbelievers' plots against the Prophet Muhammad(pbuh) and their attempts to undermine the Quran. It serves as a reminder that their plans are futile against the divine word.

This verse encourages believers to reflect on the profound nature of the Quran and to heed its message with seriousness and sincerity.

Verse 14 offers a warning to those who reject the truth while also providing solace to the Prophet Muhammad (peace be upon him) by assuring him that Allah's plan will ultimately prevail.

Verse 15

Innahum yakeedoona kaidaa

"Indeed, they are plotting a plan,"

This refers to the disbelievers' attempts to undermine the message of Islam and the Prophet Muhammad (peace be upon him). The verse highlights their schemes and efforts to extinguish the light of faith. However, the subsequent verse, "And I am also planning a plan," emphasizes that Allah is also plotting, implying that the disbelievers' plans will ultimately fail, and the believers will be victorious. The overall message is one of reassurance to the Prophet and his followers, assuring them that Allah is in control and will support them.

The disbelievers were actively trying to thwart the spread of Islam and the Prophet's message engaging in various plots and schemes to undermine the faith.

This verse highlights Allah's counter-plan, demonstrating that He is fully aware of the disbelievers' schemes and has His own plan to ultimately defeat them. Allah's plan is described as a way to make the plots of the disbelievers fail and to grant victory to the believers.

The verse collectively signifies that while the disbelievers are actively plotting against the truth, Allah is also planning, and His plan is superior and will ultimately prevail. This provides reassurance and encouragement to the Prophet and his followers, reminding them that they are not alone in their struggle and that Allah is their ultimate protector.

Verse 16

Wa akeedu kaidaa

"And I (too) am planning a plan"

In the context of the surah, this verse signifies that while disbelievers may plot against the truth and the Prophet (peace be upon him), Allah is also planning, and His plan is ultimately superior and will prevail. It's a reassurance to the Prophet that he is not alone in his struggle and that Allah's plan will overcome the disbelievers' schemes.

The previous verse, (inna hum yakidūna kaydan), highlights the disbelievers' attempts to undermine the Prophet's message and the truth of Islam. They are depicted as actively plotting against the Prophet's call to Islam and trying to extinguish the light of faith.

The overall message is one of reassurance for the Prophet and the believers. It highlights that while the disbelievers may be actively plotting, Allah is in control and His plan will ultimately prevail. The believers should not be disheartened by the disbelievers' schemes, but rather remain steadfast in their faith and trust in Allah's plan.

The tafseer emphasizes that the disbelievers' schemes will ultimately be defeated and exposed, and the truth of Islam will prevail. The conquest of Mecca and the humiliation of the Quraysh are often cited as examples of how Allah's plan ultimately unfolded.

Verse 17

Famahhilil kaafireena amhilhum ruwaidaa

Give respite to them gently (for awhile),"

This verse is instructing the Prophet Muhammad (PBUH) to be patient and give the disbelievers a temporary respite. It means that Allah is in control and will ultimately judge them, and there is no need for immediate punishment. The verse is teaching us that despite their plotting and disbelief, Allah will deal with them in His own time and way.

This further clarifies the nature of the respite. It's not a complete abandonment, but rather a period of time given to allow the disbelievers to reflect on their actions and potentially come to believe. The term "gently" suggests a compassionate approach, even in the face of their opposition. Some interpretations suggest that this respite could refer to both this worldly life and the afterlife, where Allah will ultimately judge their deeds.

Islamic scholars explain that this verse offers reassurance to the Prophet (PBUH) by indicating that Allah is aware of the disbelievers' plots and schemes, and He has a plan to deal with them. Some commentaries note that this respite is a test for both the believers and the disbelievers, allowing believers to remain steadfast and giving disbelievers an opportunity to change their ways. The verse also highlights Allah's absolute power and control over all affairs.

LESSONS TO BE LEARNT FROM SURAH AT-TARIQ

- **Accountability and Judgment:**

Surah At-Tariq emphasizes that every soul is watched and their deeds are recorded. It reminds believers that they will be brought before Allah on the Day of Judgment and held accountable for their actions.

- **Certainty of Resurrection:**

The Surah uses the creation of man from a humble drop of fluid as evidence of Allah's ability to resurrect him after death. The helpless state of man on the Day of Judgment is contrasted with Allah's power and ability to examine the secrets of all deeds.

- **Divine Nature of the Quran:**

Surah At-Tariq declares that the Quran is a decisive word from Allah, not mere amusement, and is protected from human alteration or falsification.

- **Guidance and Trust in Allah:**

The Surah encourages believers to trust in Allah's divine plan and wisdom, reminding them that their destinies are in His hands. It also highlights the importance of seeking Allah's help and remaining steadfast in faith.

- **Reflecting on Allah's Creation:**

The Surah urges believers to reflect on the creation of the heavens and the earth, recognizing Allah's power and wisdom in the alternation of night and day.

SURAH TARIQ – SURAH 86

Questions

1. What is the primary theme of Surah Al-Tariq?
2. What does the term "Al-Tariq" refer to in this Surah?
3. How is the sky described in Surah Al-Tariq?
4. What is the significance of the "piercing star" mentioned in the Surah?
5. How does Surah Al-Tariq emphasize the creation of man?
6. What does the Surah say about the preservation and protection of the Quran?
7. According to Surah Al-Tariq, what will happen on the Day of Judgment?
8. How does the Surah describe the power and knowledge of Allah?
9. What comparison is made to emphasize the inevitability of resurrection?
10. What is the central message of Surah Al-Tariq regarding human accountability?

Answers

1. The primary theme of Surah Al-Tariq is the inevitability of resurrection and the accountability of human actions, emphasizing the power and knowledge of Allah.

2. The term "Al-Tariq" refers to the "night visitor" or "piercing star," highlighting the imagery of a star that appears at night.

3. The sky in Surah Al-Tariq is described as having a "returning" nature, symbolizing the cyclical and ordered nature of the universe created by Allah.

4. The "piercing star" signifies something that penetrates the darkness and is used to draw attention to the certainty and clarity of Allah's signs.

5. Surah Al-Tariq emphasizes the creation of man by reminding humans of their origin from a drop of fluid, highlighting Allah's power in creation and the eventual return for judgment.

6. The Surah assures that the Quran is preserved and protected by Allah, underscoring its authenticity and lasting guidance.

7. On the Day of Judgment, all secrets will be exposed, and individuals will be held accountable for their deeds.

8. The Surah describes Allah's power and knowledge as encompassing all things, highlighting His ability to create, preserve, and resurrect.

9. The comparison made is between the resurrection and the natural processes like rain returning from the sky, emphasizing the certainty and ease with which Allah will bring about the resurrection.

10. The central message regarding human accountability is that every soul will be questioned about its actions, and nothing will be hidden from Allah's knowledge.

These questions and answers provide a structured way to understand the key themes and messages of Surah Al-Tariq.

Multiple Choice Questions

1. What does the term "Al-Tariq" refer to in Surah Al-Tariq?

    a) The sun

    b) The moon

    c) The night visitor or piercing star

    d) The morning light

2. How is the sky described in Surah Al-Tariq?

    a) As a vast void

    b) As having a returning nature

    c) As unchanging and static

    d) As dark and mysterious

3. What is the significance of the "piercing star" mentioned in the Surah?

    a) It represents a hidden danger

    b) It symbolizes clarity and certainty of Allah's signs

    c) It is a metaphor for wealth

    d) It refers to a past prophet

4. How does Surah Al-Tariq emphasize the creation of man?

    a) By describing the complexity of human emotions

    b) By highlighting the physical strength of humans

    c) By reminding humans of their origin from a drop of fluid

    d) By focusing on human intelligence

5. What does Surah Al-Tariq say about the preservation of the Quran?

    a) It is left to human effort

    b) It is protected by angels

    c) It is preserved and protected by Allah

    d) It is vulnerable to alteration

6. According to Surah Al-Tariq, what will happen on the Day of Judgment?

    a) All secrets will be exposed

    b) Only the righteous will be judged

    c) The earth will become a paradise

    d) Everyone will be forgiven

7. How does Surah Al-Tariq describe Allah's power and knowledge?

    a) Limited to the spiritual realm

    b) Encompassing all things

    c) Focused only on the believers

    d) Restricted to the afterlife

8. What natural process is used to emphasize the inevitability of resurrection in Surah Al-Tariq?

    a) The change of seasons

    b) The movement of the stars

    c) The rain returning from the sky

    d) The growth of plants

9. What is the central message of Surah Al-Tariq regarding human accountability?

    a) Only major sins will be judged

    b) Every soul will be questioned about its actions

    c) Actions are judged collectively

    d) Accountability is based on wealth

Answers

1. *Answer:* c) The night visitor or piercing star
2. *Answer:* b) As having a returning nature
3. *Answer:* b) It symbolizes clarity and certainty of Allah's signs
4. *Answer:* c) By reminding humans of their origin from a drop of fluid
5. *Answer:* c) It is preserved and protected by Allah
6. *Answer:* a) All secrets will be exposed
7. *Answer:* b) Encompassing all things
8. *Answer:* c) The rain returning from the sky
9. *Answer:* b) Every soul will be questioned about its actions

These questions and answers can help in understanding the key messages and themes of Surah Al-Tariq in a multiple-choice format.

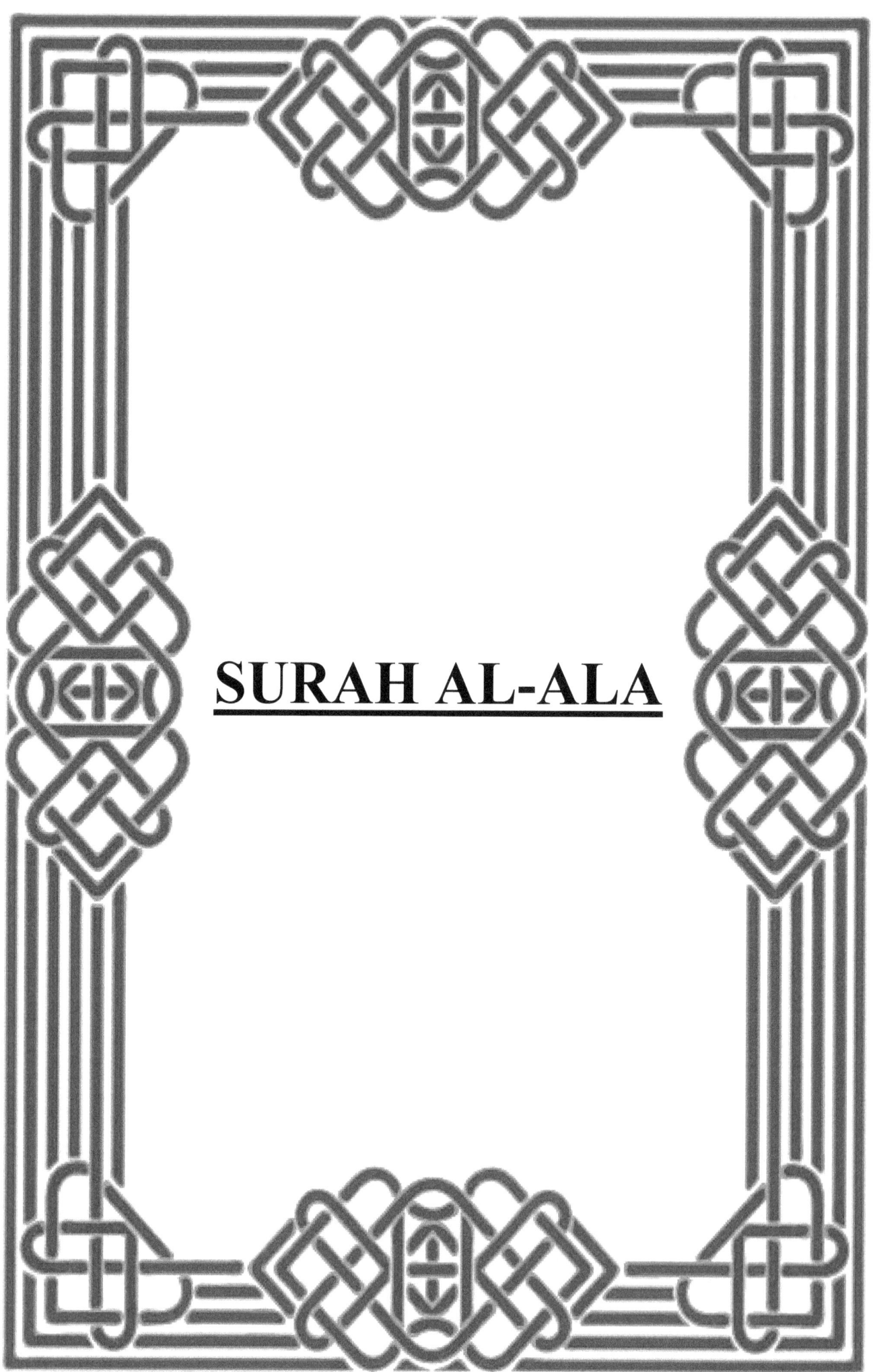
SURAH AL-ALA

SURAH AL-ALA

Bismillahi ar-Rahmani ar-Raheem

Verse 1

Sabbihisma Rabbikal A'laa

"Glorify the name of thy Guardian-Lord Most High"

This is a command from Allah to Prophet Muhammad (peace be upon him) to extol and venerate Allah's name, emphasizing His supreme position and attributes. It signifies that Allah should be remembered and addressed with names that befit His perfection, avoiding any that might imply deficiency or resemblance to creation. This verse is a call for purification of one's understanding and remembrance of Allah, starting with the correct use of His names.

- **The Command:**

The verse uses the imperative verb "sabbih" (صَبِّحْ), which means to glorify, extol, or celebrate. It directs the Prophet (and by extension, all believers) to purify their thoughts and actions by glorifying Allah.

- **The Name of the Lord:**

The verse demonstrates the importance of using the most appropriate names for Allah, reflecting His attributes of Lordship (Rabb) and Supreme Highness (al-A'la).

- **Tawhid (Oneness of Allah):**

The verse is a concise expression of the core concept of Tawhid, emphasizing Allah's unique and unparalleled nature.

- **Significance of Names:**

The selection of names for Allah is crucial. It is not merely a matter of preference but rather a reflection of one's understanding of Allah's attributes and actions.

- **Purification:**

The verse calls for purification in two ways: purification of the heart from polytheism and other vices, and purification of one's understanding of Allah's names.

This first verse sets the tone for the entire Surah, which continues to discuss Allah's creation, guidance, and the ultimate accountability in the Hereafter.

The Prophet (peace be upon him) is reported to have responded to this verse by saying "Subhana Rabbi al-A'la" (Glory to my Lord, the Most High), demonstrating the practical application of the verse.

This verse is among the earliest revelations of the Quran, highlighting its foundational importance.

Verse 2

Allazee khalaqa fasawwaa

"Who hath created, and further, given order and proportion,"

This is showing Allah's role as the creator who not only brings things into existence but also meticulously designs and structures them with precise balance and harmony. This verse highlights the intricate order and proportion found throughout creation, from the smallest atom to the largest galaxy, as evidence of Allah's divine plan and wisdom.

- **"Who hath created"**:

This part acknowledges Allah's role as the ultimate creator, the one who brought everything into existence from nothing.

- **"and further, given order and proportion"**:

This highlights Allah's role in establishing the intricate balance, harmony, and design within creation. It implies that everything is not just created, but also meticulously crafted with a specific purpose and function, demonstrating a divine plan and wisdom.

This verse essentially points to the perfection and intricacy of Allah's creation as evidence of His lordship and divine attributes. The order and proportion found throughout the universe, from the smallest organisms to the vast cosmos, are not random occurrences but rather the result of Allah's design and wisdom.

Verse 3

Wallazee qaddara fahadaa

"Who hath ordained laws. And granted guidance"

Allah declares His attribute of ordaining and guiding. It signifies that He has established the natural laws and order of the universe and has also provided guidance to His creation, particularly mankind, to understand right from wrong and follow the path of righteousness.

- **"Who has ordained"**: This part of the verse refers to Allah's role in creating everything and establishing the specific functions and purposes for each creation. It encompasses the idea of divine decree or destiny, where Allah has preordained the nature and course of all things.

- **"and then guided"**: This signifies Allah's provision of guidance to His creation, enabling them to fulfill their intended purpose. For humans, this guidance includes the revelation of the Quran and the Prophet Muhammad (peace be upon him) as a guide, showing the path to righteousness and success. It also includes the natural instincts and abilities He has given to all creatures to guide them towards their needs and survival.

In summary, this verse highlights Allah's complete sovereignty and wisdom in creation and guidance, emphasizing that He is the ultimate source of order and direction in the universe and for humanity

Verse 4

Wallazeee akhrajal mar'aa

And Who bringeth out the (green and luscious) pasture

This signifies Allah's power in bringing forth vegetation from the earth. It highlights the transition of this greenery into dry, black stubble, symbolizing life's cycles and the transient nature of the world. The verse serves as a reminder of Allah's creative force and the eventual return to Him.

The verse emphasizes Allah's power and wisdom in managing the natural world, particularly the cycle of plant life.

It also serves as a reminder of the transient nature of worldly life, as the lush pasture eventually gives way to dry stubble, symbolizing the cycle of life and death.

The verse encourages reflection on Allah's actions and His control over creation, urging believers to contemplate His attributes and remember Him.

Verse 5

Faja'alahoo ghusaaa'an ahwaa

"And then doth make it (but) swarthy stubble"

This refers to the Divine power of Allah to bring forth vegetation, specifically green pasture, and then transform it into dark, dried stubble. This transformation signifies the cycle of life and death, growth and decay, and ultimately points to Allah's ultimate power over all creation.

This transformation highlights Allah's power to create and destroy, bringing forth life and then ending it. It also symbolizes the fleeting nature of worldly life and the eventual return to Allah.

Verse 6

Sanuqri'uka falaa tansaaa

"By degrees shall We teach thee to declare (the Message), so thou shalt not forget"

Allah assures the Prophet Muhammad (peace be upon him) that He will make him recite the Quran and that he will not forget it. This verse offers a double blessing: first, the Prophet is spared the burden of memorizing the Quran through his own effort, and second, Allah guarantees the preservation of the Quran in his memory.

- **"We shall make thee recite"**:

This signifies that Allah is the one who will enable the Prophet to recite the Quran, not just through revelation, but also by ensuring it is firmly fixed in his memory.

- **"so thou shalt not forget":**

This is a divine guarantee that the Prophet will not forget any part of the Quran that is revealed to him. It highlights the miraculous nature of the Quran's preservation in the Prophet's memory.

The verse also highlights Allah's grace and mercy in relieving the Prophet of the burden of memorization and guaranteeing the preservation of His word.

The Prophet's initial anxiety about forgetting the verses is addressed by this verse, assuring him that Allah would take care of the preservation.

Verse 7

Illaa maa shaaa'al laah; innahoo ya'lamul jahra wa maa yakhfaa

"Except as Allah wills: For He knoweth what is manifest and what is hidden,"

This is telling us of Allah's absolute knowledge and control over all things, including the possibility of forgetting something temporarily. It emphasizes that while Allah has promised the Prophet Muhammad (peace be upon him) that he will not forget the Quran, there is always the implicit exception of what Allah wills, highlighting His ultimate authority.

- **"Except as Allah wills":**

This phrase acts as a reminder that despite the promise of not forgetting the Quran, Allah's will is ultimately supreme. It implies that if Allah were to will it, He could cause the Prophet (peace be upon him) to forget a part of the revelation, though this is not a permanent forgetting, as verses can be remembered later.

- **"For He knoweth what is manifest and what is hidden":**

This part of the verse highlights Allah's comprehensive knowledge. He is aware of everything, both what is openly declared (the manifest) and what is concealed (the hidden), including thoughts, intentions, and secrets.

- **Divine Wisdom:**

Some interpretations suggest that Allah may temporarily cause the Prophet to forget a verse or part of the revelation for a specific wisdom known only to Him. This could be to test faith, to demonstrate the importance of seeking knowledge, or for other reasons.

This verse can be seen as an encouragement to seek knowledge and not rely solely on memory. It emphasizes that even with divine guidance, understanding and retaining the message requires effort and reliance on Allah's will.

Ultimately, the verse serves as a reminder of Allah's absolute power and knowledge, emphasizing that His will is supreme and that everything is subject to His control.

Verse 8

Wa nu-yassiruka lilyusraa

"And We will make it easy for thee (to follow) the simple (Path),"

This signifies that Allah will facilitate the Prophet Muhammad's path towards righteousness and ease of practice within the Islamic faith. This ease is not merely about physical comfort, but also about spiritual ease and guidance, making the path of Islam clear and accessible.

- **"...the simple (Path)"**:

This refers to the straightforward nature of Islam, which is characterized by clear principles and ease of practice, in contrast to the complexities and burdens of other systems.

  - **Spiritual Ease:** The implies that Allah will predispose the Prophet (PBUH) to the Islamic way of life, making it natural and easy for him to embody its teachings.

  - **Facilitation of Practice:** It highlights Allah's support in making the practical aspects of Islam, such as worship and interactions, smooth and accessible for the Prophet (PBUH).

  - **Guidance and Support:** The verse emphasizes that Allah's guidance and support will be with the Prophet (PBUH) in his journey of spreading the message of Islam.

  - **Contrast with Difficulty:** The mention of "the simple (Path)" also serves to contrast Islam with the complexities and hardships of other systems or paths.

  - **Emphasis on Divine Grace:** The verse underscores that the ease with which the Prophet (PBUH) can follow the path of Islam is a result of Allah's grace and divine assistance.

Verse 9

Fazakkir in nafa'atizzikraa

"So remind, if the reminder should benefit".

This verse, following the description of Allah's facilitation for the Prophet's mission, commands him to continue reminding people of Allah's message. The "if" in the verse is not meant to be conditional, but rather emphasizes that reminding is always beneficial and should be continued, as there will always be those who will benefit from it.

- **The Command to Remind:**

The verse instructs the Prophet (and by extension, all believers) to continue reminding people of the message of Islam.

- **"If the Reminder Should Benefit":**

The "if" clause doesn't mean that the reminder should be given only if it will definitely be beneficial. Instead, it implies that even if some might not initially heed the reminder, there will always be those who will benefit from it.

- **Emphasis on Continuous Reminding:**

The verse highlights the importance of persistent and consistent conveying of the message, as it will inevitably find fertile ground in at least some hearts.

- **No Discouragement:**

The verse should not be interpreted as a reason to stop reminding those who initially reject the message. It encourages perseverance in delivering the message, as its benefits will become apparent over time.

Verse 10

Sa yazzakkaru maiyakhshaa

"He who fears Allah will be reminded." This verse signifies that those who possess true fear and reverence for Allah, coupled with an awareness of His greatness and their accountability to Him, will be receptive to and benefit from reminders and admonishments. They will be mindful of their actions and strive to align themselves with Allah's will.

- **Fear of Allah (Taqwa):**

The verse emphasizes the importance of Taqwa, which encompasses not just fear, but also reverence, awe, and consciousness of Allah. This fear is not a paralyzing fear, but rather a motivating force that leads to righteous actions and avoidance of what displeases Allah.

- **Receptivity to Reminders:**

Those who possess Taqwa are described as those who will be reminded. This means they are open to receiving guidance and advice, recognizing its source and purpose. They understand that the reminders are for their benefit and strive to implement them in their lives.

- **Distinction between Believers and the Unbelievers:**

The verse highlights a clear distinction between those who fear Allah and those who do not. The latter group, lacking Taqwa, will not be receptive to reminders and may even reject them.

Guidance and Success:

By being receptive to reminders, those who fear Allah are paving the way for guidance and success in both this world and the hereafter. They are actively seeking to please Allah and are more likely to follow His path.

- **Connection to other verses:**

This verse is closely linked to the previous verse, which encourages giving reminders when they are likely to benefit. It also connects to the overall theme of Surah Al-Ala, which emphasizes the importance of glorifying Allah, remembering Him, and striving for righteousness.

Verse 11

Wa yatajannabuhal ashqaa

"But the wretched one will avoid it,"

This is refering to those who, due to their wickedness and lack of fear of Allah, will reject and turn away from the reminder and guidance offered by the Prophet Muhammad (peace be upon him). They are described as "wretched" because they deliberately choose a path that leads to destruction and the Hellfire, despite having been warned.

- **"The wretched one"**:

This refers to individuals who are fundamentally opposed to righteousness and guidance. They are characterized by their stubbornness, arrogance, and refusal to accept the truth.

- **"Will avoid it"**:

This highlights the conscious choice of these individuals to reject the message of Islam and the warnings given by the Prophet. They actively distance themselves from anything that might lead them to repentance and a change in their ways.

This verse signifies that not everyone will accept the Prophet's message. While the Prophet is tasked with delivering the reminder, those with a hardened heart and a lack of fear of Allah will inevitably turn away from it.

This avoidance is not without consequence. Those who reject the guidance will face the severe punishment of the Hellfire in the afterlife, as mentioned in subsequent verses (87:12-13).

The verse contrasts the "wretched" with those who fear Allah and benefit from the reminder. These individuals, recognizing their accountability to Allah, will heed the warning and strive for righteousness.

Verse 12

Allazee yaslan Naaral kubraa

"He who will burn in the greatest Fire"

Here we are learning about the Great Fire, The Fire of Hell. The verse is stating that whoever enters it will neither die nor live, experiencing unending torment. A point to note here if you die with Tauheed, but your bad deeds outweigh your good ones, you will be reprieved. That person stay in the hellfire will not be everlasting.

Hence, this verse is a warning about the consequences of rejecting faith and guidance. It is teaching us the severity and permanence of punishment in the Hellfire, highlighting that it is a state of perpetual suffering without relief.

- **"Neither dying therein nor living"**:

This highlights the excruciating nature of the fire. It is not a temporary suffering, nor is it a state of death that offers relief. It is a continuous, agonizing experience.

- **The Great Fire (an-nar al-kubra)**:

This is a specific term used in the Quran to denote the Hellfire, emphasizing its intensity, duration, and scope. It is the ultimate consequence for those who choose to disobey Allah.

Verse 13

Summa laa yamootu feehaa wa laa yahyaa

"Then he will not die therein, nor will he live."

This verse describes the state of those who reject the message of guidance and fall into the Hellfire, emphasizing that they will neither find death (and thus rest) nor a life of benefit.

In the afterlife, death is often seen as a finality, a way to escape pain and punishment. However, for those in Jahannam (Hell), this escape is denied.

- **"...nor will he live."**:

This part of the verse highlights that the life they experience in Jahannam is not a life of fulfillment, purpose, or even relative comfort. It is a life of constant torment and despair. It is a life devoid of any of the positive aspects associated with living.

- **The contrast with success**:

The verse contrasts the state of those in Hell with those who heed the message and achieve success in the afterlife by purifying themselves, remembering their Lord, and praying. The success mentioned in previous verses implies both worldly and spiritual well-being, while this verse depicts the ultimate failure of those who reject the truth.

The verse serves as a warning, emphasizing the dire consequences of rejecting Allah's guidance and the Prophet's message. It highlights the eternal nature of punishment in the Hereafter for those who choose to disregard the truth.

Verse 14

Qad aflaha man tazakkaa

"Then he will not die therein, nor will he live."

This verse describes the state of those who reject the message of guidance and fall into the Hellfire, demonstrating that they will neither find death (and thus rest) nor a life of benefit.

- **"Then he will not die therein..."**:

This refers to the inhabitants of the Hellfire who will not experience death as a release from their suffering. In the afterlife, death is often seen as a finality, a way to escape pain and punishment. However, for those in Jahannam (Hell), this escape is denied.

- **"...nor will he live."**:

This part of the verse highlights that the life they experience in Jahannam is not a life of fulfillment, purpose, or even relative comfort. It is a life of constant torment and despair. It is a life devoid of any of the positive aspects associated with living.

- **The contrast with success**:

The verse contrasts the state of those in Hell with those who heed the message and achieve success in the afterlife by purifying themselves, remembering their Lord, and praying. The success mentioned in previous verses implies both worldly and spiritual well-being, while this verse depicts the ultimate failure of those who reject the truth.

- **Emphasis on consequences**:

The verse serves as a warning, emphasizing the dire consequences of rejecting Allah's guidance and the Prophet's message. It highlights the eternal nature of punishment in the Hereafter for those who choose to disregard the truth.

Verse 14

Qad aflaha man tazakkaa

"He has certainly succeeded who purifies himself,"

This verse is telling us the importance of spiritual purification for achieving true success. This purification involves cleansing oneself from sins, bad character, and polytheism, while also embracing faith and good deeds.

The ultimate goal for every human being should be to attain success, not just in this life, but also in the Hereafter.

- **"...who purifies himself"**:

The word "purifies" (tazakka) in this context refers to more than just physical cleanliness. It encompasses the purification of one's heart and soul from negative traits and actions.

- **Purification as a means to success**:

The verse suggests that achieving success is directly linked to the process of self-purification.

Verse 15

Wa zakaras ma Rabbihee fasallaa

"And remembers the name of his Lord and prays."

This verse highlights two key aspects of a successful believer: remembering Allah through both heart and tongue, and demonstrating that remembrance by performing the prayer. It emphasizes that true success comes from purifying oneself and actively engaging with Allah's remembrance and worship.

We have to engage in the remembrance of Allah both inwardly (in the heart) and outwardly (through the tongue). It means constantly keeping Allah in one's thoughts and mentioning His name in praise and devotion.

- **"and prays"**:

This signifies that a believer does not merely remember Allah verbally, but also demonstrates their faith through action, specifically by performing the obligatory prayers. Prayer is a practical demonstration of obedience to Allah and a way to strengthen one's connection with Him.

- **Success**:

The verse implies that those who engage in both remembrance and prayer are on the path to success, both in this life and the hereafter. This is because they are actively purifying themselves and striving for closeness to their Lord.

In essence, verse 15 of Surah Al-A'la calls for a holistic approach to faith, where remembrance of Allah is not just a verbal exercise, but also a way of life that is manifested through prayer and other acts of worship.

Verse 16

Bal tu'siroonal hayaatad dunyaa

"But you prefer the worldly life, while the Hereafter is better and more enduring."

This verse highlights the human tendency to prioritize the immediate pleasures and material gains of this world over the eternal rewards of the Hereafter.

Hence, it is a criticism of this tendency to be preoccupied with worldly matters, such as material possessions, fleeting desires, and immediate gratification.

- **"...while the Hereafter is better and more enduring"**:

This contrasts the worldly life with the Hereafter, emphasizing that the rewards and blessings of the Hereafter are superior in quality and permanence. The Hereafter is described as better in terms of its rewards, virtue, and happiness, and more enduring because its blessings are everlasting.

The verse essentially points out that humans often make choices that favour the temporary comforts of this world, overlooking the long-term and eternal benefits of the Hereafter. This short-sightedness is a source of regret and ultimately leads to a loss in the Hereafter.

Thus, the verse serves as a reminder to consider the bigger picture and prioritize actions that will lead to success in both worlds, rather than being solely consumed by the fleeting nature of this life.

Verse 17

Wal Aakhiratu khairunw wa abqaa

"But you prefer the worldly life, while the Hereafter is better and more enduring."

This verse highlights the contrast between the fleeting nature of worldly life and the eternal nature of the Hereafter, demonstrating that the latter is superior. It serves as a reminder to prioritize spiritual well-being and preparation for the eternal life over the transient pleasures of this world.

Humans tend to be engrossed in the immediate pleasures and concerns of this world. It acknowledges that people often prioritize material possessions, worldly achievements, and immediate gratification over spiritual growth and preparation for the afterlife.

- **"...while the Hereafter is better and more enduring"**:

This contrasts the temporary nature of worldly life with the everlasting nature of the Hereafter. The Hereafter, or the afterlife, is described as superior because it offers eternal rewards and blessings, unlike the fleeting and often deceptive pleasures of this world. The verse encourages believers to strive for the eternal rewards of the Hereafter rather than being solely preoccupied with worldly affairs.

In summary, the verse serves as a wake-up call, urging individuals to reflect on their priorities and to choose a path that leads to lasting success and fulfillment in the Hereafter, rather than being captivated by the temporary allure of this world.

Verse 18

Inna haazaa lafis suhu fil oolaa

"And this is in the Books of the earliest (Revelation)"

This verse indicates that the message of the Quran, particularly the emphasis on the oneness of God and the importance of the Hereafter, is not new but has been revealed in earlier scriptures, specifically those of Prophet Abraham and Prophet Moses.

The verse demonstrates the continuity of divine revelation. It emphasizes that the core message of Islam, which is the worship of one God and the belief in the Day of Judgment, has been consistently revealed throughout history by different prophets.

It specifically mentions the scriptures of Abraham and Moses, indicating that the teachings found in the Quran are not contradictory to the teachings of these earlier prophets. This connection serves as a validation of the Quranic message and strengthens the faith of Muslims.

By referring to the scriptures of Abraham and Moses, the verse also suggests that the message of Islam is not limited to a specific time or people but has a universal appeal, relevant to all humanity.

The verse is also a warning to those who reject the Quranic message, reminding them that the same message has been revealed before, and they are essentially rejecting a universal truth that has been consistently conveyed throughout history.

In conclusion, verse 18 of Surah Al-Ala emphasizes the continuity and universality of the divine message, connecting the teachings of the Quran to earlier revelations and highlighting the importance of understanding these timeless truths.

Verse 19

Suhufi Ibraaheema wa Moosaa

"Indeed, this is in the former scriptures – The scriptures of Abraham and Moses."

This verse essentially asserts that the core message of the Quran, emphasizing belief in one God, the Day of Judgment, and good deeds, is not a new revelation but was also present in the scriptures revealed to Prophet Abraham and Prophet Moses. It highlights the continuity of divine guidance throughout history and strengthens the Prophet Muhammad's message by connecting it to earlier prophets.

The verse underscores that the fundamental principles of Islam, as presented in the Quran, are not unique to this revelation. They were also part of the earlier scriptures revealed to previous prophets, particularly Abraham and Moses.

This connection to earlier scriptures serves to validate the Prophet Muhammad's message and demonstrate its consistency with the divine guidance given to earlier prophets. It strengthens the claim that the Quran is not a fabrication but a continuation of God's message.

By highlighting the presence of similar teachings in the scriptures of Abraham and Moses, the verse highlights the idea that divine guidance is not limited to a specific time or people, but is a consistent thread throughout history.

The verse implies that the core message found in the scriptures of Abraham and Moses included belief in one God, the Day of Judgment, and the importance of good deeds. These are also central themes in the Quran, further emphasizing the continuity of divine guidance.

By stating that the message of the Quran was also present in the scriptures of previous prophets, the verse serves as a confirmation of the prophethood of Muhammad (peace be upon him) and the divine origin of his message.

LESSONS TO BE LEARNT FROM SURAH AL-ALA

1. The Praise of Allah's Name and Creation:** The surah begins by praising Allah for His mighty and beautiful creation, reminding us to recognize and appreciate His blessings.
2. The Importance of Prayer and Worship: It emphasizes the significance of establishing prayer and focusing on Allah's worship as a means to attain success.
3. The Value of Remembrance and Reflection: The surah encourages us to remember Allah frequently and reflect on His signs in the universe as a way to purify our hearts.
4. The Reward for Righteousness: It teaches that those who strive to do good and follow Allah's guidance will be successful and rewarded.
5. Encouragement to Seek Knowledge: The surah inspires believers to learn and understand the teachings of Islam and to develop a conscious connection with Allah.
6. The Power of Allah's Speech: It reminds us that Allah's words are powerful and true, and that His promises will always be fulfilled.

These lessons promote faith, worship, reflection, and righteousness, guiding believers to live a meaningful and God-conscious life.

SUMMARY OF SURAH AL – ALA

Surah Al-Ala (The Most High), is the 87th chapter of the Quran and was revealed in Mecca. It talks about praising Allah and His qualities, especially His creation and guidance. It reminds believers of Allah's blessings, the importance of remembering Him through prayer, and what happens in the afterlife based on faith or disbelief. The surah also explains that the Prophet's job is to deliver Allah's message, which was also given to earlier prophets like Abraham and Moses.

Summary:

Praising Allah: The surah starts by telling the Prophet to praise Allah, the Most High.

Creation and Guidance: It describes how Allah made everything perfectly and guides them to their purpose, showing His power and wisdom.

Revelation and Memory: It reassures that the Quran will be kept safe by Allah.

Remembering Allah: It emphasizes that remembering Allah is important and helpful for those who fear Him.

Life and the Afterlife: It explains that worldly life is temporary, but rewards in the hereafter last forever. It talks about what happens to believers and non-believers.

Same Message for All Prophets: It ends by saying that other prophets like Abraham and Moses also received this message from Allah, showing that Allah's guidance has always been the same.

SURAH AL-ALA – SURAH 87

Questions

1. What does the name "Al-Ala" mean, and why is this surah titled with this name?
2. In the first few verses, what attributes of Allah are highlighted, and why are they significant?
3. How does the surah describe the process of creation and guidance provided by Allah?
4. What is the importance of remembering and glorifying Allah as mentioned in the surah?
5. Which aspects of human nature and the world does the surah encourage reflection upon?
6. How does the surah differentiate between those who succeed and those who fail in the hereafter?
7. What role does the concept of purification play in achieving success according to the surah?
8. How is the Quran described in this surah, and what is its significance for believers?
9. What message does the surah convey about the transient nature of this world compared to the hereafter?
10. How can the themes of this surah be applied to daily life for personal and spiritual growth?

Answers

1. What does the name "Al-Ala" mean, and why is this surah titled with this name?
   - "Al-Ala" means "The Most High." The surah is titled this way because it begins with the command to glorify the name of Allah, the Most High, reflecting His supreme nature and majesty.

2. In the first few verses, what attributes of Allah are highlighted, and why are they significant?
   - The surah highlights Allah as the Creator, the One who perfectly proportions and guides His creation. These attributes signify Allah's ability to create with precision and purpose, reminding us of His ultimate authority and wisdom.

3. How does the surah describe the process of creation and guidance provided by Allah?
   - The surah describes Allah as the One who creates, gives form, and guides. This process emphasizes His comprehensive knowledge and control over the universe and signifies that everything follows a divine plan and purpose.

4. What is the importance of remembering and glorifying Allah as mentioned in the surah?
   - Remembering and glorifying Allah is important as it keeps the believer conscious of their Creator, strengthens faith, and aligns actions with divine guidance, leading to spiritual success.

5. Which aspects of human nature and the world does the surah encourage reflection upon?
   - The surah encourages reflection on the cycles of life and death, the growth of plants, and the transient nature of worldly life. These reflections remind us of Allah's power and the temporality of material existence.

6. How does the surah differentiate between those who succeed and those who fail in the hereafter?
   - Success is attributed to those who purify themselves, remember Allah, and follow His guidance, while failure is linked to those who are heedless and prefer the temporary pleasures of this world over the eternal hereafter.

7. What role does the concept of purification play in achieving success according to the surah?
   - Purification, both of the soul and actions, is essential for success. It involves cleansing oneself from sins and developing good character, leading to spiritual elevation and closeness to Allah.

8. How is the Quran described in this surah, and what is its significance for believers?
   - The Quran is described as a reminder that is preserved on honored pages, indicating its divine origin and purity. Its significance lies in its role as a guide for living a life pleasing to Allah and achieving success in the hereafter.

9. What message does the surah convey about the transient nature of this world compared to the hereafter?
   - The surah conveys that while the pleasures of this world are temporary and fleeting, the hereafter is everlasting. It encourages believers to prioritize eternal rewards over short-lived worldly gains.

10. How can the themes of this surah be applied to daily life for personal and spiritual growth?
    - By regularly remembering and glorifying Allah, striving for personal purification, and reflecting on the temporary nature of worldly life, individuals can align their lives with divine guidance, leading to spiritual growth and fulfillment.

These answers provide a deeper understanding of Surah Al-Ala and can facilitate thoughtful discussion or personal reflection.

Multiple Choice Questions

1. What does the name "Al-Ala" mean?

    - A) The Most Merciful

    - B) The Most High

    - C) The Most Forgiving

    - D) The Most Wise

2. What is the primary command given to the Prophet Muhammad (peace be upon him) in the opening verse of Surah Al-Ala?

    - A) Seek forgiveness

    - B) Be patient

    - C) Glorify the name of your Lord

    - D) Give charity

3. Which of the following attributes of Allah is NOT mentioned in Surah Al-Ala?

    - A) Creator

    - B) Guide

    - C) Forgiver

    - D) Proportioner

4. What does the surah say about the nature of the world?

    - A) It is everlasting

    - B) It is full of suffering

    - C) It is transient and temporary

    - D) It is perfect and permanent

5. According to Surah Al-Ala, who will achieve success?

    - A) The wealthy

    - B) Those who remember Allah and purify themselves

    - C) The powerful

    - D) Those who seek knowledge

6. What does the surah say about the Quran?

    - A) It is difficult to understand

    - B) It is a reminder preserved in honored pages

    - C) It is meant only for scholars

    - D) It is only for past generations

7. How does the surah emphasize the importance of the hereafter compared to this world?

    - A) By describing the luxuries of paradise

    - B) By emphasizing the eternal nature of the hereafter

    - C) By outlining the punishments for sinners

    - D) By stating that this world is more valuable

8. What activity is encouraged in Surah Al-Ala for spiritual growth?

    - A) Traveling

    - B) Reflecting on nature

    - C) Glorifying and remembering Allah

    - D) Accumulating wealth

Answers

1. *Answer:* B) The Most High
2. *Answer:* C) Glorify the name of your Lord
3. *Answer:* C) Forgiver
4. *Answer:* C) It is transient and temporary
5. *Answer:* B) Those who remember Allah and purify themselves
6. *Answer:* B) It is a reminder preserved in honored pages
7. *Answer:* B) By emphasizing the eternal nature of the hereafter
8. *Answer:* C) Glorifying and remembering Allah

These questions and answers can be used for educational purposes, quizzes, or discussions to enhance understanding of Surah Al-Ala.

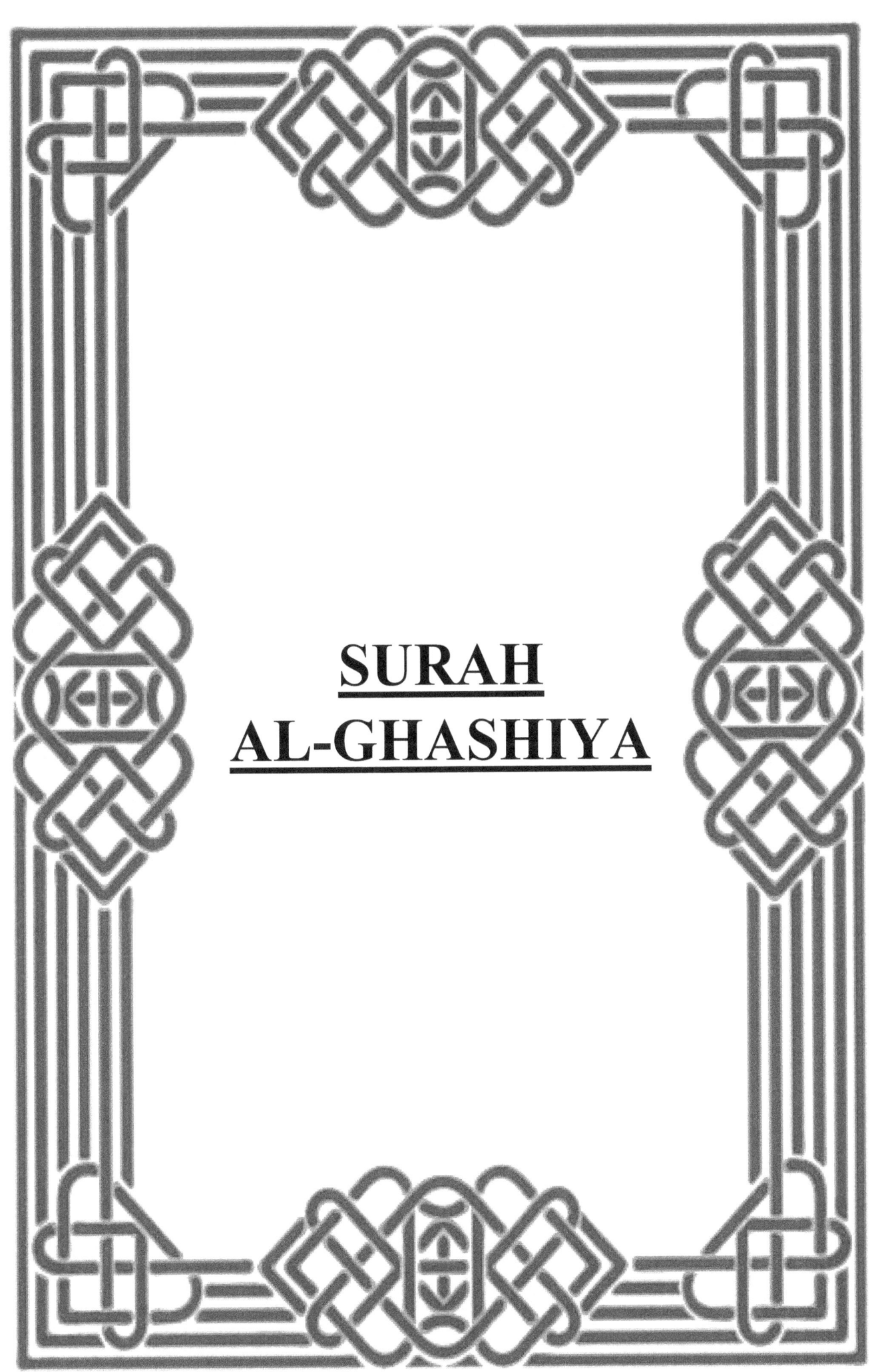

SURAH AL-GHASHIYA

AL-GHASHIYA

Bismillahi ar-Rahmani ar-Raheem

Verse 1

"Has the news reached you, [O Muhammad], of the overwhelming event?".

This verse introduces the Day of Judgment (Yawm al-Ghashiyah) as a momentous, overwhelming event that will impact all of humanity. The verse serves as a powerful reminder of the afterlife and encourages reflection on its significance.

- **"Has the news reached you"**:

This rhetorical question immediately grabs the listener's attention and emphasizes the importance of the message to follow.

- **"of the overwhelming event"**:

The Arabic word "al-Ghashiyah" refers to something that covers, envelops, or overwhelms, signifying the Day of Judgment, which will encompass all creation. This event is not just any day, but a day of immense consequence, a day of reckoning and judgment.

- **Purpose**:

The verse aims to awaken the Prophet (and by extension, all believers) to the reality of the Hereafter and the impending Day of Judgment. It highlights the need to prepare for this event, which will be a turning point for all of humanity.

- **Contrast**:

The verse sets the stage for contrasting the fates of those who believe and those who disbelieve. It foreshadows the joy and contentment of the believers and the humiliation and suffering of the disbelievers on that day.

Verse 2

Wujoohuny yawma 'izin khaashi'ah

"Some faces, that Day, will be humiliated"

This verse describes the state of some faces on the Day of Judgment as being "downcast and humbled, being humiliated."

This verse paints a picture of deep sadness and despair, indicating a state of regret and humiliation for those who will experience this on that great Day. The verse highlights the contrast between those who will be joyful and those who will be filled with sorrow on the Day of Judgment.

- **"Some faces..."**:

This phrase indicates that not all faces will be in this state. There will be a clear distinction between those who are humbled and those who are radiant with joy.

- **"on that Day..."**:

This refers to the Day of Judgment, a significant event in Islamic belief where humanity will be resurrected and judged.

- **"downcast and humbled"**:

This describes the physical manifestation of inner turmoil and regret. The Arabic word "khashi'ah" (خَاشِعَةٌ) suggests a state of humility, submissiveness, and even shame. This is in contrast to the faces that will be radiant with joy and pleasure.

This verse is often interpreted in conjunction with verse 3, which describes the faces as "toiling and worn-out". Together, these verses paint a picture of those who will be facing the consequences of their actions in this life, particularly those who lived without guidance and whose efforts in this world did not lead to lasting benefit.

Verse 3

Aamilatun naasibah

"Labouring (hard), weary"

They will be "labouring, weary," or "toiling and worn-out". This refers to those who exerted themselves in worldly actions, particularly in acts of worship that were not accepted by Allah, and thus will be in a state of exhaustion and humiliation on that day.

- **"'āmilah"** (عَامِلَةٌ):

This word implies effort, work, and action. In the context of this verse, it signifies the actions and deeds performed by the disbelievers in their worldly life.

- **"nāṣibah"** (نَّاصِبَةٌ):

This word means "weary," "exhausted," or "toiling." It indicates the fatigue and hardship experienced as a result of those actions.

- **Interpretation:**

The verse is often interpreted to mean that these individuals will be in a state of misery and regret on the Day of Judgment, having exerted themselves in worldly pursuits without earning any divine reward or benefit. Their efforts were ultimately in vain, leading to exhaustion and disappointment in the Hereafter.

- **Contrast with Believers:**

This description is in stark contrast to the state of the believers, who will be joyful and content with their deeds, having strived in the path of Allah and earning His pleasure.

Verse 4

Taslaa naaran haamiyah

"Into a blazing Fire."

Verse 4 describes the fate awaiting those who reject the truth with the words "Into a blazing Fire." This verse serves as a clear warning to disbelievers about the severe consequences of denying the message of Islam. The "blazing Fire" symbolizes Hell, representing a place of intense punishment for those who choose to ignore divine guidance.

The imagery of a "blazing" fire highlights the intensity and severity of the punishment, designed to instill fear and encourage reflection among its audience. It urges those who hear it to reconsider their stance and turn towards faith and righteousness. This vivid depiction is meant to convey the moral and spiritual consequences of rejecting the divine message, prompting individuals to recognize the seriousness of their actions in this life and their impact on the afterlife.

This verse is part of a larger narrative in Surah Al-Ghashiya, which contrasts the fates of the righteous and the wicked. While disbelievers are warned of Hell, believers are promised rewards in Paradise. This duality aims to motivate individuals to choose the path of faith and good deeds, emphasizing the importance of embracing faith and following the guidance of Allah.

VVerse 5 of Surah Al-Ghashiya describes the punishment awaiting disbelievers in the Hereafter: "Given to drink from a boiling spring." This verse follows the depiction of the blazing fire in the previous verse, intensifying the image of suffering for those who reject the truth. The metaphor of being forced to drink from a boiling spring is meant to convey the extreme discomfort and torment that will be experienced by those who turn away from divine guidance.

The imagery of a "boiling spring" serves to highlight the harshness and severity of the punishment. In a region where water is precious and life-sustaining, the concept of water being a source of agony rather than relief would be especially poignant. This detail underscores the total reversal of comfort and security for those who have denied the message of Islam.

By presenting such vivid and unsettling imagery, the verse aims to provoke reflection and reconsideration among its audience. It serves as a stark reminder of the consequences of disbelief and a cautionary tale about the spiritual and moral repercussions of turning away from faith. This verse, like others in the Surah, is intended to motivate individuals to embrace the teachings of Islam and strive towards righteousness, emphasizing the importance of aligning one's actions with divine guidance to avoid such dire outcomes in the afterlife.

Verse 5

Tusqaa min 'aynin aaniyah

"Given to drink from a boiling spring."

Verse 5 describes the punishment awaiting disbelievers in the Hereafter: This verse follows the depiction of the blazing fire in the previous verse, intensifying the image of suffering for those who reject the truth. The metaphor of being forced to drink from a boiling spring is meant to convey the extreme discomfort and torment that will be experienced by those who turn away from divine guidance.

The imagery of a "boiling spring" serves to highlight the harshness and severity of the punishment. In a region where water is precious and life-sustaining, the concept of water being a source of agony rather than relief would be especially poignant. This detail underscores the total reversal of comfort and security for those who have denied the message of Islam.

By presenting such vivid and unsettling imagery, the verse aims to provoke reflection and reconsideration among its audience. It serves as a stark reminder of the consequences of disbelief and a cautionary tale about the spiritual and moral repercussions of turning away from faith. This verse, like others in the Surah, is intended to motivate individuals to embrace the teachings of Islam and strive towards righteousness, emphasizing the importance of aligning one's actions with divine guidance to avoid such dire outcomes in the afterlife.

Verse 6

Laisa lahum ta'aamun illaa min daree'

"No food will there be for them but a bitter Dhari"

This verse continues the description of the harsh conditions awaiting disbelievers in the Hereafter, further emphasizing the severity of their punishment.

The term "dari" refers to a type of thorny plant that is bitter and lacks any nutritional value. In the context of this verse, it symbolizes the inadequate and unpleasant sustenance that will be available to those who have rejected the truth. This imagery serves to highlight the absence of comfort and satisfaction for the disbelievers in the afterlife, contrasting sharply with the nourishment and blessings promised to the believers.

By using such vivid and unsettling imagery, the verse aims to instill a sense of urgency and reflection in its audience. It serves as a powerful reminder of the consequences of ignoring divine guidance and the importance of embracing faith and righteousness. The description of such dire conditions is intended to motivate individuals to consider their actions in this life and to choose the path that leads to spiritual fulfillment and eternal reward.

Verse 7

Laa yusminu wa laa yughnee min joo'

"Which will neither nourish nor satisfy hunger,"

Verse 7 elaborates on the nature of the sustenance provided to disbelievers in the afterlife, stating: "Which will neither nourish nor satisfy hunger." This verse expands on the previous mention of "dari," a bitter and thorny plant, by emphasizing its ineffectiveness in providing any real sustenance or relief.

The verse highlights the inadequacy of the food available to those who rejected the truth. Unlike nourishing food, which provides energy and satisfies hunger, the "dari" in the hereafter will offer no such benefits. It neither nourishes the body nor alleviates the discomfort of hunger, symbolizing the utter deprivation and lack of fulfillment that disbelievers will experience.

This imagery serves as a stark contrast to the rewards and blessings promised to the faithful. While believers are assured of abundant and satisfying provisions in Paradise, disbelievers are faced with the prospect of unrelenting deprivation. The verse aims to underscore the consequences of ignoring divine guidance and to prompt reflection on the spiritual and moral choices individuals make in this life.

By presenting such vivid depictions of the afterlife for disbelievers, the verse seeks to motivate people to choose the path of faith and righteousness. It reminds the audience of the importance of aligning one's actions with divine teachings to avoid such dire outcomes and to ensure spiritual fulfillment and eternal reward.

Verse 8

Wujoohuny yawma 'izin naa'imah

"(Other) faces that Day will be joyful",

Verse 8 shifts the focus from the grim fate of the disbelievers to the contrasting experience of the believers, stating: "Other faces that Day will be joyful." This verse introduces a sense of hope and positivity by describing the radiant and joyful expressions of the righteous on the Day of Judgment.

The "faces" mentioned in the verse symbolize the countenances of those who have embraced faith and lived righteously. Their joyfulness reflects the inner contentment and satisfaction that come from knowing they have attained the pleasure of Allah and the rewards of the afterlife. This stands in stark contrast to the distressed and anguished faces of the disbelievers previously described.

By depicting the joy and radiance of the believers, the verse emphasizes the rewards awaiting those who follow divine guidance. Their happiness is a result of their steadfastness in faith and their commitment to righteous deeds. This imagery serves as an encouragement for individuals to strive for such fulfillment and success in the afterlife.

Overall, this verse is part of the larger narrative within Surah Al-Ghashiya, which contrasts the outcomes of the righteous and the wicked. It serves as a reminder of the ultimate rewards of faith and righteousness, motivating individuals to seek a life aligned with spiritual values and divine guidance.

Verse 9

Lisa'yihaa raadiyah

"Pleased with their striving",

This verse refers to the faces of the believers on the Day of Judgment. It depicts the scene where those who have lived righteously and have strived in the way of Allah will be content and satisfied with the efforts they have made in the worldly life. Their hard work, sacrifices, and perseverance in adhering to their faith and performing good deeds will result in a sense of fulfillment and joy in the Hereafter. They will be pleased with the results of their endeavours because they will be rewarded with eternal bliss and the pleasure of Allah.

This verse highlights the Quranic theme of accountability and the promise of reward for those who remain steadfast in their faith and actions, offering encouragement and motivation to lead a life that aligns with Islamic teachings.

Verse 10

Fee jannatin 'aaliyah

"In a garden So High"

This verse refers to the elevated and lofty gardens of Paradise that the righteous will inhabit in the Hereafter. The phrase "elevated garden" signifies not just the physical beauty and high status of the location but also the spiritual elevation and honour bestowed upon the believers. It suggests a place of dignity, peace, and eternal happiness, far removed from the struggles and hardships of the worldly life.

The use of the word "elevated" implies exclusivity and distinction, emphasizing the honour and reward that await those who have committed themselves to a life of faith and good deeds. It serves as a promise of the ultimate success and a source of motivation for believers to continue striving in their spiritual and moral efforts in this world.

Verse 11

Laa tasma'u feehaa laaghiyah

"Wherein they will hear no unsuitable speech."

This verse describes one of the aspects of the blissful environment of Paradise: the complete absence of any negative, vain, or inappropriate talk. In the world, people often encounter harmful, offensive, or frivolous speech, which can lead to misunderstandings, conflicts, or discomfort.

In contrast, the verse assures the believers that Paradise will be free from such negativity. The speech in Paradise will be pure, meaningful, and pleasing, contributing to the overall peace and harmony of the afterlife. This absence of unsuitable speech reflects the perfection and serenity of the eternal life that the righteous will enjoy.

The emphasis on the purity of speech in Paradise highlights the moral and ethical elevation in the Hereafter, where only goodness and truth prevail, further enhancing the joy and contentment of the inhabitants.

Verse 12

Feehaa 'aynun jaariyah

"Within it is a flowing spring."

This verse highlights one of the physical pleasures of Paradise: the presence of a flowing spring. Flowing water is often associated with life, purity, and refreshment, symbolizing the abundance and eternal nature of the blessings in Paradise.

The mention of a flowing spring suggests a setting of tranquility and beauty, where the inhabitants of Paradise can enjoy a serene and refreshing environment. This imagery is meant to convey the idea of continuous and limitless pleasure and satisfaction, contrasting with the temporary and often flawed pleasures of the worldly life.

The flowing spring also signifies the eternal and unending nature of the rewards in Paradise, assuring the believers of perpetual comfort and joy. This adds to the overall depiction of Paradise as a place of ultimate fulfillment and peace for those who have lived righteously.

Verse 13

Feehaa sururum marfoo'ah

"Within it are couches raised high."

This verse describes the elevated couches or thrones in Paradise, signifying honour, comfort, and luxury. The imagery of "couches raised high" suggests a setting of dignity and prestige, where the inhabitants of Paradise can relax and enjoy their rewards in a majestic and comfortable manner.

The elevated nature of these couches conveys a sense of prominence and distinction, reflecting the elevated status of those who have been rewarded with Paradise. It implies a life of ease and restfulness, free from the hardships and struggles of the worldly life.

Overall, the verse contributes to the portrayal of Paradise as a place of ultimate comfort, honour, and eternal joy, reinforcing the message of reward for those who have led a life of faith and righteousness.

Verse 14

Wa akwaabum mawdoo'ah

"And cups put in place."

This verse describes cups or vessels that are readily available and arranged for the inhabitants of Paradise. The imagery of "cups put in place" suggests an environment where everything is perfectly arranged for convenience and enjoyment. These cups are likely filled with delightful drinks, representing abundance and the ease with which the residents of Paradise can access what they desire.

The mention of cups being set out implies a setting of hospitality and readiness, where all needs and pleasures are anticipated and immediately met. This contributes to the overall sense of luxury, ease, and satisfaction that characterizes the life in Paradise.

This verse, along with the surrounding verses, emphasizes the idea that Paradise is a place of perfect and endless comfort, with every detail carefully prepared to ensure the ultimate pleasure and contentment of its inhabitants.

Verse 15

Wa namaariqu masfoofah

"And cushions set in rows."

This verse continues the description of the comforts and luxuries in Paradise. It portrays an image of cushions arranged in an orderly fashion, indicating a setting of comfort and relaxation. The arrangement of cushions "set in rows" suggests an environment of hospitality and leisure, where the inhabitants of Paradise can recline and converse in a tranquil and pleasant atmosphere.

The imagery of cushions set in rows reflects the meticulous preparation and attention to detail in Paradise, ensuring that everything is perfectly arranged for the enjoyment and satisfaction of its residents. This depiction adds to the overall picture of Paradise as a place of ultimate comfort and eternal happiness, where every need and desire is fulfilled in the most delightful manner.

Verse 16

Wa zaraabiyyu mabsoosah

"And carpets spread around."

This verse highlights the presence of carpets spread out, adding to the imagery of comfort and opulence in Paradise. The mention of "carpets spread around" suggests an environment that is inviting and beautifully arranged, enhancing the ambiance of relaxation and ease for the inhabitants of Paradise.

The spread carpets symbolize luxury and meticulous preparation, ensuring that the residents of Paradise experience ultimate comfort and aesthetic pleasure. This detail contributes to the overall portrayal of Paradise as a place of extraordinary beauty, comfort, and eternal joy, where every aspect is designed to provide complete satisfaction and delight.

These verses, focusing on the luxurious details of Paradise, serve to motivate and inspire believers to live a life of righteousness and faith, with the promise of such rewards in the Hereafter.

Verse 17

Afalaa yanzuroona ilalibili kaifa khuliqat

"Do they not look at the camels—how they are created?"

This verse invites people to contemplate the creation of the camel, an animal that held great significance in the daily lives of the people in the Arabian Peninsula. The camel is particularly noteworthy due to its unique adaptations that allow it to thrive in harsh desert conditions, such as its ability to go without water for extended periods and its specialized body structure.

By posing the question, "Do they not look at the camels—how they are created?" the verse encourages individuals to observe and reflect on the intricate design and functionality of the camel as a sign of divine wisdom and power. This reflection is intended to inspire recognition of Allah's creative excellence and to foster a sense of gratitude and awe for the Creator.

This verse, along with the subsequent verses that also highlight various aspects of creation, serves as a reminder to consider the natural world as a source of spiritual insight and understanding, urging people to recognize the signs of Allah in the world around them.

Verse 18

Wa ilas samaaa'i kaifa rufi'at

"And at the sky—how it is raised high?"

This verse encourages contemplation of the sky, emphasizing its vastness and the way it is elevated above the earth without any visible support. The sky's grandeur and expanse serve as a powerful reminder of Allah's creative power and the meticulous order within the universe.

By urging people to consider "how it is raised high," the verse highlights the sky's stability and the intricate balance maintained in creation. This reflection is meant to inspire awe and recognition of Allah's sovereignty and mastery over all things.

The verse encourages believers and listeners to look beyond the mundane and appreciate the signs of divine craftsmanship present in the natural world. This contemplation fosters a deeper understanding of Allah's presence and encourages gratitude and humility in acknowledgment of His greatness.

Verse 19

Wa ilal jibaali kaifa nusibat

"And at the mountains—how they are set up?"

This verse invites people to ponder the creation of mountains, focusing on their stability and grandeur. Mountains are often seen as symbols of strength and permanence, and their presence across the earth serves as a testament to the power and precision of Allah's creation.

By asking people to consider "how they are set up," the verse highlights the deliberate and purposeful design of mountains, which play a crucial role in maintaining the ecological balance of the earth. Their formation and the way they are anchored in the earth reflect Allah's wisdom and mastery over creation.

This reflection on mountains, along with the other natural phenomena mentioned in the surrounding verses, encourages individuals to recognize the signs of divine power and to develop a sense of awe and gratitude towards the Creator. It serves as a reminder of the importance of observing and contemplating the natural world to gain spiritual insight and reinforce faith.

Verse 20

Wa ilal ardi kaifa sutihat

"And at the earth—how it is spread out?"

In this verse, the Quran invites people to contemplate the earth and consider how it has been spread out and made suitable for life. The earth's vast plains and varied landscapes are designed to support human habitation and the needs of all living beings.

By directing attention to "how it is spread out," the verse emphasizes the earth's functionality, stability, and the ease it provides for traveling, cultivating, and building. This reflection is meant to inspire recognition of Allah's wisdom and precision in creating an environment perfectly suited for life.

The verse is part of a larger call to observe and appreciate the signs of divine wisdom in the natural world. It encourages individuals to look beyond the ordinary and recognize the intricate design and balance in creation, which point to the existence and greatness of Allah. This reflection fosters a sense of gratitude, humility, and awareness of the Creator's presence and power.

Verse 21

Fazakkir innama anta Muzakkir

"So remind, [O Muhammad]; you are only a reminder."

This verse addresses the Prophet Muhammad, instructing him to continue his mission of reminding people of the truth. The verse emphasizes that the Prophet's primary role is to deliver the message and remind people of their duties to Allah, the reality of the Hereafter, and the signs evident in the natural world and divine revelation.

The phrase "you are only a reminder" underscores that the Prophet's task is to convey the message clearly and persuasively, but he is not responsible for people's responses or for compelling them to believe. Guidance and acceptance ultimately depend on the individual's willingness and Allah's will.

This verse serves as both an instruction and an encouragement to the Prophet, affirming the importance of his mission and the need for perseverance in the face of challenges. It also reminds the audience of the significance of the message being delivered and the responsibility to heed the reminders given by the Prophet.

Verse 22

Lasta 'alaihim bimusaitir

"You are not a controller over them."

This verse reiterates the idea presented in the previous verse, emphasizing that the Prophet Muhammad's role is solely to deliver the message and remind people of their obligations to Allah. The phrase "You are not a controller over them" highlights that the Prophet is not responsible for compelling people to accept the message or to ensure their belief and obedience.

The verse underscores the notion of free will in matters of faith and belief. While the Prophet is tasked with conveying the message clearly and effectively, individuals are ultimately responsible for their responses and choices. Guidance and belief are matters of the heart, influenced by one's own willingness and Allah's guidance.

This verse serves as a reminder of the Prophet's mission and the limits of his responsibility. It also encourages patience and perseverance in the face of resistance or rejection, reinforcing that the ultimate accountability rests with each individual.

Verse 23

"Except for he who turns away and disbelieves."

This verse specifies an exception to the general statement made in the previous verse about the Prophet not being a controller over the people. It acknowledges that there will be those who consciously choose to turn away from the message and persist in disbelief despite receiving the reminders and guidance.

The phrase "Except for he who turns away and disbelieves" highlights the personal responsibility of individuals for their reaction to the message. While the Prophet's role is to convey the message, those who actively reject it and choose disbelief are accountable for their choices.

This verse serves as a reminder that while guidance is offered, acceptance is not guaranteed, and each person is responsible for their decisions regarding faith. It underscores the importance of personal accountability in matters of belief and the consequences of turning away from the truth.

Verse 24

Fa yu'azzibuhul laahul 'azaabal akbar

"Then Allah will punish him with the greatest punishment."

This verse warns of the severe consequences awaiting those who turn away from the message of Islam and persist in disbelief. "The greatest punishment" refers to the punishment in the Hereafter, which is more severe and enduring than any worldly suffering.

The verse serves as a reminder of the seriousness of rejecting the divine message after it has been clearly conveyed. It underscores the ultimate accountability to Allah and the reality of the consequences in the afterlife for those who choose disbelief.

This warning aims to encourage reflection and reconsideration among those who are indifferent or hostile to the message. It also reinforces the importance of the Prophet Muhammad's mission to remind and guide people, while ultimately emphasizing that each individual is responsible for their own choices and their consequences.

Verse 25

Innaa ilainaaa iyaabahum

"Indeed, to Us is their return."

This verse emphasizes the ultimate return of all individuals to Allah. It serves as a reminder that, regardless of one's actions or beliefs in this world, every person will ultimately return to their Creator. This return signifies the moment when individuals will be held accountable for their deeds and face the consequences, whether reward or punishment, based on their choices in life.

The verse reinforces the concept of divine justice and accountability, reminding believers and disbelievers alike that their earthly actions are not without consequence. The inevitability of returning to Allah serves as a powerful motivator for individuals to reflect on their lives, make righteous choices, and adhere to the guidance provided by the Prophet Muhammad.

Overall, this verse underscores the transient nature of worldly life and the permanence of the Hereafter, urging people to live with an awareness of their ultimate return to Allah.

Verse 26

Summa inna 'alainaa hisaabahum

"And at the earth—how it is spread out?"

In this verse, the Quran invites people to contemplate the earth and consider how it has been spread out and made suitable for life. The earth's vast plains and varied landscapes are designed to support human habitation and the needs of all living beings.

By directing attention to "how it is spread out," the verse emphasizes the earth's functionality, stability, and the ease it provides for traveling, cultivating, and building. This reflection is meant to inspire recognition of Allah's wisdom and precision in creating an environment perfectly suited for life.

The verse is part of a larger call to observe and appreciate the signs of divine wisdom in the natural world. It encourages individuals to look beyond the ordinary and recognize the intricate design and balance in creation, which point to the existence and greatness of Allah. This reflection fosters a sense of gratitude, humility, and awareness of the Creator's presence and power.

LEESONS TO BE LEARNT FROM SURAH AL GHASHIYA

Surah Al-Ghashiya, the 88th chapter of the Quran, offers several profound lessons and reflections for believers. Here are some key teachings and lessons that can be drawn from this Surah:

11. Awareness of the Hereafter: The Surah begins by describing the events of the Day of Judgment, emphasizing the reality of the Hereafter. It serves as a reminder to live with an awareness of the eternal consequences of our actions.
12. The Fate of the Believers and Disbelievers: The Surah contrasts the fates of the righteous and the disbelievers, highlighting the bliss and rewards awaiting the former and the punishment that awaits the latter. This contrast encourages individuals to strive for righteousness and avoid actions leading to regret in the afterlife.
13. Reflection on Creation: Verses in the Surah invite believers to contemplate the natural world, including the creation of camels, the sky, mountains, and the earth. This reflection is intended to inspire awe and recognition of Allah's power and wisdom, fostering a deeper appreciation for the Creator.
14. The Prophet's Role: The Surah underscores the role of the Prophet Muhammad as a messenger tasked with reminding people of the truth. It emphasizes that his duty is to convey the message clearly, while individuals are responsible for their responses.
15. Personal Accountability: Throughout the Surah, there is a strong emphasis on personal responsibility and accountability. Each individual is reminded that they will return to Allah and be judged based on their actions and choices in this life.
16. Encouragement for Patience and Perseverance: The Prophet and believers are reminded that their responsibility is to communicate the message, not to compel belief. This encourages patience and perseverance in the face of rejection or disbelief.
17. Gratitude and Humility: By reflecting on the wonders of creation and the blessings provided by Allah, believers are encouraged to cultivate gratitude and humility, recognizing their dependence on the Creator.

Overall, Surah Al-Ghashiya serves as a powerful reminder of the transient nature of worldly life, the certainty of the Hereafter, and the importance of living a life aligned with divine guidance. It encourages reflection, gratitude, and a sincere commitment to righteousness.

SUMMARY OF AL-GHASHIYA

The Surah gets its name from the word "al-ghishiyah" found in the first verse.

Time of Revelation

The topics covered in this Surah suggest it was revealed early on when the Prophet Muhammad (peace be upon him) began openly sharing his message. At that time, the people of Makkah were hearing his message but ignoring it without much thought.

Main Ideas

To understand the message of the Surah, it's important to know that early on, the Prophet focused on two main ideas: the oneness of Allah (Tauhid) and the Hereafter. The people of Makkah were rejecting both ideas. Let's look at what this Surah talks about and how it presents its message.

The Surah begins by asking people if they know about a time when a great disaster will happen. It goes on to describe this event, explaining that people will be split into two groups: one group will end up in Hell and face punishment, while the other will go to a wonderful Paradise and enjoy blessings.

After this warning, the Surah shifts focus, asking why people who doubt the teachings about Allah's oneness and the Hereafter don't pay attention to everyday things. For instance, how camels, essential to their desert life, are perfectly made for their needs. It asks them to think about the sky, mountains, and earth and consider how they came to be. Did all these things come about without a wise and powerful Creator? If they believe that a Creator made all of this, why don't they accept Him as their only Lord? And if they believe that Allah has the power to create everything, why do they doubt His ability to resurrect people or create Heaven and Hell?

After explaining the truth with clear reasoning, the Surah addresses the Prophet. It tells him that if people don't accept the truth, he shouldn't force them. His job is only to remind and warn them. In the end, everyone will return to Allah, who will judge them and punish those who don't believe.

SURAH AL-GHASHIYA. SURAH 88

Questions

1. What does the term "Al-Ghashiya" refer to, and why is the surah named after it?
2. How are the faces of the disbelievers described on the Day of Judgment in Surah Al-Ghashiya?
3. What specific punishments are mentioned for those who turn away from the truth?
4. How are the faces of the believers depicted on the Day of Judgment in this surah?
5. What rewards are promised to the believers in Paradise according to Surah Al-Ghashiya?
6. Which natural phenomena and creations does the surah encourage people to reflect upon?
7. How does the surah emphasize the power and capability of Allah through His creations?
8. What is the role of the Prophet Muhammad (peace be upon him) as outlined in this surah?
9. How does the surah address the concept of accountability and the inevitability of the Day of Judgment?
10. What lessons can be drawn from Surah Al-Ghashiya about living a life that aligns with divine guidance?

Answers

1. What does the term "Al-Ghashiya" refer to, and why is the surah named after it?
   - "Al-Ghashiya" refers to "the overwhelming event," which is the Day of Judgment. The surah is named after it to highlight the inevitable and all-encompassing nature of that day.

2. How are the faces of the disbelievers described on the Day of Judgment in Surah Al-Ghashiya?
   - The faces of the disbelievers are described as humbled and weary, indicating their regret and suffering due to their actions in the worldly life.

3. What specific punishments are mentioned for those who turn away from the truth?
   - The surah mentions that they will suffer in a scorching fire and be given boiling water to drink, symbolizing intense punishment for their disbelief.

4. How are the faces of the believers depicted on the Day of Judgment in this surah?
   - The faces of the believers are depicted as radiant and joyful, reflecting their satisfaction and happiness due to their righteous deeds.

5. What rewards are promised to the believers in Paradise according to Surah Al-Ghashiya?
   - The surah promises that believers will enjoy soft couches, delicious drinks, and other comforts in a blissful environment.

6. Which natural phenomena and creations does the surah encourage people to reflect upon?
   - The surah encourages reflection on the creation of the camels, the sky, the mountains, and the earth, urging people to recognize the signs of Allah's power and wisdom.

7. How does the surah emphasize the power and capability of Allah through His creations?
   - By highlighting the complexity and beauty of natural phenomena, the surah emphasizes Allah's supreme power and capability as the Creator of all things.

8. What is the role of the Prophet Muhammad (peace be upon him) as outlined in this surah?
   - The surah outlines his role as a warner and a reminder, emphasizing his responsibility to convey the message of Allah and remind people of the consequences of their actions.

9. How does the surah address the concept of accountability and the inevitability of the Day of Judgment?
   - The surah asserts that everyone will be questioned about their deeds, reinforcing the concept of accountability and the certainty of the Day of Judgment.

10. What lessons can be drawn from Surah Al-Ghashiya about living a life that aligns with divine guidance?
    - The surah teaches the importance of reflecting on the signs of Allah, acknowledging the consequences of one's actions, and striving for righteousness to achieve success in the hereafter.

These questions and answers can be used for educational purposes, study sessions, or discussions to enhance understanding of Surah Al-Ghashiya.

Multiple Choice Questions

1. What does the term "Al-Ghashiya" refer to?

    - A) The blessed night

    - B) The overwhelming event

    - C) The peaceful morning

    - D) The day of victory

2. How are the faces of the disbelievers described on the Day of Judgment in Surah Al-Ghashiya?

    - A) Happy and radiant

    - B) Laughing and joyful

    - C) Humbled and weary

    - D) Confident and proud

3. What specific punishments are mentioned for those who turn away from the truth?

    - A) Eternal darkness

    - B) Isolation and loneliness

    - C) Scorching fire and boiling water

    - D) Endless wandering

4. How are the faces of the believers depicted on the Day of Judgment in this surah?

    - A) Gloomy and fearful

    - B) Radiant and joyful

    - C) Tired and anxious

    - D) Indifferent and calm

5. What rewards are promised to the believers in Paradise according to Surah Al-Ghashiya?

    - A) Gardens and flowing rivers

    - B) Palaces and treasures

    - C) Soft couches and delicious drinks

    - D) Endless wealth and power

6. Which natural phenomena does the surah encourage people to reflect upon?

    - A) The rising sun and moon

    - B) The stars and planets

    - C) The mountains, sky, and earth

    - D) The oceans and seas

7. What is the role of the Prophet Muhammad (peace be upon him) as outlined in this surah?

    - A) He is a ruler over people

    - B) He is a warner and reminder

    - C) He is a judge and arbitrator

    - D) He is a miracle worker

8. How does the surah address the concept of accountability?

    - A) By emphasizing personal responsibility

    - B) By stating that everyone will be questioned

    - C) By denying the Day of Judgment

    - D) By promising forgiveness for all

Answers

1. *Answer:* B) The overwhelming event
2. *Answer:* C) Humbled and weary
3. *Answer:* C) Scorching fire and boiling water
4. *Answer:* B) Radiant and joyful
5. *Answer:* C) Soft couches and delicious drinks
6. *Answer:* C) The mountains, sky, and earth
7. *Answer:* B) He is a warner and reminder
8. *Answer:* B) By stating that everyone will be questioned

These multiple-choice questions and answers can be used for educational purposes, quizzes, or self-study to enhance understanding of Surah Al-Ghashiya.

SURAH
AL-FAJIR

SURAH AL-FAJIR

Bismillahi ar-Rahmani ar-Raheem

Verse 1

Wal-Fajr

"By the break of Day"

Allah swears by the dawn (Fajr), signifying a new beginning and the start of a new day. This oath emphasizes the importance of the time of Fajr and its connection to seeking sustenance and divine blessings. Some interpretations also relate it to the Fajr prayer specifically.

The dawn symbolizes a new beginning, both in the natural world with the start of a new day, and potentially in a spiritual sense, with the potential for renewed faith and action.

The time of Fajr is often associated with people going out to seek their daily provision, making it a time of effort and activity.

Some scholars connect the oath to the Fajr prayer specifically, highlighting its importance and the presence of angels who witness the prayer.

The verse highlights that time is a valuable resource, and the time of Fajr is a special time for seeking Allah's blessings and engaging in righteous deeds.

Verse 2

Wa layaalin 'ashr

By the Nights twice five"

This refers to the ten nights of Dhul-Hijjah, the month of the Hajj pilgrimage. These days are considered highly significant in Islam, with righteous deeds performed during them being especially beloved to Allah.

The verse begins with an oath, which Allah uses to draw attention to something important. In this case, the oath is by the dawn and the ten nights.

These days are highlighted as a period when good deeds are particularly cherished by Allah.

Many scholars and commentators link these nights to the Hajj pilgrimage, as it is a time when millions of Muslims travel to Mecca to perform the rituals.

The verse serves as a reminder for Muslims to maximize their worship and good deeds during these blessed days, seeking closeness to Allah and His love.

Verse 3

Wash shaf'i wal watr

"By the even and odd (contrasted)"

This discusses the concept of "even and odd" as a form of oath, suggesting that Allah swears by the pairs and the singular in His creation. The verse is interpreted as highlighting the duality and unity in the universe, emphasizing that everything exists in pairs except for Allah, who is the One.

Surah Al-Fajr begins with oaths, specifically by the dawn, the ten nights, and then by the even and the odd (shaf' and watr).

- **Interpretation of "shaf' and watr":**

This is understood in several ways:

  - **All creation in pairs:** Some scholars interpret "shaf'" as referring to everything Allah created in pairs (e.g., day and night, male and female, sun and moon), and "watr" as referring to the One, Allah Himself.

  - **Specific days of Hajj:** Others connect "shaf' and watr" to specific days of Hajj, with the even days representing the days of ritual and the odd day being the Day of Arafah, which is considered a unique and distinct day.

  - **General concept of duality:** Ultimately, the verse points to a general concept of duality in creation, with Allah as the ultimate singular entity.

- **Purpose of the oath:**

The oaths in the beginning of the surah serve to draw attention to the significance of the verses that follow, emphasizing the consequences of actions and the eventual reckoning.

- **Connection to the rest of the surah:**

The oaths, including the one by the even and the odd, are followed by verses that discuss the destruction of past nations (Ad, Thamud, Pharaoh) for their disobedience and corruption. This comparison highlights the idea that actions have consequences and that Allah is watchful of His creation.

Verse 4

Wallaili izaa yasr

"And by the Night when it passeth away"

This verse is part of Allah's oath, emphasizing the significance of the night. Here, Allah is swearing by the night when it concludes or passes away.

The night represents a time of rest and tranquility, but it also passes away, making way for the dawn. This passage of the night signifies the natural cycle of time that Allah Has created. It reminds us that everything in life, including darkness and hardship, is temporary and part of Allah's divine plan.

Meaning and Reflection:

By swearing by the night when it ends, Allah draws attention to the temporary nature of difficulties and dark times. Just as the night passes and gives way to the light of dawn, hardships in life will also pass, bringing relief and hope. This serves as a reminder for believers to be patient during tough times and to trust in Allah's mercy.

The verse encourages us to reflect on the passing of the night as a sign of Allah's control over the cycles of time, and as a reminder that difficulties don't last forever. Peace and relief will come with the arrival of dawn.

Verse 5

Hal fee zaalika qasamul lizee hijr

"Have there not been in aiding of the heavens and the earth signs for those who believe?"

This verse encourages us to reflect on the signs in the universe—specifically, the heavens (sky, stars, planets) and the earth—to recognize Allah's existence and His power.

Allah is asking, "Haven't there been clear signs in the way the sky and the earth are created and maintained?" These signs include the stars, the sun, the moon, the mountains, rivers, and other natural formations. They all function in perfect harmony and show evidence of Allah's great wisdom and power.

What does it mean?

It means that for those who believe, these signs should serve as proof of Allah's existence and His control over everything. The universe's design and order are signs that point us toward recognizing Allah's greatness. For believers, contemplating these signs helps strengthen faith and trust in Allah.

In conclusion, the verse reminds us to look at the universe thoughtfully and realize that its existence is evidence of a powerful Creator. It encourages believers to reflect on Allah's creation as proof of His divine presence, which should increase their faith.

Verse 6

Alam tara kaifa fa'ala rabbuka bi'aad

"Seest thou not how thy Lord dealt with the 'Ad (people)"

"Have you not considered how your Lord dealt with 'Aad?"**

This verse is a question posed by Allah, inviting us to reflect on the story of the people of 'Aad.

In this verse, Allah is asking if we have thought about what happened to the ancient tribe of 'Aad. The people of 'Aad were known for their strength, wealth, and pride. They were a powerful nation that rejected Allah's message and defied His laws. As a result, Allah sent a severe wind that destroyed them completely.

This verse encourages us to think about how Allah dealt with a mighty, arrogant nation that ignored His signs and disobeyed His messengers. It reminds us that no matter how strong or wealthy a nation becomes, Allah's power is greater, and those who oppose Him will face consequences.

Verse 7

Iramaa zaatil 'imaad

"Of the (city of) Iram, with lofty pillars"

This verse continues to tell us about the tribe of `Aad and their city Iram, known for its lofty pillars. The verse highlights their strength and architectural prowess, but also implicitly their arrogance and transgression, as they are mentioned in the context of Allah's power and judgment.

Their city Iram was famous for its towering structures and architectural achievements. The phrase "lofty pillars" (or "with many-columned Iram") is used to describe the city's impressive buildings.

The verse is not just about describing a historical tribe but also symbolizes the dangers of arrogance, excessive pride in worldly achievements, and the eventual consequences of defying divine authority.

In essence, verse 7 uses the example of `Aad and Iram to warn against the pitfalls of pride and transgression, emphasizing that even the most powerful civilizations are subject to Allah's judgment.

Verse 8

Allatee lam yukhlaq misluhaa fil bilaad

"The likes of whom have never been created in the Land"

The verse continues to describe the ancient tribe of 'Aad, specifically their physical strength and architectural prowess, stating that such a people had not been created before in the land.

The phrase "the likes of whom had never been created in the land" emphasizes that the 'Ad were unparalleled in their time, both in terms of physical stature and their ability to build towering structures, such as those with lofty pillars.

By mentioning the 'Aad and their destruction, the verse encourages believers to reflect on the transient nature of worldly power and to strive for righteousness and submission to Allah.

Verse 9

Wa samoodal lazeena jaabus sakhra bil waad

"And [with] Thamud, who carved out the rocks in the valley?".

This verse refers to the people of Thamud, an ancient Arab tribe known for their skill in carving dwellings from the rocks in the valley. The verse prompts reflection on how Allah dealt with them, highlighting their specific transgression and the consequences they faced.

The Thamud are a people known for their architectural prowess in carving homes and structures into the mountains and cliffs, particularly in the valley.

The phrase "carved out the rocks in the valley" points to their unique ability to shape the landscape to their needs.

They existed after the people of `Aad.

By questioning what happened to the Thamud, the verse encourages believers to learn from the past and avoid the mistakes that led to their downfall.

Verse 10

Wa fir'awna zil awtaad

"And with Pharaoh, holder of the stakes."

This verse refers to Pharaoh, the ruler of Egypt in the time of Prophet Moses. The phrase "holder of the stakes" (or "lord of the stakes") is understood by scholars as describing a specific method of punishment used by Pharaoh or his officials.

Historically, during Pharaoh's reign, some of his punishments for enemies or for those who opposed him involved the use of stakes or poles. These could have been used to execute or intimidate people, such as impaling or displaying enemies on stakes.

In the context of the Quran, this phrase symbolizes Pharaoh's cruelty, arrogance, and oppressive power. It highlights how tyrants often use brutal measures to suppress others and enforce their authority.

The verse draws a comparison between the story of Prophet Moses and Pharaoh's tyranny, reminding us of the severe punishment and tyranny led by Pharaoh against his enemies and oppressed people. It serves as a warning about injustice, cruelty, and defying Allah's commandments.

Verse 11

Allazeena taghaw fil bilaad

All of whom oppressed within the lands"—we can understand it in the context of the stories of past nations such as the people of Aad, Thamud, and Pharaoh.

These communities are prime examples of oppressed peoples who acted unjustly and arrogantly in their lands. The people of Aad were known for their arrogance and pride, living in tall structures and defying Allah's commandments. Despite their strength, Allah sent a fierce wind to destroy them because of their oppression and disbelief.

The people of Thamud were similarly a powerful civilization that rejected the signs of Allah and mistreated their Prophet Salih. Their arrogance and immoral behaviour led to their punishment, which included a mighty earthquake and a loud sound that destroyed their city.

Pharaoh, the ruler of Egypt, oppressed the people ruthlessly. His tyranny included slavery, cruelty, and the attempted killing of Prophet Moses, along with arrogance in denying Allah's message. His oppressive rule and injustice ultimately led to his drowning in the Red Sea when he pursued Moses and the believers.

Verse 11 reminds us that past civilizations—Aad, Thamud, and Pharaoh—oppressed others within their lands through arrogance, cruelty, and disbelief. Their oppression and unjust actions resulted in Allah's severe punishment, serving as a warning for us today to avoid tyranny and to uphold justice and righteousness.

Verse 12

Fa aksaroo feehal fasaad

"And brought about great corruption therein"

Verse 12 Quran refers to the actions of past nations that were destroyed due to their excessive corruption and wrongdoing. The verse is part of a passage that recounts the fate of ancient peoples who defied divine guidance and engaged in widespread corruption. Specifically, this verse highlights the behaviour of those who contributed to moral and social decay, leading to their eventual downfall.

The context of this verse is important to understand its message. Surah Al-Fajr addresses themes of divine retribution and the consequences of human arrogance and corruption. It serves as a reminder of the fate that befell previous communities that ignored the warnings of their prophets and continued in their unjust and oppressive ways.

The "great corruption" mentioned in the verse can be interpreted as encompassing various forms of moral, social, and economic injustices that these communities engaged in. This corruption could include oppression, deceit, exploitation, and other actions that undermine social harmony and violate ethical principles.

Overall, this verse serves as a cautionary reminder of the importance of righteousness and justice, emphasizing that societies that perpetuate corruption and ignore moral guidance are ultimately subject to divine accountability.

Verse 13

Fasabba 'alaihim Rabbuka sawta 'azaab

"And therefore thy sustainer let loose upon them a scourge of suffering"

Verse 13 of Surah Al-Fajr continues the narrative from the previous verses, describing the consequences faced by those nations that engaged in great corruption. This verse states that as a result of their persistent wrongdoing and moral decay, Allah unleashed a "scourge of suffering" upon them.

The term "scourge of suffering" refers to the divine punishment or calamities that befell these communities as a consequence of their actions. This punishment serves as a direct response to their defiance and corruption, highlighting the principle of divine justice. The specific form of suffering or calamity is not detailed in this verse, but it is understood to be a severe and fitting response to their transgressions.

In the broader context of Surah Al-Fajr, these verses serve as a warning to all readers about the consequences of turning away from righteousness and engaging in unjust practices. They illustrate the Quranic theme that societies which indulge in corruption and ignore the moral and ethical guidance provided by Allah are ultimately held accountable.

The passage encourages reflection on the importance of upholding justice, morality, and humility, underscoring the idea that enduring prosperity and success are contingent upon adherence to these values.

The term "scourge of suffering," as used in the context of Surah Al-Fajr, relates to the concept of divine justice by illustrating the principle that actions have consequences, particularly when it comes to moral and ethical conduct. In the Quranic worldview, Allah is portrayed as just and fair, rewarding righteousness and punishing wrongdoing. The "scourge of suffering" serves as a manifestation of this divine justice, where those who engage in persistent corruption and defiance of Allah's guidance are subject to punishment.

This concept of divine justice is central to many narratives in the Quran, where past communities that indulged in wrongdoing faced severe repercussions. These stories serve as moral and spiritual lessons for readers, emphasizing that while individuals and societies have the free will to choose their actions, they are ultimately accountable to Allah for those choices.

Divine justice, as represented by the "scourge of suffering," is meant to remind believers of the importance of adhering to ethical and moral principles. It underscores the idea that while Allah's mercy and forgiveness are abundant, there is also a clear expectation for humans to strive towards justice and righteousness. The consequences faced by corrupt nations serve as cautionary tales highlighting that persistent injustice and moral decay can lead to divine retribution.

Verse 14

Inna Rabbaka labil mirsaad

"For verily, thy sustainer is ever on the watch"

This verse emphasizes Allah's constant awareness and vigilance over His creation. It serves as a reminder that nothing escapes Allah's notice, including the actions and intentions of individuals and communities.

In the context of the preceding verses, which discuss the consequences faced by corrupt nations, this verse underscores the idea that Allah is fully aware of human behaviour and the moral state of societies. It reassures believers that justice will ultimately be served, as Allah observes everything with complete knowledge and wisdom.

The phrase "ever on the watch" conveys the notion of Allah's omnipresence and omniscience. It highlights that Allah is not distant or detached but is actively engaged in overseeing the moral order of the universe. This awareness serves both as a source of comfort for those who strive for righteousness and as a warning for those who engage in wrongdoing.

Ultimately, this verse reinforces the concept of accountability, reminding individuals that their actions are observed and will be judged by Allah. It encourages believers to maintain a sense of moral responsibility and integrity, knowing that they are always in the presence of their Sustainer.

Verse 15

Fa ammal insaanu izaa mab talaahu Rabbuhoo fa akramahoo wa na' 'amahoo fa yaqoolu Rabbeee akraman

"But as for man, whenever his Sustainer tries him by His generosity and by letting him enjoy a life of ease, he says, 'My Sustainer has been [justly] generous towards me.'"

Verse 15 addresses a common human tendency in the way people perceive prosperity and adversity. The verse highlights how individuals often interpret their circumstances, particularly when they experience ease and abundance.

This verse points to the tendency of people to equate material success and comfort with divine favour. When individuals are granted prosperity and ease, they may interpret these blessings as a sign that Allah is pleased with them. This mindset can lead to a superficial understanding of one's relationship with Allah, where material wealth is seen as the primary indicator of divine approval.

However, the use of the word "tries" in this verse is significant. It indicates that prosperity is a form of test from Allah, just as adversity is. The test lies in how individuals react to blessings: whether they remain grateful, humble, and just, or whether they become arrogant and complacent, forgetting their responsibilities and duties towards others and Allah.

The Quran often emphasizes that both prosperity and hardship are tests of faith and character. This verse serves as a reminder that material wealth and comfort are not inherently indicative of one's moral or spiritual standing. Instead, it urges individuals to maintain gratitude, humility, and righteousness regardless of their material circumstances. True success in the Quranic sense is measured by one's faith, character, and actions rather than material possessions.

Verse 16

Wa ammaaa izaa mabtalaahu faqadara 'alaihi rizqahoo fa yaqoolu Rabbeee ahaanan

Verse 16 complements the previous verse by highlighting the contrasting human response to adversity. It reads: "whereas, whenever He tries him by straitening his means of livelihood, he says, 'My Sustainer has disgraced me!'"

This verse illustrates how people often misinterpret hardship and challenges. When individuals face difficulties, such as financial constraints or a lack of resources, they might perceive these conditions as a sign of divine displeasure or disgrace. This reflects a common human tendency to view material success and failure as direct indicators of one's standing with Allah.

The verse continues to emphasize the idea that both prosperity and adversity are tests from Allah. The "straitening of means" is another form of trial, intended to test a person's patience, resilience, and faith. Just as prosperity should not lead to arrogance or complacency, adversity should not lead to despair or a loss of faith.

The underlying message of verses 15 and 16 is to encourage a deeper understanding of one's relationship with Allah, beyond material circumstances. It calls for maintaining faith, gratitude, and integrity in both good times and bad, recognizing that material conditions are temporary and not the ultimate measure of one's spiritual worth or divine favour.

In essence, these verses remind believers to look beyond the surface and understand that life's ups and downs are part of a broader divine plan, serving as opportunities for spiritual growth and development. The true measure of success lies in how one responds to these tests, maintaining trust in Allah and striving to uphold moral and ethical conduct.

Verse 17

Kalla bal laa tukrimooo nal yateem

Verse 17 shifts the focus from the abstract concepts of prosperity and adversity to concrete actions, emphasizing moral and social responsibilities. The verse states: "But nay, nay, [O men, consider all that you do and fail to do:] you are not generous towards the orphan."

This verse calls attention to a specific moral failing: the lack of generosity and care for orphans. In the context of the Quran, orphans often symbolize the vulnerable and marginalized members of society who require protection and assistance. Caring for orphans is frequently highlighted in Islamic teachings as a significant moral obligation.

By pointing out the neglect of orphans, the verse critiques those who, despite their material wealth or comfort, fail to fulfill their social responsibilities. It serves as a reminder that true righteousness is not solely about one's personal relationship with Allah but also about how one treats others, particularly the disadvantaged.

The mention of orphans underscores the broader Quranic theme of social justice and compassion. It urges believers to reflect on their actions and attitudes, highlighting the importance of generosity, empathy, and active support for those in need. This focus on social responsibility is a crucial aspect of living a life that aligns with Islamic values.

Overall, verse 17 is a call to action, encouraging individuals to go beyond superficial measures of success and instead prioritize ethical conduct and social welfare. It challenges people to assess their behaviour towards others, reminding them that fulfilling these responsibilities is an integral part of true faith and righteousness.

Islamic teachings place a strong emphasis on the moral obligations of believers towards the vulnerable members of society. These obligations are deeply rooted in the principles of justice, compassion, and community welfare.

Verse 18

Wa laa tahaaaddoona 'alaata'aamil miskeen

Verse 18 continues to address the moral shortcomings of individuals in their social responsibilities. It states: "and you do not urge one another to feed the needy."

This verse highlights the lack of collective encouragement and action in addressing the needs of the less fortunate, specifically the hungry and impoverished. It underscores the importance of not only individual acts of charity but also the communal responsibility to promote and facilitate support for those in need.

The phrase "urge one another" suggests that social responsibility is a shared obligation. It is not enough for individuals to act in isolation; there must be a community-wide culture of compassion and generosity. This involves actively encouraging and reminding each other to care for the needy, thereby fostering a society that prioritizes the welfare of all its members.

The emphasis on feeding the needy reflects a fundamental Islamic principle: ensuring that everyone's basic needs are met. Providing food to the hungry is one of the most direct and essential forms of assistance, addressing immediate physical needs and alleviating suffering.

This verse, like the ones preceding it, calls for self-reflection and action. It challenges individuals and communities to evaluate their priorities and behaviours, urging them to cultivate a spirit of empathy and solidarity. By doing so, they fulfill a core aspect of their faith, aligning with the Quranic vision of a just and compassionate society.

Overall, verse 18 reinforces the idea that true piety and righteousness are demonstrated not only through personal devotion but also through active engagement in uplifting and supporting those who are vulnerable and in need.

Providing food to the needy aligns closely with several fundamental Islamic principles, reflecting the religion's emphasis on compassion, justice, and community welfare.

Verse 19

Wa ta'kuloona at-turaatha aklan lammaa

"And you consume inheritance, devouring it altogether,"

This verse highlights a behaviour where people unjustly consume or seize the wealth and inheritance that rightfully belongs to others. It criticizes those who greedily take over the inheritances of others, often leaving the rightful heirs, such as orphans and the vulnerable, without their due share. This behaviour is condemned as it reflects greed and a lack of social justice, which are contrary to Islamic values.

In the broader context of Surah Al-Fajr, these verses serve as a reminder of the moral and ethical decay that can occur when people prioritize material wealth and power over fairness, equity, and compassion. The Surah as a whole calls for reflection on the consequences of such actions and the importance of adhering to divine guidance.

Verse 20
Wa tuḥibboonal-maala ḥubban jammā

"And you love wealth with immense love."

This verse points out the intense love and attachment that some people have for wealth. It highlights a materialistic attitude where acquiring and accumulating wealth becomes a primary focus, often at the expense of ethical and moral values.

In the context of the Surah, this verse serves as a caution against allowing the love of wealth to overshadow one's duties to others and to Allah. It emphasizes the importance of balancing material pursuits with spiritual and moral responsibilities, and it warns against the potential consequences of unchecked greed and materialism. The broader message is a reminder to use wealth in a way that is just and beneficial to society, rather than hoarding it or using it solely for personal gain.

Kallā 'idhā dukkati l-'arḍu dakkan dakkan

"No! When the earth has been leveled, pounded and crushed,"

This verse introduces a scene of the Day of Judgment, emphasizing the formidable and awe-inspiring events that will occur. The imagery of the earth being levelled and crushed serves as a powerful reminder of the ultimate reality that all worldly matters, including wealth and power, will come to an end. It underscores the insignificance of material possessions in the face of divine judgment and the inevitable transformation of the world.

The use of the word "Kallā" (No!) at the beginning of the verse serves as a strong refutation of the misguided priorities and false sense of security that people may have due to their love for wealth. It marks a transition from the critique of human behaviour to the consequences that await if they do not heed the warnings and change their ways.

In the broader context, this verse is a call to reflection and repentance, urging people to prepare for the afterlife by adhering to moral and ethical principles, rather than being consumed by material pursuits.

Verse 22
Wa jā'a rabbuka wa al-malaku ṣaffan ṣaffā

"And your Lord has come and the angels, rank upon rank,"

This verse describes a scene of divine majesty and orderliness on the Day of Judgment. The phrase "your Lord has come" is understood to mean the manifestation of Allah's command and authority, signifying the commencement of judgment. The depiction of angels arranged in ranks illustrates the structured and solemn nature of the proceedings on that day.

The imagery of angels standing in ranks signifies their readiness to fulfill Allah's commands and the organized manner in which the events of the Day of Judgment will unfold. It emphasizes the seriousness and the grandeur of the occasion, reminding people of the ultimate accountability before Allah.

In the broader context of Surah Al-Fajr, this verse serves as a powerful reminder of the reality of the afterlife and the inevitability of divine judgment. It calls on people to reflect on their actions and to live their lives in accordance with Allah's guidance, mindful of the ultimate consequences.

Verse 23

Wa jī'a yawma'idhin bi-jahannama; yawma'idhin yatadhakkaru l-insānu wa-annā lahu adh-dhikrā

"And Hell is brought [forth] that Day. On that Day, man will remember, but what good to him will be the remembrance?"

This verse vividly portrays the moment when Hell is brought into view on the Day of Judgment. It serves as a stark reminder of the reality and seriousness of the consequences awaiting those who have neglected their duties to Allah and humanity.

The phrase "man will remember" suggests that on that day, people will reflect on their past actions and realize the errors and missed opportunities for righteousness. However, the verse also points out the futility of such remembrance at that point, as it will be too late to change one's fate or rectify past wrongs.

In the broader context of Surah Al-Fajr, this verse underscores the importance of living a life of mindfulness and responsibility before it is too late. It calls on people to heed the warnings of the Quran and to act upon them while they still have the chance, rather than waiting until the Day of Judgment when regret will be of no benefit.

Verse 24

Yaqoolu yālaytanī qaddamtu li-ḥayātī

"He will say, 'Oh, I wish I had sent ahead [some good] for my life.'"

In this verse, the individual expresses deep regret and longing for having not prepared for the afterlife while they had the opportunity. The phrase "Oh, I wish" captures the despair and helplessness felt by those who realize too late that they squandered their chances to do good and secure a favourable outcome in the hereafter.

The use of the term "my life" shows the eternal nature of the afterlife compared to the transient nature of worldly life. It serves as a reminder that the true "life" is the one that comes after death, and the time spent in this world should be used to prepare for that eternal existence.

This verse reinforces the call to action for individuals to live righteously and to prioritize their spiritual and moral obligations over mere material pursuits. It serves as a poignant reminder to take advantage of the present to invest in one's future in the hereafter, avoiding the regret and sorrow depicted in this verse.

Verse 25

Fa yawma'idhin lā yuʿadhdhibu ʿadhābahū ʾaḥad

"So on that Day, none will punish [as severely] as His punishment,"

This verse underscores the unparalleled nature of Allah's punishment on the Day of Judgment. It conveys the idea that no one can inflict a punishment as severe and just as that which Allah will administer. The emphasis is on the unique and ultimate justice that will be executed by Allah against those who have committed wrongs and ignored the warnings provided to them.

This verse serves as a stern warning to those who persist in their wrongdoing and neglect their moral and spiritual responsibilities. It highlights the seriousness of divine retribution and the importance of living a life in accordance with Allah's guidance to avoid such severe consequences.

Together with the preceding verses, it calls on individuals to reflect on their actions and to make amends while they still have the opportunity, thereby avoiding the regret and punishment described in these passages.

Verse 26

Wa lā yūthiqu wathāqahū ʾaḥad

"And none will bind as severely as His binding [of the evildoers]."

This verse looks at the unparalleled nature of Allah's ability to bind or restrain those who have committed wrongs. Similar to the previous verse, it highlights the exclusivity and severity of divine retribution. The "binding" here can be understood as a metaphor for the inescapable and ultimate nature of Allah's justice, illustrating that no one can escape or mitigate the consequences of their actions when judged by Allah.

These verses serve as a strong reminder of the inevitable accountability that everyone will face. They highlight the importance of living a life aligned with divine principles, emphasizing that ignoring these principles will lead to severe consequences that only Allah can administer.

These verses collectively urge individuals to reflect on their lives, to act righteously, and to prepare for the ultimate judgment, avoiding the regret and punishment that await those who fail to do so.

Verse 27

Yā ʾayyatuhā an-nafsu l-muṭmaʾinnah

"[To the righteous it will be said], 'O reassured soul,'"

In this verse, Allah addresses the "reassured soul," a term that refers to the soul at peace, content, and secure in its faith and actions. This soul is characterized by its tranquility and certainty in the truth of Allah's guidance and the afterlife.

The verse serves as a comforting promise to those who have lived their lives in accordance with divine guidance, maintaining faith and righteousness even amidst life's challenges. It signifies a transition to the rewards and peace that await such individuals in the hereafter.

This verse provides a stark contrast to the preceding descriptions of regret and punishment. It highlights the ultimate reward for those who have been steadfast in their faith and have led a life of righteousness. The subsequent verses further elaborate on the blessings and honour that await the reassured soul in the presence of Allah.

Verse 28

Irjiʿī ʾilā rabbiki rāḍiyatan marḍiyyah

"Return to your Lord, well-pleased and pleasing [to Him]."

This verse is a divine invitation to the "reassured soul" to return to Allah. It is looking at a state of mutual satisfaction and acceptance: the soul is content and satisfied with its deeds and the rewards it is about to receive, and Allah is pleased with the soul's faithfulness and righteousness.

The phrase "well-pleased and pleasing" highlights a harmonious relationship between the servant and the Creator, where the soul's efforts in life are acknowledged and rewarded by Allah's grace. This mutual pleasure signifies the ultimate success and fulfillment for believers who have lived a life of devotion and integrity.

This verse, along with the surrounding verses, provides a hopeful and positive conclusion for those who adhere to divine guidance. It serves as an encouragement to strive for a life that leads to such a blessed state, contrasting sharply with the earlier verses that warn of the consequences of neglect and wrongdoing.

Verse 29

Fadkhulee fee 'ibaadee

"Enter among My servants."

This verse is part of a sequence where Allah addresses the soul that has achieved a state of inner peace and contentment.

In this context, "Enter among My servants" is an invitation for the soul to join the ranks of the righteous and faithful servants of Allah. It suggests inclusion in a community of believers who have lived their lives in devotion and obedience. This invitation is a significant honour, as it implies acceptance and recognition from Allah, allowing the soul to be part of a blessed group that is favoured in the sight of the Divine.

This verse signifies the transition from worldly life to a spiritual existence among others who have similarly fulfilled their purpose by living a life of faith and righteousness. It underscores the importance of community and fellowship in the spiritual journey and the eventual reward for a life well-lived in accordance with divine guidance.

Verse 30

Wadkhulee jannatee

"And enter My Paradise."

This verse extends the ultimate invitation and promise to the reassured soul to enter Paradise, signifying the culmination of a life well-lived in accordance with divine guidance. The possessive "My Paradise" underscores the personal and direct relationship between Allah and the believer, highlighting the divine approval and grace bestowed upon the righteous.

This final verse serves as a powerful conclusion to the message of the chapter. It contrasts the fate of the righteous with the earlier warnings of regret and punishment for those who neglected their duties. The promise of Paradise is the ultimate reward for those who have maintained faith and righteousness, offering eternal peace and fulfillment.

These closing verses (27-30) collectively provide hope and encouragement for believers, reinforcing the importance of living a life aligned with spiritual and moral values to achieve the ultimate success in the hereafter.

LESSONS LEARNT FROM SURAH FAJIR

Surah Al-Fajr (Chapter 89 of the Quran) imparts several important lessons and reflections that are relevant to believers. Here are some key lessons that can be drawn from this Surah:

1. The Transience of Worldly Power and Wealth: The Surah begins by referencing historical examples of powerful nations and individuals who were ultimately destroyed due to their arrogance and wrongdoing. This serves as a reminder of the fleeting nature of worldly power and wealth, emphasizing that true success lies in righteousness and humility.
2. Accountability and Justice: The Surah underscores the inevitability of the Day of Judgment, where everyone will be held accountable for their actions. It highlights the importance of living a life of integrity and justice, knowing that all deeds will be scrutinized and judged by Allah.
3. The Perils of Materialism and Greed: Through its critique of those who excessively love wealth and consume it unjustly, the Surah warns against materialism and greed. It calls for a balanced approach to wealth, where one's material pursuits do not overshadow ethical and spiritual responsibilities.
4. The Reality of Regret for the Negligent: The Surah vividly depicts the regret that will be felt by those who neglected their spiritual duties and prioritized worldly desires. This serves as a cautionary tale, urging individuals to reflect on their lives and make amends before it's too late.
5. The Reward for the Righteous: In its concluding verses, the Surah offers a message of hope and reassurance to the righteous by describing the peaceful and honored state of the reassured soul. It promises eternal reward and satisfaction for those who have lived in accordance with divine guidance.
6. Divine Invitation to Paradise: The Surah ends with an invitation to the righteous to enter Paradise, highlighting the ultimate success and fulfillment that await those who are faithful to Allah. It encourages believers to strive for this eternal reward by adhering to moral and spiritual principles.

Overall, Surah Al-Fajr encourages reflection on one's life choices, urging individuals to prioritize righteousness, justice, and humility over fleeting worldly gains. It serves as both a warning to the heedless and a promise of eternal peace to the faithful.

SUMMARY OF SURAH AL- FAJIR

Surah Al-Fajr starts by drawing attention to the beautiful and meaningful signs in nature, such as the dawn, the night, and the sky. These signs serve as reminders from Allah of His power and creation. They encourage people to think about Allah's greatness and to be grateful for His blessings.

The surah then shares the stories of two ancient and powerful nations: the people of 'Aad and the people of Thamud. Both groups were very wealthy and proud of their strength. However, they rejected the messages of their prophets and chose to ignore Allah's guidance. Because of their arrogance and disobedience, Allah punished them severely. The people of 'Aad were destroyed by a strong wind that came suddenly, and the people of Thamud were destroyed by a loud, destructive sound. These stories teach us that no matter how strong or wealthy people become, they will face punishment if they turn away from Allah and act unjustly.

The surah emphasizes that Allah's punishment comes as a reminder for people to stay humble and obedient to Him. It also explains that those who do good deeds—such as helping others, giving charity, praying, and being mindful of Allah—will be rewarded with paradise. On the other hand, those who are proud, greedy, and ignore Allah's guidance will face the punishment of hell. This shows that everyone will be held responsible for their actions in this life.

Toward the end, the surah reminds us that humans are tested by the blessings Allah gives, like wealth and children. Some people become proud and arrogant because of these blessings, but the surah warns us that Allah can take away what He has given if we are ungrateful or dishonest. It urges everyone to be mindful of their deeds and to prepare for the life after death, where everyone will be rewarded or punished based on their actions.

Overall, Surah Al-Fajr teaches us to recognize Allah's signs, learn from the stories of past nations, stay humble and obedient, and always try to do good. It reminds us that our actions matter and that Allah is just and merciful. It encourages us to seek righteousness and to fear Allah's punishment, knowing that He is watching over all of us.

SURAH AL-FAJIR (SURAH 89)

Questions

1. What does the term "Al-Fajr" refer to, and why is the surah named after it?
2. What are the oaths mentioned at the beginning of Surah Al-Fajr, and what is their significance?
3. Which historical nations are mentioned in Surah Al-Fajr as examples of those who were punished for their transgressions?
4. What does the surah say about the human tendency to forget Allah's favors when in comfort?
5. How does the surah describe the reaction of people when they face trials or loss?
6. What message does the surah convey about wealth and the treatment of orphans and the needy?
7. How does Surah Al-Fajr depict the Day of Judgment for the righteous soul?
8. What is the ultimate destination for the soul that is satisfied and content according to the surah?
9. How does the surah address the concept of accountability and the consequences of one's actions?
10. What lessons can be drawn from Surah Al-Fajr about leading a life that aligns with divine guidance?

Answers

1. What does the term "Al-Fajr" refer to, and why is the surah named after it?
   - "Al-Fajr" refers to "the dawn." The surah is named after it because it begins with an oath by the dawn, emphasizing the significance of this time as a symbol of new beginnings and divine order.

2. What are the oaths mentioned at the beginning of Surah Al-Fajr, and what is their significance?
   - The surah begins with oaths by the dawn, the ten nights, the even and the odd, and the night as it departs. These oaths highlight the importance of time and specific periods as witnesses to divine truth and human actions.

3. Which historical nations are mentioned in Surah Al-Fajr as examples of those who were punished for their transgressions?
   - The surah mentions the people of 'Ad, Thamud, and Pharaoh as examples of powerful nations that were destroyed due to their arrogance and wrongdoing.

4. What does the surah say about the human tendency to forget Allah's favors when in comfort?
   - The surah describes how people often become arrogant and ungrateful when blessed with comfort and ease, forgetting Allah's favors and failing to acknowledge His role in their prosperity.

5. How does the surah describe the reaction of people when they face trials or loss?
   - The surah notes that when people face trials or loss, they often despair and become despondent, questioning Allah's wisdom and neglecting patience and gratitude.

6. What message does the surah convey about wealth and the treatment of orphans and the needy?
   - The surah criticizes those who hoard wealth and neglect their duty to care for orphans and the needy, emphasizing the importance of charity and justice.

7. How does Surah Al-Fajr depict the Day of Judgment for the righteous soul?
   - The surah describes the righteous soul as one that will be addressed with peace and invited to return to its Lord, satisfied and content, and enter paradise.

8. What is the ultimate destination for the soul that is satisfied and content according to the surah?
   - The ultimate destination for the satisfied and content soul is paradise, where it will join other righteous servants in eternal bliss.

9. How does the surah address the concept of accountability and the consequences of one's actions?
   - The surah emphasizes that every individual will be held accountable for their actions, and those who transgress will face consequences, while the righteous will be rewarded.

10. What lessons can be drawn from Surah Al-Fajr about leading a life that aligns with divine guidance?
    - Surah Al-Fajr teaches the importance of humility, gratitude, justice, and compassion. It encourages reflection on past lessons, awareness of one's actions, and preparation for the hereafter.

These questions and answers can be used for educational purposes, study sessions, or discussions to enhance understanding of Surah Al-Fajr.

Multiple Choice Questions

1. What does the term "Al-Fajr" refer to?

    - A) The night

    - B) The dawn

    - C) The midday

    - D) The sunset

2. Which time periods are mentioned in the oaths at the beginning of Surah Al-Fajr?

    - A) The morning, the afternoon, and the evening

    - B) The dawn, the ten nights, the even and the odd, and the departing night

    - C) The sunrise, the sunset, and the full moon

    - D) The winter, the spring, and the summer

3. Which historical nations are cited in Surah Al-Fajr as examples of those punished for their transgressions?

    - A) The people of Sodom and Gomorrah

    - B) The people of 'Ad, Thamud, and Pharaoh

    - C) The people of Nineveh and Babylon

    - D) The people of Rome and Persia

4. What does the surah say about people's attitude when they are blessed with comfort?

    - A) They become grateful and humble

    - B) They tend to forget Allah's favors and become arrogant

    - C) They pray more frequently

    - D) They help the poor more often

5. How does the surah describe people's reaction to trials or loss?

    - A) They remain patient and hopeful

    - B) They despair and become despondent

    - C) They seek guidance from others

    - D) They increase their charitable acts

6. What criticism does Surah Al-Fajr make regarding wealth?

    - A) It is inherently evil

    - B) It should be accumulated without concern for others

    - C) It leads to arrogance if not used to help orphans and the needy

    - D) It should be spent quickly

7. How does the surah describe the Day of Judgment for the righteous soul?

    - A) It will be filled with fear and anxiety

    - B) It will be greeted with peace and invited to paradise

    - C) It will be indifferent and unchanged

    - D) It will face a long journey

8. What ultimate destination is promised to the soul that is satisfied and content in Surah Al-Fajr?

    - A) Eternal darkness

    - B) A simple life in paradise

    - C) Eternal bliss in paradise

    - D) Rebirth into a new life

Answers

1. *Answer:* B) The dawn
2. *Answer:* B) The dawn, the ten nights, the even and the odd, and the departing night
3. *Answer:* B) The people of 'Ad, Thamud, and Pharaoh
4. *Answer:* B) They tend to forget Allah's favors and become arrogant
5. *Answer:* B) They despair and become despondent
6. *Answer:* C) It leads to arrogance if not used to help orphans and the needy
7. *Answer:* B) It will be greeted with peace and invited to paradise
8. *Answer:* C) Eternal bliss in paradise

These questions and answers can be used for educational purposes, quizzes, or study sessions to deepen understanding of Surah Al-Fajr.

SURAH BALAD

SURAH BALAD

Bismillahi ar-Rahmani ar-Raheem

Verse 1

Verse 1 of Surah Al-Balad (The City) begins with an oath, which is a common stylistic feature in the Quran. The verse states:

Laaa uqsimu bihaazal balad

"I swear by this city (Makkah)."

This verse immediately draws attention to the significance of the city of Makkah. By swearing an oath by the city, the verse demonstrates its sacredness and importance. Makkah is not only the birthplace of Prophet Muhammad but also the location of the Kaaba, the holiest site in Islam. Historically, Makkah has been a center of pilgrimage and spirituality for Muslims.

The use of an oath serves to highlight the gravity of the message that follows in the Surah. It sets the stage for discussing the trials and struggles faced by humans, particularly the challenges faced by the Prophet Muhammad(pbu) in Makkah. The verse underscores Makkah's religious and historical importance, making it a powerful starting point for the Surah's themes.

Verse 2

Wa anta hillum bihaazal balad

"And you, [O Muhammad], are free of restriction in this city."

This verse highlights the unique status of Prophet Muhammad(pbuh) in Makkah. It suggests that although Makkah is a sacred and protected place where violence and bloodshed are traditionally forbidden, there was an exception made for the Prophet. This could refer to a future time when the Prophet would be given the divine mandate to fight against the oppression and persecution of the Muslims, specifically during the conquest of Makkah.

The verse underlines the special circumstances surrounding the Prophet's mission and the challenges he faced in his own city. Despite Makkah being a sanctuary, the Prophet was subjected to hostility and persecution there. This verse serves to acknowledge his struggles and the eventual change in his status within the city, emphasizing his pivotal role in transforming Makkah into a center of Islam.

Verse 3

Wa waalidinw wa maa walad

"And [by] the father and that which was born [of him],"

This verse is another oath, continuing from the oaths in the previous verses. The "father" and "that which was born [of him]" are generally interpreted to refer to the broader concept of human lineage, starting from Adam as the first human and all his descendants. This interpretation highlights the significance of human creation and the continuity of the human race.

By swearing an oath on this relationship, the verse underscores the importance of human life and the inherent struggles and responsibilities that come with it. It sets the stage for discussing the moral and ethical choices faced by humans, emphasizing the interconnectedness of all people and the shared human experience. This links back to the themes of the Surah, which focus on the trials and efforts required to lead a righteous life.

Verse 4

Laqad khalaqnal insaana fee kabad

"Certainly We have created man into hardship."

This verse highlights the inherent nature of human life, which involves facing challenges and difficulties. It emphasizes that struggle and toil are integral parts of the human experience. From birth to death, individuals encounter various forms of hardship, whether physical, emotional, or spiritual.

The verse sets the context for the themes of the Surah, which discuss the choices humans make in the face of these challenges. It underscores the idea that life is not meant to be a journey of ease and comfort but one where effort and perseverance are necessary. This understanding encourages individuals to strive for righteousness and moral integrity, despite the difficulties they may encounter. Overall, the verse serves as a reminder of the trials inherent in life and the importance of enduring them with patience and resilience.

Verse 5

Ayahsabu al-lai yaqdira 'alaihi ahad

"Does he think that no one has power over him?"

This verse questions the mindset of a person who believes they are beyond accountability or control. It challenges the arrogance and self-deception of those who act as if they can do whatever they please without any consequences. The verse serves as a reminder that, despite human efforts and achievements, there is a higher power—Allah—who oversees everything and holds people accountable for their actions.

By highlighting this misconception, the verse encourages humility and awareness of one's limitations. It underscores the importance of recognizing that ultimate power and authority belong to Allah, and it warns against the false sense of security that can come from wealth, status, or personal achievements. This message aligns with the Surah's broader themes of accountability and the moral choices individuals must make in life.

Verse 6

Yaqoolu ahlaktu maalal lubadaa

"He says, 'I have spent wealth in abundance.'"

This verse reflects the boastful attitude of someone who takes pride in spending large amounts of money, possibly for show or self-glorification. It highlights a mindset where wealth is squandered on extravagant or ostentatious displays, rather than being used for meaningful or virtuous purposes.

The verse serves as a critique of those who are proud of their material wealth and use it to impress others, without considering the moral implications or responsibilities that come with such resources. It points out the superficiality of equating wealth with success or worthiness, especially when it is not used to help others or contribute positively to society. This connects to the Surah's broader themes of moral accountability and the proper use of one's resources in the face of life's inherent challenges.

Verse 7

Ayahsabu al lam yarahooo ahad

"Does he think that no one has seen him?"

This verse addresses the misconception of those who believe that their actions, particularly how they use their wealth, go unnoticed. It points to a false sense of security where individuals assume they are not accountable for their actions because no one is observing them.

The verse serves as a reminder that Allah is always aware of what people do, even if they think they are acting in secrecy. It emphasizes the idea of divine oversight and accountability, reinforcing the message that one's actions, intentions, and the use of their resources are all known to Allah. This connects to the Surah's themes by highlighting the importance of being mindful of one's actions and the need for integrity and righteousness, even when no one else seems to be watching.

Verse 8

Alam naj'al lahoo 'aynayn

"Does he think that no one has seen him?"

This verse highlights the faculties and abilities that Allah has given to humans, starting with the gift of sight. By mentioning the eyes, the verse draws attention to the physical and intellectual capacities that enable humans to observe, understand, and make sense of the world around them.

The mention of eyes symbolizes not just physical sight but also insight and the ability to distinguish between right and wrong. This verse serves as a reminder of the blessings and resources humans have been endowed with, which come with the responsibility to use them wisely and justly. It reinforces the Surah's themes of accountability and moral choice by emphasizing that these gifts should guide individuals in making ethical decisions and leading a life aligned with divine guidance.

Verse 9

Wa lisaananw wa shafatayn

"And a tongue and two lips?"

This verse continues from the previous one, listing the faculties and abilities that Allah has given to humans. The mention of "a tongue and two lips" highlights the gift of speech and communication. These abilities enable humans to express thoughts, share knowledge, and interact with others.

The verse emphasizes that these faculties are not just physical features but are essential tools for understanding, learning, and moral decision-making. By highlighting these gifts, the Surah reminds individuals of the responsibility to use them wisely and ethically. This includes speaking truthfully, promoting good, and fostering understanding and harmony in society. The verse contributes to the Surah's broader themes by underscoring the idea that with these abilities comes the accountability for how they are used in daily life.

Verse 10

Wa hadaynaahun najdayn

"And have shown him the two ways?"

This verse highlights that Allah has provided humans with guidance and the ability to discern between two distinct paths: the path of righteousness and the path of wrongdoing. It underscores the concept of free will, where individuals are given the choice to follow either the way of good or the way of evil.

By mentioning "the two ways," the verse emphasizes that humans are not left without direction or purpose. They are equipped with the knowledge and faculties necessary to make informed decisions about their actions and moral conduct. This verse ties into the Surah's themes by reinforcing the idea of accountability and the importance of making ethical choices in life. It serves as a reminder that while the right path may be challenging, it ultimately leads to a fulfilling and virtuous life aligned with divine guidance.

Verse 11

Falaq tahamal-'aqabah

"But he has not broken through the difficult pass."

This verse uses the metaphor of a "difficult pass" or "steep path" to describe the challenging moral and ethical choices that individuals often avoid. It suggests that many people prefer taking the easier, more comfortable route rather than confronting and overcoming the challenges that come with living a life of righteousness and virtue.

The "difficult pass" represents the path of self-restraint, sacrifice, and doing good deeds, which often require effort and perseverance. By pointing out that this path has not been taken, the verse emphasizes the need for individuals to rise above their base desires and strive for higher moral standards.

This connects to the Surah's themes by highlighting the importance of making tough but rewarding choices in life, encouraging believers to embrace the challenges of doing what is right, even when it is difficult. It serves as a call to action to break free from complacency and actively pursue a path of virtue and righteousness.

Verse 12

Wa maaa adraaka mal'aqabah

"And what will make you know what is [breaking through] the difficult pass?"

This verse prompts reflection and curiosity about the nature of the "difficult pass" mentioned in the previous verse. It asks the listener or reader to consider deeply what it means to overcome the challenges and obstacles that life presents, particularly in the moral and ethical realm.

The verse serves to prepare the reader for the explanation that follows in the subsequent verses, which describe the specific actions and attributes that constitute breaking through the difficult pass. It emphasizes the significance and value of understanding and undertaking this challenging path. By posing this rhetorical question, the verse engages the audience, encouraging them to think about what true moral and spiritual effort involves and why it is important.

This question sets the stage for the following verses, which detail the acts of kindness, charity, and compassion that characterize the path of righteousness, thereby reinforcing the Surah's themes of moral choice and accountability.

Verse 13

Fakku raqabah

"It is the freeing of a slave."

This verse begins to explain what "breaking through the difficult pass" entails by highlighting a specific act of righteousness: freeing a slave. In the context of the time when the Quran was revealed, slavery was a common practice, and the act of liberating a slave was considered a significant and noble deed.

Freeing a slave is an example of a selfless act that requires personal sacrifice and compassion for others. It represents a commitment to justice and humanity, reflecting a willingness to use one's resources to improve the lives of others and correct societal wrongs.

By emphasizing this particular action, the verse underscores the importance of acts that promote freedom, equality, and dignity. It ties into the Surah's broader themes by illustrating that overcoming the challenges of the "difficult pass" involves making choices that align with ethical and moral values, even when they require effort and sacrifice.

Verse 14

Aw it'aamun fee yawmin zee masghabah

"Or feeding on a day of severe hunger."

This verse continues to describe the actions that constitute "breaking through the difficult pass." It highlights the act of feeding the hungry, especially during times of severe need or famine. This act of charity and compassion is another example of selflessness and generosity.

Providing food to those who are hungry, particularly when resources are scarce, demonstrates a commitment to helping others and alleviating suffering. It embodies the principles of kindness and empathy, encouraging individuals to consider the needs of others and to act in ways that benefit the community as a whole.

This verse reinforces the Surah's themes by illustrating that righteous actions often involve personal sacrifice and a willingness to support those who are less fortunate. It emphasizes that true moral strength lies in the ability to perform good deeds, especially during challenging times, thereby aligning one's life with values of compassion and justice.

Verse 15

Yateeman zaa maqrabah

"An orphan of near relationship."

This verse elaborates on the types of charitable acts that constitute "breaking through the difficult pass." It highlights the importance of caring for orphans, particularly those who are related to you or are close in proximity.

Taking care of an orphan, especially one who is near or related, underscores the values of compassion, family responsibility, and community support. Orphans, being vulnerable and without parental care, are in need of kindness and assistance. Providing for them is a noble deed that requires empathy and a sense of duty towards those who are disadvantaged.

This verse ties into the Surah's broader themes by emphasizing the significance of performing acts of kindness and generosity, especially towards those who are most in need. It encourages individuals to extend their support to the vulnerable, thereby fostering a caring and just society. The inclusion of orphans in this context highlights the moral responsibility to support and nurture those who cannot care for themselves.

Verse 16

Aw miskeenan zaa matrabah

"Or a needy person in misery."

This verse continues to describe the actions that exemplify "breaking through the difficult pass." It emphasizes the importance of assisting those who are in severe need and distress. The verse highlights the moral and ethical obligation to help individuals who are suffering due to poverty or difficult circumstances.

Helping a needy person in misery involves acts of charity and support that alleviate their hardship and improve their situation. It reflects compassion, kindness, and a sense of social responsibility. By urging individuals to care for those in dire situations, the verse underscores the importance of empathy and the commitment to uplifting others.

This verse reinforces the Surah's themes by illustrating that true righteousness involves taking tangible actions to assist those who are less fortunate. It encourages believers to actively seek out opportunities to make a positive impact in the lives of others, thereby fostering a more equitable and just society. The focus on helping those in misery highlights the value of selflessness and the moral duty to support those in need.

Verse 17

"Thumma kāna mina alladhīna āmanū wa tawāṣaw biṣ-ṣabri wa tawāṣaw bil-marḥamah."

"Then he is of those who believe and advise one another to patience and to compassion."

This verse highlights the qualities and actions that align with true belief. It emphasizes that, in addition to performing acts of charity and kindness, a person should also be among those who have faith. Furthermore, they should encourage and advise each other to practice patience and compassion.

- Patience (ṣabr): This refers to enduring hardships, persevering through difficulties, and maintaining steadfastness in faith and righteousness.

Compassion (marḥamah): This involves showing kindness, empathy, and a caring attitude toward others, ensuring that one's actions are guided by mercy and understanding.

The verse underscores the importance of community and mutual support among believers. It suggests that true believers not only act righteously themselves but also encourage others to embody these values, thereby strengthening the bonds of faith and fostering a supportive and empathetic community. This reflects the Surah's broader themes of moral responsibility, accountability, and the pursuit of a righteous life.

Verse 18

"Ulā'ika aṣ-ḥābu al-maymanah."

"Those are the companions of the right."

This verse refers to the people who embody the virtues and actions described in the preceding verses. These individuals are characterized by their belief, their acts of charity, their encouragement of patience and compassion, and their moral integrity.

Being "companions of the right" signifies that these people are on the path of righteousness and will receive favourable outcomes in the hereafter. In Islamic teachings, those on the right are often associated with those who will enter Paradise, as they have led a life aligned with divine guidance and have upheld the values of faith and good deeds.

This verse ties into the Surah's broader themes by highlighting the rewards and positive status of those who choose the path of virtue and strive to overcome life's challenges through righteous actions and support for others. It serves as encouragement for believers to aspire to be among these companions by living a life of faith, patience, and compassion.

Verse 19

"Wa alladhīna kafarū biāyātinā hum aṣ-ḥābu al-mash'amah."

"But they who disbelieved in Our signs - those are the companions of the left."

This verse contrasts the fate of those who reject faith and the signs of Allah with those who believe and act righteously. The "companions of the left" are those who deny or ignore the divine guidance and choose not to follow the path of righteousness.

In Islamic teachings, being on the left is often associated with those who face negative consequences in the hereafter, as opposed to the companions of the right who are rewarded. This verse serves as a warning about the consequences of disbelief and the rejection of Allah's signs.

The Surah's broader themes of moral choice, accountability, and the importance of following divine guidance are reinforced in this verse. It emphasizes that one's actions and beliefs have significant implications for their ultimate fate, encouraging individuals to reflect on their choices and align themselves with the path of faith and righteousness.

Verse 20

Alayhim nārun mu'ṣadah.

"Over them will be fire closed in."

This verse describes the consequence for those who are "the companions of the left," as mentioned in the previous verse. It depicts a scene of punishment where those who disbelieve and reject Allah's signs will face a fire that is enclosed around them. The imagery of a closed-in fire suggests an intense, inescapable, and suffocating punishment.

This verse serves as a stark warning about the spiritual and moral consequences of turning away from the path of righteousness and faith. It underscores the seriousness of disbelief and the turning away from divine guidance, reinforcing the Surah's themes of accountability and the importance of adhering to a life of faith, patience, and compassion.

By presenting the contrasting fates of the companions of the right and the left, the Surah encourages individuals to reflect on their actions and beliefs, urging them to choose the path that leads to favourable outcomes in this life and the hereafter.

Surah Al-Balad offers several important lessons and themes that are relevant for personal reflection and moral guidance:

1. Life's Challenges and Struggles: The Surah begins by highlighting that human life is inherently filled with challenges and hardships. This serves as a reminder that difficulties are a part of life, and overcoming them is essential for personal growth and moral development.
2. Moral Accountability: Throughout the Surah, there is an emphasis on accountability for one's actions. The idea that Allah is always aware of what we do encourages individuals to live with integrity and mindfulness, knowing that their deeds are observed and will be judged.

3. Free Will and Choice: The Surah underscores the concept of free will and the ability to choose between right and wrong. Individuals are given the faculties and guidance needed to make informed decisions, highlighting the responsibility that comes with free will.
4. Acts of Compassion and Charity: The Surah details specific acts of righteousness, such as freeing slaves and helping the needy, underscoring the importance of selflessness, empathy, and generosity. It emphasizes that true moral strength involves making sacrifices to help others.
5. Community and Support: There is a call for believers to support one another in patience and compassion. This highlights the importance of community and mutual encouragement in fostering a society that upholds moral and ethical values.
6. Consequences of Disbelief: The Surah contrasts the fate of the righteous with those who deny Allah's signs, illustrating the consequences of disbelief. This serves as a warning and encourages reflection on one's beliefs and actions.
7. Value of Righteousness and Patience: The Surah encourages perseverance in the face of adversity and the pursuit of righteousness despite challenges. It promotes the idea that a life of virtue, patience, and compassion leads to favorable outcomes both in this world and the hereafter.

Overall, Surah Al-Balad encourages individuals to reflect on the moral choices they make, to strive toward compassion and generosity, and to remain steadfast in their faith and ethical conduct despite life's challenges.

SUMMARY OF SURAH AL-BALAD

When It Was Revealed

The Surah's style and subject suggest it was revealed in the early days in Makkah when the disbelievers decided to oppose Prophet Muhammad and felt justified in their harsh treatment of him.

Main Ideas and Subject

This Surah packs a lot into a few sentences, showing how the Quran can explain complex ideas simply. It explains that humans are given the choice to follow either the path of good or evil and the ability to choose wisely. The world is not meant for comfort but for hard work, and one's future depends on their efforts.

In the Surah, Makkah and the Prophet's struggles are mentioned to show that life is about toil and struggle, not ease. This ties into a verse from another Surah that says people get only what they strive for. This part of the Surah also addresses the mistaken belief that people can do whatever they want without accountability.

The Surah criticizes the idea that wasting wealth for show is admirable, pointing out that Allah sees how wealth is obtained and used. It emphasizes using knowledge and understanding to choose the right path and explains that Allah has shown people both good and bad ways. The easy path leads to moral decay, while the difficult path requires self-control but leads to moral heights.

Allah explains that the right path involves spending wealth to help those in need, believing in Allah, and working with others to build a compassionate and virtuous society. Those who follow this path will receive Allah's mercy, while those who don't will face punishment.

The Surah begins with a "Nay" and an oath, indicating that the disbelievers' way of life in Makkah, which was focused on enjoyment without accountability, was wrong. They didn't believe in life after death or being held accountable for their actions.

Makkah, referred to as "this city," was significant because of its history and sacredness. Abraham settled his family there, and it became a religious and commercial center. The Surah hints at the challenges the Prophet faced in this city, where he had no peace despite its sanctity.

The Surah suggests that humans are meant to endure hardship and toil. Makkah's development and the Prophet's struggles are examples of this. From birth to death, humans face challenges, showing that life is not about ease but overcoming difficulties.

It questions the belief that people can act without consequences, pointing out that even in this world, forces beyond human control can disrupt their plans. The Surah criticizes those who waste wealth for show and reminds them that Allah is aware of their actions.

The Surah highlights that humans have been given the ability to understand and choose between good and evil. It criticizes the choice to follow the easy path of moral decay instead of the challenging path of virtue.

Ultimately, the Surah encourages believers to join together, support each other in patience and compassion, and strive for a virtuous life. It highlights the importance of community and mutual support in living a life of faith and good deeds.

SURAH AL-BALAD (Surah 90)

Questions

1. What does the term "Al-Balad" refer to, and why is the surah named after it?
2. What is the significance of the city mentioned at the beginning of Surah Al-Balad?
3. What does the surah say about the human condition and the nature of life?
4. How does Surah Al-Balad describe the challenges that humans face?
5. What does the surah indicate about the human perception of wealth and power?
6. What moral actions does the surah emphasize as important for believers?
7. How does the surah describe those who fail to take the challenging path of righteousness?
8. What does Surah Al-Balad say about the consequences for those who choose the path of immorality?
9. How does the surah encourage compassion and care for others?
10. What are some lessons that can be drawn from Surah Al-Balad about leading a virtuous life?

Answers

1. What does the term "Al-Balad" refer to, and why is the surah named after it?
   - "Al-Balad" refers to "the city," specifically Mecca. The surah is named after it because it begins with an oath by this sacred city, emphasizing its significance in Islamic tradition.

2. What is the significance of the city mentioned at the beginning of Surah Al-Balad?
   - The city, Mecca, is significant because it is the birthplace of the Prophet Muhammad (peace be upon him) and a central site of pilgrimage for Muslims. It holds a special spiritual and historical importance.

3. What does the surah say about the human condition and the nature of life?
   - The surah acknowledges that humans are created into a life of toil and struggle, highlighting the inherent challenges and responsibilities faced in the journey of life.

4. How does Surah Al-Balad describe the challenges that humans face?
   - The surah describes the challenges as a series of tests and trials that require perseverance and moral strength to overcome.

5. What does the surah indicate about the human perception of wealth and power?
   - The surah suggests that humans often take pride in their wealth and power, mistakenly believing these to be everlasting or a measure of their success.

6. What moral actions does the surah emphasize as important for believers?
   - The surah emphasizes the importance of freeing captives, feeding the hungry, caring for orphans, and assisting those in need, promoting acts of charity and compassion.

7. How does the surah describe those who fail to take the challenging path of righteousness?
   - The surah describes them as those who avoid acts of kindness and charity, ultimately failing to fulfill their moral duties.

8. What does Surah Al-Balad say about the consequences for those who choose the path of immorality?
   - The surah warns that those who choose the path of immorality will face negative consequences and will not find success in this life or the hereafter.

9. How does the surah encourage compassion and care for others?
   - The surah encourages compassion by urging believers to support the vulnerable, highlighting the spiritual rewards of such actions.

10. What are some lessons that can be drawn from Surah Al-Balad about leading a virtuous life?
    - Surah Al-Balad teaches the value of perseverance in the face of difficulties, the importance of moral integrity, and the need for compassion and generosity toward others.

These questions and answers can be used for educational purposes, study sessions, or discussions to enhance understanding of Surah Al-Balad.

Multiple Choice Questions

1. What does the term "Al-Balad" refer to in the context of this surah?

    - A) The night

    - B) The city

    - C) The mountain

    - D) The river

2. Which city is referenced in the opening of Surah Al-Balad?

    - A) Medina

    - B) Jerusalem

    - C) Mecca

    - D) Cairo

3. What does the surah say about the nature of human life?

    - A) It is meant to be easy and carefree

    - B) It is full of toil and struggle

    - C) It is predestined and unchangeable

    - D) It is a journey of wealth accumulation

4. How does Surah Al-Balad describe the common human perception of wealth?

    - A) As a temporary loan

    - B) As a source of eternal happiness

    - C) As a measure of success and pride

    - D) As a burden to be avoided

5. Which moral actions are highlighted as important in Surah Al-Balad?

    - A) Hoarding wealth and gaining power

    - B) Traveling extensively

    - C) Freeing captives, feeding the hungry, and caring for orphans

    - D) Pursuing personal ambitions

6. What does the surah indicate about those who avoid the path of righteousness?

    - A) They will eventually find success

    - B) They will face challenges but remain content

    - C) They will fail to fulfill their moral duties and face consequences

    - D) They will be rewarded for their independence

7. How does Surah Al-Balad encourage believers to treat others?

    - A) With indifference and neutrality

    - B) With competition and rivalry

    - C) With compassion and generosity

    - D) With suspicion and caution

8. What is the ultimate message of Surah Al-Balad regarding human actions?

    - A) Actions have no real consequences

    - B) Only wealth matters in the end

    - C) Moral integrity and compassion lead to success

    - D) Personal happiness is the ultimate goal

Answers

1. *Answer:* B) The city
2. *Answer:* C) Mecca
3. *Answer:* B) It is full of toil and struggle
4. *Answer:* C) As a measure of success and pride
5. *Answer:* C) Freeing captives, feeding the hungry, and caring for orphans
6. *Answer:* C) They will fail to fulfill their moral duties and face consequences
7. *Answer:* C) With compassion and generosity
8. *Answer:* C) Moral integrity and compassion lead to success

These questions and answers can be used for quizzes, educational discussions, or self-study to enhance understanding of Surah Al-Balad.

SURAH ASH-SHAMS

SURAH ASH SHAMS

Bismillahi ar-Rahmani ar-Raheem

Verse 1

Wash shamsi wa duhaa haa

"By the Sun and his (glorious) splendour"

In the opening verse, Allah swears by the sun, highlighting its significance as a central celestial body crucial for life on Earth. The sun is a vital source of light, warmth, and energy, sustaining the ecological balance necessary for all living beings. By swearing by the sun, the verse draws attention to its remarkable importance and the intricate design inherent in the universe. The sun's role in maintaining life underscores the broader theme of divine order and precision in creation.

Symbolism of the Sun

The sun is often seen as a symbol of guidance, clarity, and enlightenment. Just as the sun illuminates the physical world, providing light and dispelling darkness, divine guidance serves to illuminate the moral and spiritual paths for humanity. The oath emphasizes the necessity for individuals to recognize and follow this guidance, drawing a parallel between the physical light provided by the sun and the spiritual light provided by divine wisdom.

"And its Brightness"

The phrase "ḍuḥāhā" refers to the morning brightness or the full light of day when the sun is at its peak and its light is most intense. This highlights the clarity and distinction between light and darkness, symbolizing the clear demarcation between truth and falsehood, and between good and evil. The brightness of the sun represents the potential for clarity in understanding and decision-making in human lives.

Purpose of the Oath

In classical Arabic, oaths are employed to emphasize the importance and truth of the message that follows. The oath by the sun and its brightness sets the stage for the surah's central message concerning human nature and moral responsibility. It underscores the weight and seriousness of the subsequent verses, urging the reader to pay close attention to the moral lessons being conveyed.

Reflection on Creation

This verse invites believers to reflect on the natural world as a manifestation of Allah's power and wisdom. The regularity and precision of the sun's movement reflect the perfection of divine creation. By pondering these signs, believers are encouraged to strengthen their faith and gain a deeper appreciation for the divine order that governs the universe.

Connection to Human Behavior

The sun's brightness also serves as a metaphor for potential clarity in human understanding and behavior. Just as the sun reveals the world around us, divine guidance reveals the path of righteousness. This sets the foundation for the surah's exploration of human morality, urging individuals to choose the path of righteousness illuminated by divine insight.

In summary, the first verse of Surah Ash-Shams uses the sun and its brightness as powerful symbols to convey the importance of divine guidance, the clarity of truth, and the necessity for humans to reflect on the signs of Allah in the universe. This sets a foundational context for the surah's exploration of human moral responsibility and the consequences of one's actions.

Verse 2

"Wal-qamari idhā talāhā"

"And [by] the moon when it follows it"

Oath by the Moon

In this verse, Allah swears by the moon, which is another significant celestial body. The moon follows the sun, reflecting its light and illuminating the night. This sequence of day following night and the moon following the sun highlights the natural order and harmony in the universe. It serves as a reminder of the constant and dependable cycles created by Allah, reflecting His wisdom and control over all things.

The Cycle of Day and Night

The reference to the moon following the sun illustrates the cyclical nature of time, marked by the alternation between day and night. This cycle is essential for the balance of life on Earth, affecting natural phenomena, biological rhythms, and human activities. By swearing by both the sun and the moon, the Quran draws attention to the seamless transition and interdependence of these celestial bodies, emphasizing the intricate design and purpose within creation.

Symbolism of the Moon

The moon is often associated with reflection and illumination in darkness. Just as the moon reflects the sun's light, providing guidance during the night, the verse symbolizes how divine guidance serves to illuminate the moral and spiritual paths during times of uncertainty or moral darkness. The moon's phases also symbolize the changes and stages in life, reminding believers of the transient nature of worldly matters and the permanence of divine truth.

Purpose of the Oaths

The oaths by the sun and the moon underscore the importance of the message that follows in the surah. They serve to direct the reader's attention to the lessons of human nature and morality that are to be discussed. By invoking these powerful natural phenomena, the verse stresses the certainty and significance of the teachings about human behavior, accountability, and the consequences of one's actions.

Reflection on Creation

This verse invites reflection on the natural order and the signs of Allah's creative power. The precise movement and phases of the moon, along with its ability to reflect light, are manifestations of divine wisdom. Believers are encouraged to contemplate these phenomena as evidence of Allah's sovereignty and to strengthen their faith through understanding the signs present in the universe.

In summary, the second verse of Surah Ash-Shams uses the moon and its following of the sun as symbols of the natural order, reflection, and guidance. These celestial phenomena emphasize the themes of divine wisdom, the balance of creation, and the need for humans to seek and follow divine guidance in their lives. This continues to set the stage for the surah's exploration of human morality and ethical responsibility.

Verse 3

"Wan-nahāri idhā jallāhā"

"And [by] the day when it displays it"

Oath by the Day

In this verse, Allah swears by the day, specifically highlighting its role in displaying the sun. The day is a time when the sun's light is most apparent, illuminating the world and allowing life to thrive. This oath emphasizes the significance of daylight in revealing the world around us, showcasing the wonders of creation and facilitating human activity.

The Clarity of Daylight

The phrase "when it displays it" indicates the clarity and visibility that daylight brings. Just as the day reveals the sun and illuminates the Earth, it symbolizes the clarity with which truth and divine guidance can illuminate the human mind and soul. The day is a time of activity and productivity, reflecting the potential for enlightenment and understanding in our daily lives.

Symbolism of Daylight

Daylight serves as a metaphor for knowledge, awareness, and the discernment of truth. In a spiritual sense, the clarity of day represents the ability to distinguish between right and wrong, good and evil. By swearing by the day, the verse underscores the importance of seeking and embracing truth and enlightenment in our lives.

Purpose of the Oaths

The series of oaths by the sun, the moon, and the day serves to underscore the importance and certainty of the message that follows in the surah. These natural phenomena are invoked to draw attention to the lessons of human nature and morality. The clarity and order in the natural world mirror the clarity and order that should be sought in human conduct and spiritual understanding.

Reflection on Creation

This verse invites believers to reflect on the natural world as evidence of Allah's wisdom and power. The regular occurrence and predictability of day and night cycles are signs of divine order and precision. By contemplating these cycles, believers are encouraged to recognize the signs of Allah in creation and strengthen their faith.

In summary, the third verse of Surah Ash-Shams uses the day and its role in displaying the sun to symbolize clarity, enlightenment, and the discernment of truth. These natural phenomena emphasize the themes of divine wisdom and the need for humans to seek and follow clear guidance in their lives. This continues to set the stage for the surah's exploration of human morality and ethical responsibility.

Verse 4
"Wal-layli idhā yaghshāhā"

"And [by] the night when it covers it"

Oath by the Night

In this verse, Allah swears by the night, particularly focusing on its characteristic of covering or enveloping the daylight. The night follows the day, bringing darkness and a time of rest. This natural transition from light to darkness demonstrates the cycle of time and the balance inherent in creation.

The Covering of Night

The phrase "when it covers it" refers to the way night conceals the brightness of the day. This covering is symbolic of the transitions and contrasts in life, such as the movement from activity to rest, and from clarity to obscurity. It serves as a reminder of the temporary nature of both light and darkness in the world, pointing to the cyclical nature of life and the balance ordained by Allah.

Symbolism of Night

Night is often associated with rest, reflection, and introspection. Just as the day represents clarity and activity, the night provides an opportunity for contemplation and recuperation. Spiritually, the night can symbolize times of uncertainty or challenge, during which one must rely on faith and inner guidance to navigate.

Purpose of the Oaths

The sequence of oaths by the sun, moon, day, and night serves to emphasize the certainty and importance of the lessons that follow in the surah. These natural phenomena highlight the order and balance in the universe, mirroring the balance that should exist in human behaviour and morality. The oaths draw attention to the themes of human nature and ethical responsibility that are central to the surah.

Reflection on Creation

This verse invites believers to reflect on the natural order and the signs of Allah's wisdom in creation. The predictable transition between day and night is a manifestation of divine order, encouraging believers to acknowledge the signs of Allah in the world and to strengthen their faith through understanding these cycles.

In summary, the fourth verse of Surah Ash-Shams uses the night and its role in covering the day to symbolize the balance and cyclical nature of life. These natural phenomena emphasize the themes of divine wisdom and the need for humans to seek balance and guidance in their lives. This continues to set the stage for the surah's exploration of human morality and ethical responsibility.

Verse 5

"Wassamā'i wa mā banāhā"

"And [by] the sky and He who constructed it"

Oath by the Sky

In this verse, Allah swears by the sky, focusing onu the vastness and structure of the heavens. The sky, with its expanse and complexity, represents one of the most awe-inspiring aspects of creation. This oath draws attention to the majesty and precision involved in its creation.

The Construction of the Sky

The phrase "and He who constructed it" highlights the divine act of creation. The sky's construction is a testament to Allah's power, wisdom, and artistry. The vastness and order of the heavens serve as a powerful reminder of the Creator's capability and the intricate balance maintained in the universe.

Symbolism of the Sky

The sky symbolizes vastness, limitlessness, and the grandeur of creation. It often evokes a sense of wonder and reflection on the Creator's magnificence. Spiritually, the sky can represent the loftiness of divine attributes and the boundless scope of divine mercy and power.

Purpose of the Oaths

This series of oaths by various elements of creation underscores the importance and truth of the message that follows in the surah. By invoking the sky, the verse highlights the themes of divine order and precision, drawing attention to the moral and ethical lessons that the surah imparts. It encourages believers to reflect on the signs of Allah in the universe and to consider the implications for human behaviour and responsibility.

Reflection on Creation

This verse invites believers to contemplate the creation of the sky as a sign of Allah's infinite power and wisdom. The sky's beauty and order are manifestations of divine perfection, encouraging believers to strengthen their faith and recognize the signs of Allah in the world around them.

In summary, the fifth verse of Surah Ash-Shams uses the sky and its construction to symbolize the majesty and precision of divine creation. This natural phenomenon emphasizes the themes of divine wisdom and the need for humans to reflect on the signs of Allah in their lives. This continues to set the stage for the surah's exploration of human morality and ethical responsibility.

Verse 6

"Wal-arḍi wa mā ṭaḥāhā"

"And [by] the earth and He who spread it"

Oath by the Earth

In this verse, Allah swears by the earth, highlighting its role and the way it has been spread out for life. The earth is a foundational element of creation, providing a stable and nurturing environment for living beings. This oath emphasizes the importance and intricacy of the earth's design.

The Spreading of the Earth

The phrase "and He who spread it" refers to the way Allah has shaped and prepared the earth to support life. This includes the earth's surface, its resources, and its ability to sustain diverse ecosystems. The earth's spread is a testament to Allah's provision and mercy, as it accommodates the needs of all living creatures.

Symbolism of the Earth

The earth symbolizes stability, sustenance, and the nurturing aspect of creation. It serves as a reminder of Allah's generosity and care in providing for His creation. Spiritually, the earth can represent the foundation of faith and the grounding of human existence in divine wisdom and provision.

Purpose of the Oaths

The series of oaths by various elements of creation underscores the importance and truth of the message that follows in the surah. By invoking the earth, the verse highlights themes of divine care, provision, and the intricate balance that sustains life. It encourages believers to reflect on the signs of Allah in the natural world and to consider their responsibilities towards it, as well as the moral and ethical lessons imparted by the surah.

Reflection on Creation

This verse invites believers to contemplate the creation of the earth as a sign of Allah's power and wisdom. The earth's ability to sustain life and its resources are manifestations of divine mercy, encouraging believers to acknowledge the signs of Allah and strengthen their faith.

In summary, the sixth verse of Surah Ash-Shams uses the earth and its spreading to symbolize the provision and care inherent in divine creation. This natural phenomenon emphasizes the themes of divine wisdom and the need for humans to reflect on the signs of Allah in their lives. This continues to set the stage for the surah's exploration of human morality and ethical responsibility.

Verse 7

"Wa nafsin wa mā sawwāhā"

"And [by] the soul and He who proportioned it"

Oath by the Soul

In this verse, Allah swears by the human soul, emphasizing its significance and the meticulous care with which it has been fashioned. The soul represents the essence of human life, encompassing consciousness, intellect, and moral capacity. This oath highlights the profound nature of the soul and its central role in human existence.

The Proportioning of the Soul

The phrase "and He who proportioned it" refers to the way Allah has created and balanced the soul, endowing it with the ability to discern, choose, and incline towards both good and evil. This proportioning indicates the inherent potential within the soul for moral and ethical development, as well as the responsibility that comes with such endowment.

Symbolism of the Soul

The soul symbolizes the inner dimension of human beings, including their spiritual and ethical aspects. It represents the capacity for awareness, reflection, and moral decision-making. The soul's creation and balance are a testament to Allah's wisdom and the trust placed in humans to uphold moral integrity.

Purpose of the Oaths

The series of oaths by various elements of creation emphasizes the importance and certainty of the message that follows in the surah. By invoking the soul, the verse highlights the themes of human potential, moral responsibility, and the divine trust endowed upon individuals. It serves as a prelude to the lessons on human morality and ethical conduct that are central to the surah.

Reflection on Human Nature

This verse invites believers to reflect on the nature of the soul as a sign of Allah's creative power and wisdom. The soul's capacity for moral discernment and choice underscores the importance of adhering to divine guidance and striving for spiritual growth. Believers are encouraged to acknowledge this profound gift and to cultivate their souls in alignment with divine will.

In summary, the seventh verse of Surah Ash-Shams uses the soul and its proportioning to highlight the profound nature of human existence and the moral responsibility endowed upon individuals. This focus on the inner dimension of humanity emphasizes the themes of divine wisdom and the need for humans to reflect on their moral and ethical responsibilities. This continues to set the stage for the surah's exploration of human morality and ethical accountability.

Verse 8

"Fa-alhamahā fujūrahā wa taqwāhā"

"And inspired it [with discernment of] its wickedness and its righteousness"

Inspiration of the Soul

This verse describes how Allah has inspired the human soul with an innate understanding of both wickedness and righteousness. This divine inspiration endows individuals with the capacity to distinguish between right and wrong, guiding them in moral and ethical decision-making.

Discernment of Wickedness and Righteousness

The terms "fujūrahā" (its wickedness) and "taqwāhā" (its righteousness) refer to the dual inclinations within the human soul. On one hand, the soul has the potential to incline towards wrongdoing and moral corruption. On the other hand, it has the ability to pursue righteousness, piety, and moral virtue. This dual capacity underscores the responsibility of individuals to exercise their free will in choosing the path of righteousness.

Human Moral Responsibility

The verse highlights the moral responsibility placed upon individuals to nurture their righteousness and resist their inclinations toward wickedness. This internal moral compass is a testament to Allah's wisdom in creating humans with the ability to self-reflect and strive for ethical conduct.

Purpose of the Message

This verse serves as a pivotal point in the surah, emphasizing the themes of moral responsibility and ethical accountability. It underscores the importance of heeding divine guidance and making conscious choices that align with righteousness. The verse prepares the reader for the subsequent discussion on the consequences of one's moral choices.

Reflection on Human Nature

Believers are encouraged to reflect on their inner capacities for discernment and moral choice. The ability to distinguish between good and evil is a sign of Allah's favour and trust placed in humanity. This reflection should inspire individuals to cultivate their righteousness and seek divine guidance in their actions.

In summary, the eighth verse of Surah Ash-Shams highlights the divine inspiration within the human soul, granting it the ability to discern between wickedness and righteousness. This emphasis on moral discernment and responsibility is central to the surah's exploration of human morality and ethical accountability.

Verse 9
"Qad aflaha man zakkāhā"

"He has succeeded who purifies it"

Success Through Purification

This verse emphasizes that true success is attained by those who purify their souls. The term "zakkāhā" refers to the purification and nurturing of the soul, which involves cultivating righteousness, piety, and moral integrity. This process of purification is central to achieving spiritual success and fulfillment.

The Concept of Purification

Purification of the soul involves self-discipline, self-reflection, and adherence to moral and ethical principles. It requires individuals to strive against their base desires and inclinations toward wrongdoing, seeking instead to align their actions and intentions with divine guidance and righteousness.

Definition of Success

In the context of this verse, success is not defined by worldly achievements or material gains but by the spiritual and moral development of the individual. True success is measured by the state of the soul and its alignment with divine will, leading to eternal rewards in the hereafter.

Encouragement for Self-Improvement

This verse serves as an encouragement for believers to engage in continuous self-improvement and spiritual growth. It highlights the importance of being mindful of one's actions and intentions, striving to purify the soul from negative traits such as greed, envy, and arrogance.

Connection to Previous Verses

This verse follows the explanation of the dual capacities of the soul for wickedness and righteousness. It underscores the importance of choosing the path of righteousness and actively working to purify the soul, aligning with the divine inspiration mentioned earlier.

In summary, the ninth verse of Surah Ash-Shams highlights the success achieved by those who purify their souls. This emphasis on spiritual purification and moral integrity is central to the surah's exploration of human morality and ethical responsibility, encouraging believers to strive for righteousness and spiritual growth.

Verse 10

"Qad aflaha man zakkāhā"

"He has succeeded who purifies it"

Success Through Purification

This verse emphasizes that true success is attained by those who purify their souls. The term "zakkāhā" refers to the purification and nurturing of the soul, which involves cultivating righteousness, piety, and moral integrity. This process of purification is central to achieving spiritual success and fulfillment.

The Concept of Purification

Purification of the soul involves self-discipline, self-reflection, and adherence to moral and ethical principles. It requires individuals to strive against their base desires and inclinations toward wrongdoing, seeking instead to align their actions and intentions with divine guidance and righteousness.

Definition of Success

In the context of this verse, success is not defined by worldly achievements or material gains but by the spiritual and moral development of the individual. True success is measured by the state of the soul and its alignment with divine will, leading to eternal rewards in the hereafter.

Encouragement for Self-Improvement

This verse serves as an encouragement for believers to engage in continuous self-improvement and spiritual growth. It highlights the importance of being mindful of one's actions and intentions, striving to purify the soul from negative traits such as greed, envy, and arrogance.

Connection to Previous Verses

This verse follows the explanation of the dual capacities of the soul for wickedness and righteousness. It underscores the importance of choosing the path of righteousness and actively working to purify the soul, aligning with the divine inspiration mentioned earlier.

In summary, the ninth verse of Surah Ash-Shams highlights the success achieved by those who purify their souls. This emphasis on spiritual purification and moral integrity is central to the surah's exploration of human morality and ethical responsibility, encouraging believers to strive for righteousness and spiritual growth.

Verse 11

"Kadhdhabat Thamūdu biṭaghwāhā"

"Thamud denied [their prophet] by reason of their transgression"

Reference to the People of Thamud

This verse introduces the historical example of the people of Thamud, an ancient tribe known for their advanced civilization but also for their arrogance and defiance of divine guidance. The Thamud people were sent the prophet Salih, who called them to righteousness and worship of Allah alone.

Denial Due to Transgression

The term "biṭaghwāhā" refers to the transgression and rebellion of the Thamud people. Their denial of the prophet Salih and his message was rooted in their excessive pride, disobedience, and indulgence in sinful behaviour. This transgression led them to reject the divine message and ultimately face severe consequences.

Lessons from the Thamud

The mention of Thamud serves as a warning and a lesson for all humanity. Their story illustrates the dangers of arrogance, moral corruption, and the refusal to heed divine guidance. It underscores the consequences of allowing transgression to overshadow the innate capacity for righteousness and discernment.

Connection to Previous Verses

This verse connects to the earlier discussion about the soul's capacity for both wickedness and righteousness. It provides a historical example of a people who allowed their transgression to dominate, leading to their downfall. This serves as a cautionary tale for readers to reflect on their own choices and avoid the path of corruption.

Moral and Ethical Implications

The story of Thamud emphasizes the importance of humility, obedience to divine guidance, and the pursuit of righteousness. It highlights the need for individuals and communities to be mindful of their actions and to strive for moral and ethical integrity, avoiding the pitfalls of arrogance and rebellion.

In summary, the eleventh verse of Surah Ash-Shams highlights the denial of the Thamud people due to their transgression. This serves as a powerful reminder of the consequences of rejecting divine guidance and allowing transgression to overshadow righteousness, reinforcing the surah's themes of moral responsibility and ethical accountability.

Verse 12

"Idhin baʿatha ashqāhā"

"When the most wicked of them was sent forth"

The Most Wicked Among Them

This verse refers to a specific incident involving the people of Thamud, where the most wicked individual among them took a leading role in their transgression. According to Islamic tradition, this person was identified as the one who acted to harm the she-camel that was sent as a sign and a test to the Thamud by Allah through the prophet Salih.

The She-Camel as a Test

The she-camel was a miraculous sign provided to Thamud to test their obedience and faith. They were instructed not to harm it and to allow it to graze freely. However, their arrogance and defiance led them to disregard this command, and the most wicked among them took the initiative to harm the camel, leading to severe consequences for the entire community.

Symbolism of Wickedness

This verse highlights the role of individuals who incite and lead others into wrongdoing and transgression. The actions of the "most wicked" serve as a catalyst for communal sin, illustrating how individual actions can have far-reaching negative impacts on society.

Connection to the Theme of Accountability

The mention of this incident underscores the importance of moral responsibility and the consequences of defying divine commands. It serves as a reminder of the potential for destruction when individuals and communities allow wickedness to prevail over righteousness.

Moral and Ethical Lessons

This verse, along with the surrounding narrative of Thamud, emphasizes the need for vigilance against following or supporting those who lead others astray. It highlights the importance of maintaining moral integrity and adhering to divine guidance, even in the face of societal pressure or temptation to do otherwise.

In summary, the twelfth verse of Surah Ash-Shams refers to the emergence of the most wicked individual among the Thamud, illustrating the dangers of transgression and the significant consequences of defying divine guidance. This reinforces the surah's themes of moral responsibility and the importance of choosing righteousness over wickedness.

Verse 13

"Faqāla lahum rasūlu Allāhi nāqata Allāhi wa suqyāhā"

"And the messenger of Allah [Salih] said to them, '[Do not harm] the she-camel of Allah and [prevent her from] her drink.'"

The Messenger's Warning

In this verse, the prophet Salih, referred to as the "messenger of Allah," is depicted warning his people, the Thamud, not to harm the she-camel, which was a miraculous sign from Allah. He emphasizes the importance of respecting the she-camel and ensuring it receives its rightful share of water.

The She-Camel of Allah

The she-camel is described as belonging to Allah, highlighting its significance as a divine sign and test for the Thamud. It was meant to be a symbol of Allah's power and a test of their obedience and faith. The community was instructed to allow the camel to graze and drink freely as part of their covenant with Allah.

Importance of the Warning

The warning from Salih underscores the gravity of the situation. It reflects the mercy and patience of Allah, giving the Thamud ample opportunity to heed the warning and avoid the consequences of their transgression. Salih's message was clear: respect the divine sign and adhere to the command to avoid incurring divine wrath.

Symbolism of the Divine Test

The she-camel's presence and the command to respect it symbolize a broader test of faith and obedience. It serves as a metaphor for the tests and trials that individuals and communities face, requiring them to choose between following divine guidance and succumbing to transgression.

Moral and Ethical Lessons

This verse highlights the importance of heeding prophetic warnings and respecting the signs of Allah. It serves as a reminder of the consequences of ignoring divine guidance and the responsibility to act in accordance with moral and ethical principles.

In summary, the thirteenth verse of Surah Ash-Shams recounts the warning given by the prophet Salih to the people of Thamud concerning the she-camel. It underscores the importance of respecting divine signs and adhering to Allah's commands, reinforcing the surah's themes of moral responsibility and the consequences of transgression.

Verse 14

"Fakadhdhabūhu faʿaqarūhā fadamdama ʿalayhim rabbuhum bidhambihim fasawwāhā"

"But they denied him and hamstrung her, so their Lord brought down upon them destruction for their sin and made it equal upon all of them."

Denial and Defiance

This verse describes the reaction of the Thamud people to the prophet Salih's warning. Despite the clear sign and command, they denied Salih's message and proceeded to harm the she-camel. Their action of hamstringing the camel reflects their blatant defiance and rejection of divine guidance.

Consequences of Their Actions

As a result of their sin, Allah brought down severe punishment upon the Thamud. The phrase "fadamdama ʿalayhim" refers to the overwhelming destruction that befell them. This reflects the divine justice meted out in response to their transgression and defiance.

Equal Punishment

The verse emphasizes that the punishment was made equal upon all of them. This indicates that the entire community bore the consequences of the collective sin, highlighting the shared responsibility and the impact of communal wrongdoing.

Lessons on Divine Justice

This verse serves as a powerful reminder of the consequences of rejecting divine guidance and engaging in transgression. It underscores the concept of divine justice, where actions have consequences, and communities are held accountable for their collective behaviour.

Moral and Ethical Implications

The story of Thamud illustrates the dangers of arrogance, defiance, and the refusal to heed prophetic warnings. It emphasizes the importance of maintaining moral integrity, respecting divine signs, and adhering to ethical principles to avoid the consequences of collective wrongdoing.

In summary, the fourteenth verse of Surah Ash-Shams recounts the denial and defiance of the Thamud people, leading to their destruction as a consequence of their sin. It reinforces the surah's themes of moral responsibility, divine justice, and the importance of adhering to divine guidance to avoid the severe consequences of transgression.

Verse 15

"Wa lā yakhāfu ʿuqbāhā"

"And He does not fear the consequence thereof."

Divine Confidence in Justice

This verse concludes the account of the Thamud by emphasizing that Allah does not fear the consequences of the punishment He decrees. It underscores the absolute authority and sovereignty of Allah in administering justice. Unlike human actions, which may have unforeseen consequences, divine justice is executed with complete wisdom and certainty.

The Nature of Divine Justice

Allah's justice is perfect and flawless. This verse highlights the fact that when Allah enacts His will, it is done with full knowledge and wisdom, without concern for any repercussions. It serves to remind believers of the perfection and infallibility of divine decisions.

Assurance of Accountability

This verse reassures that all actions, particularly those involving transgressions and defiance against divine guidance, are subject to Allah's judgment. It emphasizes that nothing escapes Allah's knowledge and that justice will be served without any flaw or fear of error.

Moral and Ethical Implications

For the believers, this verse serves as a reminder of the importance of aligning one's actions with divine guidance, knowing that Allah's justice is comprehensive and inevitable. It encourages individuals to reflect on their actions, strive for righteousness, and be mindful of their responsibilities.

Conclusion of the Narrative

As the concluding verse of the surah, it ties together the themes of divine justice, moral responsibility, and the consequences of transgression. It serves as a powerful reminder of the ultimate accountability to Allah and the importance of heeding divine guidance.

In summary, the fifteenth verse of Surah Ash-Shams emphasizes Allah's absolute authority and confidence in administering justice. It reinforces the surah's themes of moral responsibility, divine justice, and the importance of adhering to divine guidance to avoid the severe consequences of transgression.

Key lessons to be learned from Surah Ash-Shams:

1. Distinction Between Good and Evil: Surah Ash-Shams emphasizes the clear difference between righteousness and wickedness, much like the differences between natural phenomena such as day and night, or the sun and the moon.
2. Innate Moral Compass: Humans are endowed with an innate ability to discern right from wrong. This natural inspiration guides us to recognize good as good and evil as evil.
3. Moral Responsibility: The surah highlights the importance of using our capacity for judgment to nurture good traits and suppress negative tendencies. Success is achieved by purifying the soul and fostering righteousness.

4. Consequences of Actions: Through the story of the people of Thamud, the surah illustrates the severe consequences of rejecting divine guidance and indulging in transgression. It serves as a warning about the dangers of arrogance and defiance.
5. Divine Justice: The surah underscores the certainty and inevitability of divine justice, where actions have consequences, and accountability is assured.
6. Need for Prophetic Guidance: While humans have an innate sense of morality, the surah also highlights the necessity of prophetic guidance to provide clear and detailed instructions on living a righteous life.

By reflecting on these lessons, individuals are encouraged to align their lives with moral and ethical principles, seeking to purify their souls and live in accordance with divine guidance.

SUMMARY OF
SURAH ASH SHAMS- SURAH 91

The chapter is called "Ash-Shams" because it starts with that word, meaning "the sun."

It was revealed early in the Prophet Muhammad's (peace be upon him) mission in Mecca, during a time of strong opposition.

Themes and Structure:

The chapter talks about the difference between good and evil and warns people who choose to follow the wrong path.

It is divided into two parts: the first part is verses 1-10, and the second part is verses 11-15.

First Part (Verses 1-10):

1. Natural Differences: Just like the sun and moon, day and night, and earth and sky are different, so are good and evil.
2. Built-In Guidance: Allah has given humans an inner sense to tell right from wrong.
3. Moral Responsibility: Success comes from developing good traits and overcoming bad ones.

Second Part (Verses 11-15):

Story of Thamud: This part tells the story of the people of Thamud to show why prophets are needed. Even though people have an inner sense of right and wrong, they often need clear guidance from prophets.

Prophet Salih's Warning: The Thamud rejected their prophet, Salih, and harmed a special camel sent by Allah, which led to their destruction.

SURAH ASH-SHAMS

Questions

1. What is the primary theme of Surah Ash-Shams?
2. Which celestial bodies and natural phenomena are mentioned in the oaths at the beginning of the surah?
3. How does the surah describe the human soul in relation to righteousness and wickedness?
4. What example from history is mentioned in Surah Ash-Shams to illustrate the consequences of moral corruption?
5. How does the surah emphasize the importance of self-purification?
6. What is the significance of the oaths taken at the beginning of the surah?
7. What lesson can be learned from the fate of the people mentioned in the surah?
8. How does Surah Ash-Shams describe the successful individual?
9. What does the surah imply about the balance between divine guidance and human free will?
10. How can the teachings of Surah Ash-Shams be applied to contemporary life?

Answers

1. What is the primary theme of Surah Ash-Shams?
   - The primary theme of Surah Ash-Shams is the contrast between righteousness and wickedness and the importance of self-purification and moral integrity.

2. Which celestial bodies and natural phenomena are mentioned in the oaths at the beginning of the surah?
   - The surah begins with oaths by the sun, the moon, the day, the night, the sky, and the earth, highlighting the natural order and balance created by Allah.

3. How does the surah describe the human soul in relation to righteousness and wickedness?
   - The surah states that every soul has been inspired with both its wickedness and its righteousness, emphasizing the responsibility of individuals to choose the path of purity.

4. What example from history is mentioned in Surah Ash-Shams to illustrate the consequences of moral corruption?
   - The surah mentions the story of the people of Thamud and their destruction as a consequence of rejecting divine guidance and moral corruption.

5. How does the surah emphasize the importance of self-purification?
   - The surah declares that success is achieved by those who purify their souls, while failure befalls those who neglect their moral duties.

6. What is the significance of the oaths taken at the beginning of the surah?
   - The oaths underscore the divine order and balance in the universe, serving as a reminder of the importance of adhering to moral and spiritual principles.

7. What lesson can be learned from the fate of the people mentioned in the surah?
   - The lesson is that rejecting divine guidance and indulging in moral corruption leads to destruction, while righteousness leads to success.

8. How does Surah Ash-Shams describe the successful individual?
   - The successful individual is described as one who purifies their soul, adhering to righteousness and moral integrity.

9. What does the surah imply about the balance between divine guidance and human free will?
   - The surah suggests that while divine guidance is provided, it is up to each individual to choose between righteousness and wickedness, highlighting human free will.

10. How can the teachings of Surah Ash-Shams be applied to contemporary life?
    - The teachings encourage self-reflection, personal accountability, and the pursuit of moral integrity, urging individuals to make ethical choices and purify their souls in daily life.

These questions and answers can be used for educational purposes, study sessions, or discussions to enhance understanding of Surah Ash-Shams.

Multiple Choice Questions

1. What celestial bodies are mentioned in the oaths at the beginning of Surah Ash-Shams?

    - A) The sun and the stars

    - B) The sun and the moon

    - C) The earth and the mountains

    - D) The ocean and the rivers

2. Which natural phenomena are included in the oaths at the beginning of the surah?

    - A) The rain and the wind

    - B) The thunder and lightning

    - C) The day and the night

    - D) The seasons and the tides

3. How does Surah Ash-Shams describe the human soul?

    - A) As inherently evil

    - B) As inspired with both wickedness and righteousness

    - C) As naturally pure and good

    - D) As indifferent to moral choices

4. What historical example is mentioned in Surah Ash-Shams to illustrate the consequences of moral corruption?

    - A) The people of Sodom

    - B) The people of Thamud

    - C) The people of Babylon

    - D) The people of Nineveh

5. According to Surah Ash-Shams, who achieves success?

    - A) Those who accumulate wealth

    - B) Those who purify their souls

    - C) Those who gain power and influence

    - D) Those who travel widely

6. What is the fate of those who neglect their moral duties, as described in the surah?

    - A) They achieve happiness

    - B) They find peace

    - C) They face failure

    - D) They gain respect

7. How does the surah emphasize the importance of self-purification?

    - A) By stating that wealth leads to success

    - B) By highlighting the example of the prophets

    - C) By declaring that purification of the soul leads to success

    - D) By focusing on physical strength

8. What does the surah imply about the relationship between divine guidance and human free will?

    - A) Divine guidance is irrelevant

    - B) Human free will does not exist

    - C) Humans are free to choose between righteousness and wickedness

    - D) Divine guidance forces people to be righteous

Answers

1. B) The sun and the moon
2. C) The day and the night
3. B) As inspired with both wickedness and righteousness
4. B) The people of Thamud
5. B) Those who purify their souls
6. C) They face failure
7. C) By declaring that purification of the soul leads to success
8. C) Humans are free to choose between righteousness and wickedness

These questions and answers can be used for quizzes, educational discussions, or self-study to enhance understanding of Surah Ash-Shams.

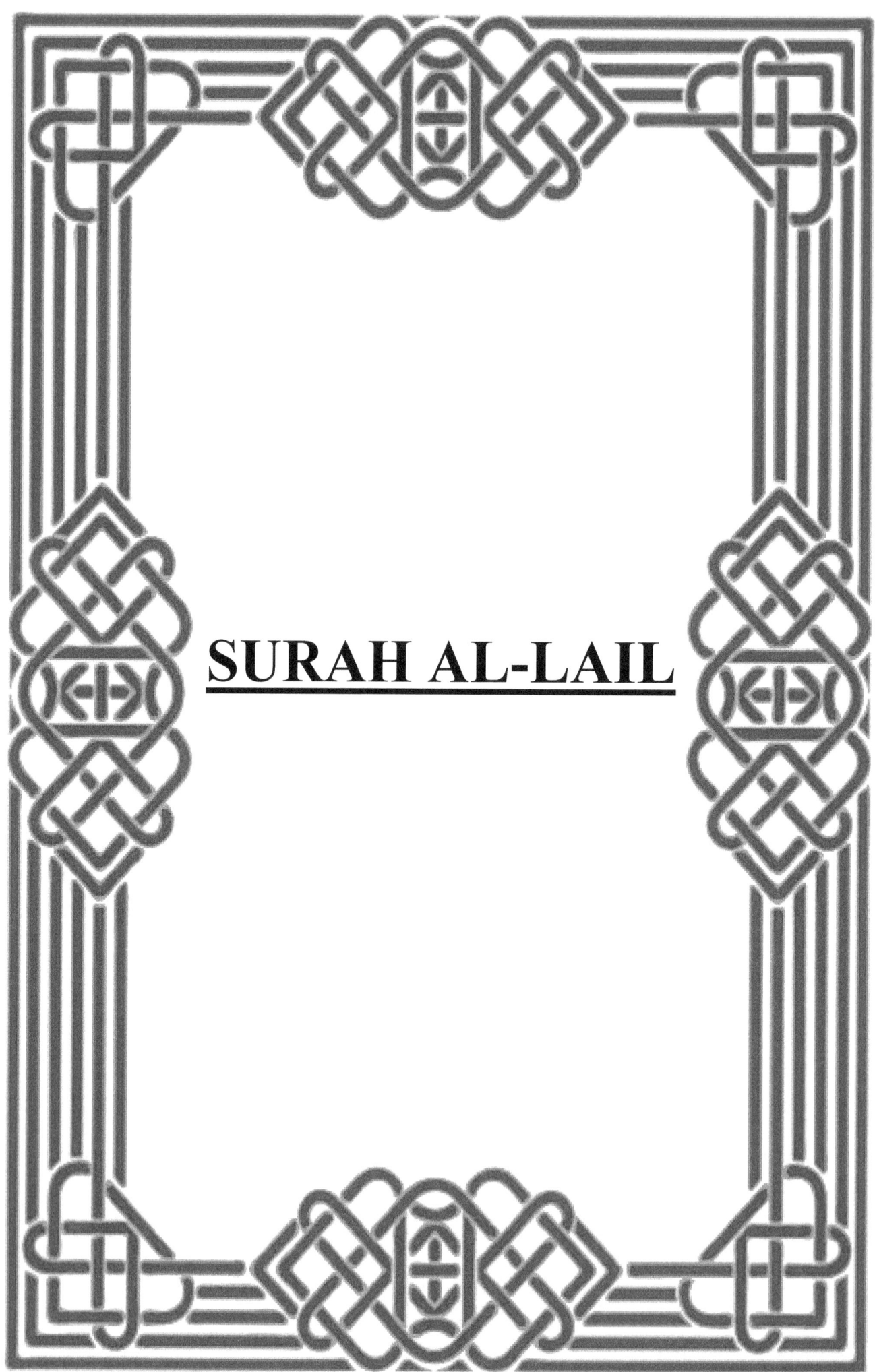

SURAH AL-LAIL

SURAH AL-LAIL

Bismillahi ar-Rahmani ar-Raheem

Verse 1

"Wal-layli idha yaghsha"

Translation: "By the night when it covers"

This verse begins with an oath, as many verses in the Quran do, to emphasize the significance of the message that will follow. The night is used as a symbol here, specifically focusing on the time when it envelops or covers everything in darkness. This imagery of the night covering the world serves as a powerful metaphor for various concepts, such as the transitions and contrasts in life, the hidden and the apparent, or even the different paths and choices individuals face.

In the context of the Surah, the night represents one of the natural phenomena created by Allah, highlighting His power and wisdom. By swearing an oath by the night, the verse calls attention to the natural order and balance in the universe, setting the stage for the subsequent discussion about the two divergent paths of human life and their ultimate outcomes. The night, with its encompassing nature, serves as a reminder of the enveloping presence and authority of Allah over all creation.

Verse 2

Wannahaari izaa tajalla

"And [by] the day when it appears in brightness"

This verse continues the use of natural phenomena to emphasize the message. Here, the day is highlighted, specifically focusing on the time when it becomes bright and everything is illuminated. The day, with its clarity and light, contrasts with the night mentioned in the previous verse, underscoring the theme of duality and contrast that runs throughout the Surah.

By swearing an oath by the day as it shines and reveals all things, the verse draws attention to the cycles and balance in the natural world created by Allah. This serves as a reminder of the clarity and guidance that can be found in life, paralleling the contrast between right and wrong, or guidance and misguidance, which are key themes in the Surah. The juxtaposition of night and day sets the stage for exploring the different paths people choose in life and their ultimate consequences.

Verse 3

"Wa ma khalaqa adh-dhakara wal-untha"

"And [by] He who created the male and female"

This verse continues the pattern of oaths used in the Surah to emphasize the importance of the message. Here, the focus shifts from the natural phenomena of night and day to the creation of male and female. By referencing the creation of gender, the verse highlights the diversity and duality present within human existence, which is another aspect of the natural order established by Allah.

The mention of male and female serves as a reminder of the complementary roles and balance in creation. It underscores the theme of duality, reflecting the broader contrasts between different ways of living and the choices individuals make. Just as night and day are distinct yet part of a harmonious cycle, so too are male and female part of the balance in human life.

This verse, therefore, emphasizes Allah's power and wisdom in creating such balance and diversity in the world. It sets the stage for the subsequent discussion about the different paths people take in life, highlighting that just as there are clear differences in creation, there are also clear distinctions between the righteous and unrighteous paths individuals can follow.

Verse 4

"Inna sa'yakum lashatta"

"Indeed, your efforts are diverse."

This verse shifts the focus to human actions and efforts. It acknowledges that people engage in various kinds of efforts and pursuits in their lives. The term "diverse" emphasizes the wide range of activities, goals, and paths that individuals choose to follow.

By highlighting the diversity of human effort, this verse introduces the central theme of the Surah, which is the contrast between the different paths that people take and their respective outcomes. Some pursue paths of righteousness, generosity, and Allah-consciousness, while others may follow paths of miserliness, heedlessness, and rejection of good.

This acknowledgment of diverse efforts sets the stage for the verses that follow, which elaborate on the consequences of these different paths. It serves as a reminder that although human endeavors are varied, they are not equal in terms of their moral and spiritual value, and they lead to different ultimate ends.

Verse 5

"Fa-amma man a'ṭā wattaqā"

Translation: "So as for he who gives and fears [Allah]"

This verse begins a description of one of the two main paths of human behavior mentioned in the Surah. It refers to the person who is generous ("gives") and is conscious of Allah ("fears [Allah]"). Giving here implies spending in charity and helping others, reflecting a selfless and compassionate nature. Fearing Allah, or having Allah-consciousness (taqwa), involves living a life in accordance with divine guidance, being aware of one's responsibilities towards Allah and avoiding actions that incur His displeasure.

This verse highlights the positive moral and spiritual characteristics of a person who chooses the righteous path. It signifies a life led by generosity, piety, and a deep sense of accountability to Allah. Such actions are portrayed as virtuous and are implied to lead to a favorable outcome, as elaborated in the subsequent verses. This sets the groundwork for contrasting this behavior with the other type of path, which involves different, less commendable attributes.

Verse 6

"Wa ṣaddaqa bil-ḥusnā"

Translation: "And believes in the best [reward]."

This verse continues to describe the characteristics of the person who follows the righteous path. It highlights the importance of belief, specifically in "the best," which can be understood as the best reward or the ultimate good. This belief refers to having faith in the promises of Allah, such as the rewards of the Hereafter and the truth of His guidance.

By believing in the best, this person affirms their trust in Allah's promises and acts with the conviction that their good deeds and righteous conduct will lead to positive outcomes, both in this life and the Hereafter. This belief motivates them to continue on the path of righteousness, characterized by generosity and Allah-consciousness.

Overall, this verse emphasizes the importance of faith in divine rewards as a driving force behind ethical and moral behavior, reinforcing the idea that belief and action are interconnected in the journey towards spiritual success.

Verse 7

"Fasanu yassiruhu lil-yusra"

Translation: "So We will ease him toward ease."

This verse promises that for the person who is generous, Allah-conscious, and believes in the best reward (as described in the previous verses), Allah will make the path of ease accessible for them. The "ease" referred to here can be understood as a life that aligns with goodness, righteousness, and spiritual contentment.

This means that Allah will facilitate the journey for those who choose the righteous path by making it easier for them to perform good deeds and live a life in accordance with divine guidance. Their hearts and circumstances will be inclined towards what is good, and they will find it easier to avoid sin and wrongdoing.

The verse underscores a reciprocal relationship: when individuals strive to act righteously and maintain faith in Allah's rewards, Allah, in turn, supports and guides them, making their path smoother and more fulfilling. It highlights the divine assistance and blessings that accompany sincere faith and good actions.

Verse 8

"Wa amma man bakhila wastaghna"

Translation: "But as for he who withholds and considers himself free of need,"

This verse begins to describe the characteristics of the person who follows the opposite path to that of righteousness. It highlights two key traits: miserliness and a sense of self-sufficiency or independence from Allah.

1. Withholds (Bakhila): This refers to being stingy or miserly, particularly with wealth. Instead of being generous and giving to others, this person hoards their resources, unwilling to spend in the way of Allah or for the benefit of others.
2. Considers himself free of need (Wastaghna): This describes an attitude of self-reliance or arrogance, where a person believes they do not need Allah or divine guidance. They may feel self-sufficient due to their wealth, status, or abilities, leading them to neglect their spiritual responsibilities and dependence on Allah.

This verse sets up a contrast with the previous description of the righteous person. It suggests that the path of miserliness and arrogance leads away from divine favor and guidance, as will be further elaborated in the following verses.

Verse 9

"Wa kadhdaba bil-ḥusnā"

Translation: "And denies the best [reward]."

This verse continues to describe the characteristics of the person who follows the path opposite to righteousness. It highlights the act of denying or rejecting "the best," which can be understood as the best reward or ultimate good promised by Allah.

By denying the best reward, this person lacks faith in the promises of Allah, such as the rewards of the Hereafter and the truth of His guidance. This disbelief or rejection of divine promises often leads to a life focused on immediate, worldly gains rather than spiritual or moral values.

This verse emphasizes the contrast between those who believe in and work towards the ultimate good and those who reject it, choosing instead a path characterized by miserliness, arrogance, and disbelief. It sets the stage for the consequences of such choices, which will be further detailed in the following verses.

Verse 10

"Fasanu yassiruhu lil-'usra"

"So We will ease him toward difficulty."

This verse explains the consequence for the person who chooses the path of miserliness, arrogance, and disbelief, as described in the preceding verses. It states that Allah will make the path of difficulty accessible for them.

The "difficulty" here refers to a life that is spiritually challenging and morally problematic. For someone who withholds, feels self-sufficient, and denies divine guidance, their path in life becomes fraught with obstacles, making it easier for them to engage in wrongdoings and harder to find peace and fulfillment.

This verse underscores the idea that just as Allah facilitates the path of ease for those who are righteous and believe in His rewards, He also allows those who choose the opposite path to face the natural consequences of their choices. It highlights the principle of divine justice, where individuals are guided or left to their chosen paths based on their actions and beliefs.

Verse 11

"Wa mā yugh'nī 'anhu māluhu idhā taraddā"

"And his wealth will not avail him when he falls."

This verse emphasizes that the wealth of a person who follows the path of miserliness and disbelief will be of no benefit to them in the end. The phrase "when he falls" can be understood as referring to the ultimate downfall or demise of such an individual, particularly in the context of the Hereafter.

The verse underscores the idea that material wealth, no matter how abundant, cannot save a person from the consequences of their spiritual and moral failures. When a person prioritizes wealth over righteousness and divine guidance, they may find temporary comfort in this world, but this wealth holds no value in the face of divine judgment.

This verse serves as a reminder that true success and salvation depend not on material possessions but on one's faith, actions, and adherence to the path of righteousness. It highlights the futility of relying solely on worldly assets when confronted with the realities of life and the Hereafter.

Verse 12

"Inna 'alaynā lal-hudā"

"Indeed, [incumbent] upon Us is guidance."

This verse asserts that it is Allah's responsibility to provide guidance to humanity. It emphasizes that Allah has undertaken the task of showing people the right path, ensuring they are not left without direction or knowledge of what is good and righteous.

The verse reassures that guidance is part of Allah's divine plan and wisdom. He provides it through various means, such as sending prophets, revealing scriptures, and instilling an innate sense of right and wrong within human beings. This guidance is accessible to all, but it is up to individuals to choose whether to follow it.

This verse highlights the benevolence and justice of Allah, affirming that He has not left humanity without the means to distinguish between right and wrong. It also underscores the importance of seeking and adhering to this divine guidance for a successful and fulfilling life.

Verse 13

"Wa innā lanā lal-ākhirata wal-ūlā"

"And indeed, to Us belongs the Hereafter and the first [life]."

This verse emphasizes Allah's sovereignty over both the present life (referred to as "the first") and the Hereafter. It underscores that Allah has complete control and ownership over all aspects of existence, both in this world and the next.

By declaring that both realms belong to Him, the verse reminds believers that their ultimate accountability is to Allah, who governs both this life and the life to come. It serves to reinforce the idea that while humans may focus on their worldly pursuits, the true purpose and end lie beyond this life, in the Hereafter.

This understanding encourages individuals to align their actions with divine guidance, recognizing that success and fulfillment in both worlds depend on their relationship with Allah. It is a call to prioritize spiritual and moral values over temporary, worldly gains.

Verse 14

"Fa-andhartukum nāran talaẓẓā"

"So I have warned you of a Fire which is blazing."

In this verse, Allah warns of a severe punishment in the form of a blazing fire, which refers to Hell. The warning serves as a serious reminder of the consequences for those who choose to reject divine guidance and follow the path of miserliness, arrogance, and disbelief, as described in the earlier verses.

The imagery of a "blazing" fire underscores the intensity and severity of the punishment, highlighting the serious nature of the choices individuals make in their lives. This verse acts as a strong admonition, urging people to reflect on their actions and beliefs and to consider the ultimate consequences of their choices.

The warning is meant to encourage individuals to turn towards righteousness, generosity, and belief in the divine reward, thus avoiding the dire consequences of a life led astray. It is a call to heed the guidance provided by Allah and to live in a way that aligns with His commandments.

Verse 15

"Lā yaṣlāhā illā l-ashqā"

"None will enter it except the most wretched."

This verse highlights that the blazing fire, or Hell, is specifically reserved for "the most wretched" individuals. It implies that those who will face this severe punishment are those who have chosen to live in a way that rejects divine guidance, characterized by miserliness, disbelief, and arrogance.

"The most wretched" refers to those who have persistently turned away from the truth and lived a life of moral and spiritual corruption. It emphasizes that entering the fire is not a random occurrence, but a consequence of one's actions and choices.

This verse serves as a warning and a call to self-reflection, encouraging individuals to examine their lives and ensure they are not among those who are heedless of the guidance provided by Allah. It underscores the importance of aligning one's life with righteousness and faith to avoid being counted among those who are destined for such a fate.

Verse 16

"Alladhī kadhdhaba watawallā"

"He who had denied and turned away."

This verse specifies the behavior and characteristics of "the most wretched" mentioned in the previous verse. It describes two key actions:

1. "Denied" (Kadhdhaba): This refers to rejecting or denying the truth and the message brought by the prophets and the revelations from Allah. It implies disbelief in the divine guidance and the ultimate truths about life and the Hereafter.
2. "Turned away" (Tawallā): This means turning away from the path of righteousness and ignoring the guidance that was provided. It indicates a willful abandonment of one's responsibilities towards Allah and a refusal to follow the moral and ethical teachings prescribed in the divine message.

Together, these actions lead to the wretched state mentioned earlier, as they signify a conscious choice to reject and avoid the path of guidance and good. This verse serves as a caution to avoid such attitudes and behaviors and underscores the importance of embracing faith and righteousness.

Verse 17

"Wa sayujannabuhā al-atqā"

"But the righteous one will be kept away from it."

This verse provides a contrast to the fate of "the most wretched" by highlighting the destiny of "the righteous one" or "the most pious." It reassures that those who are righteous and Allah-fearing will be saved from the blazing fire of Hell.

"The righteous one" refers to individuals who have lived their lives in accordance with divine guidance, characterized by belief, piety, generosity, and adherence to moral and ethical principles. These are the people who strive to align their actions with the teachings of Allah and work towards spiritual and moral excellence.

This verse serves as a source of hope and encouragement for believers, affirming that sincere faith and righteous conduct lead to protection from the severe punishment described in previous verses. It emphasizes the importance of striving for piety and righteousness to attain salvation and divine favour.

Verse 18

"Alladhī yu'tī mālahu yatazakkā"

"He who gives from his wealth to purify himself."

This verse describes one of the key characteristics of "the righteous one" mentioned in the previous verse. It highlights the act of giving wealth as a means of self-purification.

1. "Gives from his wealth" refers to the act of charity and generosity. It involves using one's financial resources to help others, support good causes, and fulfill social and religious obligations such as zakat (almsgiving).
2. "To purify himself" indicates that the motivation behind this generosity is self-purification. This means that the act of giving is not just for show or personal gain, but is intended to cleanse one's heart and soul, drawing closer to Allah and seeking His pleasure.

The verse underscores the importance of charitable giving as a path to spiritual growth and purification. It emphasizes that true righteousness involves using one's resources in a way that aligns with divine guidance and benefits both the individual and the broader community.

Verse 19

"Wa mā li'aḥadin 'indahu min ni'matin tujzā"

"And not [giving] for anyone who has [done him] a favor to be rewarded."

This verse emphasizes the sincerity and purity of the intentions behind the righteous person's acts of charity and generosity. It highlights that their giving is not motivated by a desire to repay someone for a favor they received or to gain something in return.

Instead, the righteous person gives selflessly, without any expectation of worldly rewards or reciprocation from others. Their actions are driven by a genuine desire to purify themselves, seek Allah's pleasure, and fulfill their moral and spiritual obligations.

This verse underscores the concept of altruism in Islam, where acts of kindness and generosity are performed sincerely for the sake of Allah, reflecting true piety and devotion. It serves as a reminder of the importance of maintaining pure intentions in all charitable activities.

Verse 20

"Illā ib'tighā'a wajhi rabbihi l-a'lā"

Translation: "But only seeking the countenance of his Lord, Most High."

This verse further clarifies the motivation behind the charitable acts of the righteous person described in the previous verses. It emphasizes that their giving is done solely for the purpose of seeking the pleasure and approval of Allah, the "Most High."

The expression "seeking the countenance" of Allah signifies striving for His favor and closeness, reflecting a deep sense of devotion and sincerity. The righteous person's actions are not driven by material or worldly gains but by the desire to attain spiritual fulfillment and divine acceptance.

This verse highlights the ultimate goal of a believer's efforts in this world: to live a life that earns the approval of Allah. It serves as a reminder that true success lies in aligning one's intentions and actions with the pursuit of Allah's pleasure, above all else.

Verse 21

"Wa lasawfa yarḍā"

Translation: "And he is going to be satisfied."

This verse concludes the description of the righteous person by assuring them of contentment and satisfaction. It implies that the person who gives selflessly and seeks the pleasure of Allah will ultimately find true contentment and fulfillment.

The satisfaction referred to here can be understood as encompassing both this world and the Hereafter. In this life, the person will experience inner peace and a sense of fulfillment from their righteous actions. In the Hereafter, they will be rewarded with Allah's pleasure and the eternal joys of Paradise.

This verse serves as a powerful reminder that genuine happiness and satisfaction come from living a life aligned with divine values and seeking Allah's approval. It reassures believers that their efforts and sacrifices for the sake of Allah will not be in vain, and they will be rewarded with lasting contentment.

Surah Al-Lail offers several valuable lessons that can guide individuals in their daily lives. Here are some of the key lessons:

1. The Importance of Choices:

The Surah highlights the two divergent paths people can take: one of righteousness and generosity, and the other of miserliness and disbelief. This emphasizes the importance of making conscious choices that align with moral and spiritual values.

2. The Role of Generosity:

- Generosity is portrayed as a virtuous act that leads to self-purification and divine favor. It teaches that sharing wealth and resources, without expecting anything in return, is a noble deed that brings one closer to Allah.

3. Divine Guidance:

- The Surah reassures that Allah provides guidance to humanity, and it is up to individuals to seek and follow this guidance. This underscores the importance of staying connected to divine teachings through the Quran and prophetic traditions.

4. Consequences of Actions:

- There is a clear distinction between the outcomes for those who choose to follow the righteous path and those who do not. The Surah warns of the severe consequences of ignoring divine guidance, serving as a reminder of accountability in the Hereafter.

5. Sincerity in Worship and Deeds:

- The intention behind actions is crucial. Acts of worship and charity should be performed with sincerity, seeking only the pleasure of Allah, rather than worldly recognition or repayment.

6. Allah's Sovereignty:

- The Surah emphasizes that both this life and the Hereafter belong to Allah. Recognizing Allah's sovereignty helps individuals maintain humility and rely on Him for guidance and support.

7. Contentment through Righteousness:

- The Surah promises satisfaction and contentment for those who live righteously. This teaches that true happiness and peace come from aligning one's life with divine values and seeking Allah's approval.

8. Encouragement and Hope:

- For those who strive to follow the righteous path, the Surah offers encouragement and hope, assuring them of divine assistance and a favorable outcome in both this world and the Hereafter.

Overall, Surah Al-Lail provides a comprehensive framework for living a life that is pleasing to Allah, highlighting the importance of ethical behavior, sincere intentions, and the pursuit of spiritual growth

SUMMARY OF SURAH AL-LAIL- SURAH 92

Surah Al-Lail (The Night) in the Quran discusses two contrasting ways of life and their different outcomes. It is closely related to Surah Ash-Shams, with both Surahs covering similar themes and likely revealed around the same time.

The first part of Surah Al-Lail (verses 1-11) describes human actions as divergent, like the differences between night and day or male and female. It outlines two sets of moral characteristics. The first set encourages spending wealth for good, being conscious of Allah, and recognizing goodness. Those who follow this path find it easy to do good deeds, as Allah makes their way easy. In contrast, the second set involves miserliness, ignoring Allah's pleasure, and rejecting goodness. Those who follow this path find it easy to do wrong, as Allah makes the path of evil easy for them. The section concludes by reminding that worldly wealth won't benefit a person after death.

The second part (verses 12-21) presents three truths: First, Allah has provided guidance on the right way of living, via His Messenger and the Quran. Second, Allah is the master of both the world and the Hereafter, and it's up to individuals to choose what they seek from Him. Third, those who reject divine guidance face dire consequences, while those who spend their wealth sincerely for Allah's pleasure will be blessed.

The Surah uses the example of day and night, and male and female, to illustrate the differences in human endeavours and their outcomes. It highlights that those who choose the righteous path will find ease and fulfillment, while those who follow the wrong path will struggle and face difficulties. The Surah ends by emphasizing the sincerity of the pious, who seek Allah's pleasure without expecting worldly rewards, exemplified by figures like Abu Bakr, who selflessly helped others for the sake of Allah.

SURAH AL-LAIL (SURAH 92)

Questions

1. What does the term "Al-Lail" refer to, and why is the surah named after it?

2. Which natural phenomena are mentioned in the oaths at the beginning of Surah Al-Lail?

3. How does the surah describe the contrasting paths that people can take in life?

4. What are the characteristics of those who take the path of righteousness according to Surah Al-Lail?

5. What outcome does the surah promise for those who are generous and conscious of Allah?

6. How does the surah describe the characteristics of those who take the path of wickedness?

7. What warning does Surah Al-Lail give to those who are miserly and deny the truth?

8. How does the surah emphasize the concept of personal responsibility and free will?

9. What does Surah Al-Lail say about the ultimate source of guidance and the role of the Prophet Muhammad (peace be upon him)?

10. How can the teachings of Surah Al-Lail be applied to contemporary life to lead a virtuous and fulfilling life?

Answers

1. What does the term "Al-Lail" refer to, and why is the surah named after it?
   - "Al-Lail" refers to "the night." The surah is named after it because it begins with an oath by the night as it covers, emphasizing the contrasting phases of night and day as a metaphor for the different paths in life.

2. Which natural phenomena are mentioned in the oaths at the beginning of Surah Al-Lail?
   - The surah mentions the night as it covers, the day as it brightens, and the creation of male and female, highlighting the natural order and balance.

3. How does the surah describe the contrasting paths that people can take in life?
   - The surah describes two paths: the path of righteousness, characterized by generosity and consciousness of Allah, and the path of wickedness, characterized by miserliness and denial.

4. What are the characteristics of those who take the path of righteousness according to Surah Al-Lail?
   - Those on the path of righteousness are generous, conscious of Allah, and strive to purify themselves, ultimately seeking divine pleasure.

5. What outcome does the surah promise for those who are generous and conscious of Allah?
   - The surah promises that those who are generous and conscious of Allah will find ease and be led to a state of satisfaction and success.

6. How does the surah describe the characteristics of those who take the path of wickedness?
   - Those on the path of wickedness are described as miserly, denying the truth, and turning away from righteousness, leading to hardship and dissatisfaction.

7. What warning does Surah Al-Lail give to those who are miserly and deny the truth?
   - The surah warns that those who are miserly and deny the truth will face difficulty and failure in their lives, ultimately leading to a negative outcome.

8. How does the surah emphasize the concept of personal responsibility and free will?
   - The surah emphasizes that every individual has the choice to follow either the path of righteousness or wickedness, highlighting personal responsibility and free will in determining one's destiny.

9. What does Surah Al-Lail say about the ultimate source of guidance and the role of the Prophet Muhammad (peace be upon him)?
   - The surah implies that ultimate guidance comes from Allah and that the Prophet Muhammad (peace be upon him) is a messenger to convey this guidance and remind people of their choices and responsibilities.

10. How can the teachings of Surah Al-Lail be applied to contemporary life to lead a virtuous and fulfilling life?
    - The teachings encourage individuals to be generous, conscious of their actions, and strive for righteousness, emphasizing personal responsibility and the pursuit of a balanced and ethical life.

These questions and answers can be used for educational purposes, study sessions, or discussions to enhance understanding of Surah Al-Lail.

Multiple Choice Questions

1. What does the term "Al-Lail" refer to?

    - A) The morning
    - B) The night
    - C) The sun
    - D) The earth

2. Which natural phenomena are mentioned in the oaths at the beginning of Surah Al-Lail?

    - A) The rain and the clouds
    - B) The mountains and the valleys
    - C) The night as it covers and the day as it brightens
    - D) The sea and the river

3. How does Surah Al-Lail describe the two contrasting paths in life?

    - A) The path of wealth and the path of poverty
    - B) The path of righteousness and the path of wickedness
    - C) The path of knowledge and the path of ignorance
    - D) The path of strength and the path of weakness

4. What are the characteristics of those who take the path of righteousness according to Surah Al-Lail?

    - A) They are wealthy and powerful
    - B) They are generous and conscious of Allah
    - C) They are famous and influential
    - D) They are silent and reserved

5. What outcome does the surah promise for those who are generous and conscious of Allah?

    - A) They will face hardship
    - B) They will be led to a state of satisfaction and success
    - C) They will gain material wealth
    - D) They will be isolated

6. How does the surah describe the characteristics of those who take the path of wickedness?

    - A) They are hardworking and diligent
    - B) They are miserly and deny the truth
    - C) They are friendly and sociable
    - D) They are intelligent and wise

7. What warning does Surah Al-Lail give to those who are miserly and deny the truth?

    - A) They will be rewarded with wealth

    - B) They will face ease and comfort

    - C) They will face difficulty and failure

    - D) They will be respected by all

8. How does the surah emphasize the concept of personal responsibility and free will?

    - A) By stating that everyone is forced to follow a predetermined path

    - B) By highlighting that individuals have the choice to follow either righteousness or wickedness

    - C) By denying the existence of free will

    - D) By encouraging reliance on others for guidance

9. What does Surah Al-Lail say about the ultimate source of guidance and the role of the Prophet Muhammad (peace be upon him)?

    - A) Guidance comes from wealth and power

    - B) Guidance comes from Allah, and the Prophet is a messenger to convey it

    - C) Guidance is unnecessary for success

    - D) Guidance is only for the knowledgeable

10. How can the teachings of Surah Al-Lail be applied to contemporary life?

    - A) By focusing solely on wealth accumulation

    - B) By emphasizing personal responsibility, generosity, and ethical living

    - C) By ignoring moral and ethical considerations

    - D) By isolating oneself from society

Answers

1. *Answer:* B) The night
2. *Answer:* C) The night as it covers and the day as it brightens
3. *Answer:* B) The path of righteousness and the path of wickedness
4. *Answer:* B) They are generous and conscious of Allah
5. *Answer:* B) They will be led to a state of satisfaction and success
6. *Answer:* B) They are miserly and deny the truth
7. *Answer:* C) They will face difficulty and failure
8. *Answer:* B) By highlighting that individuals have the choice to follow either righteousness or wickedness
9. *Answer:* B) Guidance comes from Allah, and the Prophet is a messenger to convey it
10. *Answer:* B) By emphasizing personal responsibility, generosity, and ethical living

These questions and answers can be used for quizzes, educational discussions, or self-study to enhance understanding of Surah Al-Lail.

SURAH DUHA

SURAH DUHA

Bismillahi ar-Rahmani ar-Raheem

Verse 1

Wad duhaa

"By the morning brightness."

This verse begins with an oath, where Allah swears by the bright morning light. Imagine waking up and seeing the sun shining brightly after a dark night. The morning light makes everything look fresh and new, filling the world with warmth and energy. It symbolizes the start of a new day, full of possibilities and hope.

The morning brightness is a promise of a new beginning. Just like how the light of the morning always follows the darkness of the night, this verse reminds us that after difficult times, better days are sure to come. It's a comforting message that tells us no matter how challenging things might seem, there is always hope for improvement and renewal.

This verse serves as a symbol of hope. It encourages us to be patient and trust that Allah will bring light after darkness. Even when things seem tough or uncertain, we can remember that, just like the sun rises every day, Allah will bring ease and joy after hardship.

Overall, this verse reminds us of Allah's constant care and presence in our lives. It shows us that Allah is always there, ready to bring us comfort and guidance, just like He brings the morning after the night. So, whenever you see the bright morning light, think of this verse and feel hopeful that good things are always on their way!

Verse 2

"Wal-laili idhā sajā"

"And [by] the night when it covers with darkness"

1. The Night's Stillness:

- This verse talks about the night when it becomes calm and still. Just as the morning represents brightness and new beginnings, the night represents rest and peace.

2. A Time for Rest:

- Night time is when the world becomes quieter, and people rest after a busy day. It's a time to relax and recharge for the next day.

3. Balance in Nature:

- The mention of both morning and night in these verses shows the balance in nature that Allah has created. Just like life has its ups and downs, day and night come and go, each serving its purpose.

4. Symbol of Tranquility:

- The peacefulness of the night can also be a symbol of tranquility and calmness, reminding us that even in the quiet moments, there is beauty and purpose.

Why It's Important:

- Reassurance: This verse reassures us that just as night follows the day, every phase of life has its time and purpose, and Allah is in control of it all.

- Understanding Life's Cycles: It helps us understand that life is full of cycles, and each one, whether bright or dark, is important for our growth and well-being.

So, when you look at the calm night sky, remember this verse and feel at peace, knowing that Allah has a plan for every moment, whether it's filled with light or wrapped in darkness.

Verse 3

"Mā waddaʿaka rabbuka wamā qalā"

"Your Lord has not forsaken you, nor has He detested you."

1. Allah's Constant Presence:

- This verse reassures the Prophet Muhammad (peace be upon him) that Allah has not left him alone. It emphasizes that Allah is always present and caring, even when times seem difficult.

2. No Displeasure:

- The verse makes it clear that Allah is not upset or angry with the Prophet. It counters any feelings of doubt or worry that might have arisen during the pause in the revelation.

3. Comfort and Reassurance:

- For the Prophet, this message was a source of immense comfort. It reminded him that Allah's love and support were constant, regardless of the challenges he faced.

4. A Message for Everyone:

- While this message was directly for the Prophet, it also serves as a reminder to all of us that Allah never abandons His believers. Even if we go through tough times, Allah's love and guidance are always with us.

Why It's Important:

- Emotional Support: This verse provides emotional support and reassurance that Allah's care is unwavering.

- Strength in Faith: It helps strengthen our faith, reminding us that Allah never forgets or forsakes those who believe in Him.

Whenever you feel alone or unsure, remember this verse. It's a comforting reminder that Allah is always by your side, supporting and watching over you with love.

Verse 4
"Inna sa'yakum lashatta"

"Indeed, your efforts are diverse."

This verse shifts the focus to human actions and efforts. It acknowledges that people engage in various kinds of efforts and pursuits in their lives. The term "diverse" emphasizes the wide range of activities, goals, and paths that individuals choose to follow.

By highlighting the diversity of human effort, this verse introduces the central theme of the Surah, which is the contrast between the different paths that people take and their respective outcomes. Some pursue paths of righteousness, generosity, and God-consciousness, while others may follow paths of miserliness, heedlessness, and rejection of good.

This acknowledgment of diverse efforts sets the stage for the verses that follow, which elaborate on the consequences of these different paths. It serves as a reminder that although human endeavours are varied, they are not equal in terms of their moral and spiritual value, and they lead to different ultimate ends.

Verse 5
"Walasaofa yuʿṭīka rabbuka fatarḍā"

"And your Lord is going to give you, and you will be satisfied."

1. Promise of Blessings:

- This verse contains a promise from Allah to the Prophet Muhammad (peace be upon him) that He will bless him abundantly. It is a reassuring message that Allah has great plans and rewards in store.

2. Future Contentment:

- The verse assures that the blessings Allah will bestow will bring satisfaction and happiness. It's a promise of future joy and fulfillment.

3. A Source of Hope:

- For the Prophet and for all believers, this verse is a source of hope. It reminds us that Allah knows our needs and is ready to provide us with what is best for us.

4. Trust in Allah:

- It encourages us to trust in Allah's wisdom and timing, knowing that He will give us what we need when the time is right.

Why It's Important:

- Encouragement: This verse provides encouragement during challenging times, reminding us that good things are on the horizon.

- Strengthening Faith: It helps strengthen our faith in Allah's plans, reassuring us that He always has our best interests at heart.

When you feel uncertain about the future, remember this verse. It's a beautiful promise that Allah will provide for you in ways that will bring joy and contentment.

Verse 6

"Alam yajidka yatīman faāwā"

"Did He not find you an orphan and give [you] refuge?"

1. Reminder of Past Blessings:

- This verse reminds the Prophet Muhammad (peace be upon him) of Allah's care and protection during his early years. The Prophet was an orphan, and Allah ensured that he was looked after and cared for.

2. Allah's Protection:

- Even in the Prophet's vulnerable state as an orphan, Allah provided him with a loving family and support, showing His deep care and protection.

3. Evidence of Allah's Love:

- This is a reminder of Allah's continuous love and support throughout the Prophet's life. It serves as evidence of how Allah has always been there for him.

4. Gratitude and Trust:

- The verse encourages gratitude for past blessings and trust in Allah's ongoing care and support, reminding us that just as Allah helped in the past, He will continue to do so in the future.

Why It's Important:

- Reflection on Blessings: This verse encourages us to reflect on the blessings we have received in our own lives, even in difficult times.

- Assurance of Allah's Care: It reassures us that Allah's care is constant, reminding us of His protection and support throughout our lives.

Whenever you feel alone or in need, remember this verse. It's a comforting reminder that Allah has always been looking after you and will continue to do so.

Verse 7

"Wawajadaka ḍāllan fahadā"

"And He found you lost and guided [you]."

Explanation:

1. Guidance from Allah:

- This verse highlights how Allah guided the Prophet Muhammad (peace be upon him) when he was searching for the truth. Before receiving revelation, the Prophet was seeking the right path, and Allah provided him with guidance and clarity.

2. Spiritual Enlightenment:

The "lost" here refers to the Prophet's search for spiritual truth and meaning in a world filled with ignorance and idolatry. Allah enlightened him with the message of Islam, providing the guidance he needed.

3. Allah's Help in Finding the Way:

- This verse is a reminder of Allah's active role in guiding people to the right path, especially those who are earnestly seeking it.

4. Gratitude for Guidance:

- It encourages gratitude for the guidance and wisdom that Allah provides, reminding us of the importance of seeking and valuing divine guidance.

Why It's Important:

- Personal Transformation: This verse illustrates the transformative power of Allah's guidance in a person's life, turning confusion into clarity and purpose.

- Encouragement to Seek Guidance: It encourages us to seek Allah's guidance in our own lives, trusting that He will lead us to what is right and true.

Whenever you feel unsure or in need of direction, remember this verse. It's a reminder that Allah is always there to guide you towards the best path.

Verse 8 of Surah Duha is:

"Wawajadaka ʿāʾilan fa-aghnā"

"And He found you poor and made [you] self-sufficient."

1. Allah's Provision:

- This verse reminds the Prophet Muhammad (peace be upon him) of a time when he had limited resources, and how Allah provided for him and made him self-sufficient.

2. Transition from Need to Contentment:

- The Prophet, who started with very little, was blessed by Allah in many ways, including through his marriage to Khadijah, which brought not only emotional support but also financial stability.

3. Recognition of Blessings:

- This verse highlights the importance of recognizing and being grateful for the blessings Allah bestows, particularly in terms of provision and sustenance.

4. Assurance of Support:

- It reassures us that Allah is aware of our needs and provides for us in ways that lead to contentment and sufficiency.

Why It's Important:

- Gratitude for Provision: This verse encourages us to be thankful for the provisions and resources we have, recognizing them as blessings from Allah.

- Trust in Allah's Care: It strengthens our trust in Allah's ability to provide for us, turning scarcity into sufficiency.

Whenever you feel worried about your needs, remember this verse. It's a comforting reminder that Allah is always there to provide and take care of you.

Verse 9

"Fa-ammā l-yatīma falā taqhar"

"So as for the orphan, do not oppress [him]."

Explanation:

1. Compassionate Treatment:

- This verse instructs us to treat orphans with kindness and compassion. It emphasizes the importance of not mistreating or oppressing those who are vulnerable.

2. A Reminder of the Prophet's Past:

- Since the Prophet Muhammad (peace be upon him) was once an orphan himself, this verse serves as a reminder of his past and encourages all believers to be mindful and caring towards orphans.

3. Social Responsibility:

- It underscores the responsibility of the community to protect and support orphans, ensuring that they are not subjected to hardship or injustice.

4. Encouragement of Kindness:

- The verse encourages kindness, empathy, and fairness, reminding us to be considerate and supportive to those in need.

Why It's Important:

- Promotes Empathy: This verse encourages empathy and compassion, guiding us to care for others, especially the vulnerable.
- Strengthens Community: By looking after orphans and those in need, we build a stronger and more caring community.

Whenever you encounter someone in need or without support, remember this verse. It's a call to action to treat them with dignity, care, and respect.

Verse 10

"Wa-ammā s-sā'ila falā tanhar"

"And as for the petitioner, do not repel [him]."

Explanation:

1. Treating Seekers Kindly:

- This verse advises us to treat those who ask for help or guidance with kindness and respect. It emphasizes the importance of not turning them away harshly or rudely.

2. Helping Those in Need:

- "The petitioner" can refer to anyone asking for assistance, whether it's material help or seeking knowledge. The verse encourages generosity and patience in responding to their needs.

3. Encouragement of Generosity:

- It promotes a spirit of generosity and understanding, reminding us to be compassionate and considerate towards those who reach out for support.

4. Building a Caring Society:

- By treating petitioners with kindness, we contribute to a more supportive and empathetic community where people feel valued and respected.

Why It's Important:

- Encourages Compassion: This verse encourages us to be compassionate and helpful, recognizing the needs of others and responding with kindness.

- Fosters Positive Interaction: It promotes positive and respectful interactions, ensuring that everyone feels heard and cared for.

Whenever someone asks for your help or guidance, remember this verse. It's a gentle reminder to respond with understanding and generosity.

Verse 11

"Wa-ammā biniʿmati rabbika faḥaddith"

"But as for the favour of your Lord, report [it]."

1. Acknowledging Allah's Blessings:

- This verse encourages us to recognize and speak about the blessings and favours that Allah has bestowed upon us. It's an invitation to be grateful and to share our gratitude with others.

2. Sharing Goodness:

- By talking about Allah's favours, we can inspire others and remind them of the blessings in their own lives. It's about spreading positivity and recognizing the good that Allah provides.

3. Gratitude and Humility:

- The act of acknowledging blessings fosters a sense of gratitude and humility. It helps us remember that everything we have is due to Allah's generosity and kindness.

4. Encouragement to Use Blessings Wisely:

- By recognizing Allah's favours, we are encouraged to use these blessings wisely and for good purposes, benefiting ourselves and others.

Why It's Important:

- Promotes Gratitude: This verse encourages us to be grateful and to express our gratitude, which can lead to a more positive outlook on life.

- Inspires Others: By sharing our blessings, we can inspire others to recognize their own and foster a community of thankfulness and appreciation.

Whenever you reflect on the good in your life, remember this verse. It's a beautiful reminder to speak of Allah's blessings and to share the positivity with those around you.

LESSONS LEARNT FROM SURAH DUHA

Surah Duha offers several valuable lessons that can be understood and appreciated, even by young children. Here's a simple explanation of the lessons we can learn from this beautiful chapter:

Trust in Allah's Plan

One of the key lessons from Surah Duha is to trust in Allah's plan for us. The Surah reassures us that Allah never leaves us alone, even during challenging times. Just like the Prophet Muhammad (peace be upon him) was reminded that Allah had not forsaken him, we too should remember that Allah is always with us, guiding and supporting us through every situation.

Gratitude for Blessings

Surah Duha teaches us to be grateful for the blessings we receive. It reminds us of the importance of acknowledging Allah's favours and sharing them with others. By being thankful, we can see the good in our lives, even when things are tough, and this gratitude helps us to be more positive and content.

Kindness and Compassion

The Surah emphasizes the importance of treating others with kindness and compassion, especially those who are vulnerable, like orphans, and those who ask for help. We are encouraged to be generous and gentle, ensuring that we help and support others whenever we can. This builds a caring and supportive community.

Hope and Optimism

Another lesson from Surah Duha is the message of hope and optimism. It reminds us that after every difficulty, there will be ease, just like morning follows night. This teaches us to remain hopeful and patient, knowing that better times are always ahead.

Using Blessings Wisely

Finally, Surah Duha encourages us to use the blessings we have in a wise and positive way. By recognizing and speaking about Allah's favors, we are reminded to use our gifts and resources to help others and make the world a better place.

These lessons from Surah Duha remind us of the importance of faith, gratitude, kindness, hope, and wise use of our blessings. They encourage us to live a life that is pleasing to Allah and beneficial to those around us.

SUMMARY OF SURAH DUHA-SURAH 93

A long time ago, when Prophet Muhammad (peace be upon him) was in Makkah, something special happened. For a while, there were no new messages from Allah, and this made the Prophet feel worried and sad. He thought maybe he did something wrong. But then, Allah sent him a beautiful message to make him feel better. This message is called Surah Duha.

What the Surah Tells Us:

1. Morning and Night: Allah starts by talking about the bright morning and the quiet night. This was to show the Prophet that just like the day and night have a purpose, the pause in messages also had a reason.
2. Allah's Love: Allah told the Prophet that He did not leave him and was not angry with him. Allah promised that the future would be even better than the past and that the Prophet would be very happy with what Allah would give him.
3. Blessings and Guidance: Allah reminded the Prophet of His blessings. He was an orphan, and Allah took care of him. He was unsure of the right way, and Allah guided him. He was not rich, and Allah made him content and provided for him.
4. Being Kind and Thankful: Allah told the Prophet to be kind to orphans and to help those in need. He reminded him to always be thankful for the blessings he received and to share the message of Allah with others.

Why This Surah is Important:

This Surah teaches us that even when things seem tough, Allah is always with us. He has a plan and purpose for everything. It also reminds us to be grateful for what we have, to help others, and to trust in Allah's wisdom and timing.

So, whenever you feel a bit down or worried, remember Surah Duha and how Allah is always there to guide and support us, just like He did for Prophet Muhammad (peace be upon him).

SURAH AD-DHUHA (SURAH 93)

Questions

1. What does the term "Ad-Duha" refer to, and why is the surah named after it?
2. Which natural phenomena are mentioned in the oaths at the beginning of Surah Ad-Duha?
3. What reassurance is given to the Prophet Muhammad (peace be upon him) in this surah?
4. How does the surah describe the state of the Prophet before receiving revelation?
5. What promise does Surah Ad-Duha make regarding the future of the Prophet Muhammad (peace be upon him)?
6. How does the surah address the concept of divine favor and guidance?
7. What instructions are given to the Prophet Muhammad (peace be upon him) concerning orphans and the needy?
8. How does the surah encourage gratitude and acknowledgment of Allah's blessings?
9. What is the overall tone of Surah Ad-Duha, and how does it aim to comfort the Prophet?
10. How can the teachings of Surah Ad-Duha be applied to contemporary life to find comfort and reassurance?

Answers

1. What does the term "Ad-Duha" refer to, and why is the surah named after it?
   - "Ad-Duha" refers to "the morning brightness" or "forenoon." The surah is named after it because it begins with an oath by the morning brightness, symbolizing hope and renewal.

2. Which natural phenomena are mentioned in the oaths at the beginning of Surah Ad-Duha?
   - The surah begins with oaths by the morning brightness (Ad-Duha) and the night as it covers, highlighting the cycles of day and night.

3. What reassurance is given to the Prophet Muhammad (peace be upon him) in this surah?
   - The surah reassures the Prophet that his Lord has neither forsaken him nor is displeased with him, addressing concerns during a period of pause in revelation.

4. How does the surah describe the state of the Prophet before receiving revelation?
   - The surah mentions that the Prophet was an orphan, and Allah provided him care and guidance, highlighting divine assistance in times of need.

5. What promise does Surah Ad-Duha make regarding the future of the Prophet Muhammad (peace be upon him)?
   - The surah promises that the future will be better for the Prophet than the past, offering hope and assurance of continued blessings.

6. How does the surah address the concept of divine favor and guidance?
   - The surah emphasizes that Allah's favor and guidance are always present, and the Prophet has been blessed with divine care throughout his life.

7. What instructions are given to the Prophet Muhammad (peace be upon him) concerning orphans and the needy?
   - The surah instructs the Prophet not to oppress the orphan and not to repel the beggar, emphasizing compassion and generosity.

8. How does the surah encourage gratitude and acknowledgment of Allah's blessings?
   - The surah encourages expressing gratitude by proclaiming the bounties of the Lord, acknowledging and sharing the blessings received.

9. What is the overall tone of Surah Ad-Duha, and how does it aim to comfort the Prophet?
   - The overall tone is one of reassurance and comfort, aiming to alleviate the Prophet's concerns and reminding him of Allah's continuous support and care.

10. How can the teachings of Surah Ad-Duha be applied to contemporary life to find comfort and reassurance?
    - The teachings encourage individuals to remain hopeful and patient during difficult times, emphasizing gratitude, compassion, and trust in divine guidance.

These questions and answers can be used for educational purposes, study sessions, or discussions to enhance understanding of Surah Ad-Duha.

Multiple Choice Questions

1. What does the term "Ad-Duha" refer to?

    - A) The night

    - B) The morning brightness

    - C) The sunset

    - D) The moon

2. Which natural phenomena are mentioned in the oaths at the beginning of Surah Ad-Duha?

    - A) The stars and the sea

    - B) The morning brightness and the night as it covers

    - C) The mountains and the valleys

    - D) The rain and the clouds

3. What reassurance is given to the Prophet Muhammad (peace be upon him) in this surah?

    - A) That his wealth will increase

    - B) That his Lord has neither forsaken him nor is displeased

    - C) That he will become a king

    - D) That he will live forever

4. How does the surah describe the state of the Prophet before receiving revelation?

    - A) As a wealthy merchant

    - B) As an orphan whom Allah provided care and guidance

    - C) As a farmer

    - D) As a powerful leader

5. What promise does Surah Ad-Duha make regarding the future of the Prophet Muhammad (peace be upon him)?

    - A) The future will be worse than the past

    - B) The future will be better than the past

    - C) The future will be uncertain

    - D) The future will be the same as the past

6. What instructions are given to the Prophet concerning orphans and the needy?

    - A) Ignore them

    - B) Oppress them

    - C) Do not oppress the orphan and do not repel the beggar

    - D) Take advantage of them

7. How does the surah encourage gratitude and acknowledgment of Allah's blessings?

    - A) By keeping them private

    - B) By proclaiming the bounties of the Lord

    - C) By sharing them only with family

    - D) By ignoring them

8. What is the overall tone of Surah Ad-Duha?

    - A) Reassurance and comfort

    - B) Fear and intimidation

    - C) Indifference and neutrality

    - D) Anger and frustration

Answers

1. *Answer:* B) The morning brightness
2. *Answer:* B) The morning brightness and the night as it covers
3. *Answer:* B) That his Lord has neither forsaken him nor is displeased
4. *Answer:* B) As an orphan whom Allah provided care and guidance
5. *Answer:* B) The future will be better than the past
6. *Answer:* C) Do not oppress the orphan and do not repel the beggar
7. *Answer:* B) By proclaiming the bounties of the Lord
8. *Answer:* A) Reassurance and comfort

These questions and answers can be used for quizzes, educational discussions, or self-study to enhance understanding of Surah Ad-Duha.

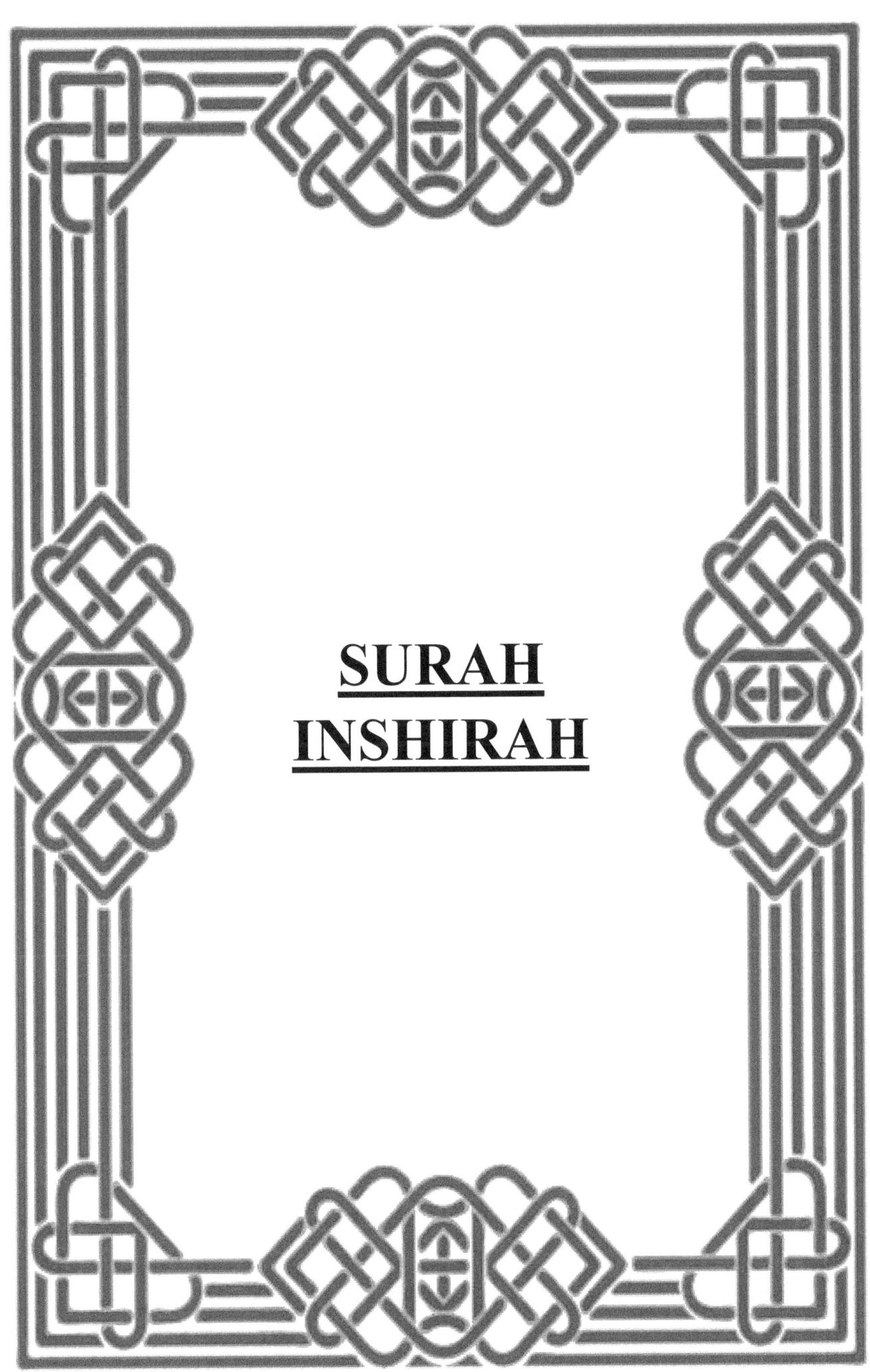

SURAH INSHIRAH

SURAH INSHIRAH

Bismillahi ar-Rahmani ar-Raheem

Verse 1

Alam nashraḥ laka ṣadrak

"Did We not expand for you, [O Muhammad], your breast?"

Tafseer:

This verse refers to the spiritual and emotional expansion granted to the Prophet Muhammad (peace be upon him) by Allah. It signifies the opening of the heart to faith, wisdom, and patience. The "expansion" can also be understood as the capacity to bear the mission of prophethood and its accompanying challenges, providing relief and tranquility amidst adversity.

Verse 2

Wa waḍa'nā 'anka wizrak

"And We removed from you your burden"

Tafseer:

The "burden" mentioned here refers to the difficulties and challenges the Prophet faced in his mission to spread the message of Islam. Allah reassures him that these burdens have been lifted, symbolizing divine support and relief from the weight of challenges.

Verse 3

Alladhī anqaḍa ẓahrak

"Which had weighed upon your back"

Tafseer:

This verse continues the theme from the previous one, emphasizing the heaviness of the challenges that felt like a physical weight on the Prophet's back. It reassures him that Allah has alleviated these burdens, providing comfort and strength to continue his mission.

Verse 4
Wa rafa'nā laka dhikrak

"And raised high for you your repute"

Tafseer:

Allah assures the Prophet(pbuh) that his reputation and status have been elevated. This can be interpreted as the exaltation of his name and mission, both in this world and the hereafter. It signifies the honour and respect granted to the Prophet, ensuring his message reaches far and wide.

Verse 5
Fa inna ma'al-'usri Yusra

"For indeed, with hardship [will be] ease."

Tafseer:

This verse provides a profound message of hope and resilience, indicating that every difficulty is accompanied by ease. It serves as a reminder that challenges are temporary and that relief will follow, encouraging believers to maintain faith and patience during tough times.

Verse 6
Inna ma'al-'usri Yusra

"Indeed, with hardship [will be] ease."

Tafseer:

The repetition of this verse reinforces the promise that ease accompanies difficulty. It emphasizes that believers should not despair during trials, as Allah's support and relief are always near.

Verse 7

Fa idhā faraghta fa inṣab

"So when you have finished [your duties], then stand up [for worship]."

Tafseer:

After completing worldly responsibilities and tasks, the verse encourages turning to worship and devotion. This highlights the importance of maintaining a connection with Allah through prayer and supplication, reinforcing the need for spiritual grounding.

Verse 8

Wa ilā rabbika farghab

"And to your Lord direct [your] longing."

Tafseer:

The final verse advises directing one's aspirations and hopes towards Allah. It underscores the importance of reliance on Allah and seeking His guidance and support in all matters, encouraging believers to prioritize their relationship with the Divine.

Overall, Surah Al-Inshirah offers comfort and encouragement, reminding us of the transient nature of difficulties and the enduring presence of divine mercy and support. It encourages maintaining faith, patience, and devotion throughout life's journey.

LESSONS LEARNT FROM SURAH INSHIRAH

Surah Inshirah offers a profound message of hope and resilience, emphasizing that with every hardship comes ease. This reassures us that challenges are temporary and relief will follow, encouraging patience and perseverance. The surah highlights the importance of spiritual and emotional growth, reminding us that seeking strength and wisdom from Allah can help us navigate life's difficulties. It assures us of divine support, underscoring that Allah is aware of our struggles and will provide comfort and assistance. The mention of elevating the Prophet's status teaches that sincere efforts in righteousness are recognized and rewarded. Additionally, the surah emphasizes the need for balance between fulfilling worldly duties and maintaining spiritual devotion, highlighting the significance of prayer and connection with Allah.

The overarching theme is one of hope and optimism, encouraging believers to maintain a positive outlook in challenging times and to focus their aspirations and reliance on the Divine.

Overall, Surah Inshirah provides comfort and motivation, reminding us of the transient nature of difficulties and the enduring presence of divine mercy and support.

SUMMARY OF SURAH INSHIRAH-SURAH 94

Surah Inshirah is a special chapter in the Quran that was sent to comfort and encourage Prophet Muhammad when he was feeling sad and burdened. The following is a simplified explanation:

Time of Revelation:

Surah Inshirah was revealed in Makkah, soon after another chapter called Surah Ad-Duha. Both chapters were given to the Prophet during a time when he was facing many challenges.

Main Message:

The surah starts by reminding the Prophet of the blessings he has received. Allah has given him three important gifts:

1. Opening of the Heart: Allah helped the Prophet feel confident and at peace with the message he was given to share.
2. Removing Burdens: Before becoming a prophet, the Prophet felt worried about the troubles in his society. Allah removed these worries by guiding him to the right path.
3. Raising his Honor: Although at first people were against him, Allah promised that the Prophet's name and message would be respected and honored all over the world.

The surah then reassures the Prophet that with every difficulty, there will be ease. This means that even though times may be tough now, better days are coming soon. It's a promise that hard times won't last forever and things will get better.

Instruction for the Prophet:

Finally, the surah advises the Prophet to stay dedicated to worship and focus on his connection with Allah. When he finishes his tasks, he should use his free time to pray and seek strength from Allah.

In summary, Surah Inshirah is a comforting message to the Prophet, reminding him of Allah's blessings, promising relief after hardships, and encouraging him to stay devoted to his mission and faith.

SURAH AL-INSHIRAH (SURAH 94)

Questions

1. What is the primary theme of Surah Al-Inshirah?
2. How does the surah describe the Prophet Muhammad's (peace be upon him) experiences of hardship and ease?
3. What metaphor is used in the surah to describe the relief given to the Prophet?
4. What promise is made about the relationship between hardship and ease?
5. How does the surah emphasize the importance of perseverance and patience?
6. What reassurance is given to the Prophet regarding the burdens he faces?
7. How does the surah encourage the Prophet to respond after completing his tasks?
8. What does the surah suggest about the nature of struggles and challenges in life?
9. How can the teachings of Surah Al-Inshirah be applied to contemporary life?
10. What is the overall tone of Surah Al-Inshirah, and how does it aim to comfort the Prophet and the believers?

Answers

1. What is the primary theme of Surah Al-Inshirah?
   - The primary theme is the reassurance of ease and relief following hardship, emphasizing patience and perseverance.

2. How does the surah describe the Prophet Muhammad's (peace be upon him) experiences of hardship and ease?
   - The surah acknowledges the difficulties faced by the Prophet and reassures him that these burdens have been relieved and his path made easier.

3. What metaphor is used in the surah to describe the relief given to the Prophet?
   - The metaphor of expanding the chest is used to describe the relief and comfort given to the Prophet, symbolizing spiritual and emotional ease.

4. What promise is made about the relationship between hardship and ease?
   - The surah promises that with every hardship comes ease, repeating this assurance to emphasize its certainty.

5. How does the surah emphasize the importance of perseverance and patience?
   - The surah highlights that enduring hardship with patience will eventually lead to ease and relief, encouraging perseverance.

6. What reassurance is given to the Prophet regarding the burdens he faces?
   - The surah reassures the Prophet that his burdens have been lifted and his mission made easier, providing comfort and support.

7. How does the surah encourage the Prophet to respond after completing his tasks?
   - The surah advises the Prophet to continue striving and turn to Allah in devotion and worship after completing his tasks.

8. What does the surah suggest about the nature of struggles and challenges in life?
   - The surah suggests that struggles and challenges are temporary and that perseverance will lead to eventual relief and ease.

9. How can the teachings of Surah Al-Inshirah be applied to contemporary life?
   - The teachings encourage individuals to remain patient during difficult times, trust in eventual relief, and maintain devotion and perseverance.

10. What is the overall tone of Surah Al-Inshirah, and how does it aim to comfort the Prophet and the believers?
    - The overall tone is one of reassurance and comfort, aiming to alleviate the Prophet's concerns and provide hope and encouragement to the believers.

These questions and answers can be used for educational purposes, study sessions, or discussions to enhance understanding of Surah Al-Inshirah.

Multiple Choice Questions

1. What is the primary theme of Surah Al-Inshirah?

    - A) The importance of wealth

    - B) The reassurance of ease following hardship

    - C) The significance of power and influence

    - D) The inevitability of suffering

2. Which metaphor is used in the surah to describe the relief given to the Prophet Muhammad (peace be upon him)?

    - A) Opening the gates of heaven

    - B) Expanding the chest

    - C) Lighting the path

    - D) Moving mountains

3. What promise is repeatedly made in Surah Al-Inshirah about hardship?

    - A) Hardship will last forever

    - B) Hardship is a sign of divine displeasure

    - C) With every hardship comes ease

    - D) Hardship is a test of wealth

4. How does the surah describe the Prophet's burdens?

    - A) As increasing day by day

    - B) As being ignored by others

    - C) As having been lifted and eased

    - D) As overwhelming and insurmountable

5. What does Surah Al-Inshirah encourage the Prophet to do after completing his tasks?

    - A) Rest and relax

    - B) Turn to Allah in devotion and worship

    - C) Seek assistance from others

    - D) Pursue worldly ambitions

6. What is the overall tone of Surah Al-Inshirah?

    - A) Reassurance and comfort

    - B) Warning and punishment

    - C) Fear and anxiety

    - D) Indifference and neutrality

7. How does the surah suggest the Prophet should deal with challenges?

    - A) By ignoring them

    - B) By persevering and trusting in Allah's plan

    - C) By seeking material solutions

    - D) By avoiding them at all costs

8. How can the teachings of Surah Al-Inshirah be applied to contemporary life?

    - A) By focusing solely on material success

    - B) By remaining patient, trusting in eventual relief, and maintaining devotion

    - C) By avoiding challenges and struggles

    - D) By isolating oneself from society

Answers

1. *Answer:* B) The reassurance of ease following hardship
2. *Answer:* B) Expanding the chest
3. *Answer:* C) With every hardship comes ease
4. *Answer:* C) As having been lifted and eased
5. *Answer:* B) Turn to Allah in devotion and worship
6. *Answer:* A) Reassurance and comfort
7. *Answer:* B) By persevering and trusting in Allah's plan
8. *Answer:* B) By remaining patient, trusting in eventual relief, and maintaining devotion

These questions and answers can be used for quizzes, educational discussions, or self-study to enhance understanding of Surah Al-Inshirah.

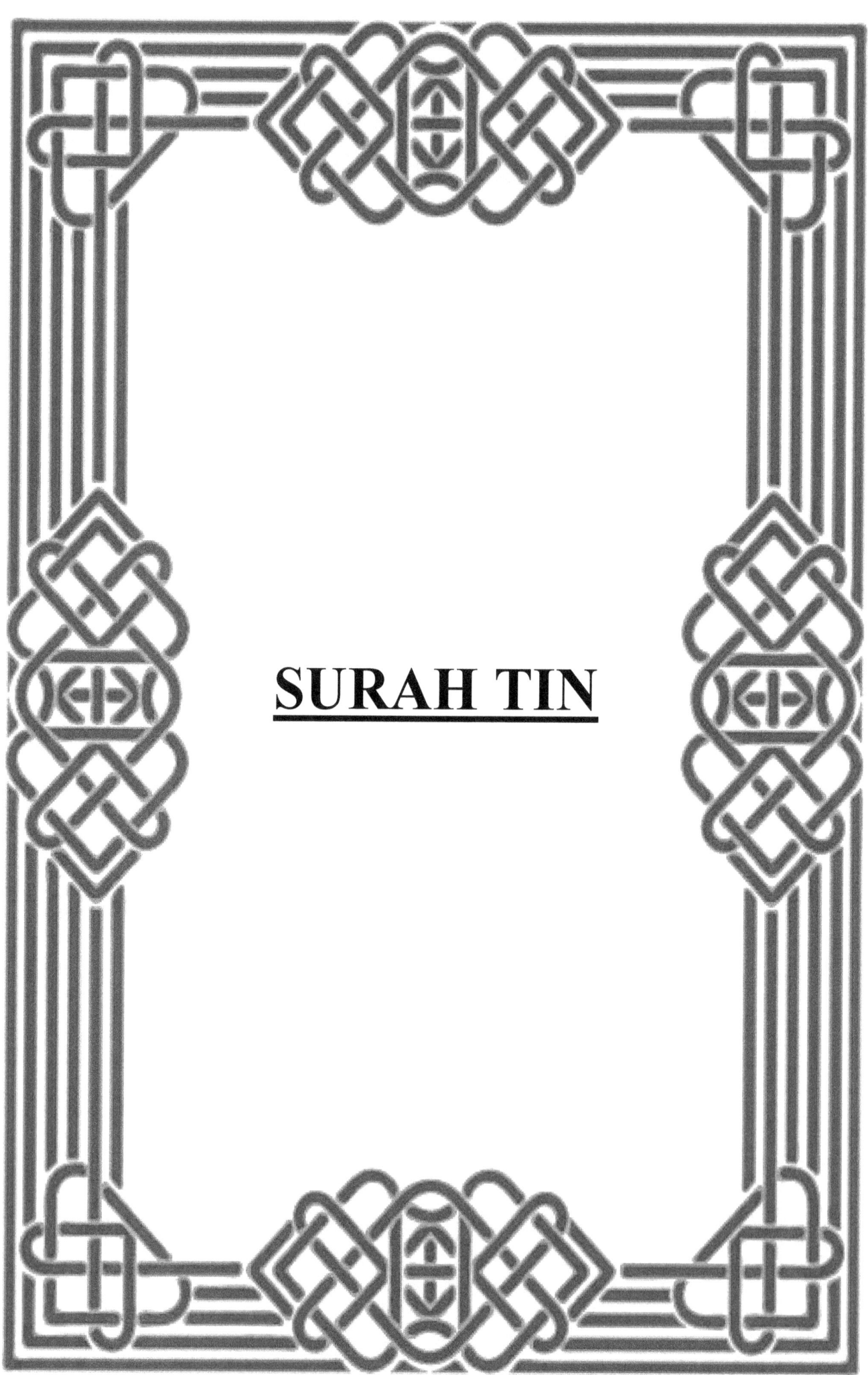

SURAH TIN

SURAH TIN

Bismillahi ar-Rahmani ar-Raheem

Surah At-Tin (Chapter 95)

Verse 1

Wa at-teen wa az-zaytoon

By the fig and the olive

Tafseer:

Allah swears by the fig and the olive, which are significant both as fruits and as symbols. Some interpretations suggest that these refer to lands where these fruits are abundant, like Palestine and the surrounding regions, which are historically significant in Abrahamic religions.

Verse 2

Wa toori sineen

And [by] Mount Sinai

Tafseer:

Mount Sinai is where Prophet Moses received the Ten Commandments. It is a place of great significance in the history of divine revelation.

Verse 3

Wa haadha al-balad al-ameen

And [by] this secure city [Makkah]

Tafseer:

The secure city refers to Mecca, the birthplace of the Prophet Muhammad and a sacred city in Islam. It emphasizes the importance and holiness of Mecca.

Verse 4

Laqad khalaqna al-insana fee ahsani taqweem

We have certainly created man in the best of stature

Tafseer:

This verse highlights the nobility and excellence of human creation. Humans are endowed with intellect, morality, and the potential for spiritual elevation.

Verse 5

Thumma radadnaahu asfala saafileen

Then We return him to the lowest of the low

Tafseer:

Despite being created in the best form, humans can fall to the lowest state if they neglect their moral and spiritual duties. This decline is a result of turning away from righteousness.

Verse 6

Illa allatheena aamanoo wa 'amiloo as-saalihaati falahum ajrun ghayru mamnoon

Except for those who believe and do righteous deeds, for they will have a reward uninterrupted

Tafseer:

Those who maintain their faith and engage in righteous actions are promised an eternal reward. This highlights the importance of belief paired with good deeds.

Verse 7

Fama yukaththibuka ba'du bid-deen

So what yet causes you to deny the Recompense?

Tafseer:

The verse questions what reasons one might have to deny the Day of Judgment and divine justice after understanding the purpose and accountability of human life.

Verse 8

Alaysa Allahu bi-ahkami al-haakimeen

Is not Allah the most just of judges?

Tafseer:

The surah concludes with a rhetorical question affirming Allah's ultimate justice and wisdom. It reassures believers of the fairness and righteousness of Allah's judgment.

This surah, through its symbols and statements, calls upon individuals to recognize their inherent dignity and responsibility, urging them to uphold faith and righteousness to achieve eternal success.

Key lessons we can learn from this surah:

1. Appreciation of Divine Creation: The surah begins with oaths by elements of nature and significant locations, underscoring the beauty and importance of these creations. It encourages us to appreciate the natural world and recognize the signs of Allah in it.
2. Human Dignity and Potential: Humans are created in the best of forms, signifying inherent dignity and potential. This reminds us of our unique position in creation and the responsibility to live up to this potential through moral and spiritual development.
3. Consequences of Moral Decline: Despite being created in an excellent state, humans can fall to the lowest of the low if they deviate from righteousness. This serves as a warning about the dangers of neglecting ethical and spiritual values.
4. Importance of Faith and Righteousness: The surah emphasizes that belief in Allah and righteous deeds lead to eternal rewards. It highlights the importance of pairing faith with good actions to achieve success in this life and the hereafter.
5. Divine Justice and Accountability: The rhetorical questions towards the end of the surah affirm the certainty of divine justice and the existence of the Day of Judgment. This encourages believers to remain conscious of their actions and their ultimate accountability to Allah.
6. Reflecting on Divine Wisdom: By ending with a question about Allah's justice, the surah invites reflection on the wisdom and fairness of Allah's decrees. It reassures believers of the ultimate balance and justice in the divine plan.

Overall, Surah At-Tin offers a reminder of the balance between human potential and the need for spiritual discipline, encouraging us to lead lives of faith, integrity, and awareness of our ultimate return to Allah.

SUMMARY OF SURAH TIN-SURAH 95

Surah At-Tin, the 95th chapter of the Quran, is a short surah consisting of eight verses. It is named after the mention of "the fig" (At-Tin) in its opening verse. Here is a summary of its themes and messages:

1. Oaths and Symbolism: The surah begins with a series of oaths by significant natural symbols: the fig, the olive, Mount Sinai, and the secure city of Mecca. These symbols are often interpreted to represent places of spiritual and historical significance in Islam and other Abrahamic faiths.
2. Creation of Humans: The surah highlights the noble creation of humans, stating that they were created in the best of forms. This reflects the inherent dignity and potential of human beings.
3. Human Decline and Accountability: It mentions the decline of humans to the lowest of the low if they turn away from righteousness. This serves as a reminder of the consequences of moral and spiritual neglect.
4. Reward for the Righteous: The surah reassures that those who believe and perform righteous deeds will have an unending reward, emphasizing the importance of faith and good actions.
5. Divine Justice: It concludes with rhetorical questions about the truthfulness and justice of Allah, reinforcing the belief in divine accountability and the ultimate judgment.

Overall, Surah At-Tin underscores the potential for human excellence and the importance of maintaining faith and righteousness to achieve eternal rewards.

SURAH AT-TIN (SURAH 96)

Questions

1. What does the term "At-Tin" refer to, and why is the surah named after it?
2. Which significant locations are mentioned in the oaths at the beginning of Surah At-Tin?
3. How does the surah describe the creation of humans?
4. What does the surah say about the potential for humans to reach a state of moral excellence?
5. How does the surah address the potential for moral decline in humans?
6. What does Surah At-Tin say about the role of faith and righteous deeds in achieving the best of stature?
7. How does the surah emphasize the concept of divine judgment?
8. What rhetorical question is posed at the end of Surah At-Tin, and what does it imply?
9. How does the surah encourage reflection on the consequences of one's actions?
10. How can the teachings of Surah At-Tin be applied to contemporary life to promote moral integrity?

Answers

1. What does the term "At-Tin" refer to, and why is the surah named after it?
   - "At-Tin" refers to "the fig." The surah is named after it because it begins with an oath by the fig, highlighting the significance of certain creations and locations.

2. Which significant locations are mentioned in the oaths at the beginning of Surah At-Tin?
   - The surah mentions the fig, the olive, Mount Sinai, and the secure city (Mecca), each representing important aspects of spiritual and religious history.

3. How does the surah describe the creation of humans?
   - The surah describes humans as being created in the best of stature, emphasizing the potential for moral and physical excellence.

4. What does the surah say about the potential for humans to reach a state of moral excellence?
   - The surah acknowledges that humans are created with the potential to achieve the highest moral standards through faith and righteous deeds.

Multiple Choice Questions

1. What does the term "At-Tin" refer to in the context of this surah?

    - A) The olive

    - B) The fig

    - C) The mountain

    - D) The city

2. Which significant locations are mentioned in the oaths at the beginning of Surah At-Tin?

    - A) The fig, the olive, Mount Sinai, and the secure city (Mecca)

    - B) The desert, the sea, the valley, and the forest

    - C) The sun, the moon, the stars, and the sky

    - D) The river, the mountain, the plain, and the hill

3. How does the surah describe the creation of humans?

    - A) In the best of stature

    - B) As inherently sinful

    - C) As weak and flawed

    - D) As angels

4. What does the surah say about the potential for humans to reach a state of moral excellence?

    - A) It is impossible to achieve

    - B) It is only for prophets

    - C) Humans are created with the potential to achieve it through faith and righteous deeds

    - D) It is an illusion

5. How does the surah address the potential for moral decline in humans?

    - A) Humans are immune to moral decline

    - B) Humans can be reduced to the lowest of the low if they fail to uphold moral values

    - C) Moral decline is inevitable

    - D) Moral decline is irrelevant

6. What does Surah At-Tin say about the role of faith and righteous deeds in achieving the best of stature?

    - A) They have no impact

    - B) They are only for the privileged

    - C) They ensure that individuals maintain their excellent stature and are rewarded

    - D) They are optional

7. How does the surah emphasize the concept of divine judgment?

    - A) By denying divine judgment

    - B) By stating that everyone will be equally rewarded

    - C) By reminding that Allah is the ultimate judge and will hold individuals accountable

    - D) By emphasizing material wealth

8. What rhetorical question is posed at the end of Surah At-Tin, and what does it imply?

    - A) "Is not wealth the most important?" implying material success
        - B) "Is not knowledge the greatest?" implying the superiority of knowledge

    - C) "Is not Allah the most just of judges?" implying the certainty of Allah's just judgment

    - D) "Is not power the ultimate goal?" implying the pursuit of power

Answers

1. *Answer:* B) The fig
2. *Answer:* A) The fig, the olive, Mount Sinai, and the secure city (Mecca)
3. *Answer:* A) In the best of stature
4. *Answer:* C) Humans are created with the potential to achieve it through faith and righteous deeds
5. *Answer:* B) Humans can be reduced to the lowest of the low if they fail to uphold moral values
6. *Answer:* C) They ensure that individuals maintain their excellent stature and are rewarded
7. *Answer:* C) By reminding that Allah is the ultimate judge and will hold individuals accountable
8. *Answer:* C) "Is not Allah the most just of judges?" implying the certainty of Allah's just judgment

These questions and answers can be used for quizzes, educational discussions, or self-study to enhance understanding of Surah At-Tin.

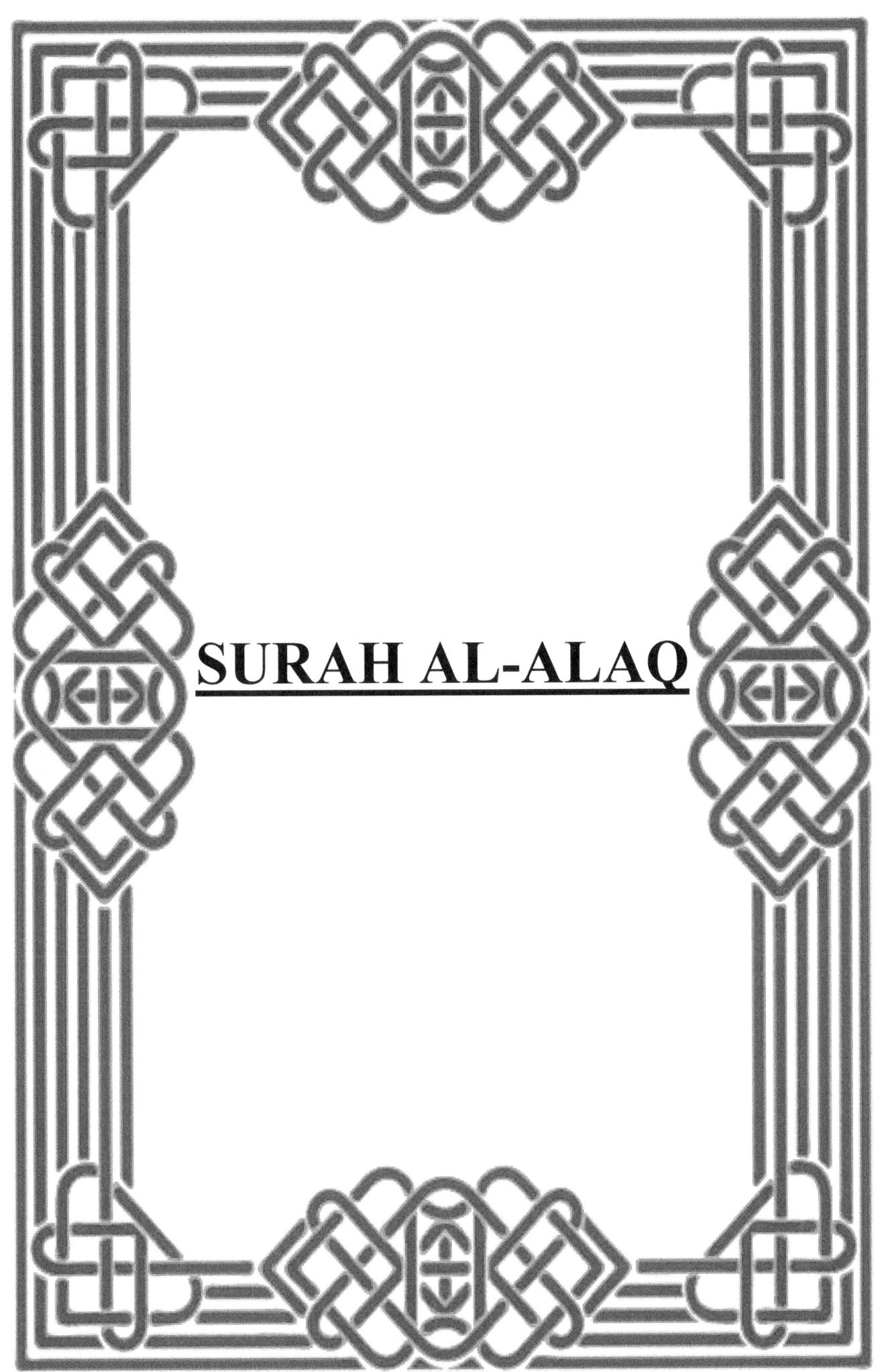

SURAH AL-ALAQ

SURAH AL-ALAQ

Bismillahi ar-Rahmani ar-Raheem

Verse 1

Iqra' bismi rabbika allathee khalaq

Read in the name of your Lord who created.

Explanation: This verse marks the beginning of the first revelation to Prophet Muhammad (peace be upon him). The angel Gabriel instructed him to read, emphasizing the importance of seeking knowledge. The command to "read" signifies the beginning of a journey of learning and understanding. By invoking "the name of your Lord," it highlights that all knowledge should be pursued with an awareness of Allah as the Creator of everything.

Verse 2

Khalaqa al-insana min alaq

Created man from a clinging substance.

Explanation: This verse describes the humble beginnings of human creation. The "clinging substance" refers to the embryonic state, emphasizing the miraculous development of humans from simple origins. It serves as a reminder of our dependence on Allah for life and creation.

Verse 3

Iqra' warabbuka alakram

Read, and your Lord is the Most Generous.

Explanation: The repetition of "read" reinforces the importance of knowledge, while "your Lord is the Most Generous" highlights Allah's kindness in granting humans the ability to learn and grow. Allah's generosity is seen in the countless opportunities for learning and discovery provided to humanity.

Verse 4

Allathee 'allama bilqalam

Who taught by the pen.

Explanation: The "pen" symbolizes the tool of writing and recording knowledge. This verse underscores the significance of writing as a means of sharing and preserving knowledge across generations. The ability to write is a divine gift that allows humans to document and communicate ideas, fostering intellectual growth.

Verse 5

'Allama al-insana ma lam ya'lam

Taught man that which he knew not.

Explanation: This verse acknowledges that all knowledge originates from Allah. Humans are born without knowledge, and it is through Allah's guidance that they learn and acquire information. This reinforces the idea that intellectual and spiritual growth are possible through divine favour.

Verse 6

Kalla inna al-insana layatgha

No! [But] indeed, man transgresses.

Explanation: This verse warns against human arrogance and pride. When people forget their humble beginnings and the source of their knowledge, they may become rebellious and overstep boundaries, leading to moral and ethical failures.

Verse 7

An ra'ahu istaghna

Because he sees himself self-sufficient.

Explanation: Human beings often become proud and self-reliant when they feel they have achieved wealth, power, or knowledge. This sense of self-sufficiency can lead individuals to neglect their dependence on Allah and overlook their responsibilities.

Verse 8

Inna ila rabbika ar-ruj'a

Translation: Indeed, to your Lord is the return.

Explanation: This verse serves as a reminder that regardless of one's achievements or status, everyone will eventually return to Allah. This return signifies accountability and the ultimate judgment by Allah, encouraging a life of humility and righteousness.

Verse 9

Ara-ayta allathee yanha

Have you seen the one who forbids

Explanation: The verse introduces a scenario where someone tries to prevent a believer from performing acts of worship, such as prayer. It highlights the opposition faced by those who are committed to their faith.

Verse 10

Abdan itha salla

A servant when he prays?

Explanation: This refers to an individual who attempts to stop a devoted servant of Allah from praying. It focuses on the unjust interference in personal acts of worship, which are sacred and significant.

Verse 11

Ara'ayta in kana 'ala alhuda

Have you seen if he is upon guidance

Explanation: This rhetorical question invites reflection on the possibility that the one praying is following the correct path and Allah's guidance. It challenges the actions of those who oppose acts of faith.

Verse 12

Aw amara bittaqua

Or enjoins righteousness?

Explanation: The verse continues the reflection by considering if the person praying is also encouraging others to do good and be righteous. It highlights the positive influence of faith and practice.

Verse 13

Ara'ayta in kaththaba watawalla

Have you seen if he denies and turns away

Explanation: This verse contrasts the earlier scenario by considering the one who denies the truth and turns away from guidance. It underscores the consequences of rejecting faith and moral teachings.

Verse 14

Alam ya'lam bi-anna Allaha yara

Does he not know that Allah sees?

Explanation: This verse reminds those who oppose or deny the truth that Allah is always watching. It serves as a warning that all actions are observed by Allah and will be accounted for.

Verse 15

Kalla la-in lam yantahi lanasfa'an bin-nasiyah

No! If he does not desist, We will surely drag him by the forelock –

Explanation: This verse warns of severe consequences for those who persist in wrongdoing and arrogance. The "forelock" symbolizes control, indicating that Allah has power over all.

Verse 16

Nasiyatin kathibatin khati'ah

A lying, sinning forelock.

    Explanation: The verse describes the forelock as belonging to someone who lies and sins. It emphasizes the moral failings of those who oppose truth and righteousness.

Verse 17

Fal yad'u nadiyah

Translation: Then let him call his associates;

    Explanation: This challenges the wrongdoer to call upon others for support, highlighting the futility of relying on people rather than Allah.

Verse 18

Sanad'u az-zabaniyah

We will call the angels of Hell.

    Explanation: If the wrongdoer persists, Allah will summon the angels responsible for punishing evildoers, illustrating the seriousness of divine justice.

Verse 19

Kalla la tuti'hu wasjud waqtarib

No! Do not obey him. But prostrate and draw near [to Allah].

    Explanation: The final verse encourages believers to ignore those who oppose them and continue to worship Allah through prayer. "Prostrate and draw near" emphasizes the importance of maintaining a close relationship with Allah through acts of devotion.

SURAH AL-ALAQ – SURAH 96

Summary of the key points from Surah Al-Alaq:

1. Revelation Begins: Surah Al-Alaq marks the beginning of the Quranic revelation to Prophet Muhammad (peace be upon him). It starts with the command to "Read" in the name of Allah, highlighting the importance of knowledge and learning.
2. Creation of Humans: The surah emphasizes the miraculous creation of humans from a simple, clinging substance, urging reflection on our origins and dependence on Allah's power.
3. Importance of Knowledge: Allah is described as the one who taught humans by the pen, underscoring the significance of writing and knowledge as divine gifts that enable learning and growth.
4. Human Arrogance: The surah warns against the arrogance that can arise when people feel self-sufficient and forget their reliance on Allah. This pride can lead to moral and ethical transgressions.
5. Accountability and Return: It reminds everyone that they will ultimately return to Allah, who will judge their actions. This serves as a call to humility and righteousness.
6. Opposition to Worship: The surah addresses those who try to prevent others from worshipping Allah, highlighting the unjust nature of such interference and the importance of staying true to one's faith.
7. Allah's Watching and Justice: It reassures believers that Allah sees everything, and those who oppose or deny the truth will face consequences. Divine justice will prevail.
8. Encouragement to Worship: The final verses encourage believers to continue their prayers and devotion, drawing nearer to Allah despite any opposition they may face.

Overall, Surah Al-Alaq emphasizes the themes of creation, knowledge, humility, accountability, and steadfastness in worship, encouraging believers to maintain their faith and trust in Allah's guidance and justice.

ADDITIONAL INFORMATION

The first five verses of Surah Al-Alaq were revealed in one go and are considered the first revelation received by Prophet Muhammad (peace be upon him). This event took place while he was in the Cave of Hira, marking the beginning of his prophethood. The initial revelation began with the command to "Read" and continued through the first five verses, highlighting themes of creation, knowledge, and the significance of learning.

The remaining verses of Surah Al-Alaq (verses 6-19) were revealed later, addressing different circumstances and themes, such as human arrogance, accountability, and opposition to worship. This pattern of revelation, where parts of a surah are revealed at different times, is common in the Quran.

The Cave of Hira holds profound significance in Islamic history as the site where Prophet Muhammad (peace be upon him) received the first revelation of the Quran. It was in this secluded cave that the angel Gabriel (Jibril) appeared to him and instructed him to "Read" (Iqra), marking the beginning of his prophethood. This moment is pivotal as it signifies the start of the final and complete revelation from Allah to humanity. Before this transformative event, Prophet Muhammad frequently visited the Cave of Hira to meditate and engage in spiritual reflection. He sought solitude there to contemplate the injustices and idolatry prevalent in Meccan society at the time, and this period of reflection prepared him for his future mission as a prophet.

The experience in the Cave of Hira represents a turning point in the Prophet's life, transforming him from a seeker of truth into a messenger tasked with conveying Allah's message to humanity. It symbolizes spiritual awakening and marks the beginning of his role as a guide for all people. The initial verses revealed in the cave emphasize the importance of knowledge, the miraculous nature of creation, and the acknowledgment of Allah as the Creator. These themes form the foundation of the Quranic message and highlight the significance of the revelation received in the cave.

For Muslims, the Cave of Hira is a place of historical and religious importance, serving as a physical location that connects believers to a crucial event in the history of Islam. Many Muslims who visit Mecca for pilgrimage also visit the cave to remember and reflect on the profound moment of the first revelation. Thus, the Cave of Hira is significant not only as the site of the first revelation but also as a symbol of spiritual preparation and the Prophet's transition into his role as the final messenger of Allah.

SURAH AL ALAQ (SURAH 96)

Questions

1. What is the significance of Surah Al-Alaq in the context of the Quranic revelation?
2. What does the term "Al-Alaq" refer to, and why is the surah named after it?
3. What are the first words revealed to the Prophet Muhammad (peace be upon him) in this surah?
4. How does the surah describe the creation of humans?
5. What is the importance of knowledge and learning as emphasized in Surah Al-Alaq?
6. How does the surah address the concept of arrogance and defiance against divine guidance?
7. What warning does Surah Al-Alaq give about those who hinder others from following the path of righteousness?
8. How does the surah emphasize the consequences of ignoring divine guidance?
9. What is the significance of the command to "prostrate and draw near" at the end of the surah?
10. How can the teachings of Surah Al-Alaq be applied to contemporary life to encourage personal growth and humility?

Answers

1. What is the significance of Surah Al-Alaq in the context of the Quranic revelation?
   - Surah Al-Alaq contains the first verses revealed to the Prophet Muhammad (peace be upon him), marking the beginning of the Quranic revelation and the Prophet's mission.

2. What does the term "Al-Alaq" refer to, and why is the surah named after it?
   - "Al-Alaq" refers to "the clot" or "a clinging substance," referring to the early stage of human embryonic development. The surah is named after it because it highlights the creation of humans from a humble beginning.

3. What are the first words revealed to the Prophet Muhammad (peace be upon him) in this surah?
   - The first words revealed are "Read in the name of your Lord who created."

4. How does the surah describe the creation of humans?
   - The surah describes humans as being created from a clinging substance (alaq), emphasizing the humble origins and intricate creation by Allah.

5. What is the importance of knowledge and learning as emphasized in Surah Al-Alaq?
   - The surah highlights the importance of reading and learning, portraying knowledge as a means to understand divine guidance and fulfill human potential.

6. How does the surah address the concept of arrogance and defiance against divine guidance?
   - The surah warns against arrogance and defiance, particularly criticizing those who believe they are self-sufficient and reject divine guidance.

7. What warning does Surah Al-Alaq give about those who hinder others from following the path of righteousness?
   - The surah warns that those who hinder others from prayer and righteousness will face dire consequences and be held accountable by Allah.

8. How does the surah emphasize the consequences of ignoring divine guidance?
   - The surah emphasizes that ignoring divine guidance leads to moral and spiritual decline and that such individuals will face accountability.

9. What is the significance of the command to "prostrate and draw near" at the end of the surah?
   - The command signifies submission to Allah and encourages believers to seek closeness to their Creator through worship and humility.

10. How can the teachings of Surah Al-Alaq be applied to contemporary life to encourage personal growth and humility?
    - The teachings encourage the pursuit of knowledge, humility, and adherence to divine guidance, promoting personal growth and a deeper connection with Allah.

These questions and answers can be used for educational purposes, study sessions, or discussions to enhance understanding of Surah Al-Alaq.

Multiple Choice Questions

1. What is the significance of Surah Al-Alaq in the context of Quranic revelation?

    - A) It contains the last verses revealed

    - B) It contains the first verses revealed to the Prophet Muhammad (peace be upon him)

    - C) It is the longest surah in the Quran

    - D) It was revealed in Medina

2. What does the term "Al-Alaq" refer to?

    - A) The pen

    - B) The clot or a clinging substance

    - C) The mountain

    - D) The river

3. What are the first words revealed to the Prophet Muhammad (peace be upon him) in this surah?

    - A) Pray in the name of your Lord

    - B) Fast for your Lord

    - C) Read in the name of your Lord who created

    - D) Give charity in the name of your Lord

4. How does the surah describe the creation of humans?

    - A) From dust

    - B) From a clinging substance (alaq)

    - C) From clay

    - D) From light

5. What is emphasized as a means to understand divine guidance in Surah Al-Alaq?

    - A) Wealth

    - B) Knowledge and learning

    - C) Physical strength

    - D) Silence

6. How does the surah address those who are arrogant and defiant against divine guidance?

    - A) It praises them

    - B) It warns against arrogance and defiance

    - C) It ignores them

    - D) It rewards them

7. What warning does Surah Al-Alaq give about those who hinder others from righteousness?

    - A) They will be honoured

    - B) They will face dire consequences and accountability

    - C) They will be rewarded

    - D) They will be forgotten

8. What is the command given at the end of the surah?

    - A) Fight and conquer

    - B) Prostrate and draw near to Allah

    - C) Accumulate wealth

    - D) Seek vengeance

Answers

1. *Answer:* B) It contains the first verses revealed to the Prophet Muhammad (peace be upon him)
2. *Answer:* B) The clot or a clinging substance
3. *Answer:* C) Read in the name of your Lord who created
4. *Answer:* B) From a clinging substance (alaq)
5. *Answer:* B) Knowledge and learning
6. *Answer:* B) It warns against arrogance and defiance
7. *Answer:* B) They will face dire consequences and accountability
8. *Answer:* B) Prostrate and draw near to Allah

These questions and answers can be used for quizzes, educational discussions, or self-study to enhance understanding of Surah Al-Alaq.

SURAH AL-QADR

SURAH AL-QADR

Bismillahi ar-Rahmani ar-Raheem

Verse 1

Innaa anzalnaahu fee lailatil qadr

"Indeed, We sent it [the Quran] down during the Night of Decree."

Explanation:

This verse begins by asserting the revelation of the Quran during Laylat al-Qadr. The "We" refers to Allah, emphasizing His majesty and authority. The use of "sent it down" indicates the Quran's descent from the divine realm to the earthly plane, marking a crucial moment in Islamic history. Laylat al-Qadr is believed to be the night when the Quran was revealed from the Preserved Tablet to the lowest heaven, from where it was subsequently revealed to the Prophet Muhammad over 23 years.

Verse 2

Wa maa adraaka ma lailatul qadr

"And what can make you know what is the Night of Decree?"

Explanation:

This rhetorical question underscores the exceptional nature of Laylat al-Qadr. It suggests that human comprehension of this night's full significance and value is limited. The verse invites believers to reflect on its profound spiritual impact and the magnitude of Allah's mercy and blessings associated with it.

Verse 3

Lailatul qadri khairum min alfee shahr

"The Night of Decree is better than a thousand months."

Explanation:

This verse quantifies the spiritual value of Laylat al-Qadr. Worship and good deeds performed during this night are more rewarding than those carried out over a thousand months, equivalent to more than 83 years. This immense merit encourages Muslims to seek out and maximize their devotion during this time, as it offers unparalleled opportunities for spiritual growth and forgiveness.

Verse 4

Tanaz zalul malaa-ikatu war roohu feeha bi izni-rab bihim min kulli amr

"The angels and the Spirit descend therein by permission of their Lord for every matter."

Explanation:

This verse describes the descent of angels and the Spirit, commonly interpreted as Angel Gabriel, on Laylat al-Qadr. Their descent signifies the execution of divine commands and the distribution of decrees for the coming year. The presence of angels and Gabriel highlights the night's sanctity and the celestial harmony accompanying this blessed event.

Verse 5

Salaamun hiya hattaa mat la'il fajr

"Peace it is until the emergence of dawn."

Explanation:

The surah concludes by describing Laylat al-Qadr as a night of peace and tranquility that lasts until dawn. This peace encompasses both a spiritual serenity experienced by worshippers and a reflection of Allah's mercy and forgiveness. The mention of "until the emergence of dawn" indicates the specific timing during which believers are encouraged to engage in prayers, reflection, and remembrance of Allah.

In summary, Surah Al-Qadr emphasizes the profound significance of the Night of Decree, urging believers to seek it out through increased devotion and reflection. It highlights the Quran's divine origin and the continued relevance of Allah's guidance and mercy. Reflection and Application

Personal Reflection:

Believers are encouraged to reflect on their lives, seek personal improvement, and strengthen their relationship with Allah during this period.

- Community and Solidarity: Laylat al-Qadr also fosters a sense of community, as Muslims worldwide engage in collective worship and reflection, reinforcing bonds of faith and solidarity.

Surah Al-Qadr, with its focus on the Night of Decree, serves as a powerful reminder of the Quran's revelation and the ongoing presence of divine mercy and guidance. It encourages Muslims to seize the spiritual opportunities presented by Laylat al-Qadr and to strive towards a more profound connection with Allah.

SUMMARY OF
SURAH AL-QADR – SURAH 97

Surah Al-Qadr is a short chapter in the Quran that emphasizes the significance of the Night of Decree (Laylat al-Qadr), which is considered one of the holiest nights in Islam. The surah highlights that this night is better than a thousand months, during which angels, including Angel Jibreel (Gabriel), descend by Allah's permission to bring peace and tranquility. It also underscores that on this night, Allah's blessings and mercy are plentiful, and sins are forgiven. The surah serves as a reminder of the immense spiritual benefits associated with Laylat al-Qadr and encourages believers to seek this night through prayer and worship.

SURAH AL-QADR – SURAH 97

Questions

1. What does the term "Al-Bayyina" mean, and why is the surah named after it?
2. What is the "clear evidence" mentioned in Surah Al-Bayyina?
3. According to the surah, what divided the People of the Book before the clear evidence came to them?
4. How does the surah describe those who reject faith after the clear evidence has come?
5. What does Surah Al-Bayyina say about the fate of those who disbelieve?
6. How does the surah describe the characteristics of those who believe and do righteous deeds?
7. What ultimate reward is promised to the believers according to Surah Al-Bayyina?
8. What are the key commandments outlined in the surah for those who receive the clear evidence?
9. How does the surah emphasize the importance of sincerity in worship?
10. How can the teachings of Surah Al-Bayyina be applied to contemporary life to foster faith and righteous actions?

Answers

1. What does the term "Al-Bayyina" mean, and why is the surah named after it?
   - "Al-Bayyina" means "the clear evidence." The surah is named after it because it discusses the coming of clear evidence, specifically the Prophet Muhammad (peace be upon him) and the Quran.

2. What is the "clear evidence" mentioned in Surah Al-Bayyina?
   - The "clear evidence" refers to the Prophet Muhammad (peace be upon him) and the Quran, which provide guidance and distinguish between truth and falsehood.

3. According to the surah, what divided the People of the Book before the clear evidence came to them?
   - The People of the Book were divided due to differing beliefs and interpretations, but the clear evidence was meant to clarify the truth.

4. How does the surah describe those who reject faith after the clear evidence has come?
   - The surah describes them as being in a state of denial and destined for severe consequences in the hereafter.

5. What does Surah Al-Bayyina say about the fate of those who disbelieve?
   - It states that those who disbelieve will be in the fire of Hell, abiding therein eternally, as they are the worst of creatures.

6. How does the surah describe the characteristics of those who believe and do righteous deeds?
   - It describes them as the best of creatures, highlighting their faith and righteous actions.

7. What ultimate reward is promised to the believers according to Surah Al-Bayyina?
   - Believers are promised eternal gardens of bliss in Paradise, where they will dwell forever.

8. What are the key commandments outlined in the surah for those who receive the clear evidence?
   - The surah commands sincere worship of Allah, establishing prayer, and giving charity, as these are integral aspects of faith.

9. How does the surah emphasize the importance of sincerity in worship?
   - The surah emphasizes worshiping Allah alone with sincerity, highlighting that this is the essence of true faith.

10. How can the teachings of Surah Al-Bayyina be applied to contemporary life to foster faith and righteous actions?
    - The teachings encourage individuals to seek clarity in faith, practice sincerity in worship, and engage in righteous actions to achieve spiritual success.

These questions and answers can be used for educational purposes, study sessions, or discussions to enhance understanding of Surah Al-Bayyina.

Multiple Choice Questions

1. What does the term "Al-Bayyina" mean?

    - A) The night

    - B) The clear evidence

    - C) The mountain

    - D) The promise

2. What is referred to as the "clear evidence" in Surah Al-Bayyina?

    - A) The miracles of Jesus

    - B) The wealth of the people

    - C) The Prophet Muhammad (peace be upon him) and the Quran

    - D) The strength of the believers

3. What caused division among the People of the Book before the clear evidence came to them?

    - A) Political conflicts

    - B) Lack of resources

    - C) Differing beliefs and interpretations

    - D) Natural disasters

4. How does the surah describe those who reject faith after the clear evidence has come?

    - A) As being misguided but forgiven

    - B) As being in a state of denial and destined for severe consequences

    - C) As wise and knowledgeable

    - D) As wealthy and powerful

5. What does Surah Al-Bayyina say about the fate of those who disbelieve?

    - A) They will be wealthy in this life

    - B) They will be in the fire of Hell, abiding eternally

    - C) They will be revered by others

    - D) They will live in peace and harmony

6. How does the surah describe the characteristics of those who believe and do righteous deeds?

    - A) As the best of creatures

    - B) As the most intelligent

    - C) As the wealthiest

    - D) As the most powerful

7. What ultimate reward is promised to the believers according to Surah Al-Bayyina?

    - A) Great wealth in this world

    - B) Eternal gardens of bliss in Paradise

    - C) Political power and influence

    - D) Long life and health

8. What are the key commandments outlined in the surah for those who receive the clear evidence?

    - A) Pursue wealth and power

    - B) Engage in constant warfare

    - C) Worship Allah sincerely, establish prayer, and give charity

    - D) Seek fame and recognition

9. How does the surah emphasize the importance of sincerity in worship?

    - A) By encouraging competition among believers

    - B) By emphasizing worship of Allah alone with sincerity

    - C) By promoting material wealth

    - D) By discouraging acts of charity

Answers

1. *Answer:* B) The clear evidence
2. *Answer:* C) The Prophet Muhammad (peace be upon him) and the Quran
3. *Answer:* C) Differing beliefs and interpretations
4. *Answer:* B) As being in a state of denial and destined for severe consequences
5. *Answer:* B) They will be in the fire of Hell, abiding eternally
6. A) As the best of creatures
7. *Answer:* B) Eternal gardens of bliss in Paradise
8. *Answer:* C) Worship Allah sincerely, establish prayer, and give charity
9. *Answer:* B) By emphasizing worship of Allah alone with sincerity

These questions and answers can be used for quizzes, educational discussions, or self-study to enhance understanding of Surah Al-Bayyina.

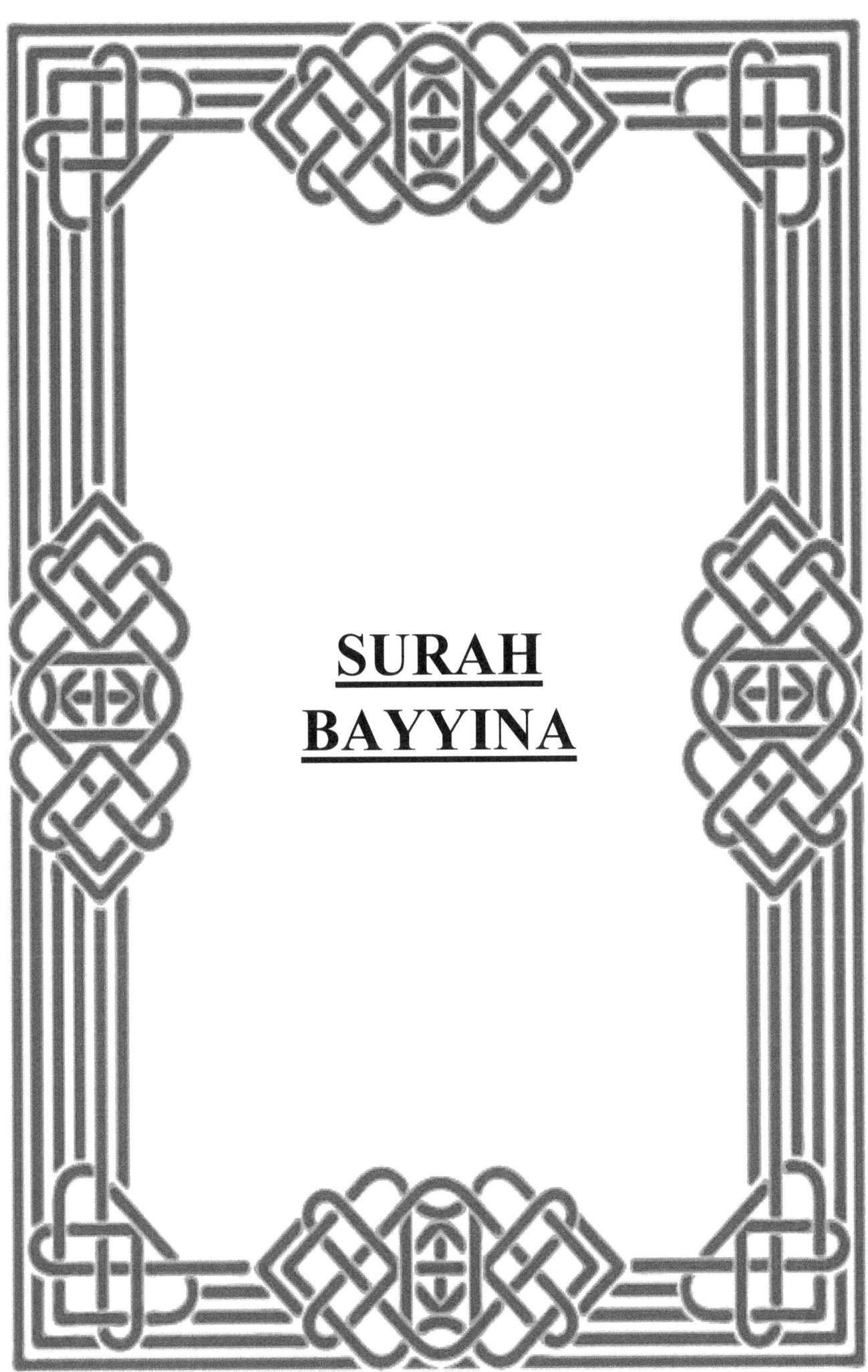

SURAH BAYYINA

SURAH BAYYINA

Bismillahi ar-Rahmani ar-Raheem

Verse 1

Lam yakuni allatheena kafaroo min ahli alkitabi walmushrikeena munfakkeena hatta ta/tiyahumu albayyina

Those who disbelieved among the People of the Scripture and the polytheists were not to be parted [from misbelief] until there came to them clear evidence.

Explanation:

This verse addresses the disbelievers among the People of the Scripture (Jews and Christians) and the polytheists, stating that they remained in their disbelief until the "clear evidence" came to them. The "clear evidence" refers to the Prophet Muhammad and the Quran, which provided undeniable proof and guidance necessary to distinguish truth from falsehood.

Verse 2

Rasoolun mina Allahi yatloo suhufan mutahhara

A Messenger from Allah, reciting purified scriptures.

Explanation:

The "Messenger from Allah" is identified as the Prophet Muhammad, who recites "purified scriptures," referring to the Quran. The word "purified" highlights the Quran's divine origin, free from corruption or error, and emphasizes the role of the Prophet as the bearer of a clear and untainted message.

Verse 3

Feeha kutubun qayyima

Within which are correct writings.

Explanation:

This verse describes the Quranic revelations as containing "correct writings" or teachings. These teachings are comprehensive, aligning perfectly with divine wisdom, and provide a complete framework for leading a righteous life. The Quran is presented as a guide to truth and moral integrity.

Verse 4

Wama tafarraqa allatheena ootoo alkitaba illa min baAAdi ma jaat-humu albayyina

Nor did those who were given the Scripture become divided until after there had come to them clear evidence.

Explanation:

This verse addresses the divisions among the People of the Scripture, noting that their disagreements arose after receiving the "clear evidence." This implies that their sectarian splits were due to a failure to fully accept and adhere to the divine message, highlighting human tendencies to deviate from clear guidance.

Verse 5

Wama omiroo illa liyaAAbudoo Allaha mukhliseena lahu alddeena hunafaa wayuqeemoo alssalata wayu/too alzzakata wathalika deenu alqayyima

And they were not commanded except to worship Allah, [being] sincere to Him in religion, inclining to truth, and to establish prayer and to give zakah. And that is the correct religion.

Explanation:

This verse outlines the core tenets of faith: sincere worship of Allah, regular prayer, and zakah (charitable giving). It emphasizes sincerity and truthfulness in religion, presenting these acts as expressions of true faith and devotion. The phrase "that is the correct religion" underscores the straightforwardness and universality of these commands.

Verse 6

Inna allatheena kafaroo min ahli alkitabi walmushrikeena fee nari jahannama khalideena feeha ola-ika hum sharru albarriya

Indeed, they who disbelieved among the People of the Scripture and the polytheists will be in the fire of Hell, abiding eternally therein. Those are the worst of creatures.

Explanation:

This verse warns that disbelievers among the People of the Scripture and polytheists will face eternal punishment in Hell, described as the "worst of creatures." It highlights the severity of rejecting divine truth after it has been clearly presented, serving as a cautionary reminder of the consequences of disbelief.

Verse 7

Inna allatheena amanoo waAAamiloo alssalihati ola-ika hum khayru albarriya

Indeed, they who have believed and done righteous deeds - those are the best of creatures.

Explanation:

In contrast to the previous verse, this one praises those who believe and perform righteous deeds, describing them as "the best of creatures." The verse highlights the honour and distinction of those who follow divine guidance, reinforcing the message that faith and good deeds lead to Allah's favor and blessings.

Verse 8

Jazaoohum AAinda rabbihim jannatu AAadnin tajree min tahtiha alanharu khalideena feeha abada radiya Allahu AAanhum waradoo AAanhu thalika liman khashiya Rabbah

Their reward with Allah will be gardens of perpetual residence beneath which rivers flow, wherein they will abide forever, Allah being pleased with them and they with Him. That is for whoever has feared his Lord.

Explanation:

The surah concludes by promising believers eternal reward in paradise, depicted as gardens with flowing rivers, symbolizing eternal bliss and divine pleasure. The mutual satisfaction—Allah being pleased with them and they with Him—reflects the harmonious relationship between the Creator and His faithful servants. The verse ends by emphasizing that such a reward is reserved for those who have lived in reverence and fear of their Lord, underscoring the importance of a pious and conscious life.

In summary, Surah Al-Bayyina provides a clear distinction between those who accept and follow divine guidance and those who reject it. It emphasizes the significance of the Quran as a source of clear evidence, advocates for sincere worship and righteous deeds, and outlines the eternal consequences for both believers and disbelievers.

SUMMARY OF
SURAH AL-BAYYINA – SURAH 97

Surah Al-Bayyina, the 98th chapter of the Quran, addresses the necessity of clear evidence in distinguishing truth from falsehood. It begins by emphasizing the arrival of the Prophet Muhammad with the Quran as the definitive proof needed by those who had previously rejected the message. This revelation serves as a guidance meant to resolve doubts and divisions among people, particularly addressing the "People of the Book" (Jews and Christians). The surah notes that these groups did not dissent until after the clear evidence had been presented to them, highlighting how divine guidance was intended to unify, yet human tendencies led to division.

The surah underscores the importance of sincere worship and righteous conduct, calling upon people to worship Allah alone, maintain regular prayers, and give charity. These acts are fundamental components of Islamic practice and are portrayed as the essence of true faith and devotion. The text distinguishes between believers and disbelievers, stating that those who reject faith, including disbelievers among the People of the Book and polytheists, will face the fire of Hell. In contrast, those who believe and perform righteous deeds are considered the best of creation, promised eternal reward.

In its conclusion, Surah Al-Bayyina describes the eternal consequences of one's beliefs and actions. It assures believers who engage in good deeds of a reward in the form of Gardens of Paradise, where they will dwell eternally, enjoying the pleasure of Allah—a supreme triumph. The surah serves as a poignant reminder of the clarity and truth of the Islamic message, emphasizing the importance of faith, righteous actions, and the ultimate distinction between those who accept the truth and those who reject it. It calls for sincerity in worship and warns of the eternal repercussions based on one's response to the divine message.

SURAH BAYYINA SURAH 98

QUESTIONS

1. What does Surah Al-Bayyina talk about?
2. Who brought the "clear evidence" mentioned in Surah Al-Bayyina?
3. What does Surah Al-Bayyina say will happen to people who do good deeds and believe in Allah?
4. Who are referred to as the "People of the Book" in this Surah?
5. What are two important things that believers are asked to do in Surah Al-Bayyina?
6. What does Surah Al-Bayyina say about those who do not believe in the truth?

Answers

1. Surah Al-Bayyina talks about the clear message that Prophet Muhammad brought and the difference between those who believe and those who do not.

2. The "clear evidence" was brought by Prophet Muhammad.

3. People who do good deeds and believe in Allah will go to Paradise, a beautiful and happy place.

4. The "People of the Book" are the Jews and Christians who had received earlier scriptures from Allah.

5. Believers are asked to pray and give to charity (zakat) as part of their good deeds.

6. Those who do not believe in the truth will receive a severe punishment.

These questions are designed to engage primary school children with the key messages of Surah Al-Bayyina in a straightforward manner.

Multiple Choice Questions

1. What is the main theme of Surah Al-Bayyina?

    - A) The attributes of Allah

    - B) The clear evidence and the separation of truth from falsehood

    - C) The rewards of Jannah

    - D) Stories of past prophets

2. Who are the "People of the Book" mentioned in Surah Al-Bayyina?

    - A) Followers of Islam

    - B) Followers of Jesus

    - C) Jews and Christians

    - D) Polytheists of Makkah

3. What clear evidence is referred to in this Surah?

    - A) The miracles of previous prophets

    - B) The splitting of the moon

    - C) The coming of the Prophet Muhammad with the Quran

    - D) The Day of Judgment

4. In Surah Al-Bayyina, what are those who disbelieve promised?

    - A) Gardens beneath which rivers flow

    - B) A severe punishment

    - C) Peace and contentment

    - D) Wealth and power in this world

5. What will be the fate of the righteous, as mentioned in Surah Al-Bayyina?

    - A) They will be cast into Hell

    - B) They will be ignored

    - C) They will dwell in Paradise forever

    - D) They will face trials in this world

6. What key act of worship is highlighted in Surah Al-Bayyina as a command from Allah for believers?

    - A) Charity

    - B) Pilgrimage

    - C) Establishing prayer and giving zakat

    - D) Fasting

7. Surah Al-Bayyina emphasizes a division between which two groups of people?

    - A) Nomads and city dwellers

    - B) Rich and poor

    - C) Believers and disbelievers

    - D) Men and women

These questions can serve as a helpful study tool or quiz for those looking to deepen their understanding of Surah Al-Bayyina.

Answer

1. *Answer:* B) The clear evidence and the separation of truth from falsehood
2. *Answer:* C) Jews and Christians
3. *Answer:* C) The coming of the Prophet Muhammad with the Quran
4. *Answer:* B) A severe punishment
5. *Answer:* C) They will dwell in Paradise forever
6. *Answer:* C) Establishing prayer and giving zakat
7. *Answer:* C) Believers and disbelievers

SURAH AL-ZALZALAH

SURAH AL-ZALZALAH

Bismillahi ar-Rahmani ar-Raheem

Verses 1-2: The Earthquake

Izaa zul zilatil ardu zil zaalaha

Wa akh rajatil ardu athqaalaha

"When the earth is shaken with its [final] earthquake. And the earth discharges its burdens."

Tafseer:

These opening verses describe an extraordinary and final earthquake that will occur at the end of times. The phrase "its [final] earthquake" signifies the ultimate upheaval, beyond any natural disaster previously experienced. The Earth will convulse violently, symbolizing the commencement of the Day of Judgment. The "burdens" that the Earth discharges may refer to the dead being resurrected or the Earth's secrets being revealed. This shaking represents both a physical and spiritual transformation, indicating that the world as we know it is coming to an end.

Verses 3-4: The Earth Speaks

Wa qaalal insaanu ma laha

Yawmaa izin tuhaddithu akhbaaraha

Translation:

"And man says, 'What is [wrong] with it?' That Day, it will report its news."

Tafseer:

In these verses, humanity is depicted as bewildered by the Earth's violent upheaval, questioning what is happening. This reaction underscores human vulnerability and the realization that a significant, divine event is unfolding. The Earth "reporting its news" suggests that it will testify to all that has transpired upon it. This could include the actions of humans, both good and bad, as the Earth bears witness to the deeds performed on its surface. This idea emphasizes the comprehensive nature of divine justice and accountability.

Verse 5: Divine Command

Bi-anna rabbaka awhaa laha

"Because your Lord has commanded it."

Tafseer:

This verse underscores the sovereignty and authority of Allah over all creation. The earthquake and the Earth's testimony occur by the explicit command of Allah. It highlights that the events of the Day of Judgment are not random but are divinely orchestrated and serve a specific purpose in the fulfillment of divine justice. It reminds believers of the omnipotence of Allah and the certainty of His will being executed.

Verses 6-8: The Presentation of Deeds

Yawma iziny yas durun naasu ash tatal liyuraw a'maalahum. Famaiy ya'mal mithqala zarratin khai raiy-yarah. Wa maiy-y'amal mithqala zarratin sharraiy-yarah

"That Day, the people will depart separated [into categories] to be shown [the result of] their deeds. So whoever does an atom's weight of good will see it, and whoever does an atom's weight of evil will see it."

Tafseer:

These concluding verses describe the culmination of the Judgment Day process. Humanity will be divided into groups based on their deeds, highlighting the ultimate accountability each individual faces. The concept of deeds being shown refers to the precise and just nature of divine judgment. Every action, no matter how small, is significant and will be accounted for. The use of "an atom's weight" illustrates the meticulousness of this accountability. This serves as a powerful reminder of personal responsibility and the importance of moral conduct, encouraging believers to be conscious of their actions.

Conclusion:

Surah Al-Zalzalah is a compelling chapter that encapsulates the eschatological themes of accountability, divine justice, and the transient nature of worldly life. Through its vivid imagery and profound message, it serves as a reminder for believers to live righteously, with an awareness of the inevitable day when all deeds will be evaluated by the divine standard.

REFLECTIONS AND LESSONS LEARNT FROM SURAH ZALZALAH

Surah Al-Zalzalah, despite its briefness, offers profound reflections and lessons that have significant implications for both individual and communal aspects of life. One of the primary themes is the awareness of the Day of Judgment. The surah vividly depicts the events of this day, emphasizing its certainty and the dramatic changes it will bring. This serves as a reminder for believers to maintain a constant awareness of the afterlife. It encourages them to live with a consciousness of the transient nature of this world, preparing for the eternal life that follows.

Another central theme is the meticulous nature of divine justice and accountability. The assurance that even an atom's weight of good or evil will be accounted for highlights the precision with which Allah will judge human actions. This emphasizes the importance of being mindful of one's deeds, as nothing is too small to escape divine scrutiny. The surah teaches that every action, no matter how insignificant it may seem, holds weight in the sight of Allah. This encourages individuals to consistently engage in good deeds, fostering a mindset of generosity, kindness, and ethical behaviour in everyday life. It also serves as a caution against neglecting small sins, as they too will be accounted for.

The personification of the Earth as a witness to human actions serves as a powerful metaphor for accountability. It reminds believers that their actions are observed and recorded, not just by Allah, but by their very environment. This can inspire a deeper sense of responsibility towards ethical interactions with both people and the natural world. The dramatic portrayal of the end times prompts introspection and reflection on one's life choices. It serves as an impetus for repentance and spiritual renewal, encouraging believers to seek forgiveness for past wrongs and to strive for moral rectitude.

On the Day of Judgment, all humans will be judged equitably based on their deeds, regardless of their social status, wealth, or earthly accomplishments. This underscores the Islamic principle that true worth is determined by one's piety and actions, rather than material or worldly measures. Ultimately, the surah calls for a life lived in preparation for the hereafter. It encourages believers to prioritize their spiritual and ethical obligations, ensuring that their actions align with the teachings of Islam and contribute positively to their standing on the Day of Judgment.

In conclusion, Surah Al-Zalzalah serves as a profound reminder of the impermanence of worldly life and the importance of preparing for the eternal hereafter. Its lessons on justice, accountability, and the significance of even the smallest deeds inspire a holistic approach to living a life of faith, mindfulness, and moral integrity.

SUMMARY OF
SURAH AL-ZALZALAH-SURAH 99

Surah Al-Zalzalah, also known as "The Earthquake," is the 99th chapter of the Qur'an, consisting of eight verses. It was revealed during the Meccan period of Prophet Muhammad's (peace be upon him) prophethood. The central theme of the surah is the Day of Judgment and the transformative events that accompany it, particularly focusing on a monumental earthquake that signals the end of the world as we know it.

The surah opens with a depiction of an unprecedented earthquake that will shake the Earth with immense force. This disastrous event symbolizes the onset of the Day of Judgment, marking a transition from the temporal to the eternal realm. The intensity of the earthquake underscores the gravity of the moment and serves as a reminder of the ultimate power and authority of Allah over creation.

In a unique and thought-provoking portrayal, the Earth is personified in the subsequent verses. It is described as testifying about everything that has occurred upon it. This personification emphasizes the concept of accountability, where the Earth itself becomes a witness to human actions. The idea that the Earth will reveal its secrets reinforces the belief that nothing is hidden from divine scrutiny, and it highlights the comprehensive nature of divine justice.

The surah also captures the reaction of humanity to these unfolding events. People will be in a state of confusion and reflection, confronted by the reality of their actions and the truth of the divine message. The astonishment of individuals serves as a moment of realization, where they are faced with the consequences of their deeds, no matter how minor they might have seemed during their lifetimes.

The final verses describe the presentation of individual deeds on the Day of Judgment. Every person will be shown their actions with precise justice, emphasizing that even the smallest actions, whether good or bad, will be accounted for. This reinforces the concept of personal responsibility and the importance of moral conduct. The surah serves as a reminder that every action has significance in the eyes of Allah and will impact one's standing in the hereafter.

Overall, Surah Al-Zalzalah is a powerful reminder of personal accountability and the inevitability of divine justice. It encourages believers to live with awareness of the transient nature of this world and the permanence of the hereafter. The surah's vivid imagery and profound message prompt reflection and a call to repentance, urging individuals to live righteously and prepare for the ultimate accountability before Allah.

Surah Al-Zalzalah, also known as "The Earthquake," is a profound chapter of the Qur'an that presents vivid imagery of the Day of Judgment. Here is a tafseer, or interpretation, of the surah's verses, offering insights into their meanings and implications:

SURAH AL-ZALZALA (SURAH 98)

Questions

1. What does the term "Al-Zalzalah" refer to, and why is the surah named after it?
2. What major event is described in Surah Al-Zalzalah?
3. How does the surah describe the reaction of people on the Day of Judgment?
4. What will happen to the earth on the Day of Judgment according to this surah?
5. What will the earth reveal on the Day of Judgment?
6. How does Surah Al-Zalzalah emphasize the concept of accountability for one's deeds?
7. What does the surah say about the scale of deeds and their significance?
8. How does the surah describe the presentation of deeds to individuals?
9. What is the significance of even the smallest deeds according to Surah Al-Zalzalah?
10. How can the teachings of Surah Al-Zalzalah be applied to contemporary life to encourage mindfulness and responsibility?

Answers

1. What does the term "Al-Zalzalah" refer to, and why is the surah named after it?
   - "Al-Zalzalah" refers to "the earthquake." The surah is named after it because it describes the great shaking of the earth that will occur on the Day of Judgment.

2. What major event is described in Surah Al-Zalzalah?
   - The surah describes the shaking of the earth on the Day of Judgment, when it will release its burdens and reveal everything within it.

3. How does the surah describe the reaction of people on the Day of Judgment?
   - People will be in a state of confusion and will question what is happening to the earth.

4. What will happen to the earth on the Day of Judgment according to this surah?
   - The earth will shake violently, release its burdens, and reveal all that has happened on it.

5. What will the earth reveal on the Day of Judgment?
   - The earth will reveal everything that has been done upon it, as it will testify to the deeds of people.

6. How does Surah Al-Zalzalah emphasize the concept of accountability for one's deeds?
   - The surah emphasizes that every individual will see their deeds, no matter how small, and will be held accountable for them.

7. What does the surah say about the scale of deeds and their significance?
   - The surah states that even the smallest deeds, as little as an atom's weight, will be shown and accounted for.

8. How does the surah describe the presentation of deeds to individuals?
   - Individuals will be shown their deeds clearly, and they will see the results of their actions.

9. What is the significance of even the smallest deeds according to Surah Al-Zalzalah?
   - The surah underscores that every deed, no matter how small, is significant and will be accounted for on the Day of Judgment.

10. How can the teachings of Surah Al-Zalzalah be applied to contemporary life to encourage mindfulness and responsibility?
    - The teachings encourage individuals to be mindful of their actions, recognizing that every deed matters and will be accounted for, thus promoting ethical behavior and accountability.

These questions and answers can be used for educational purposes, study sessions, or discussions to enhance understanding of Surah Al-Zalzala.

Multiple Choice Questions

1. What does the term "Al-Zalzalah" refer to?

    - A) The storm

    - B) The earthquake

    - C) The flood

    - D) The fire

2. What major event is described in Surah Al-Zalzalah?

    - A) The rising of the sun from the west

    - B) The great shaking of the earth on the Day of Judgment

    - C) The splitting of the sea

    - D) The descent of angels

3. How does the surah describe the earth's condition on the Day of Judgment?

    - A) Calm and peaceful

    - B) Shaking violently and releasing its burdens

    - C) Covered in water

    - D) Bursting into flames

4. What will the earth do on the Day of Judgment according to this surah?

    - A) Hide its secrets

    - B) Testify to the deeds done upon it

    - C) Collapse into dust

    - D) Become a paradise

5. How does Surah Al-Zalzalah emphasize the concept of accountability for one's deeds?

    - A) By stating that only major sins will be judged

    - B) By indicating that even the smallest deeds will be shown and accounted for

    - C) By suggesting that deeds are irrelevant

    - D) By promising automatic forgiveness for all deeds

6. What does the surah say about even the smallest deeds?

    - A) They will be ignored

    - B) They are insignificant

    - C) They will be shown and accounted for

    - D) They will automatically be forgiven

7. How will individuals see their deeds according to Surah Al-Zalzalah?

    - A) In a dream

    - B) Through other people's testimonies

    - C) Clearly, as they will be presented to them

    - D) In written form only

8. What is the ultimate message of Surah Al-Zalzalah regarding human actions?

    - A) Only major actions matter

    - B) Every action, big or small, is significant and will be accounted for

    - C) Actions do not affect one's fate

    - D) Good intentions are enough

Answers

1. *Answer:* B) The earthquake
2. *Answer:* B) The great shaking of the earth on the Day of Judgment
3. *Answer:* B) Shaking violently and releasing its burdens
4. *Answer:* B) Testify to the deeds done upon it
5. *Answer:* B) By indicating that even the smallest deeds will be shown and accounted for
6. *Answer:* C) They will be shown and accounted for
7. *Answer:* C) Clearly, as they will be presented to them
8. *Answer:* B) Every action, big or small, is significant and will be accounted for

These questions and answers can be used for quizzes, educational discussions, or self-study to enhance understanding of Surah Al-Zalzalah.

SURAH AL-ADIYAT

SURAH AL-ADIYAT

Bismillahi ar-Rahmani ar-Raheem

Verse 1

Wal'aadi yaati dabha

"By the racers, panting,"

This verse begins with an oath by the warhorses that charge forward swiftly, panting as they gallop. The imagery is intended to capture the urgency and intensity of their movement.

Verse 2

Fal moori yaati qadha

"And the producers of sparks [when] striking,"

As the horses' hooves strike the ground, they produce sparks, emphasizing the speed and power with which they move. This imagery highlights the ferocity and energy of the horses as they rush into battle.

Verse 3

Fal mugheeraati subha

"And the chargers at dawn,"

The horses charge at dawn, a time often associated with military raids. This indicates the strategic nature of their movement, suggesting preparation and determination in their action.

Verse 4

Fa atharna bihee naq'a

"Stirring up thereby [clouds of] dust,"

As the horses gallop, they kick up clouds of dust, illustrating the commotion and chaos of their charge. This symbolizes the impact and disturbance caused by such a forceful action.

Verse 5

Fawa satna bihee jam'a

"Arriving thereby in the center collectively,"

The horses penetrate deep into the enemy ranks, reaching the center of their formation. This demonstrates the effectiveness and resolve of their charge, highlighting the fruits of their effort and courage.

Verse 6

Innal-insana lirabbihee lakanood

"Indeed mankind, to his Lord, is ungrateful."

This verse marks a shift from the vivid imagery of the horses to a moral lesson about human nature. Despite the blessings and signs around them, humans often remain ungrateful to their Creator.

Verse 7

Wa innahu 'alaa zaalika la Shaheed

"And indeed, he is to that a witness."

Humans themselves are witnesses to their own ingratitude. Despite being aware of their neglect and failure to appreciate Allah's blessings, they persist in their heedlessness.

Verse 8

Wa innahu lihubbil khairi la shaded

"And indeed he is, in love of wealth, intense."

This verse highlights human attachment to material wealth, indicating how this obsession often blinds people to their spiritual and moral responsibilities.

Verse 9

Afala ya'lamu iza b'uthira ma filquboor

"But does he not know that when the contents of the graves are scattered,"

The surah shifts to a stark reminder of the Day of Judgment, when the dead will be resurrected, and the contents of the graves will be exposed. This serves as a wake-up call to those engrossed in worldly pursuits.

Verse 10

Wa hussila maa fis sudor

"And that within the breasts is obtained,"

On that Day, not only will physical deeds be revealed, but also the secrets and intentions hidden within hearts will be brought to light. This emphasizes accountability for both actions and inner thoughts.

Verse 11

Inna rabbahum bihim yauma 'izil lakhabeer

"Indeed, their Lord with them, that Day, is [fully] Acquainted."

The surah concludes by affirming Allah's complete awareness and knowledge of all that people do and think. This serves as a final reminder of divine justice and the need for sincerity and righteousness.

Overall, Surah Al-Adiyat uses powerful imagery and a narrative on human behavior to underscore themes of gratitude, accountability, and the transient nature of worldly pursuits in light of the eternal hereafter.

Certainly! Here are the reflections on Surah Al-Adiyat presented in paragraph form:

Reflecting on Surah Al-Adiyat offers valuable insights into human nature, spiritual priorities, and the balance between worldly pursuits and eternal accountability. The surah begins with a vivid depiction of charging horses, symbolizing urgency and decisive action. This imagery serves as a reminder that life requires active engagement and purposeful effort, especially in spiritual matters. The intense energy of the horses can inspire individuals to approach their spiritual journey with similar vigor and commitment.

A central theme in the surah is human ingratitude towards Allah. Despite the countless blessings bestowed upon individuals, there is often a tendency to overlook divine favors. This invites self-examination and encourages the cultivation of gratitude in daily life. By acknowledging and appreciating these blessings, individuals can foster a deeper connection with Allah and a more meaningful spiritual experience.

The surah also addresses the intense love of wealth, highlighting it as a major distraction from spiritual growth. This reflection prompts a reassessment of personal priorities, urging individuals to adopt a balanced approach that values spiritual and moral wealth over mere material accumulation. By shifting focus away from materialism, one can find greater fulfillment and purpose.

The vivid imagery of the Day of Judgment underscores the inevitability of accountability, reminding individuals that actions and intentions are significant. This serves as a call to live with an awareness of ultimate accountability before Allah, motivating people to align their lives with divine values. The exposure of what lies within people's hearts on that day emphasizes the importance of sincerity and purity of intention, inspiring a commitment to align outward actions with inner beliefs.

Finally, the surah concludes with a reminder of Allah's complete awareness. This can provide comfort, knowing that one's struggles and efforts are recognized by Allah, while also serving as a caution against hypocrisy and hidden wrongdoing. The contrast between the transient nature of worldly pursuits and the permanence of the hereafter invites reflection on the ultimate purpose of life. It encourages individuals to invest in actions that have lasting value beyond this life, guiding them to prioritize what truly matters in the grand scheme of their spiritual journey.

SUMMARY OF
SURAH AL-ADIYAT SURAH 100

Surah Al-Adiyat is the 100th chapter of the Quran, consisting of 11 verses. This surah is characterized by its vivid imagery and powerful language. It begins with an oath by the charging horses, highlighting their speed and the dust they raise during battle. This imagery serves to capture attention and set the stage for a deeper message.

The core theme of the surah revolves around human ingratitude and the tendency to prioritize worldly possessions over spiritual and moral obligations. It highlights how people often become obsessed with wealth and material pursuits, neglecting their duty to Allah and overlooking the reality of the Day of Judgment.

The surah concludes with a reminder that Allah is fully aware of everything hidden within human hearts and that individuals will be held accountable for their actions in the hereafter. It serves as a powerful admonition to refocus on spiritual values and prepare for the ultimate accountability before Allah.

SURAH AL-ADIYAT (SURAH 100)

Questions

1. What does the term "Al-Adiyat" refer to, and why is the surah named after it?
2. What scene is vividly described at the beginning of Surah Al-Adiyat?
3. How does the surah illustrate the concept of urgency and power in its opening verses?
4. What human characteristic does the surah highlight as a central theme?
5. According to Surah Al-Adiyat, what is the source of human ingratitude?
6. How does the surah describe the knowledge of Allah regarding human actions?
7. What warning does Surah Al-Adiyat give about the consequences of ingratitude and heedlessness?
8. How does the surah emphasize the certainty of the Day of Judgment?
9. What role do the galloping horses play in conveying the message of the surah?
10. How can the teachings of Surah Al-Adiyat be applied to contemporary life to encourage gratitude and mindfulness?

Answers

1. What does the term "Al-Adiyat" refer to, and why is the surah named after it?
   - "Al-Adiyat" refers to "the chargers" or "the galloping horses." The surah is named after it because it begins with an oath by the horses that charge swiftly into battle, symbolizing urgency and power.

2. What scene is vividly described at the beginning of Surah Al-Adiyat?
   - The surah describes the scene of horses galloping swiftly, striking sparks with their hooves, and charging into the midst of battle.

3. How does the surah illustrate the concept of urgency and power in its opening verses?
   - The surah uses the imagery of swift, powerful horses galloping with intensity, creating sparks and dust clouds, to convey a sense of urgency and force.

4. What human characteristic does the surah highlight as a central theme?
   - The surah highlights human ingratitude and forgetfulness as central themes.

5. According to Surah Al-Adiyat, what is the source of human ingratitude?
   - The surah suggests that human ingratitude stems from a focus on material wealth and desires, leading to a neglect of spiritual and moral obligations.

6. How does the surah describe the knowledge of Allah regarding human actions?
   - The surah states that Allah is fully aware of what is in the hearts of people, indicating His complete knowledge of their intentions and actions.

7. What warning does Surah Al-Adiyat give about the consequences of ingratitude and heedlessness?
   - The surah warns that those who are ungrateful and heedless of Allah's guidance will face accountability and consequences on the Day of Judgment.

8. How does the surah emphasize the certainty of the Day of Judgment?
   - The surah emphasizes the certainty of the Day of Judgment by reminding that all hidden intentions and deeds will be exposed and judged.

9. What role do the galloping horses play in conveying the message of the surah?
   - The galloping horses symbolize urgency and power, serving as a metaphor for the swift approach of accountability and the need for vigilance in one's actions.

10. How can the teachings of Surah Al-Adiyat be applied to contemporary life to encourage gratitude and mindfulness?
    - The teachings encourage individuals to reflect on their actions, remain grateful for Allah's blessings, and be mindful of their responsibilities and the inevitable accountability in the hereafter.

These questions and answers can be used for educational purposes, study sessions, or discussions to enhance understanding of Surah Al-Adiyat.

Multiple Choice Questions

1. What does the term "Al-Adiyat" refer to?

    - A) The stars

    - B) The mountains

    - C) The galloping horses

    - D) The rivers

2. What scene is vividly described at the beginning of Surah Al-Adiyat?

    - A) A peaceful garden

    - B) Horses galloping swiftly, striking sparks with their hooves

    - C) A calm sea

    - D) An evening sunset

3. How does the surah illustrate the concept of urgency and power?

    - A) By depicting a storm

    - B) By describing horses galloping with intensity and creating dust clouds

    - C) By showing a calm and peaceful night

    - D) By narrating a story of ancient kings

4. What human characteristic is highlighted as a central theme in Surah Al-Adiyat?

    - A) Wisdom

    - B) Patience

    - C) Ingratitude

    - D) Generosity

5. According to Surah Al-Adiyat, what is the source of human ingratitude?

    - A) Lack of education

    - B) Focus on material wealth and desires

    - C) Poor health

    - D) Environmental factors

6. How does the surah describe the knowledge of Allah regarding human actions?

    - A) Limited to major sins

    - B) Full and complete, aware of what is in the hearts

    - C) Based on outward appearances

    - D) Only during times of worship

7. What warning does Surah Al-Adiyat give about the consequences of ingratitude and heedlessness?

    - A) There will be no consequences

    - B) They will face accountability and consequences on the Day of Judgment

    - C) They will be rewarded with wealth

    - D) They will be forgotten

8. How does the surah emphasize the certainty of the Day of Judgment?

    - A) By stating that all hidden intentions and deeds will be exposed and judged

    - B) By describing it as a myth

    - C) By suggesting it will be delayed indefinitely

    - D) By focusing on worldly success

Answers

1. *Answer:* C) The galloping horses
2. *Answer:* B) Horses galloping swiftly, striking sparks with their hooves
3. *Answer:* B) By describing horses galloping with intensity and creating dust clouds
4. *Answer:* C) Ingratitude
5. *Answer:* B) Focus on material wealth and desires
6. *Answer:* B) Full and complete, aware of what is in the hearts
7. *Answer:* B) They will face accountability and consequences on the Day of Judgment
8. *Answer:* A) By stating that all hidden intentions and deeds will be exposed and judged

These questions and answers can be used for quizzes, educational discussions, or self-study to enhance understanding of Surah Al-Adiyat.

SURAH AL-QARIAH

SURAH AL-QARIAH

Bismillahi ar-Rahmani ar-Raheem

Verses 1-3:

"Al-Qāriʿah, Mā al-qāriʿah, Wa mā adrāka mā al-qāriʿah"

- Explanation: The chapter opens with the powerful term "Al-Qariah," referring to the Day of Judgment, characterized as a sudden and overwhelming calamity. The repetition and rhetorical questioning ("Mā al-qāriʿah" and "Wa mā adrāka mā al-qāriʿah") stress its immense significance and mystery, urging reflection on this inevitable event that is beyond full human comprehension.

Verses 4-5:

"Yawma yakūnu an-nāsu ka-al-farāshi al-mabthūth, Wa takūnu al-jibālu ka-al-ʿihni al-manfūsh"

- Explanation: These verses describe the chaotic and tumultuous nature of the Day of Judgment. "Yawma yakūnu an-nāsu ka-al-farāshi al-mabthūth" depicts people as scattered moths, symbolizing chaos and disorientation. "Wa takūnu al-jibālu ka-al-ʿihni al-manfūsh" illustrates mountains being reduced to carded wool, highlighting the complete upheaval of the natural world and the dissolution of perceived stability and permanence.

Verses 6-7:

"Fa-ammā man thaqulat mawāzīnuhu, Fahuwa fī ʿīshatin rāḍiyah"

- Explanation: These verses introduce the concept of weighing deeds. "Fa-ammā man thaqulat mawāzīnuhu" indicates that those whose scales are heavy with good deeds will be rewarded. "Fahuwa fī ʿīshatin rāḍiyah" assures a life of satisfaction and eternal bliss for them, emphasizing the importance of accumulating righteous actions.

Verses 8-9:

"Wa ammā man khaffat mawāzīnuhu, Fa-ummuhu hāwiyah"

- Explanation: Conversely, "Wa ammā man khaffat mawāzīnuhu" refers to those whose scales are light due to insufficient good deeds. "Fa-ummuhu hāwiyah" implies that their refuge will be "Hawiyah," symbolizing a deep abyss or pit, highlighting severe punishment. This stark warning underlines the consequences of neglecting spiritual duties.

Verses 10-11:

"Wa mā adrāka mā hiyah, Nārun ḥāmiyah"

- Explanation: The surah concludes with "Wa mā adrāka mā hiyah," asking rhetorically about the nature of "Hawiyah," followed by "Nārun ḥāmiyah," which describes it as an intensely hot fire. This emphasizes the severity of the punishment and reinforces the importance of taking faith and deeds seriously, as their true nature is beyond human understanding.

Surah Al-Qariah, through its powerful imagery and messages, calls believers to reflect on their lives, urging them to prepare for the ultimate accountability by living righteously and ensuring their scales are heavy with good deeds.

Surah Al-Qariah imparts several valuable lessons that are relevant to both spiritual and practical aspects of life.

1. Awareness of the Hereafter: The surah underscores the reality of the Day of Judgment, reminding us of the certainty of an afterlife where everyone will be held accountable for their deeds. This awareness encourages us to live with a sense of purpose and responsibility, mindful of our actions and their consequences in the hereafter.
2. Impermanence of the World: The imagery used in the surah, such as people being like scattered moths and mountains like fluffed wool, highlights the transient nature of the world. This serves as a reminder that material possessions and worldly achievements are temporary and should not distract us from our spiritual goals and eternal success.
3. Significance of Deeds: The concept of weighing deeds emphasizes the importance of our actions in determining our fate in the afterlife. Every deed, whether good or bad, carries weight and contributes to the overall balance. This encourages us to engage in righteous actions consistently and avoid sinful behavior.
4. Righteous Living: The surah motivates us to live righteously, fulfilling our obligations to Allah and to other people. It highlights the rewards of a life filled with good deeds, encouraging us to cultivate virtues such as honesty, kindness, and compassion.
5. Seriousness of Consequences: The depiction of "Hawiyah" as a blazing fire serves as a stern warning about the severe consequences of neglecting one's spiritual duties. This emphasizes the importance of taking our faith seriously and striving to avoid actions that could lead to spiritual loss.
6. Reflection and Introspection: The rhetorical questions posed in the surah invite us to reflect on our own lives and readiness for the Day of Judgment. This encourages introspection and self-assessment, prompting us to make necessary changes to align our lives with the values and principles taught in the Quran.
7. Ultimate Justice: The surah reassures that ultimate justice will prevail on the Day of Judgment. Everyone will be judged fairly based on their deeds, offering comfort and motivation to live a life aligned with divine guidance, knowing that true justice is in the hands of Allah.

SUMMARY OF
SURAH AL-QARIAH – SURAH 101

Surah Al-Qariah, the 101st chapter of the Quran, is a profound and vivid depiction of the Day of Judgment, emphasizing its sudden and overwhelming nature. The surah opens with the term "Al-Qariah," which translates to "The Calamity" or "The Striking Event," immediately capturing the reader's attention and highlighting the significant impact of this day. The use of rhetorical questions serves to underscore the incomprehensible magnitude and seriousness of the event, urging believers to reflect on its inevitability and their own state of preparedness.

The imagery in Surah Al-Qariah paints a picture of chaos and upheaval, illustrating the disarray that will characterize the Day of Judgment. The surah describes people as scattered moths and mountains as carded wool, symbolizing the complete disruption of the natural order. This serves as a reminder of the impermanence of worldly possessions and status, encouraging individuals to focus on spiritual growth and the pursuit of eternal success rather than temporary material gains.

A central theme of the surah is the weighing of deeds, which determines one's fate in the hereafter. The surah makes clear that those whose good deeds outweigh their bad deeds will enjoy a pleasant life in paradise. In contrast, those whose scales are light will find their refuge in "Hawiyah," a term denoting a deep abyss or blazing fire. This stark contrast emphasizes the importance of righteous living and the serious consequences of neglecting one's spiritual duties.

In conclusion, Surah Al-Qariah serves as a powerful reminder of the transient nature of life and the ultimate accountability that awaits every individual. It calls upon believers to engage in self-reflection, assess their actions, and strive towards a life of righteousness. The surah's vivid imagery and compelling message underscore the significance of preparing for the hereafter through good deeds and a strong relationship with Allah, ensuring that one's scales are heavy on the Day of Judgment.

SURAH AT-TAKATHUR

SURAH AT-TAKATHUR

Bismillahi ar-Rahmani ar-Raheem

Verse 1

"Alhaakumu al-takaathur"

"The mutual rivalry for piling up of worldly things diverts you,"

- Interpretation: This verse highlights how humans are often distracted by the competition to accumulate more wealth, possessions, and social status. This rivalry takes their focus away from spiritual responsibilities and the remembrance of God.

Verse 2

"Hatta zurtumu al-maqaabir"

"Until you visit the graves."

- Explanation: The verse suggests that this preoccupation with material gain continues until death. The phrase "visit the graves" implies that death is a temporary transition, and the reality of life and its purpose will become clear in the hereafter.

Verse 3

"Kalla sawfa ta'lamoon"

"No! You are going to know."

- Explanation: This is a warning that people will eventually come to realize the truth about their worldly pursuits. The certainty of the knowledge that will come after death emphasizes the futility of their previous distractions.

Verse 4

"Thumma kalla sawfa ta'lamoon"

"Then, no! You are going to know."

- Explanation: This verse reinforces the warning, indicating that not only will people understand the reality after death, but they will be reminded again in the afterlife of their negligence and the consequences of their actions.

Verse 5

"Kalla law ta'lamoona 'ilma al-yaqeen"

"No! If you only knew with knowledge of certainty..."

- Explanation: If people possessed true certainty and understanding of the afterlife, they would not have been distracted by worldly gains. This verse calls for deeper reflection and awareness of the eternal life to come.

Verse 6

"Latarawunna al-jaheem"

"You will surely see the Hellfire."

- Explanation: This verse serves as a stark warning that those who wasted their lives in worldly pursuits without heed to God's guidance will face the reality of Hellfire. It underscores the gravity of ignoring spiritual obligations.

Verse 7

"Thumma latarawunnaha 'ayna al-yaqeen"

"Then you will surely see it with the eye of certainty."

- Explanation: The vision of Hellfire will be undeniable and clear, leaving no room for doubt. This reinforces the idea that the consequences of one's actions will be evident and unavoidable.

Verse 8

"Thumma latus'alunna yawma'idhin 'ani an-na'eem"

"Then you will surely be asked that Day about the pleasure."

- Explanation: On the Day of Judgment, individuals will be questioned about how they utilized the blessings and bounties they received in life. It emphasizes accountability and the need for gratitude and responsible use of resources.

Overall, the surah serves as a reminder to focus on spiritual growth and the reality of the hereafter, rather than being consumed by the ephemeral nature of worldly gains.

LESSONS AND REFFLECTIONS ON SURAH AT-TAKATHUR

1. The Futility of Materialism: One of the primary messages of Surah At-Takathur is the fleeting nature of material wealth and worldly competition. The surah cautions against allowing the pursuit of material gains to distract from one's spiritual duties and the remembrance of God. It serves as a reminder that material possessions are temporary and cannot be taken beyond the grave. Therefore, individuals should not measure their success solely by their accumulation of wealth and status.

2. Inevitability of Death: The surah underscores the certainty of death and the transition it represents from worldly life to the hereafter. It reminds individuals that no matter how engrossed they may be in worldly pursuits, they will ultimately face their mortality. This realization should prompt a reevaluation of one's priorities and encourage a focus on actions that hold eternal significance.

3. The Reality of the Afterlife: Surah At-Takathur emphasizes the reality of the afterlife and the certainty that individuals will be held accountable for their actions. It highlights that the distractions of this world will be of no value in the hereafter, where true knowledge and certainty will prevail. This serves as a call to cultivate awareness and prepare for the eternal life to come.

4. Accountability for Blessings: The chapter concludes with a powerful reminder that individuals will be questioned about how they utilized the blessings and pleasures they were granted in life. This lesson underscores the importance of gratitude, responsible stewardship, and using one's resources in ways that align with divine guidance. It encourages reflection on whether one's actions contribute positively to their spiritual growth and the well-being of others.

5. The Consequence of Negligence: Finally, the surah warns of the severe consequences of neglecting spiritual obligations and the reality of Judgment Day. It paints a vivid picture of the undeniable certainty of the Hellfire for those who remain heedless. This serves as a sobering reminder to maintain awareness of one's actions and the potential repercussions in the afterlife.

In summary, Surah At-Takathur prompts individuals to transcend the superficial allure of materialism, embrace the certainty of the afterlife, and live with a sense of accountability and purpose. It encourages a shift in focus from ephemeral worldly gains to actions that foster spiritual fulfillment and everlasting success.

SUMMARY OF
SURAH AT-TAKATHUR. SURAH 102

Surah At-Takathur is the 102nd chapter of the Quran and consists of 8 verses. The chapter is titled "The Rivalry in Worldly Increase" and addresses the human preoccupation with material wealth and competition. Here is a brief summary:

1. Distraction by Abundance: The surah begins by highlighting how the obsession with accumulating worldly possessions and rivalry in increasing wealth distracts people from their ultimate purpose and spiritual obligations.
2. Reality of the Grave: It warns that this preoccupation will continue until individuals visit their graves, implying that death is inevitable and will bring an end to worldly pursuits.
3. Knowledge of Certainty: The surah emphasizes that on the Day of Judgment, people will come to realize the futility of their worldly pursuits. It stresses the importance of having knowledge and certainty about the hereafter.
4. Vision of Hellfire: It cautions that people will be shown the Hellfire, underscoring the seriousness of the consequences of their actions and their negligence of spiritual duties.
5. Accountability for Blessings: The final verse warns that individuals will be questioned about how they used the blessings and bounties they received in life, urging them to reflect on their actions and priorities.

Overall, Surah At-Takathur serves as a reminder to prioritize spiritual growth and awareness of the afterlife over the fleeting pursuits of material wealth and status.

SURAH AT-TAKATHUR (SURAH 103)

Questions

1. What is the central theme of Surah At-Takathur?
2. How does the surah describe the effect of worldly competition on people?
3. What does the term "At-Takathur" refer to, and why is the surah named after it?
4. According to the surah, what distracts people until they visit the graves?
5. How does Surah At-Takathur emphasize the reality of the hereafter?
6. What warning does the surah give about the consequences of being overly focused on worldly possessions?
7. How does the surah encourage reflection on the ultimate reality of life?
8. What does the surah say about the knowledge people will gain after death?
9. What is the significance of the repeated phrase "You will surely know" in the surah?
10. How can the teachings of Surah At-Takathur be applied to contemporary life to promote mindfulness and spiritual awareness?

Answers

1. What is the central theme of Surah At-Takathur?
   - The central theme is the distraction caused by the competition for worldly gains and the neglect of the hereafter.

2. How does the surah describe the effect of worldly competition on people?
   - The surah describes it as a distraction that keeps people preoccupied until they visit the graves, emphasizing the temporary nature of worldly pursuits.

3. What does the term "At-Takathur" refer to, and why is the surah named after it?
   - "At-Takathur" refers to "the competition for more" or the rivalry for worldly gains. The surah is named after it because it highlights how such competition can distract people from the ultimate realities of life.

4. According to the surah, what distracts people until they visit the graves?
   - The competition for accumulating more wealth and possessions distracts people until they die.

5. How does Surah At-Takathur emphasize the reality of the hereafter?
   - The surah warns that people will eventually come to know the truth about their actions and the hereafter once they face death.

6. What warning does the surah give about the consequences of being overly focused on worldly possessions?
   - The surah warns that such focus can lead to neglect of spiritual responsibilities and ultimate accountability in the hereafter.

7. How does the surah encourage reflection on the ultimate reality of life?
   - The surah encourages reflection by reminding people that the pursuit of worldly gains is temporary and that they will eventually face the reality of the hereafter.

8. What does the surah say about the knowledge people will gain after death?
   - The surah states that people will come to realize and understand the truth about their actions and the consequences of their worldly pursuits after death.

9. What is the significance of the repeated phrase "You will surely know" in the surah?
   - The repetition emphasizes the certainty and inevitability of realizing the truth about one's actions and the reality of the hereafter.

10. How can the teachings of Surah At-Takathur be applied to contemporary life to promote mindfulness and spiritual awareness?
    - The teachings encourage individuals to prioritize spiritual awareness, reflect on the temporary nature of material pursuits, and focus on their responsibilities towards the hereafter.

These questions and answers can be used for educational purposes, study sessions, or discussions to enhance understanding of Surah At-Takathur.

Multiple-Choice Questions

1. What does the term "At-Takathur" refer to?
   - A) The night
   - B) The competition for more
   - C) The prayer
   - D) The journey

2. What is the central theme of Surah At-Takathur?
   - A) The beauty of nature
   - B) The distraction caused by worldly competition
   - C) The importance of charity
   - D) The need for patience

3. How does the surah describe the effect of worldly competition on people?
   - A) It makes them wise and humble
   - B) It distracts them until they visit the graves
   - C) It leads them to success and happiness
   - D) It brings them closer to their families

4. According to Surah At-Takathur, what distracts people until they visit the graves?
   - A) Their devotion to prayer
   - B) Their competition for accumulating more wealth
   - C) Their love for knowledge
   - D) Their acts of kindness

5. How does Surah At-Takathur emphasize the reality of the hereafter?
   - A) By describing the beauty of paradise
   - B) By warning that people will come to know the truth after death
   - C) By promising wealth and power
   - D) By emphasizing worldly success

6. What warning does the surah give about the consequences of being overly focused on worldly possessions?
   - A) It leads to ultimate happiness
   - B) It results in neglect of spiritual responsibilities
   - C) It guarantees success in this life
   - D) It is the key to paradise

7. What does the surah say about the knowledge people will gain after death?

    - A) They will remain ignorant

    - B) They will gain ultimate understanding of their actions

    - C) They will forget everything

    - D) They will become wealthy

8. What is the significance of the repeated phrase "You will surely know" in the surah?

    - A) It emphasizes uncertainty

    - B) It emphasizes the certainty and inevitability of realizing the truth

    - C) It suggests doubt

    - D) It questions one's beliefs

Answers

1. *Answer:* B) The competition for more
2. *Answer:* B) The distraction caused by worldly competition
3. *Answer:* B) It distracts them until they visit the graves
4. *Answer:* B) Their competition for accumulating more wealth
5. *Answer:* B) By warning that people will come to know the truth after death
6. *Answer:* B) It results in neglect of spiritual responsibilities
7. *Answer:* B) They will gain ultimate understanding of their actions
8. *Answer:* B) It emphasizes the certainty and inevitability of realizing the truth

These questions and answers can be used for quizzes, educational discussions, or self-study to enhance understanding of Surah At-Takathur.

SURAH ASR

SURAH ASR

Bismillahi ar-Rahmani ar-Raheem

Verse 1

"Wal-Asr"

"By the time,"

- Explanation: In this verse, Allah swears by "Asr," which is commonly understood as "time" or the late afternoon. The oath emphasizes the profound importance of time and its passage. Time is presented as a critical aspect of human life, underscoring that it is a limited and precious resource that should be used wisely. The invocation of time highlights that it is within this temporal framework that humans live, act, and ultimately meet their fate.

Verse 2

"Innal insaana lafee khusr"

"Indeed, mankind is in loss,"

- Explanation: This verse makes a general declaration about the human condition, stating that all of humanity is in a state of loss. The "loss" here refers to the spiritual and existential loss that comes from not recognizing the value of time and failing to live in accordance with divine guidance. It serves as a reminder that if individuals are left to their own devices, they are likely to waste their lives in pursuits that do not lead to true success or fulfillment. The verse sets a somber tone, illustrating the urgency of addressing this state of loss.

Verse 3

"Illa allatheena aamanoo wa 'amiloo assaalihaati watawaasaw bilhaqqi watawaasaw bissabr"

"Except for those who have believed and done righteous deeds and advised each other to truth and advised each other to patience."

- Explanation:

This verse outlines the qualities that exempt individuals from the loss mentioned in the previous verse. Four key attributes are highlighted:

- Belief (Iman): Having genuine faith in Allah and the tenets of Islam. This serves as the foundation for all other actions and attitudes.

- Righteous Deeds ('Amal Salih): Engaging in actions that are ethical, good, and in alignment with divine commands. This includes both acts of worship and good behavior towards others.

- Advising to Truth (Tawasaw bil-Haqq): Encouraging one another to uphold and speak the truth. This involves promoting justice, honesty, and integrity within the community.

- Advising to Patience (Tawasaw bil-Sabr): Supporting each other in being patient and steadfast, particularly in enduring trials and hardships. Patience is seen as a crucial virtue in maintaining faith and perseverance in the face of life's challenges.

Surah Al-Asr succinctly captures the essence of what it means to live a meaningful and successful life. It emphasizes the transient nature of time and the necessity of using it to develop faith, engage in good deeds, and foster a supportive community centered on truth and patience. This chapter serves as a powerful reminder that true success is achieved through a balanced combination of belief, action, and mutual support.

LESSONS AND REFFLECTIONS ON SURAH ASR

Surah Al-Asr, despite its brevity, conveys profound lessons that are essential for leading a meaningful and successful life. Here are the key lessons derived from this chapter:

1. The Value of Time: The surah begins with an oath by time, highlighting its immense value. It serves as a reminder that time is a limited and precious resource that is constantly passing. Individuals must be mindful of how they utilize their time, ensuring that it is spent in pursuits that bring spiritual and moral growth.
2. Humanity's Default State of Loss: The declaration that mankind is in a state of loss emphasizes the natural human tendency to waste time and engage in pursuits that do not lead to ultimate success. This serves as a wake-up call to reflect on one's life and priorities, encouraging a shift towards actions that have lasting significance.
3. The Importance of Faith: Belief in God and the teachings of Islam is foundational for escaping the state of loss. Faith provides the guiding principles and moral compass necessary for navigating life's challenges and making decisions that align with divine wisdom.
4. Righteous Deeds: The surah underscores the importance of coupling faith with righteous actions. Good deeds are a manifestation of faith and are essential for personal development and contributing positively to society. This includes acts of worship, kindness, justice, and ethical conduct.
5. Mutual Encouragement of Truth: Encouraging one another to uphold and speak the truth is vital for building a just and honest society. This lesson highlights the role of community in promoting values of integrity and accountability, as well as standing up for what is right.
6. The Power of Patience: Patience is identified as a key virtue necessary for enduring life's trials and maintaining steadfastness in faith. The surah teaches that mutual encouragement of patience strengthens individuals and communities, enabling them to persevere through difficulties with resilience and hope.
7. Interconnectedness of Faith and Action: The surah illustrates that true success is achieved through a combination of belief, action, and mutual support. It emphasizes that faith without action, and actions without faith, are insufficient. A balanced life requires both spiritual and practical dimensions working in harmony.

SUMMARY OF SURAH ASR

Surah Al-Asr is the 103rd chapter of the Quran and is comprised of just three verses. Despite its brevity, it carries a profound message about the essence of time and the qualities necessary for success in this life and the hereafter. Here is a summary of its key themes:

1. The Oath by Time: The surah begins with an oath by "al-Asr," which is often interpreted as "time" or "the passage of time." This emphasizes the significance and preciousness of time as a resource. It serves as a reminder that time is constantly passing and that individuals must use it wisely.
2. Universal Human Loss: The second verse declares that all of humanity is in a state of loss. This statement is a stark reminder of the default condition of human beings, who, if left to their own devices, tend to waste their lives in pursuits that do not lead to true success.
3. Path to Salvation: The final verse outlines the four essential qualities that can save individuals from this state of loss:

- Faith (Iman): Having true belief in Allah and the teachings of Islam.

- Righteous Deeds (Amal Salih): Engaging in actions that are good, ethical, and aligned with divine guidance.

- Mutual Encouragement of Truth (Tawasaw bil-Haqq): Encouraging one another to uphold and speak the truth.

- Mutual Encouragement of Patience (Tawasaw bil-Sabr): Supporting each other in being patient and steadfast, particularly in the face of adversity.

Surah Al-Asr succinctly encapsulates the essentials for a fulfilling and successful life. It stresses the importance of recognizing the value of time and utilizing it to cultivate faith, perform good deeds, and foster a community that upholds truth and patience. This chapter serves as a powerful reminder that true success is measured not by worldly gains but by one's adherence to these core principles.

SURAH AL-ASR (SURAH 103)

Questions

1. What does the term "Al-Asr" refer to, and why is the surah named after it?
2. How many verses are in Surah Al-Asr?
3. What is the primary theme of Surah Al-Asr?
4. According to the surah, what is the fate of humanity without certain key attributes?
5. What are the four key attributes mentioned in Surah Al-Asr that lead to success?
6. How does Surah Al-Asr emphasize the importance of time?
7. What does the surah say about the role of faith in achieving success?
8. How does the surah highlight the significance of righteous deeds?
9. What is the meaning of mutual encouragement towards truth in the context of Surah Al-Asr?
10. How can the teachings of Surah Al-Asr be applied to contemporary life to achieve spiritual and moral success?

Answers

1. What does the term "Al-Asr" refer to, and why is the surah named after it?
   - "Al-Asr" refers to "the time" or "the declining day." The surah is named after it because it begins with an oath by time, emphasizing its importance and the urgency of making the most of it.

2. How many verses are in Surah Al-Asr?
   - Surah Al-Asr consists of three verses.

3. What is the primary theme of Surah Al-Asr?
   - The primary theme is the importance of time, faith, righteous deeds, and mutual encouragement in truth and patience to avoid loss.

4. According to the surah, what is the fate of humanity without certain key attributes?
   - The surah states that humanity is in a state of loss except for those who possess certain key attributes.

5. What are the four key attributes mentioned in Surah Al-Asr that lead to success?
   - The four key attributes are faith, righteous deeds, mutual encouragement towards truth, and patience.

6. How does Surah Al-Asr emphasize the importance of time?
   - The surah begins with an oath by time, highlighting its fleeting nature and the need to use it wisely for spiritual and moral growth.

7. What does the surah say about the role of faith in achieving success?
   - The surah emphasizes that faith is essential for avoiding loss and achieving spiritual success.

8. How does the surah highlight the significance of righteous deeds?
   - The surah mentions righteous deeds as a key attribute for success, indicating that actions must align with faith to achieve spiritual fulfillment.

9. What is the meaning of mutual encouragement towards truth in the context of Surah Al-Asr?
   - It means supporting and advising one another to uphold truth and integrity, fostering a community built on ethical principles.

10. How can the teachings of Surah Al-Asr be applied to contemporary life to achieve spiritual and moral success?
    - The teachings encourage individuals to prioritize faith, engage in righteous actions, and support one another in truth and patience, thus fostering personal growth and community well-being.

These questions and answers can be used for educational purposes, study sessions, or discussions to enhance understanding of Surah Al-Asr.

Multiple Choice Questions

1. What does the term "Al-Asr" refer to in the context of this surah?

    - A) The sun

    - B) The time or the declining day

    - C) The mountain

    - D) The river

2. How many verses are in Surah Al-Asr?

    - A) Five

    - B) Three

    - C) Ten

    - D) Seven

3. What is the primary theme of Surah Al-Asr?

    - A) The importance of wealth

    - B) The significance of time, faith, and righteous deeds

    - C) The beauty of nature

    - D) The power of knowledge

4. According to Surah Al-Asr, what is the fate of humanity without certain key attributes?

    - A) Eternal happiness

    - B) Success in this world

    - C) A state of loss

    - D) Material wealth

5. What are the four key attributes mentioned in Surah Al-Asr that lead to success?

    - A) Wealth, power, knowledge, and fame

    - B) Faith, righteous deeds, mutual encouragement towards truth, and patience

    - C) Intelligence, beauty, strength, and health

    - D) Charity, prayer, fasting, and pilgrimage

6. How does Surah Al-Asr emphasize the importance of time?

    - A) By describing the changing seasons

    - B) By beginning with an oath by time

    - C) By narrating a story about time

    - D) By emphasizing the length of life

7. What does the surah say about the role of faith in achieving success?

    - A) It is irrelevant

    - B) It is essential for avoiding loss

    - C) It is only for scholars

    - D) It guarantees wealth

8. How does the surah highlight the significance of righteous deeds?

    - A) By stating they lead to material wealth

    - B) By mentioning them as a key attribute for success

    - C) By emphasizing their role in physical strength

    - D) By comparing them to worldly gains

Answers

1. *Answer:* B) The time or the declining day
2. *Answer:* B) Three
3. *Answer:* B) The significance of time, faith, and righteous deeds
4. *Answer:* C) A state of loss
5. *Answer:* B) Faith, righteous deeds, mutual encouragement towards truth, and patience
6. *Answer:* B) By beginning with an oath by time
7. *Answer:* B) It is essential for avoiding loss
8. *Answer:* B) By mentioning them as a key attribute for success

These questions and answers can be used for quizzes, educational discussions, or self-study to enhance understanding of Surah Al-Asr.

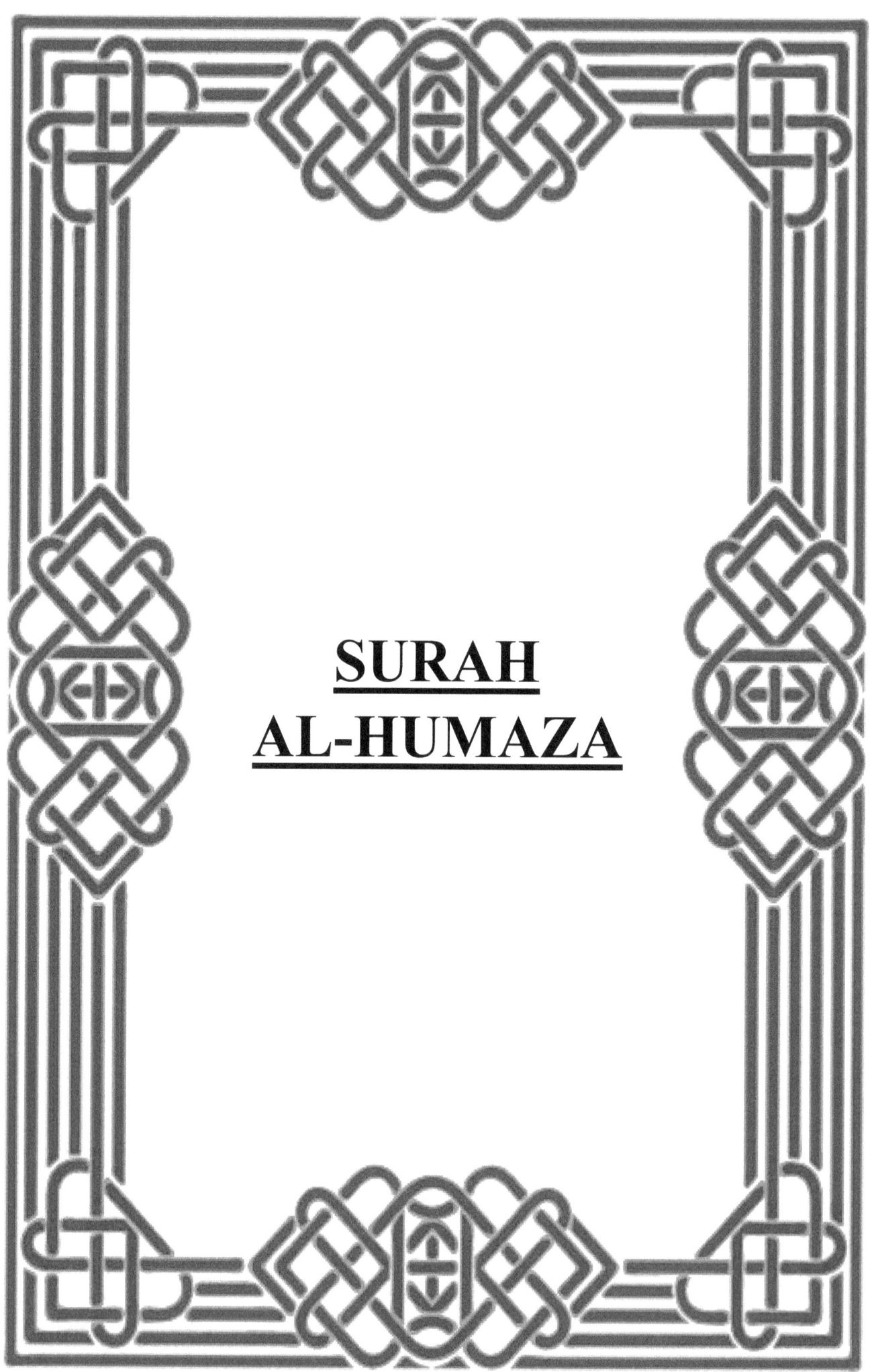

SURAH AL-HUMAZA

SURAH AL-HUMAZA

Bismillahi ar-Rahmani ar-Raheem

Verse 1

"Waylun likulli humazatin lumazah."

"Woe to every scorner and mocker."

- Explanation: This verse begins with a strong warning against those who engage in slander and mockery. The terms "humazah" and "lumazah" refer to individuals who habitually insult, belittle, or degrade others, both in their presence and behind their backs. This behavior is condemned as it spreads negativity and harms social cohesion. The verse serves as a reminder that such actions are morally reprehensible and have serious consequences.

Verse 2

"Allathee jama'a malan wa 'addadah."

"Who collects wealth and [continuously] counts it."

- Explanation: The surah criticizes those who are obsessed with amassing wealth and constantly counting or hoarding it. This behavior reflects an attachment to material possessions and a belief that wealth provides security and status. The verse highlights the futility of such pursuits, as they distract individuals from their spiritual and moral responsibilities.

Verse 3

"Yahsabu anna malahu akhladah."

"He thinks that his wealth will make him immortal."

- Explanation: This verse points out the misconception that wealth can grant one immortality or lasting security. It critiques the false sense of invulnerability and self-sufficiency that comes from dependence on material wealth. The verse underscores that true security and eternal life cannot be achieved through worldly possessions.

Verse 4

"Kalla layunbadhanna fee alhutamah."

"No! He will surely be thrown into the Crusher."

- Explanation: The verse serves as a stark warning that those who engage in slander and are obsessed with wealth will face severe punishment. "Alhutamah," or "the Crusher," refers to a devastating form of punishment, symbolizing the intense consequences awaiting such individuals. It underscores that worldly pursuits cannot protect one from divine justice.

Verse 5

"Wama adraka malhutamah."

"And what can make you know what is the Crusher?"

- Explanation: This rhetorical question invites reflection on the severity and intensity of the punishment described as "the Crusher." It emphasizes that the true nature of this punishment is beyond human comprehension, highlighting the seriousness of the consequences for those who persist in negative behaviors.

Verse 6

"Naru Allahi almoo'qadah."

"It is the fire of Allah, [eternally] fueled,"

- Explanation: The verse describes "the Crusher" as the fire of Allah, emphasizing its divine origin and relentless nature. The eternal fueling of this fire implies that it is an unending punishment, reflecting the gravity of the sins committed by those who engage in slander and hoard wealth.

Verse 7

"Allatee tattali'u 'ala al-af'idah."

"Which mounts directed at the hearts."

- Explanation: This verse indicates that the punishment specifically targets the hearts, symbolizing the core of one's intentions and character. It suggests that the consequences of slander and greed are not superficial but penetrate deeply, affecting the very essence of one's being.

Verse 8

"Innaha 'alayhim mo'sada."

"Indeed, it [i.e., the fire] will be closed down upon them."

- Explanation: The verse conveys the idea of an inescapable punishment, with the fire being closed down upon those who are condemned. This imagery of confinement underscores the permanence and inevitability of the consequences for their actions.

Verse 9

"Fee 'amadin mumaddadah."

"In extended columns."

- Explanation: The final verse describes the punishment as occurring in "extended columns," which may suggest both the intensity and the enduring nature of the confinement. It reinforces the seriousness of the divine retribution for those who persist in harmful behavior.

Overall, Surah Al-Humazah serves as a powerful warning against the moral and spiritual dangers of slander, mockery, and materialism. It calls for self-reflection and encourages individuals to move away from these negative behaviors towards a life of ethical conduct and spiritual awareness.

Surah Al-Humazah offers several lessons and reflections that are relevant to both personal conduct and broader societal interactions. Here are some key takeaways:

1. The Consequences of Slander and Mockery:

- The surah begins with a stern warning against those who engage in slander and mockery. It highlights the destructive nature of such behavior, which can harm relationships and community cohesion. Reflecting on this, individuals are reminded of the importance of maintaining respectful and kind interactions with others, avoiding gossip, and refraining from belittling or insulting others.

2. The Futility of Material Obsession:

- Surah Al-Humazah criticizes the obsession with accumulating and hoarding wealth. It points out the false sense of security that people often derive from their material possessions. This serves as a reminder that wealth is transient and cannot provide true fulfillment or protection from life's ultimate realities. The lesson here is to prioritize spiritual and moral values over materialistic pursuits.

3. The Illusion of Immortality:

- The chapter addresses the misconception that wealth can lead to immortality or lasting security. This reflects a broader human tendency to seek permanence in transient things. Reflecting on this, individuals are encouraged to acknowledge the impermanence of life and focus on actions that have lasting spiritual significance.

4. Accountability and Divine Justice:

- The surah underscores the inevitability of divine justice and accountability. It serves as a reminder that negative behaviors, such as slander and greed, will ultimately lead to severe consequences. This encourages self-reflection and a reassessment of one's actions, urging individuals to align their behavior with ethical and spiritual principles.

5. The Importance of Heartfelt Intentions:

- The punishment described in the surah is said to target the heart, symbolizing the importance of one's intentions and inner character. This emphasizes the need for sincerity and purity of heart in all actions. It calls for introspection to ensure that one's intentions are aligned with positive and ethical values.

6. Reflecting on Eternal Outcomes:

- The vivid descriptions of punishment in Surah Al-Humazah invite reflection on the eternal outcomes of one's actions. This serves as a motivation to focus on deeds that contribute to spiritual growth and eternal success, rather than temporary worldly gains.

In summary, Surah Al-Humazah serves as a powerful reminder of the moral and spiritual dangers of slander, mockery, and materialism. It encourages individuals to reflect on their conduct, prioritize ethical behaviour, and seek fulfillment through spiritual and moral growth rather than the accumulation of wealth. This chapter calls for a shift in perspective towards actions and values that lead to lasting fulfillment and success in the hereafter.

SUMMARY OF
SURAH AL-HUMAZA-SURAH 104

Surah Al-Humazah, the 104th chapter of the Quran, addresses significant moral and ethical concerns in just nine verses, focusing on the themes of slander, backbiting, and the obsession with wealth. It serves as a poignant reminder of the consequences of negative behaviour and the importance of aligning one's actions with spiritual and moral values.

The surah begins by condemning those who engage in slander and backbiting. It highlights how such behaviour is destructive and harmful to both individuals and communities. The act of mocking or belittling others, whether through words or actions, is portrayed as a serious moral failing. This emphasis on the damage caused by slander serves as a warning against the spread of negativity and the importance of maintaining respect and integrity in interactions with others.

In addition to addressing slander, Surah Al-Humazah critiques the obsession with wealth accumulation. It describes those who hoard wealth and believe that their material possessions provide them with security and immortality. This focus on wealth as a source of power and protection can lead individuals to neglect their moral and spiritual duties. The surah challenges the notion that material wealth equates to true success and security, urging a shift in perspective towards more meaningful and enduring values.

The chapter reminds readers of the inevitability of judgment and the limitations of material wealth in the afterlife. It emphasizes that those who engage in slander and are consumed by greed will face severe consequences on the Day of Judgment. The vivid description of the punishment awaiting such individuals underscores the seriousness of these behaviours and serves as a call to repentance and moral reform.

In conclusion, Surah Al-Humazah serves as a powerful reminder of the dangers of slander, backbiting, and greed. It encourages self-reflection and a revaluation of priorities, urging individuals to focus on ethical behaviour, humility, and the remembrance of the hereafter. The surah calls on believers to transcend materialistic pursuits and cultivate values that lead to spiritual growth and lasting fulfillment.

SURAH AL-HUMAZA (SURAH 104)

Questions

1. What does the term "Al-Humaza" mean, and why is the surah named after it?
2. What behavior is condemned in the opening verses of Surah Al-Humaza?
3. How does the surah describe the attitude of those who hoard wealth?
4. What false belief do the people who hoard wealth have, according to the surah?
5. What is the ultimate consequence mentioned in Surah Al-Humaza for those who engage in slander and hoarding?
6. How does the surah describe the punishment in the afterlife for those who are guilty of the condemned behaviors?
7. What is the significance of the term "Hutamah" in Surah Al-Humaza?
8. How does the surah emphasize the seriousness of backbiting and slander?
9. What does the surah imply about the relationship between material wealth and spiritual well-being?
10. How can the teachings of Surah Al-Humaza be applied to contemporary life to promote ethical behavior and social harmony?

Answers

1. What does the term "Al-Humaza" mean, and why is the surah named after it?
   - "Al-Humaza" refers to "the slanderer" or "the backbiter." The surah is named after it because it condemns the behavior of slandering and backbiting.

2. What behavior is condemned in the opening verses of Surah Al-Humaza?
   - The surah condemns the behavior of slandering, backbiting, and mocking others.

3. How does the surah describe the attitude of those who hoard wealth?
   - The surah describes them as people who are obsessed with accumulating wealth and believe it will grant them immortality.

4. What false belief do the people who hoard wealth have, according to the surah?
   - They falsely believe that their wealth will make them immortal and protect them from consequences.

5. What is the ultimate consequence mentioned in Surah Al-Humaza for those who engage in slander and hoarding?
   - The ultimate consequence is punishment in the hereafter, specifically in the crushing fire.

6. How does the surah describe the punishment in the afterlife for those who are guilty of the condemned behaviors?
   - The punishment is described as "Hutamah," a crushing fire that will engulf them, indicating severe and unescapable torment.

7. What is the significance of the term "Hutamah" in Surah Al-Humaza?
   - "Hutamah" refers to a crushing fire, symbolizing the severe and destructive nature of the punishment awaiting those who engage in slander and hoarding.

8. How does the surah emphasize the seriousness of backbiting and slander?
   - The surah highlights the destructive consequences of such behaviors, both in terms of social harmony and spiritual accountability.

9. What does the surah imply about the relationship between material wealth and spiritual well-being?
   - The surah implies that an obsession with material wealth can lead to spiritual ruin and neglect of ethical responsibilities.

10. How can the teachings of Surah Al-Humaza be applied to contemporary life to promote ethical behavior and social harmony?
    - The teachings encourage individuals to avoid slander and backbiting, prioritize ethical behavior over material accumulation, and foster social harmony and respect.

These questions and answers can be used for educational purposes, study sessions, or discussions to enhance understanding of Surah Al-Humaza.

Multiple Choice Questions

1. What does the term "Al-Humaza" refer to?

    - A) The generous

    - B) The truthful

    - C) The slanderer or backbiter

    - D) The wealthy

2. What behavior is condemned in the opening verses of Surah Al-Humaza?

    - A) Kindness and generosity

    - B) Slandering, backbiting, and mocking others

    - C) Praying regularly

    - D) Fasting and charity

3. How does the surah describe the attitude of those who hoard wealth?

    - A) Content and humble

    - B) Grateful and satisfied

    - C) Obsessive and believing it will grant them immortality

    - D) Generous and giving

4. What false belief do the people who hoard wealth have, according to the surah?

    - A) That wealth will bring them happiness

    - B) That wealth will make them immortal

    - C) That wealth will solve all their problems

    - D) That wealth will secure them paradise

5. What is the ultimate consequence mentioned in Surah Al-Humaza for those who engage in slander and hoarding?

    - A) Success and prosperity

    - B) Happiness and peace

    - C) Punishment in the crushing fire

    - D) Respect and admiration

6. How does the surah describe the punishment in the afterlife for those who are guilty of the condemned behaviors?

    - A) A light reprimand

    - B) A temporary discomfort

    - C) "Hutamah," a crushing fire

- D) A minor inconvenience

7. What is the significance of the term "Hutamah" in Surah Al-Humaza?

    - A) It represents eternal paradise

    - B) It symbolizes temporary punishment

    - C) It refers to a crushing fire, symbolizing severe punishment

    - D) It signifies wealth and prosperity

8. How does the surah emphasize the seriousness of backbiting and slander?

    - A) By describing it as a minor sin

    - B) By highlighting the severe consequences in the hereafter

    - C) By suggesting it is easily forgiven

    - D) By comparing it to charity

Answers

1. *Answer:* C) The slanderer or backbiter
2. *Answer:* B) Slandering, backbiting, and mocking others
3. *Answer:* C) Obsessive and believing it will grant them immortality
4. *Answer:* B) That wealth will make them immortal
5. *Answer:* C) Punishment in the crushing fire
6. *Answer:* C) "Hutamah," a crushing fire
7. *Answer:* C) It refers to a crushing fire, symbolizing severe punishment
8. *Answer:* B) By highlighting the severe consequences in the hereafter

These questions and answers can be used for quizzes, educational discussions, or self-study to enhance understanding of Surah Al-Humaza

SURAH AL-FIL

SURAH AL-FIL

Bismillahi ar-Rahmani ar-Raheem

Verse 1

"Alam tara kayfa fa'ala rabbuka bi' aṣḥābi l-fīl?"

"Have you not seen how your Lord dealt with the People of the Elephant?"

- Tafseer: This rhetorical question is directed at the Quraysh, encouraging them to reflect on Allah's intervention in history. It recalls the miraculous event where Allah protected the Kaaba from Abraha's army, known for its use of elephants. The verse serves as a reminder of Allah's omnipotence and His role as protector of the sacred.

Verse 2

"Alam yaj'al kaydahum fī taḍlīl?"

"Did He not make their plot go astray?"

- Tafseer: This verse emphasizes the futility of Abraha's plans against the divine will. Despite their meticulous strategy and military might, their efforts were rendered useless by Allah's intervention. It illustrates a key Quranic theme: human plans are powerless against the divine decree.

Verse 3

"Wa arsala 'alayhim ṭayran abābīl."

"And He sent against them birds in flocks,"

- Tafseer: Allah sent "Ababil" birds to confront the invaders, showcasing His ability to use even the smallest creatures to achieve His purposes. The flocks of birds symbolize unexpected divine assistance, reinforcing the notion that Allah's support can come in any form.

Verse 4

"Tarmīhim biḥijāratin min sijjīl."

"Striking them with stones of baked clay,"

- Tafseer: The birds dropped stones of "sijjīl" (baked clay) on the army, causing their destruction. This vivid imagery highlights the precision and effectiveness of divine punishment. The stones, though small, were sufficient to decimate a formidable force, underscoring Allah's control over all matters.

Verse 5

"Faja'alahum ka'aṣfin ma'kūl."

"And made them like eaten straw."

- Tafseer: The verse likens the defeated army to "eaten straw," a metaphor for their complete obliteration. It conveys the idea that those who oppose Allah's will are destined for destruction, regardless of their earthly power. This serves as a powerful reminder of the temporary nature of worldly strength and the enduring sovereignty of Allah.

Through these verses, Surah Al-Fil delivers a potent message about divine protection, the futility of defying Allah's plans, and the transient nature of earthly power

Here are some of the key lessons learned from this surah:

1. Divine Protection: The surah illustrates Allah's ability to protect what is sacred. Despite the formidable strength of Abraha's army, their efforts were futile against Allah's will. This serves as a reminder that Allah's protection is unmatched and that He safeguards His chosen sanctuaries and people.
2. The Futility of Human Plans Against Divine Will: Abraha's carefully orchestrated plan to destroy the Kaaba was thwarted by divine intervention. This underscores the idea that no matter how powerful or well-planned human endeavors might be, they cannot succeed if they go against Allah's will. It teaches humility and the importance of aligning one's actions with divine guidance.
3. The Power of the Small and Unexpected: The use of birds to defeat a mighty army demonstrates that Allah can utilize even the smallest and seemingly insignificant elements to achieve His purposes. This lesson encourages believers to recognize that strength and power are not solely determined by size or might, but by divine support and purpose.
4. Reminder of Historical Events: The surah serves as a historical reminder to the Quraysh and later generations of Allah's past interventions. It encourages reflection on history to understand Allah's role and presence in guiding and protecting the faithful.
5. The Transience of Worldly Power: The complete destruction of Abraha's army, once a symbol of might, illustrates the temporary nature of worldly power. It reminds believers that true strength lies with Allah, and reliance on worldly power alone is misguided.
6. Faith in Divine Justice: The surah reassures believers of Allah's justice. Those who seek to harm or desecrate what is sacred will ultimately face divine retribution. This instills a sense of justice and trust in Allah's ultimate plan.
7. Encouragement for the Believers: For the early Muslims, this surah was a source of encouragement, highlighting that Allah's support is with those who uphold the truth and faith. It serves as a reminder that challenges and threats can be overcome with divine assistance.

Overall, Surah Al-Fil emphasizes the themes of divine protection, the futility of opposing Allah, and the transient nature of earthly power, encouraging believers to place their trust in Allah and His plans.

SUMMARY OF SURAH AL-FIL

Surah Al-Fil, the 105th chapter of the Quran, is a short surah consisting of five verses. The name "Al-Fil" translates to "The Elephant," and the surah recounts a historical event known as the "Year of the Elephant." This event is significant in Islamic history because it is believed to have occurred in the same year as the birth of the Prophet Muhammad.

The surah describes the attempt by Abraha, the Christian ruler of Yemen, to destroy the Kaaba in Mecca with a large army that included war elephants. Abraha's intention was to divert the pilgrimage from Mecca to a grand church he had built in Yemen. However, his plan was thwarted by divine intervention. According to the surah, Allah sent flocks of birds that pelted the army with stones of baked clay, leading to their defeat and destruction.

The narrative serves as a powerful reminder of Allah's protection of the sacred Kaaba and His ability to defend against any force, no matter how formidable. It emphasizes the theme of divine justice and protection, demonstrating that those who seek to harm what is sacred will ultimately face ruin. The surah reinforces the idea of faith in Allah's power and serves as a testament to the historical and spiritual significance of Mecca.

SURAH AL FIL (SURAH 105)

Questions

1. What is the historical context of Surah Al-Fil, and why is it significant?
2. What does the term "Al-Fil" refer to, and why is the surah named after it?
3. Who was the leader of the army mentioned in Surah Al-Fil, and what was his objective?
4. How does the surah describe the miraculous event that befell the army?
5. What were the "sijjil" mentioned in the surah, and how were they used?
6. What was the fate of the army that intended to attack the Kaaba?
7. How does Surah Al-Fil demonstrate Allah's power and protection?
8. What lesson can be derived from the story recounted in Surah Al-Fil?
9. How does Surah Al-Fil emphasize the importance of the Kaaba and its protection?
10. How can the teachings of Surah Al-Fil be applied to contemporary life to inspire faith and trust in divine protection?

Answers

1. What is the historical context of Surah Al-Fil, and why is it significant?
   - The historical context is the Year of the Elephant, when Abraha, the ruler of Yemen, attempted to destroy the Kaaba with a large army that included elephants. It is significant as a demonstration of divine intervention to protect the sacred site.

2. What does the term "Al-Fil" refer to, and why is the surah named after it?
   - "Al-Fil" refers to "the elephant." The surah is named after it because it recounts the story of the army that included elephants and their failed attempt to destroy the Kaaba.

3. Who was the leader of the army mentioned in Surah Al-Fil, and what was his objective?
   - The leader of the army was Abraha, and his objective was to destroy the Kaaba to divert pilgrims to his cathedral in Yemen.

4. How does the surah describe the miraculous event that befell the army?
   - The surah describes how Allah sent flocks of birds that pelted the army with stones of baked clay, leading to their defeat.

5. What were the "sijjil" mentioned in the surah, and how were they used?
   - "Sijjil" refers to the stones of baked clay carried by the birds, which were used to destroy the invading army.

6. What was the fate of the army that intended to attack the Kaaba?
   - The army was destroyed by the stones carried by the birds, leaving them like eaten straw.

7. How does Surah Al-Fil demonstrate Allah's power and protection?
   - The surah demonstrates Allah's power and protection by recounting the miraculous defeat of a powerful army through divine intervention.

8. What lesson can be derived from the story recounted in Surah Al-Fil?
   - A key lesson is the assurance of divine protection over sacred matters and the futility of opposing Allah's will.

9. How does Surah Al-Fil emphasize the importance of the Kaaba and its protection?
   - The surah highlights that the Kaaba is under divine protection, showing its significance as a sacred site that cannot be harmed by human intentions.

10. How can the teachings of Surah Al-Fil be applied to contemporary life to inspire faith and trust in divine protection?
    - The teachings inspire believers to have faith in Allah's protection and trust that He will defend what is sacred and just, encouraging reliance on divine support in times of adversity.

These questions and answers can be used for educational purposes, study sessions, or discussions to enhance understanding of Surah Al-Fil.

Multiple Choice Questions

1. What does the term "Al-Fil" refer to?

    - A) The camel

    - B) The bird

    - C) The elephant

    - D) The lion

2. Who was the leader of the army mentioned in Surah Al-Fil, and what was his objective?

    - A) Pharaoh, to conquer Mecca

    - B) Abraha, to destroy the Kaaba

    - C) Nimrod, to capture Medina

    - D) Heraclius, to expand his empire

3. How does the surah describe the miraculous event that befell the army?

    - A) The army was swept away by a flood

    - B) The army was destroyed by lightning

    - C) Allah sent birds that pelted the army with stones of baked clay

    - D) The army was swallowed by the earth

4. What were the "sijjil" mentioned in the surah?

    - A) Gold coins

    - B) Stones of baked clay

    - C) Sacred scrolls

    - D) Pieces of armor

5. What was the fate of the army that intended to attack the Kaaba?

    - A) They were victorious and captured the city

    - B) They were turned back by the Meccans

    - C) They were destroyed and left like eaten straw

    - D) They retreated peacefully

6. How does Surah Al-Fil demonstrate Allah's power and protection?

    - A) By showing Allah's ability to create wealth

    - B) By recounting the miraculous defeat of a powerful army

    - C) By describing natural disasters

    - D) By emphasizing the strength of human armies

7. What lesson can be derived from the story recounted in Surah Al-Fil?

    - A) The importance of building strong defences

    - B) The assurance of divine protection over sacred matters

    - C) The need for strategic alliances

    - D) The value of wealth accumulation

8. How does Surah Al-Fil emphasize the importance of the Kaaba and its protection?

    - A) By showing its economic significance

    - B) By highlighting its architectural beauty

    - C) By demonstrating that it is under divine protection

    - D) By emphasizing its political power

Answers

1. *Answer:* C) The elephant
2. *Answer:* B) Abraha, to destroy the Kaaba
3. *Answer:* C) Allah sent birds that pelted the army with stones of baked clay
4. *Answer:* B) Stones of baked clay
5. *Answer:* C) They were destroyed and left like eaten straw
6. *Answer:* B) By recounting the miraculous defeat of a powerful army
7. *Answer:* B) The assurance of divine protection over sacred matters
8. *Answer:* C) By demonstrating that it is under divine protection

These questions and answers can be used for quizzes, educational discussions, or self-study to enhance understanding of Surah Al-Fil.

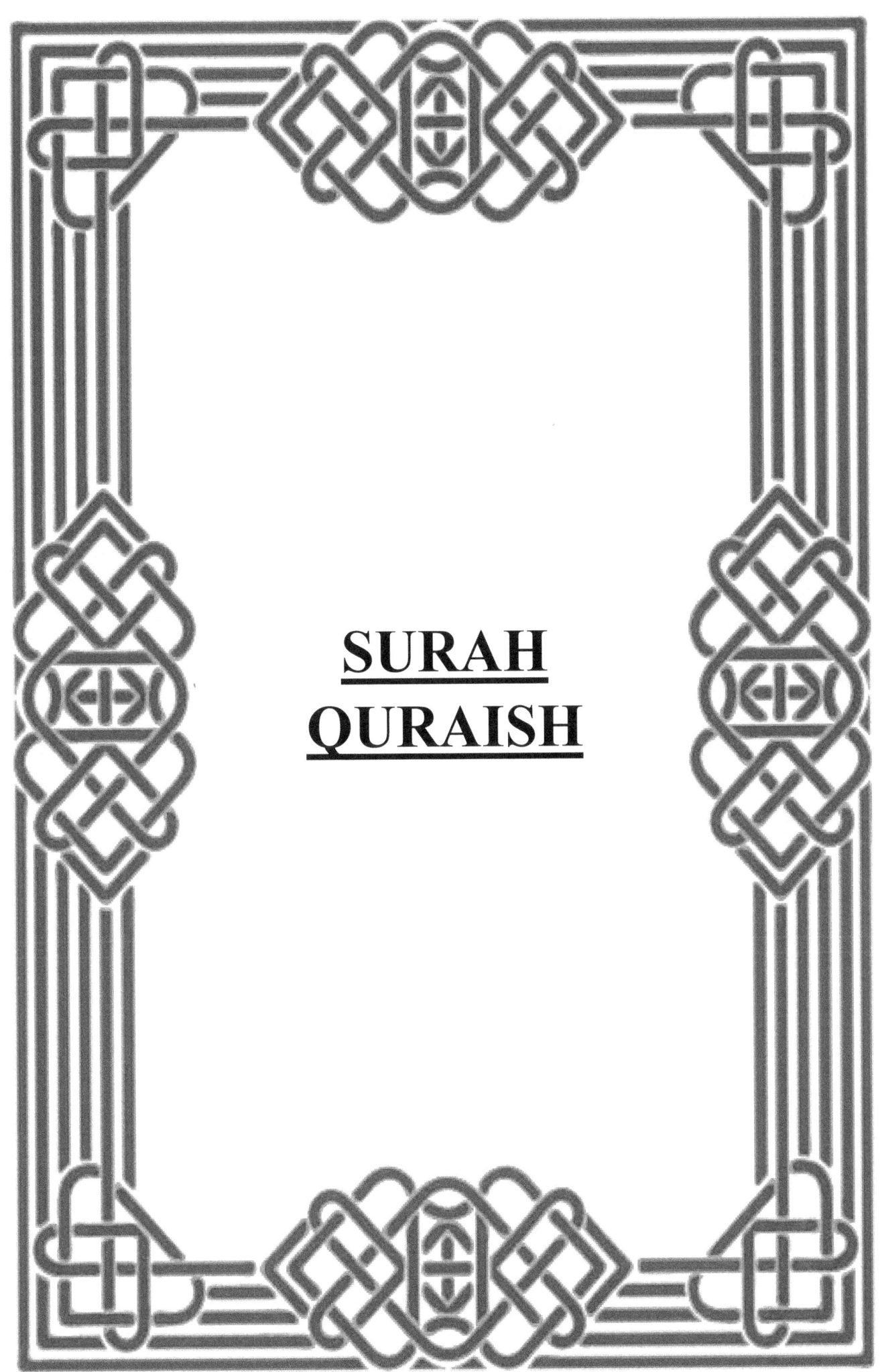

SURAH QURAISH

SURAH QURAISH

Bismillahi ar-Rahmani ar-Raheem

Verse 1

Li'ilaafi Quraish

Transliteration: ** For the protection of Quraish

Tafseer: Allah emphasizes the special agreement and protection given to Quraish, highlighting their importance and privileges.

Verse 2

Eilaafihim rihlatas-shitta'i wa-s-sayf

Transliteration: ** Their safety during winter and summer trade journeys

Tafseer: The safety and security they enjoy while traveling for trade during different seasons are signs of Allah's blessings upon them.

Verse 3

Fal-ya'budu rabbaha DHAA al-bayt

Transliteration: ** So, worship the Lord of this House (Kaaba)

Tafseer: The surah urges Quraish to worship and serve Allah, recognizing His favours upon them through their safety and prosperity.

Verse 4

Alladhi a'tamaha minal joo'i wa-'amnahum min khawfin

Transliteration: ** Who provided them food in times of hunger and security from fear

Tafseer: Allah is the One who gives them sustenance and safety, reinforcing the importance of worshipping Him with gratitude.

**Summary: **

This surah highlights Allah's blessings upon Quraish, including their safety during trade journeys, and calls them to worship Him alone, acknowledging His favours.

LESSONS TO BE LEARNT FROM SURAH QURAISH

1. Gratitude for God's Blessings: The surah reminds the Quraish of the blessings they have received from God, particularly their protection and the prosperity of their trade journeys. It serves as a reminder for all believers to acknowledge and express gratitude for the blessings they receive in their lives.
2. Security and Stability: The surah highlights the security and stability that the Quraish enjoyed in Mecca, largely due to their custodianship of the Kaaba. This security allowed them to prosper economically through trade. The lesson is that peace and stability are significant blessings that should be cherished and preserved.
3. Unity and Cooperation: The Quraish's success in trade was partly due to their unity and cooperation. This underscores the importance of working together harmoniously to achieve common goals. Unity is a source of strength and can lead to collective success and prosperity.
4. Worship and Devotion: The surah calls on the Quraish to worship the Lord of the Kaaba, who has provided for them and protected them. It emphasizes the importance of worship and devotion to God as a response to His blessings and protection.
5. Dependence on God: The surah implicitly reminds the Quraish that their prosperity and safety are not solely due to their efforts but are blessings from God. This serves as a lesson in humility and the necessity of recognizing God's role in every aspect of life.
6. Reflection on History: Like many other surahs, Surah Quraish encourages reflection on past events and the current state of affairs. Understanding and acknowledging the divine factors contributing to one's situation is crucial for maintaining faith and gratitude.
7. Encouragement to Fulfill Religious Duties: By reminding the Quraish of their blessings, the surah encourages them to fulfill their religious duties, particularly worship, as a form of gratitude. It is a reminder that religious obligations are an integral part of acknowledging God's favors.

In essence, Surah Quraish serves as a reminder of the interconnectedness of divine blessings, gratitude, worship, and community. It encourages believers to be grateful for their blessings, maintain unity, and fulfill their religious obligations as a reflection of their gratitude and recognition of God's role in their lives.

SUMMARY OF SURAH QURAISH

Surah Quraish (Chapter 106) emphasizes the importance of the tribe of Quraish, to whom the Prophet Muhammad belonged. The surah highlights how Quraish were protected and taken care of by Allah because of their role in maintaining the safety of the Kaaba and their trade routes. It reminds them of Allah's blessings and encourages them to worship Him alone, expressing gratitude for His favours to ensure their continued well-being and prosperity.

SURAH QURAISH (SURAH 106)

Questions

1. What is the primary theme of Surah Quraish?
2. Why is the surah named "Quraish"?
3. What privileges did the Quraish tribe enjoy, as mentioned in the surah?
4. How did the Quraish's custodianship of the Kaaba contribute to their status?
5. What two major journeys are referenced in Surah Quraish?
6. How does the surah emphasize the importance of worship and gratitude?
7. What does the surah imply about the relationship between security and worship?
8. What is the significance of the Kaaba mentioned in the context of Surah Quraish?
9. How does the surah encourage the Quraish to respond to their blessings?
10. How can the teachings of Surah Quraish be applied to contemporary life to foster gratitude and devotion?

Answers

1. What is the primary theme of Surah Quraish?
   - The primary theme is the security and prosperity enjoyed by the Quraish tribe due to their custodianship of the Kaaba and the subsequent call for worship and gratitude to Allah.

2. Why is the surah named "Quraish"?
   - The surah is named after the Quraish tribe, who were the custodians of the Kaaba and benefited from the trade routes and security provided by their position.

3. What privileges did the Quraish tribe enjoy, as mentioned in the surah?
   - The Quraish enjoyed security and prosperity, benefiting from established trade routes and the respect they received as custodians of the Kaaba.

4. How did the Quraish's custodianship of the Kaaba contribute to their status?
   - Their custodianship of the Kaaba elevated their status by providing them with economic and social influence, as well as protection and respect from other tribes.

5. What two major journeys are referenced in Surah Quraish?
   - The surah references the Quraish's trade journeys during the winter (to Yemen) and summer (to Syria).

6. How does the surah emphasize the importance of worship and gratitude?
   - The surah calls upon the Quraish to worship the Lord of the Kaaba, who provided them with security and sustenance, emphasizing the need for gratitude.

7. What does the surah imply about the relationship between security and worship?
   - The surah implies that the security and prosperity granted to the Quraish should lead them to worship and be grateful to Allah.

8. What is the significance of the Kaaba mentioned in the context of Surah Quraish?
   - The Kaaba is significant as the center of worship and a source of the Quraish's security and prosperity, highlighting the need for gratitude to Allah.

9. How does the surah encourage the Quraish to respond to their blessings?
   - The surah encourages the Quraish to respond to their blessings by worshiping Allah and acknowledging His role in providing for them.

10. How can the teachings of Surah Quraish be applied to contemporary life to foster gratitude and devotion?
    - The teachings encourage individuals to recognize and be grateful for their blessings, leading to devotion and worship of Allah as the provider of security and sustenance.

These questions and answers can be used for educational purposes, study sessions, or discussions to enhance understanding of Surah Quraish.

Multiple Choice Questions

1. What is the primary theme of Surah Quraish?

    - A) The wealth of the Quraish

    - B) The security and prosperity enjoyed by the Quraish and the call for worship and gratitude

    - C) The military power of the Quraish

    - D) The agricultural skills of the Quraish

2. Why is the surah named "Quraish"?

    - A) Because it details the genealogy of the Quraish

    - B) Because it discusses the migration of the Quraish

    - C) Because it highlights the privileges and responsibilities of the Quraish tribe

    - D) Because it praises the Quraish's wealth

3. What privileges did the Quraish tribe enjoy, as mentioned in the surah?

    - A) Military dominance

    - B) Security and prosperity due to their custodianship of the Kaaba

    - C) Control over all trade routes in Arabia

    - D) Political alliances with all tribes

4. How did the Quraish's custodianship of the Kaaba contribute to their status?

    - A) It provided them with economic and social influence

    - B) It granted them military power

    - C) It allowed them to control the Arabian Peninsula

    - D) It led to their agricultural success

5. What two major journeys are referenced in Surah Quraish?

    - A) Journeys to Egypt and India

    - B) Journeys to Persia and Rome

    - C) Trade journeys during the winter (to Yemen) and summer (to Syria)

    - D) Journeys to Africa and China

6. How does the surah emphasize the importance of worship and gratitude?

    - A) By calling upon the Quraish to build more temples

    - B) By urging the Quraish to worship the Lord of the Kaaba for their security and sustenance

    - C) By suggesting the Quraish donate their wealth

    - D) By instructing the Quraish to conquer new lands

7. What does the surah imply about the relationship between security and worship?

    - A) Security is unrelated to worship

    - B) Security should lead to increased wealth

    - C) Security and prosperity should lead to worship and gratitude to Allah

    - D) Security allows for political power

8. What is the significance of the Kaaba mentioned in the context of Surah Quraish?

    - A) It is a political center

    - B) It is a source of agricultural wealth

    - C) It is the center of worship and a source of the Quraish's security and prosperity

    - D) It is a military fortress

Answers

1. *Answer:* B) The security and prosperity enjoyed by the Quraish and the call for worship and gratitude
2. *Answer:* C) Because it highlights the privileges and responsibilities of the Quraish tribe
3. *Answer:* B) Security and prosperity due to their custodianship of the Kaaba
4. *Answer:* A) It provided them with economic and social influence
5. *Answer:* C) Trade journeys during the winter (to Yemen) and summer (to Syria)
6. *Answer:* B) By urging the Quraish to worship the Lord of the Kaaba for their security and sustenance
7. *Answer:* C) Security and prosperity should lead to worship and gratitude to Allah
8. *Answer:* C) It is the center of worship and a source of the Quraish's security and prosperity

These questions and answers can be used for quizzes, educational discussions, or self-study to enhance understanding of Surah Quraish.

SURAH AL-MAUN

SURAH AL-MAUN

Bismillahi ar-Rahmani ar-Raheem

Verse 1

Ara 'aytal lazee yukazzibu biddeen

"Have you seen the one who denies the Recompense?"

This verse asks the listener to consider those who do not believe in the Day of Judgment, highlighting their disbelief and its consequences on their behaviour.

Verse 2

Fazaalikal lazee yadu'ul-yateem

"For that is the one who drives away the orphan"

The denial of the Hereafter leads to a lack of compassion and justice, as depicted in the harsh treatment of orphans, who are among the most vulnerable in society.

Verse 3

Wa la yahuddu 'alaa ta'aamil miskeen

"And does not encourage the feeding of the poor."

This verse continues to describe the moral failings of those who reject faith. By not supporting or advocating for the feeding of the poor, they neglect basic human values.

Verse 4

Fa wailul-lil musalleen

"So woe to those who pray"

The focus here shifts to those who engage in worship, indicating that there are issues even among the seemingly pious.

Verse 5

Allazeena hum 'an salaatihim saahoon

"But who are heedless of their prayer"

This highlights superficial worship. These individuals are negligent in their prayers, performing it without sincerity or understanding, often for show rather than true devotion.

Verse 6

Allazeena hum yuraaa'oon

"Those who make show [of their deeds]"

This verse underscores insincerity. Acts of worship or charity done for show rather than to earn Allah's pleasure are criticized.

Verse 7

Wa yamna'oonal maa'oon

"And withhold [simple] assistance."

The Surah concludes by highlighting a lack of basic kindness. Even small acts of kindness, termed as "Ma'un" or assistance, are withheld by these individuals.

REFLECTIONS ON SURAH AL-MAUN

Surah Al-Ma'un offers a compelling insight into the integration of faith and action, emphasizing sincerity in worship and social responsibility. It critiques those who engage in religious practices merely for appearances, urging believers to ensure that their devotion is genuine and heartfelt. This Surah calls attention to the moral duty towards the vulnerable, like orphans and the poor, illustrating that true faith extends beyond rituals to compassionate and just treatment of others. It highlights the importance of small acts of kindness, reinforcing that even modest help can make a significant difference. Additionally, it invites reflection on the alignment between inner beliefs and outward actions, denouncing hypocrisy and advocating for integrity. By fostering empathy, justice, and community support, Surah Al-Ma'un guides believers towards a holistic practice of faith that embodies both personal and societal dimensions.

SUMMARY OF
SURAH AL-MAUN – SURAH 107

Surah Al-Ma'un emphasizes the importance of genuine faith and highlights the moral and social responsibilities that come with it. It criticizes those who, despite performing acts of worship, lack sincerity and fail to help the needy. The Surah specifically condemns the harsh treatment of orphans and neglect towards feeding the poor, warning against superficial worship performed for show rather than true devotion. Overall, it calls for compassion, sincerity, and integrity in both faith and actions.

SURAH AL-MAUN (SURAH 107)

Questions

1. What is Surah Al-Ma'un about?
2. How does Surah Al-Ma'un describe people who deny the Day of Judgment?
3. What does the Surah say about those who do not help orphans?
4. How are people who are neglectful in their prayers described in Surah Al-Ma'un?
5. What does Surah Al-Ma'un say about people who don't share small kindnesses?
6. Why is it important to help others, according to Surah Al-Ma'un?

Answers

1. Surah Al-Ma'un talks about the importance of helping others and being sincere in our actions and prayers.

2. The Surah describes people who deny the Day of Judgment as those who push away orphans and do not encourage feeding the needy.

3. It says that those who do not help orphans are among the ones who lie about faith and religion.

4. People who are neglectful in their prayers are described as those who pray only to show off and not out of sincerity.

5. Surah Al-Ma'un mentions that people who don't share small kindnesses are neglecting important parts of their faith.

6. It is important to help others because it shows sincerity in faith and contributes to the well-being of the community.

These questions are designed to help children understand the key teachings of Surah Al-Ma'un and their practical implications.

Multiple choice questions along with their answers based on Surah Al-Ma'un:

1. What is the primary theme of Surah Al-Ma'un?

    - A) Creation of the Universe

    - B) Importance of Sincerity in Worship and Social Responsibility

    - C) The Life of Prophet Muhammad

    - D) The Battle of Badr

2. Who is criticized in Surah Al-Ma'un?

    - A) Those who hoard wealth

    - B) Those who perform prayer for show and neglect social duties

    - C) The people of Mecca

    - D) Those who participate in wars

3. What specific group of people is mentioned as being neglected by those criticized in the Surah?

    - A) Travelers

    - B) Orphans

    - C) Merchants

    - D) Teachers

4. What kind of acts does the word "Ma'un" refer to in the Surah?

    - A) Large charitable donations

    - B) Simple, small acts of kindness and assistance

    - C) Political acts

    - D) Spiritual rituals

5. What does Surah Al-Ma'un warn against in one's prayer?

    - A) Praying too often

    - B) Praying without understanding the language

    - C) Praying without sincerity and mindfulness

    - D) Praying in public places

6. How does Surah Al-Ma'un describe those who deny the Day of Judgment?

    - A) As wise and insightful

    - B) As kind and generous

    - C) As those who repel the orphan and do not encourage feeding the poor

    - D) As those who engage in constant prayer

Answer

1. *Answer:* B) Importance of Sincerity in Worship and Social Responsibility
2. *Answer:* B) Those who perform prayer for show and neglect social duties
3. *Answer:* B) Orphans
4. *Answer:* B) Simple, small acts of kindness and assistance
5. *Answer:* C) Praying without sincerity and mindfulness
6. *Answer:* C) As those who repel the orphan and do not encourage feeding the poor

These questions are designed to test understanding of the key themes and lessons in Surah Al-Ma'un.

SURAH KAUTHAR

SURAH KAUTHAR

Bismillahi ar-Rahmani ar-Raheem

Verse 1

Innaaa a'tainaa kal kauthar

Indeed, We have granted you, [O Muhammad], al-Kauthar.

This verse affirms that Allah has bestowed upon the Prophet abundant blessings, often interpreted as a river in Paradise called "Al-Kauthar," symbolizing abundant goodness, blessings, and mercy.

Verse 2

Fasalli li rabbika wanhar

So pray to your Lord and sacrifice [to Him only].

This encourages the Prophet to establish prayer and sacrifice as acts of worship and gratitude to Allah, emphasizing worshipping Him alone.

Verse 3

Inna shaani'aka huwal abtar

Indeed, your enemy is the one cut off.

This reassures the Prophet that those who oppose him and try to diminish his message will be the ones ultimately lost and insignificant, as Allah will give him victory and support.

Overall:

The surah signifies Allah's immense blessings on the Prophet, urges gratitude and worship, and assures those who oppose him that they will be the ones deprived of success. It fosters hope and confidence, reminding believers of Allah's favor and protection.

REFLECTIONS AND LESSONS LEARNT FROM SURAH KAUTHAR

1. **Gratitude for Allah's blessings:**

The surah reminds us to be grateful for the abundant blessings Allah has given us, just as He granted Prophet Muhammad (peace be upon him) "Al-Kauthar" (abundance). Recognizing Allah's favors encourages us to worship Him sincerely and remain humble.

2. **The importance of worship and gratitude:**

The command to pray and sacrifice signifies that our acts of worship should stem from gratitude and devotion to Allah alone. It emphasizes that true success comes from sincere worship and reliance on Allah.

3. **Patience amidst challenges:**

Even during difficult times or when facing opposition, the surah reassures that Allah's support and blessings are with us. It teaches patience and steadfastness, trusting that Allah's plan is ultimately victorious.

4. **The futility of opposition:**

The verse about "the enemy being cut off" reminds us that those who oppose righteousness or challenge truth are ultimately the ones who will be the losers. It encourages believers to focus on their relationship with Allah rather than the opinions of others.

5. **Hope and reassurance:**

The surah offers hope to the Prophet and to all believers that Allah's favours are abundant, and victory is assured, even if it is not immediately visible. Trusting in divine support can motivate perseverance and dedication.

SUMMARY OF SURAH KAUTHAR – SURAH 108

Surah Kauthar (Chapter 108) is a short chapter that emphasizes Allah's abundant blessings to the Prophet Muhammad. It assures him of plentiful goodness and blessings, often interpreted as **"Kauthar"** meaning abundant river or goodness in Paradise. The surah encourages the Prophet to pray and sacrifice to Allah, and it reassures him that those who oppose him will be the ones truly lost. The core message is gratitude for Allah's blessings and reliance on Him.

SURAH AL-KAUTHER (SURAH 108)

Questions

1. What does the term "Al-Kauther" refer to, and why is the surah named after it?
2. How many verses are there in Surah Al-Kauther?
3. What is the primary message of Surah Al-Kauther to the Prophet Muhammad (peace be upon him)?
4. What does the surah promise the Prophet Muhammad (peace be upon him) in the first verse?
5. How does Surah Al-Kauther instruct the Prophet Muhammad (peace be upon him) to respond to the blessings he has received?
6. What does the surah say about those who oppose the Prophet Muhammad (peace be upon him)?
7. How does Surah Al-Kauther emphasize the importance of prayer and sacrifice?
8. What does the surah imply about the relationship between divine blessings and gratitude?
9. How does Surah Al-Kauther provide comfort and reassurance to the Prophet Muhammad (peace be upon him)?
10. How can the teachings of Surah Al-Kauther be applied to contemporary life to promote gratitude and devotion?

Answers

1. What does the term "Al-Kauther" refer to, and why is the surah named after it?
   - "Al-Kauther" refers to abundant goodness or a river in Paradise. The surah is named after it because it signifies the immense blessings granted to the Prophet Muhammad (peace be upon him).

2. How many verses are there in Surah Al-Kauther?
   - Surah Al-Kauther consists of three verses.

3. What is the primary message of Surah Al-Kauther to the Prophet Muhammad (peace be upon him)?
   - The primary message is to reassure the Prophet of the immense blessings he has received and to encourage gratitude and devotion through prayer and sacrifice.

4. What does the surah promise the Prophet Muhammad (peace be upon him) in the first verse?
   - The surah promises the Prophet Muhammad (peace be upon him) the gift of "Al-Kauther," signifying abundant blessings.

5. How does Surah Al-Kauther instruct the Prophet Muhammad (peace be upon him) to respond to the blessings he has received?
   - The surah instructs the Prophet to pray and offer sacrifice as a form of gratitude for the blessings he has received.

6. What does the surah say about those who oppose the Prophet Muhammad (peace be upon him)?
   - The surah states that those who oppose the Prophet will be cut off, implying that they will not succeed in their opposition.

7. How does Surah Al-Kauther emphasize the importance of prayer and sacrifice?
   - The surah emphasizes the importance of prayer and sacrifice as expressions of gratitude and devotion to Allah.

8. What does the surah imply about the relationship between divine blessings and gratitude?
   - The surah implies that divine blessings should be met with gratitude, expressed through acts of worship and devotion.

9. How does Surah Al-Kauther provide comfort and reassurance to the Prophet Muhammad (peace be upon him)?
   - The surah provides comfort by affirming the Prophet's blessings and promising that his opponents will be unsuccessful.

10. How can the teachings of Surah Al-Kauther be applied to contemporary life to promote gratitude and devotion?
    - The teachings encourage individuals to recognize and appreciate their blessings, and to express gratitude through regular prayer and acts of devotion.

These questions and answers can be used for educational purposes, study sessions, or discussions to enhance understanding of Surah Al-Kauther.

Multiple Choice Questions

1. What does the term "Al-Kauther" refer to in the context of the surah?

    - A) A mountain

    - B) A river in Paradise or abundant goodness

    - C) A type of bird

    - D) A marketplace

2. How many verses are there in Surah Al-Kauther?

    - A) Five

    - B) Three

    - C) Ten

    - D) Seven

3. What is the primary message of Surah Al-Kauther to the Prophet Muhammad (peace be upon him)?

    - A) To seek wealth and power

    - B) To reassure him of the immense blessings he has received

    - C) To encourage him to travel extensively

    - D) To warn him of impending danger

4. What does the surah promise the Prophet Muhammad (peace be upon him) in the first verse?

    - A) Victory in battle

    - B) The gift of "Al-Kauther"

    - C) A long life

    - D) Great wealth

5. How does Surah Al-Kauther instruct the Prophet Muhammad (peace be upon him) to respond to the blessings he has received?

    - A) By gathering an army

    - B) By building a palace

    - C) By praying and offering sacrifice

    - D) By writing a book

6. What does the surah say about those who oppose the Prophet Muhammad (peace be upon him)?

    - A) They will become powerful leaders

    - B) They will be cut off and not succeed

    - C) They will receive divine guidance

    - D) They will be wealthy

7. How does Surah Al-Kauther emphasize the importance of prayer and sacrifice?

    - A) By associating them with wealth

    - B) By linking them to other religious practices

    - C) By instructing the Prophet to engage in them as a form of gratitude

    - D) By suggesting they are optional

8. What does the surah imply about the relationship between divine blessings and gratitude?

    - A) Blessings should be met with indifference

    - B) Blessings should be met with gratitude through acts of worship

    - C) Blessings are unrelated to one's actions

    - D) Blessings should be hidden from others

Answers

1. *Answer:* B) A river in Paradise or abundant goodness
2. *Answer:* B) Three
3. *Answer:* B) To reassure him of the immense blessings he has received
4. *Answer:* B) The gift of "Al-Kauther"
5. *Answer:* C) By praying and offering sacrifice
6. *Answer:* B) They will be cut off and not succeed
7. *Answer:* C) By instructing the Prophet to engage in them as a form of gratitude
8. *Answer:* B) Blessings should be met with gratitude through acts of worship

These questions and answers can be used for quizzes, educational discussions, or self-study to enhance understanding of Surah Al-Kauther.

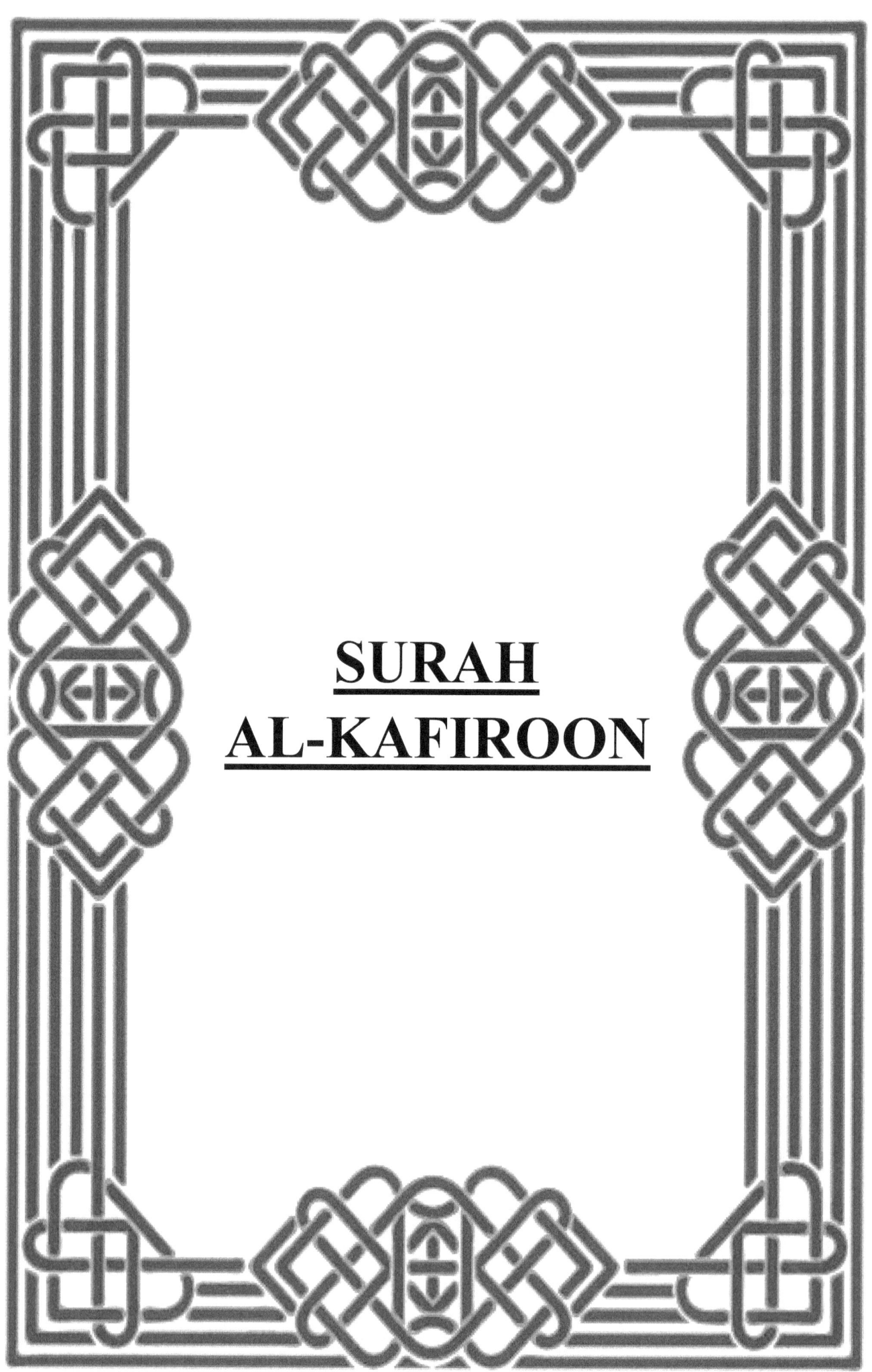

SURAH
AL-KAFIROON

SURAH AL-KAFIROON

Bismillahi ar-Rahmani ar-Raheem

Verse 1

Qul yaaa-ayyuhal kaafiroon

"Say, 'O disbelievers,

- Tafseer: This verse is a direct command to the Prophet Muhammad to address the disbelievers clearly and openly. It sets the tone for the surah by calling attention to a distinct and uncompromising message, emphasizing the importance of acknowledging differences in belief.

Verse 2

Laaa a'budu maa t'abudoon

"I do not worship what you worship."

- Tafseer: Here, the Prophet is instructed to make a clear declaration of the separation between his worship and that of the disbelievers. It affirms the commitment to monotheism and the worship of Allah alone, rejecting any form of idol worship or polytheism.

Verse 3

Wa laaa antum 'aabidoona maaa a'bud

"Nor are you worshippers of what I worship."

- Tafseer: This verse highlights the reciprocal nature of the distinction: just as the Prophet does not worship their deities, the disbelievers do not worship Allah in the manner prescribed by Islam. It underscores the fundamental differences in belief and practice.

Verse 4

Wa laaa ana 'abidum maa 'abattum

"Nor will I be a worshipper of what you worship."

- Tafseer: The repetition serves to reinforce the commitment to monotheism and the rejection of idolatry. It signifies the permanence of this stance, indicating that there will be no future compromise or change in the Prophet's dedication to Allah.

Verse 5

Wa laaa antum 'aabidoona maaa a'bud

"Nor will you be worshippers of what I worship."

- Tafseer: This reiteration emphasizes the unlikelihood of the disbelievers adopting the worship of Allah as practiced by the Prophet. It acknowledges the persistence of their disbelief and the established boundaries between the two faiths.

Verse 6

"For you is your religion, and for me is my religion."

- Tafseer: The concluding verse establishes a principle of mutual respect for religious differences. It acknowledges the coexistence of different beliefs while maintaining a clear distinction. This verse underscores the importance of religious integrity and the refusal to compromise on fundamental beliefs.

Surah Al-Kafiroon is a declaration of the distinct and unwavering nature of Islamic monotheism. It emphasizes the separation between the beliefs of the Muslims and the disbelievers, advocating for religious integrity and mutual respect without compromise.

REFLECTIONS ON SURAH AL-KAFIROON

Surah Al-Kafiroon, containing a firm and clear declaration of religious boundaries, offers several reflections that are valuable for understanding interfaith relations and personal faith integrity.

1. Clarity and Firmness in Faith: Surah Al-Kafiroon emphasizes the importance of having a clear and unwavering commitment to one's faith. It reflects the necessity for believers to understand and uphold the core principles of their religion without succumbing to external pressures or compromising on essential beliefs. This surah encourages Muslims to maintain their religious identity with confidence and clarity.
2. Respect for Religious Differences: The surah underscores a respect for religious differences by acknowledging the coexistence of various beliefs. The phrase "For you is your religion, and for me is my religion" highlights a principle of peaceful coexistence and mutual respect, allowing for religious diversity without conflict or coercion.
3. Rejection of Religious Syncretism: Surah Al-Kafiroon firmly rejects the idea of mixing or compromising religious beliefs. By repeatedly distinguishing the worship practices of Muslims from those of disbelievers, the surah reflects the Islamic stance against syncretism, where elements of different religions are combined. It advocates for a pure and unadulterated practice of faith.
4. Strength in Identity: The surah reflects the importance of maintaining a strong religious identity, especially in the face of opposition or attempts to dilute one's beliefs. It serves as a reminder for Muslims to remain steadfast in their worship of Allah and to resist any attempts to sway them from their path.
5. Peaceful Coexistence: While the surah is firm in its declaration of faith, it also promotes the idea of peaceful coexistence. By clearly stating the separation of beliefs, it sets the groundwork for living peacefully alongside those of different faiths, as long as there is mutual respect and no imposition of beliefs.
6. Relevance in Pluralistic Societies: In today's diverse and pluralistic societies, the lessons from Surah Al-Kafiroon are particularly relevant. It guides Muslims to navigate interfaith interactions with respect and integrity, upholding their beliefs while recognizing and respecting the beliefs of others.
7. Personal Reflection: On a personal level, the surah invites believers to reflect on their own faith and practices. It encourages introspection about the sincerity and purity of one's worship and the importance of maintaining a consistent and genuine relationship with God.

Overall, Surah Al-Kafiroon serves as a powerful reminder of the importance of faith integrity, respect for diversity, and the ability to coexist peacefully without compromising one's core beliefs.

SUMMARY OF
SURAH AL-KAFIROON-SURAH 109

Surah Al-Kafiroon, the 109th chapter of the Quran, is a short surah consisting of six verses. The name "Al-Kafiroon" translates to "The Disbelievers." This surah is a declaration of the distinction between the faith of the believers and that of the disbelievers.

The surah begins with a clear and firm address to the disbelievers, stating that the Prophet Muhammad does not worship what they worship, nor do the disbelievers worship what he worships. The repetition of this statement underscores the complete separation between the practices and beliefs of the two groups. It emphasizes that there is no compromise in matters of faith and worship.

The surah concludes with the declaration, "For you is your religion, and for me is my religion," reinforcing the concept of religious distinction and mutual respect for each other's choices. It highlights the importance of maintaining one's faith and identity without succumbing to pressure or blending beliefs.

Overall, Surah Al-Kafiroon serves as a powerful assertion of monotheism and the importance of religious integrity. It calls for the acceptance of religious differences while remaining steadfast in one's own beliefs, emphasizing that true faith cannot be compromised or diluted.

ADDITIONAL INFORMATION

The revelation of Surah Al-Kafiroon is associated with an event involving the Quraysh, the dominant tribe in Mecca at the time of the Prophet Muhammad. The Quraysh were polytheists who worshipped multiple gods and idols, while the Prophet Muhammad preached the message of monotheism, calling people to worship only Allah.

According to Islamic tradition, the Quraysh leaders, concerned about the growing influence of Islam and the potential disruption to their social and economic status, approached the Prophet Muhammad with a proposal. They suggested a compromise where they would worship Allah for a year if the Prophet agreed to worship their gods for a year. This offer was intended to create a mutual agreement that would allow both groups to coexist peacefully without conflict.

In response to this proposal, Surah Al-Kafiroon was revealed. The surah is a clear and unequivocal rejection of any compromise in matters of faith. It emphasizes the distinct separation between the beliefs of the Prophet and those of the disbelievers. The surah's message is that true faith cannot be compromised or diluted by blending it with polytheistic practices.

By declaring, "For you is your religion, and for me is my religion," the surah reinforces the idea that each group has its own distinct beliefs and practices, and that mutual respect for these differences is necessary. It underscores the importance of maintaining religious integrity and the refusal to compromise on core principles of faith.

This revelation served to strengthen the resolve of the early Muslims and clarified the position of Islam as a distinct and uncompromising monotheistic faith. It also highlighted the importance of standing firm in one's beliefs, even in the face of pressure to conform or compromise.

SURAH AL-KAFIROON (SURAH 109)

Questions

1. What is the primary theme of Surah Al-kafiroon?
2. How does the surah address the concept of religious differences?
3. What does the term "Al-kafiroon" mean, and why is the surah named after it?
4. How does the surah emphasize the distinction between the beliefs of the Prophet Muhammad (peace be upon him) and those of the disbelievers?
5. What does the surah convey about the concept of worship in Islam?
6. How is the message of Surah Al-kafiroon relevant to the idea of religious tolerance?
7. What response does the surah provide to those who propose compromising religious beliefs?
8. How does the surah highlight the firmness of the Prophet Muhammad (peace be upon him) in his faith?
9. What is the significance of the repeated phrase "For you is your religion, and for me is my religion" in the surah?
10. How can the teachings of Surah Al-kafiroon be applied to contemporary life to promote mutual respect and coexistence among people of different faiths?

Answers

1. What is the primary theme of Surah Al-kafiroon?
   - The primary theme is the clear distinction between Islam and disbelief, emphasizing monotheism and the respect for religious differences.

2. How does the surah address the concept of religious differences?
   - The surah explicitly states that the beliefs and practices of the Prophet and the disbelievers are separate, promoting the idea of "to you your religion, and to me mine."

3. What does the term "Al-kafiroon" mean, and why is the surah named after it?
   - "Al-kafiroon" means "the disbelievers." The surah is named after it because it addresses the Prophet's response to the disbelievers' proposals for religious compromise.

4. How does the surah emphasize the distinction between the beliefs of the Prophet Muhammad (peace be upon him) and those of the disbelievers?
   - The surah emphasizes that the Prophet will not worship what the disbelievers worship, nor will they worship what he worships, underscoring the differences in their beliefs.

5. What does the surah convey about the concept of worship in Islam?
   - The surah conveys that worship in Islam is exclusive to Allah, and there can be no compromise or mixing of religious practices.

6. How is the message of Surah Al-kafiroon relevant to the idea of religious tolerance?
   - The message promotes respect for religious differences by acknowledging distinct paths for different faiths and advocating for peaceful coexistence.

7. What response does the surah provide to those who propose compromising religious beliefs?
   - The surah firmly rejects any compromise in religious beliefs, maintaining the purity and exclusivity of Islamic worship.

8. How does the surah highlight the firmness of the Prophet Muhammad (peace be upon him) in his faith?
   - The surah underscores the Prophet's unwavering commitment to monotheism and his refusal to incorporate any form of polytheism into his worship.

9. What is the significance of the repeated phrase "For you is your religion, and for me is my religion" in the surah?
   - This phrase signifies mutual respect for religious differences and the acceptance of distinct religious identities without interference.

10. How can the teachings of Surah Al-kafiroon be applied to contemporary life to promote mutual respect and coexistence among people of different faiths?
    - The teachings encourage respecting religious diversity, maintaining one's faith without compromise, and fostering peaceful coexistence through mutual acceptance.

These questions and answers can be used for educational purposes, study sessions, or discussions to enhance understanding of Surah Al-kafiroon.

Multiple Choice Questions

1. What does the term "Al-kafiroon" mean?

    - A) The believers

    - B) The disbelievers

    - C) The hypocrites

    - D) The travellers

2. What is the primary theme of Surah Al-kafiroon?

    - A) The importance of charity

    - B) The distinct separation between the beliefs of Muslims and disbelievers

    - C) The rewards of fasting

    - D) The significance of pilgrimage

3. How does Surah Al-kafiroon address the concept of religious differences?

    - A) By encouraging the blending of religious practices

    - B) By stating that the beliefs and practices of Muslims and disbelievers are separate

    - C) By suggesting that all religions are the same

    - D) By emphasizing the superiority of wealth

4. What does the surah convey about the concept of worship in Islam?

    - A) Worship can be shared among different gods

    - B) Worship should be exclusive to Allah

    - C) Worship is optional

    - D) Worship is based on cultural practices

5. What response does the surah provide to those who propose compromising religious beliefs?

    - A) It encourages compromise for peace

    - B) It firmly rejects any compromise in religious beliefs

    - C) It suggests compromise for political gain

    - D) It remains neutral on the matter

6. How is the message of Surah Al-kafiroon relevant to the idea of religious tolerance?

    - A) It promotes the idea of peaceful coexistence by acknowledging distinct paths for different faiths

    - B) It discourages interaction with other faiths

    - C) It suggests converting others by force

    - D) It emphasizes cultural superiority

7. What is the significance of the repeated phrase "For you is your religion, and for me is my religion" in the surah?

    - A) It signifies a call to debate religious beliefs

    - B) It signifies mutual respect and acceptance of religious differences

    - C) It suggests merging different religions

    - D) It implies indifference to religious practices

8. How does the surah highlight the firmness of the Prophet Muhammad (peace be upon him) in his faith?

    - A) By showing his willingness to compromise

    - B) By reaffirming his unwavering commitment to monotheism

    - C) By depicting him as uncertain

    - D) By suggesting he change his beliefs

Answers

1. *Answer:* B) The disbelievers
2. *Answer:* B) The distinct separation between the beliefs of Muslims and disbelievers
3. *Answer:* B) By stating that the beliefs and practices of Muslims and disbelievers are separate
4. *Answer:* B) Worship should be exclusive to Allah
5. *Answer:* B) It firmly rejects any compromise in religious beliefs
6. *Answer:* A) It promotes the idea of peaceful coexistence by acknowledging distinct paths for different faiths
7. *Answer:* B) It signifies mutual respect and acceptance of religious differences
8. *Answer:* B) By reaffirming his unwavering commitment to monotheism

These questions and answers can be used for quizzes, educational discussions, or self-study to enhance understanding of Surah Al-kafiroon.

SURAH AN-NASR

SURAH AN-NASR

Bismillahi ar-Rahmani ar-Raheem

Verse 1

Iza jaaa'a nasrul-laahi walfath

"When the victory of Allah has come and the conquest,"

- Tafseer: This verse refers to the divine support and victory granted by Allah, specifically alluding to the conquest of Mecca. This event marked a significant turning point in Islamic history, as it was achieved with minimal bloodshed and led to the widespread acceptance of Islam. The victory is attributed to Allah's help, emphasizing that successes are ultimately due to divine intervention and support. The conquest of Mecca is seen as the culmination of the Prophet Muhammad's mission, fulfilling Allah's promise.

Verse 2

Wa ra-aitan naasa yadkhuloona fee deenil laahi afwajaa

"And you see the people entering into the religion of Allah in multitudes,"

- Tafseer: Following the conquest, the surah highlights the mass conversion of people to Islam. The phrase "in multitudes" signifies the large numbers of people embracing the faith, reflecting the success of the Prophet's message and the divine assistance that facilitated this movement. This verse underscores the transformative impact of Islam and the effectiveness of the Prophet's efforts over the years. It also signifies the validation of the truth of Islam, as people recognize its message and choose to follow it.

Verse 3

Fasabbih bihamdi rabbika wastaghfirh, innahoo kaana tawwaaba

"Then exalt [Him] with praise of your Lord and ask forgiveness of Him. Indeed, He is ever Accepting of repentance."

- Tafseer: The final verse provides guidance on how to respond to such a significant victory. The Prophet Muhammad is instructed to glorify Allah with praise and to seek His forgiveness. This reflects the importance of humility and gratitude, even in times of great success. It serves as a reminder that all achievements should be attributed to Allah, and that continuous self-reflection and repentance are necessary. The verse emphasizes that Allah is always willing to accept repentance, encouraging believers to maintain a relationship with Him through praise and seeking forgiveness.

Overall, Surah An-Nasr serves as a celebration of divine victory and a reminder of the responsibilities that come with success. It underscores the importance of attributing achievements to Allah's help, maintaining humility, and continuing to seek His guidance and forgiveness.

LESSONS AND REFLECTIONS ON SURAH AN-NASR

Surah An-Nasr, though brief, carries profound lessons and reflections that are applicable to both personal and communal aspects of life. Here are some key reflections and lessons from this surah:

1. Acknowledgment of Divine Support: The surah emphasizes that true victory and success come from Allah. This teaches believers to recognize and attribute their achievements to divine support rather than solely to their own efforts. It instills a sense of humility and gratitude.
2. Significance of the Conquest of Mecca: The conquest is not just a military victory but a spiritual one, marking the widespread acceptance of Islam. It reflects the culmination of the Prophet Muhammad's mission and the fulfillment of Allah's promise. This reminds believers of the importance of perseverance in the face of challenges, knowing that divine help is always near.
3. Mass Acceptance as a Validation: The mention of people entering Islam in multitudes signifies the validation of the truth of Islam. It reflects the effectiveness of conveying the message with patience and integrity. For modern believers, it underscores the importance of steadfastness and dedication in sharing and living by their faith.
4. Humility in Success: The directive to glorify Allah and seek His forgiveness even after achieving victory highlights the importance of humility. Believers are reminded that success should not lead to arrogance but to increased devotion and gratitude.
5. Continuous Self-Reflection and Repentance: The call to seek forgiveness signifies that no matter the level of success, continuous self-reflection and repentance are essential. It encourages believers to remain conscious of their actions and to seek improvement and forgiveness regularly.
6. Allah's Acceptance of Repentance: The assurance that Allah is ever accepting of repentance provides hope and encouragement. It reminds believers of the mercy and forgiveness of Allah, motivating them to turn to Him in all circumstances.
7. End of the Prophetic Mission: For the Prophet Muhammad, this surah signaled the nearing completion of his mission on earth. It serves as a reminder that life is finite, and one should strive to fulfill their duties and responsibilities with sincerity and dedication.

SUMMARY FOR SURAH AN-NASR. SURAH 110

Surah An-Nasr, the 110th chapter of the Quran, is a brief surah consisting of three verses. It is also known as "The Divine Support" or "The Help." This surah was revealed in Medina and is considered to be one of the last surahs revealed to the Prophet Muhammad.

The surah begins by acknowledging the victory and help from Allah when the conquest of Mecca takes place. It signifies the fulfillment of Allah's promise and the culmination of the Prophet's mission, as the people enter Islam in large numbers. This victory is not just a military conquest but a significant spiritual turning point, as it represents the widespread acceptance of Islam.

The second verse mentions how people will embrace Islam in crowds, highlighting the success of the Prophet's message and the divine assistance that facilitated this acceptance. It reflects the transformative impact of Islam and the Prophet's efforts over the years.

The surah concludes with a directive for the Prophet to glorify Allah with praise and seek His forgiveness. This is a reminder of the importance of humility and gratitude, even in times of success. The command to seek forgiveness also emphasizes the need for continuous self-reflection and repentance, recognizing that all accomplishments are ultimately due to Allah's support.

Overall, Surah An-Nasr serves as a celebration of victory and a reminder of the responsibilities that come with success. It underscores the importance of attributing achievements to divine support, maintaining humility, and continuing to seek Allah's guidance and forgiveness.

AL-NASR (SURAH 110)

Questions

1. What is the primary theme of Surah An-Nasr?
2. What does the term "An-Nasr" mean, and why is the surah named after it?
3. What significant event is referenced in Surah An-Nasr?
4. What does the surah instruct the Prophet Muhammad (peace be upon him) to do upon witnessing the victory and people entering Islam?
5. How does the surah emphasize the importance of seeking forgiveness?
6. What is the significance of the phrase "the victory of Allah" in the surah?
7. How does Surah An-Nasr relate to the concept of gratitude?
8. What does the surah imply about the completion of the Prophet Muhammad's (peace be upon him) mission?
9. How is the message of Surah An-Nasr relevant to the concept of humility?
10. How can the teachings of Surah An-Nasr be applied to contemporary life to encourage reflection and gratitude?

Answers

1. What is the primary theme of Surah An-Nasr?
   - The primary theme is the victory of Islam, the completion of the Prophet Muhammad's (peace be upon him) mission, and the call to praise and seek forgiveness from Allah.

2. What does the term "An-Nasr" mean, and why is the surah named after it?
   - "An-Nasr" means "the victory." The surah is named after it because it celebrates the victory of Islam and the mass acceptance of the faith.

3. What significant event is referenced in Surah An-Nasr?
   - The surah references the conquest of Mecca and the subsequent entry of people into Islam in large numbers.

4. What does the surah instruct the Prophet Muhammad (peace be upon him) to do upon witnessing the victory and people entering Islam?
   - The surah instructs the Prophet to glorify the praises of his Lord and seek His forgiveness.

5. How does the surah emphasize the importance of seeking forgiveness?
   - The surah highlights seeking forgiveness as a key aspect of gratitude and humility following a major victory.

6. What is the significance of the phrase "the victory of Allah" in the surah?
   - The phrase signifies that the victory is a divine blessing and a testament to the fulfillment of Allah's promise.

7. How does Surah An-Nasr relate to the concept of gratitude?
   - The surah encourages gratitude by instructing the Prophet to praise Allah for the victory and success granted to Islam.

8. What does the surah imply about the completion of the Prophet Muhammad's (peace be upon him) mission?
   - The surah implies that the mission is nearing completion with the widespread acceptance of Islam, signaling a time for reflection and gratitude.

9. How is the message of Surah An-Nasr relevant to the concept of humility?
   - The surah teaches humility by reminding believers to attribute successes to Allah and to seek His forgiveness and guidance.

10. How can the teachings of Surah An-Nasr be applied to contemporary life to encourage reflection and gratitude?
    - The teachings encourage individuals to acknowledge divine blessings, express gratitude, and seek forgiveness in times of success, fostering humility and spiritual growth.

These questions and answers can be used for educational purposes, study sessions, or discussions to enhance understanding of Surah An-Nasr.

Multiple Choice Questions

1. What does the term "An-Nasr" mean?

    - A) The guidance

    - B) The victory

    - C) The promise

    - D) The journey

2. What significant event is referenced in Surah An-Nasr?

    - A) The Battle of Badr

    - B) The Treaty of Hudaybiyyah

    - C) The conquest of Mecca

    - D) The migration to Medina

3. What does the surah instruct the Prophet Muhammad (peace be upon him) to do upon witnessing the victory and people entering Islam?

    - A) Build a mosque

    - B) Celebrate with a feast

    - C) Glorify the praises of his Lord and seek His forgiveness

    - D) Write a letter

4. How does the surah emphasize the importance of seeking forgiveness?

    - A) By highlighting it as a key aspect of gratitude and humility

    - B) By associating it with wealth

    - C) By making it a condition for victory

    - D) By linking it to fame

5. What is the significance of the phrase "the victory of Allah" in the surah?

    - A) It signifies military strength

    - B) It signifies a testament to the fulfillment of Allah's promise

    - C) It signifies political power

    - D) It signifies material wealth

6. How does Surah An-Nasr relate to the concept of gratitude?

    - A) It discourages gratitude

    - B) It encourages gratitude by instructing the Prophet to praise Allah for the victory

    - C) It views gratitude as unnecessary

    - D) It links gratitude to personal achievements

7. What does the surah imply about the completion of the Prophet Muhammad's (peace be upon him) mission?

    - A) The mission is incomplete

    - B) The mission is nearing completion with the widespread acceptance of Islam

    - C) The mission is only just beginning

    - D) The mission is irrelevant

8. How is the message of Surah An-Nasr relevant to the concept of humility?

    - A) It promotes arrogance

    - B) It teaches humility by reminding believers to attribute successes to Allah

    - C) It encourages pride in personal achievements

    - D) It discourages seeking forgiveness

Answers

1. *Answer:* B) The victory
2. *Answer:* C) The conquest of Mecca
3. *Answer:* C) Glorify the praises of his Lord and seek His forgiveness
4. *Answer:* A) By highlighting it as a key aspect of gratitude and humility
5. *Answer:* B) It signifies a testament to the fulfillment of Allah's promise
6. *Answer:* B) It encourages gratitude by instructing the Prophet to praise Allah for the victory
7. *Answer:* B) The mission is nearing completion with the widespread acceptance of Islam
8. *Answer:* B) It teaches humility by reminding believers to attribute successes to Allah

These questions and answers can be used for quizzes, educational discussions, or self-study to enhance understanding of Surah An-Nasr.

SURAH AL-MASADD

SURAH AL-MASADD-

Bismillahi ar-Rahmani ar-Raheem

Verse 1

"Tabbat yadā abī lahabin watab."

- Transliteration: "May the hands of Abu Lahab be ruined, and ruined is he."

- Tafseer: This verse begins with a powerful curse against Abu Lahab, one of the Prophet Muhammad's most vehement opponents. The phrase "May the hands be ruined" is an Arabic idiom expressing a wish for someone's destruction. Abu Lahab's real name was 'Abd al-'Uzza, but he was called "Lahab" (meaning "flame") possibly due to his fiery nature or reddish complexion. This verse signifies the certainty of his downfall and the futility of his efforts against the Prophet.

Verse 2

"Mā aghnā 'anhu māluhu wamā kasab."

Transliteration: "His wealth will not avail him or that which he gained."

- Tafseer: Despite Abu Lahab's significant wealth and social status, this verse declares that none of his material possessions or achievements will benefit him in the face of divine judgment. It underscores the idea that wealth and worldly success cannot shield one from the consequences of opposing Allah and His Messenger.

Verse 3

"Sa-yaṣlā nāran dhāta lahab."

- Transliteration: "He will [enter to] burn in a Fire of [blazing] flame."

- Tafseer: The verse foretells the severe punishment awaiting Abu Lahab in the Hereafter. The repetitive use of "flame" (lahab) serves as a wordplay on his nickname, emphasizing the appropriateness of his punishment. This conveys the message that those who persist in their hostility against the Prophet and the message of Islam will face dire consequences.

Verse 4

"Wa-mra-atuhu ḥammālata l-ḥaṭab."

- Transliteration: "And his wife [as well]—the carrier of firewood."

  - Tafseer: This verse includes Abu Lahab's wife, Umm Jamil, in the condemnation. She is referred to as "the carrier of firewood," which can be interpreted both literally and metaphorically. Literally, it suggests that she will contribute to her husband's punishment. Metaphorically, it implies that she actively stoked the flames of enmity against the Prophet by spreading harmful rumors and supporting her husband's antagonism.

Verse 5

"Fī jīdihā ḥablun min masad."

- Transliteration: "Around her neck is a rope of [twisted] fiber."

  - Tafseer: The imagery of a "rope of twisted fiber" around her neck symbolizes the self-inflicted nature of her punishment. Just as she used her influence and resources to harm the Prophet, she will find herself bound and punished by her own deeds. This verse serves as a stark reminder that one's actions have consequences, and those who sow discord and hatred will face retribution.

Overall, Surah Al-Masadd serves as a warning against the consequences of enmity towards the divine message and highlights the futility of relying on wealth and status to escape divine justice.

Surah Al-Masadd, also known as Surah Lahab, offers several reflections and lessons that are relevant to personal conduct, community interactions, and spiritual understanding. Here are some reflections on this surah:

1. Consequences of Hostility Toward the Divine Message: The surah directly addresses the consequences faced by Abu Lahab and his wife for their persistent antagonism towards the Prophet Muhammad and the message of Islam. It serves as a powerful reminder that opposition to divine guidance, motivated by arrogance or enmity, leads to inevitable ruin.
2. Futility of Wealth and Status: Despite Abu Lahab's wealth and social standing, the surah emphasizes that these worldly attributes cannot protect him from Allah's judgment. This illustrates the fundamental Islamic principle that material possessions and societal status are insignificant in the face of divine accountability. It encourages believers to focus on spiritual and moral integrity rather than material accumulation.
3. Accountability for One's Actions: The surah highlights that both Abu Lahab and his wife are held accountable for their actions. Umm Jamil's role as "the carrier of firewood" metaphorically underscores her active participation in spreading harm and discord. This reflects the broader lesson that individuals are responsible for their deeds and will face consequences accordingly.
4. Significance of Intentions and Actions: The punishment of Abu Lahab and his wife is not merely for their disbelief but for their active efforts to harm the Prophet and obstruct the spread of Islam. This underscores the importance of intentions and actions in Islamic teachings. It serves as a reminder that both negative intentions and harmful actions can lead to severe consequences.

5. Divine Justice and Certainty: The definitive language of the surah ("perish," "ruined") conveys the certainty of divine justice. It reassures believers that those who oppose God's messengers and work against the truth will ultimately face divine retribution. This can provide comfort to those who face opposition or injustice, knowing that ultimate justice lies with Allah.
6. Metaphorical Language and Symbolism: The use of metaphorical language, such as "a rope of twisted fiber," enriches the surah's message by symbolizing the self-destructive nature of Abu Lahab and his wife's actions. This invites reflection on how negative behaviours can entangle individuals in their own consequences.
7. Lessons in Patience and Perseverance: For the early Muslim community, the surah served as a reminder to remain patient and steadfast in the face of opposition. It encouraged them to trust in Allah's justice and continue their mission with perseverance, knowing that those who oppose the truth will not succeed in the end.

In summary, Surah Al-Masadd offers a poignant lesson on the consequences of hostility towards divine guidance, underscoring the futility of relying on material wealth and the importance of accountability, intentions, and actions. It calls for reflection on personal conduct and the assurance of divine justice.

SUMMARY OF
SURAH AL-MASADD- SURAH 112

Surah Al-Masadd, also known as Surah Lahab, is the 111th chapter of the Quran and consists of five verses. The surah is notable for its direct address and condemnation of Abu Lahab, one of the Prophet Muhammad's most ardent opponents and his paternal uncle.

The surah begins by declaring the eventual ruin of Abu Lahab, using the term "perish" to emphasize the certainty of his downfall. Despite his wealth and social standing, the surah states that his riches and efforts will not save him from destruction. This highlights the insignificance of material wealth in the face of divine judgment.

The surah also mentions Abu Lahab's wife, who is described as a partner in his hostility towards the Prophet. She is depicted as someone who will carry firewood, symbolizing her role in fueling the animosity and spreading harm. Her end is foretold as being tied with a rope of palm fiber, a metaphor for the punishment she will face.

Surah Al-Masadd serves as a warning against opposing the divine message and the consequences of persistent enmity and arrogance. It underscores the futility of relying on wealth and status to escape divine retribution. The surah is a reminder of the ultimate justice of Allah and the inevitable downfall of those who oppose His prophets and message.

SURAH MASADD (SURAH 111)

Questions

1. What is the primary theme of Surah Al-Masadd?
2. Who is Abu Lahab, and why is he mentioned in this surah?
3. What does the term "Masadd" mean, and why is the surah named after it?
4. What does the surah say about the fate of Abu Lahab?
5. How does the surah describe the consequences faced by Abu Lahab's wife?
6. What role did Abu Lahab's wife play in opposing the Prophet Muhammad (peace be upon him)?
7. How does Surah Al-Masadd illustrate the futility of wealth and power when opposed to divine will?
8. What is the significance of the phrase "the flame" in the context of this surah?
9. How does the surah emphasize the certainty of divine justice?
10. What lessons can be drawn from Surah Al-Masadd regarding opposition to truth and justice?

Answers

1. What is the primary theme of Surah Al-Masadd?
   - The primary theme is the condemnation of Abu Lahab and his wife for their persistent opposition to the Prophet Muhammad (peace be upon him) and their eventual punishment.

2. Who is Abu Lahab, and why is he mentioned in this surah?
   - Abu Lahab was the paternal uncle of the Prophet Muhammad (peace be upon him) and a staunch opponent of Islam. He is mentioned to illustrate the consequences of opposing the divine message.

3. What does the term "Masadd" mean, and why is the surah named after it?
   - "Masadd" refers to "palm fiber" or "twisted fiber," and the surah is named after it because it mentions that Abu Lahab's wife will carry firewood with a rope of twisted fiber around her neck as part of her punishment.

4. What does the surah say about the fate of Abu Lahab?
   - The surah states that Abu Lahab's wealth and gains will not benefit him, and he will be thrown into a flaming fire.

5. How does the surah describe the consequences faced by Abu Lahab's wife?
   - The surah describes that she will carry firewood and have a rope of twisted palm fiber around her neck as part of her punishment.

6. What role did Abu Lahab's wife play in opposing the Prophet Muhammad (peace be upon him)?
   - Abu Lahab's wife was complicit in opposing the Prophet and reportedly spread thorns in his path to harm him.

7. How does Surah Al-Masadd illustrate the futility of wealth and power when opposed to divine will?
   - The surah underscores that Abu Lahab's wealth and social standing will not save him from the consequences of his actions, highlighting the ultimate power of divine justice.

8. What is the significance of the phrase "the flame" in the context of this surah?
   - "The flame" signifies the fiery punishment awaiting Abu Lahab in the hereafter as a consequence of his persistent opposition to the Prophet.

9. How does the surah emphasize the certainty of divine justice?
   - The surah clearly outlines the punishment awaiting Abu Lahab and his wife, illustrating that divine justice is unavoidable for those who oppose the truth.

10. What lessons can be drawn from Surah Al-Masadd regarding opposition to truth and justice?
    - The surah teaches that opposition to truth and justice, regardless of one's wealth or status, leads to inevitable consequences under divine justice.

These questions and answers can be used for educational purposes, study sessions, or discussions to enhance understanding of Surah Al-Masadd.

Multiple Choice Questions

1. What is the primary theme of Surah Al-Masadd?

    - A) The importance of charity

    - B) The condemnation of Abu Lahab and his wife for their opposition to the Prophet Muhammad (peace be upon him)

    - C) The beauty of nature

    - D) The rewards of prayer

2. Who is Abu Lahab, and why is he mentioned in this surah?

    - A) A wealthy merchant who supported Islam

    - B) A king who built many mosques

    - C) The paternal uncle of the Prophet Muhammad (peace be upon him) and an opponent of Islam

    - D) A traveler who spread the Quran

3. What does the term "Masadd" refer to?

    - A) Gold coins

    - B) Palm fiber or twisted fiber

    - C) A type of fruit

    - D) A river in paradise

4. What does the surah say about the fate of Abu Lahab?

    - A) He will be rewarded with wealth

    - B) He will be thrown into a flaming fire

    - C) He will achieve great success

    - D) He will be honored by all

5. How does the surah describe the consequences faced by Abu Lahab's wife?

    - A) She will be praised for her kindness

    - B) She will carry firewood with a rope of twisted fiber around her neck

    - C) She will become a queen

    - D) She will be forgiven for her actions

6. What role did Abu Lahab's wife play in opposing the Prophet Muhammad (peace be upon him)?

    - A) She spread rumors to harm his reputation

    - B) She provided financial support to the Prophet

    - C) She spread thorns in the Prophet's path to harm him

    - D) She advocated for peace and reconciliation

7. How does Surah Al-Masadd illustrate the futility of wealth and power when opposed to divine will?

    - A) By stating that wealth leads to happiness

    - B) By showing that Abu Lahab's wealth cannot save him from punishment

    - C) By emphasizing the importance of social status

    - D) By suggesting wealth guarantees paradise

8. What is the significance of the phrase "the flame" in the context of this surah?

    - A) It signifies warmth and comfort

    - B) It signifies the fiery punishment awaiting Abu Lahab

    - C) It signifies light and guidance

    - D) It signifies the beauty of fire

Answers

1. *Answer:* B) The condemnation of Abu Lahab and his wife for their opposition to the Prophet Muhammad (peace be upon him)
2. *Answer:* C) The paternal uncle of the Prophet Muhammad (peace be upon him) and an opponent of Islam
3. *Answer:* B) Palm fiber or twisted fiber
4. *Answer:* B) He will be thrown into a flaming fire
5. *Answer:* B) She will carry firewood with a rope of twisted fiber around her neck
6. *Answer:* C) She spread thorns in the Prophet's path to harm him
7. *Answer:* B) By showing that Abu Lahab's wealth cannot save him from punishment
8. *Answer:* B) It signifies the fiery punishment awaiting Abu Lahab

These questions and answers can be used for quizzes, educational discussions, or self-study to enhance understanding of Surah Al-Masadd.

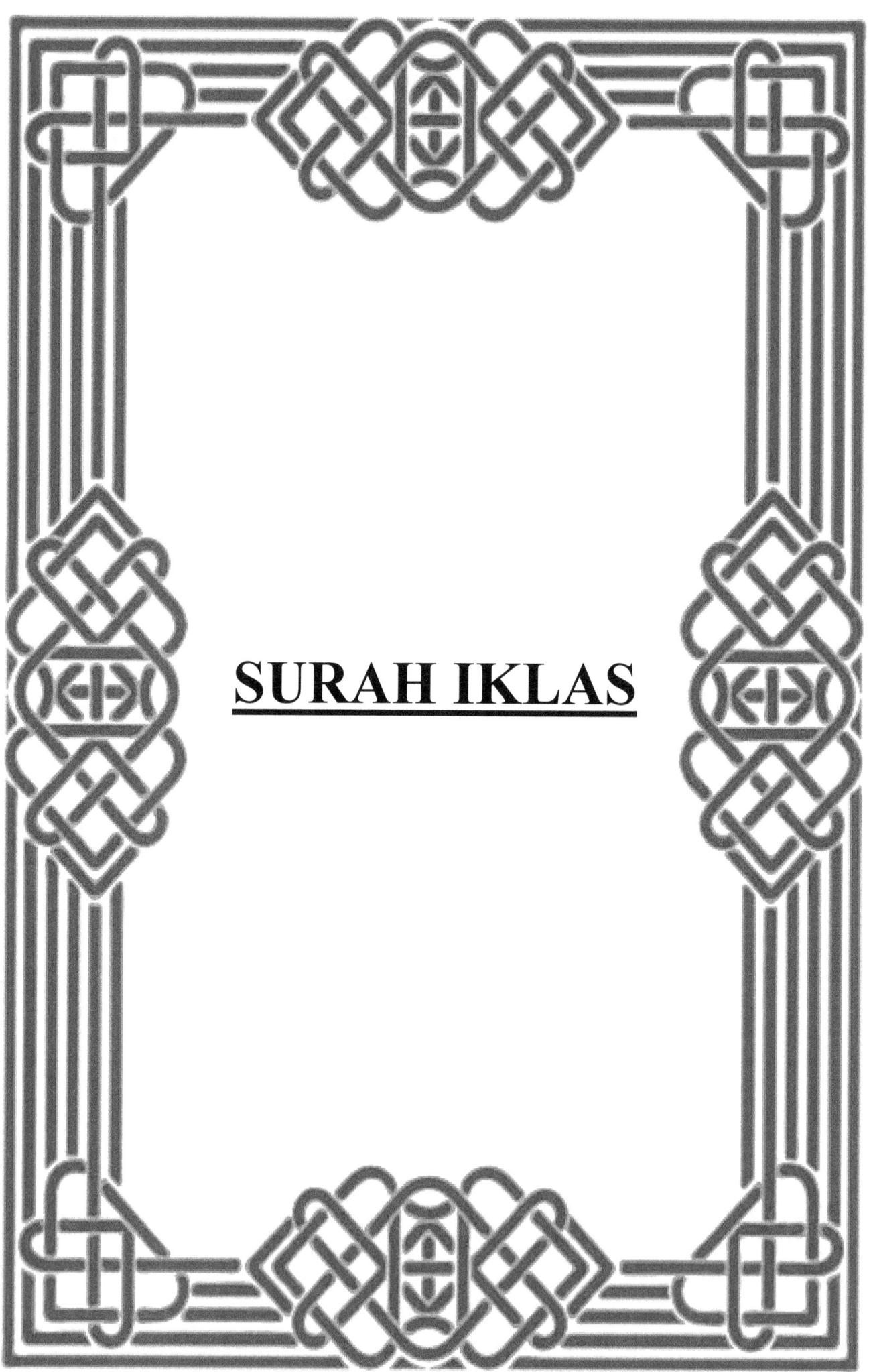

SURAH IKLAS

SURAH IKLAS

Bismillahi ar-Rahmani ar-Raheem

Verse 1

Qul huwal laahu ahad

"Say, 'He is Allah, [who is] One,'"

- Tafseer: This verse commands the Prophet Muhammad to proclaim that Allah is "Ahad," meaning singular and unique. The term "Ahad" goes beyond numerical oneness and emphasizes the absolute uniqueness and incomparability of Allah. He is not only one in being but also in His attributes and essence.

Verse 2

Allah hus-samad

"Allah, the Eternal Refuge."

- Tafseer: The term "As-Samad" is often translated as "The Eternal Refuge" or "The Self-Sufficient Master." It signifies that Allah is the one upon whom all creation depends, yet He depends on none. He is the ultimate source of support and sustenance, embodying completeness and perfection without need.

Verse 3

Lam yalid wa lam yoolad

"He neither begets nor is born,"

- Tafseer: This verse negates the possibility of Allah having offspring or being born. It refutes any form of polytheism or anthropomorphism that attributes human-like qualities to Allah. By stating that Allah does not beget, it denies the idea of lineage or descendants, and by stating He is not born, it affirms His eternal existence without beginning.

Verse 4

Wa lam yakul-lahoo kufuwan aha

"Nor is there to Him any equivalent."

- Tafseer: This verse emphasizes the unmatched and unparalleled nature of Allah. There is nothing and no one that can be compared to Him in any aspect. This affirms the concept of Tawhid, the oneness of Allah, and underscores the futility of associating partners with Him or likening Him to His creation.

Overall Reflection:

Surah Al-Ikhlas is a powerful declaration of monotheism, encapsulating the essence of Tawhid in just four verses. It serves as a clear refutation of polytheism, idolatry, and any belief systems that attribute partners or equals to Allah. The surah is often recited for its profound meaning and is considered equivalent to one-third of the Quran in terms of its significance in conveying the core message of Islam.

The surah also provides comfort and assurance to believers, reminding them of Allah's unique and all-encompassing nature. It reinforces faith in Allah's singularity and invites reflection on His eternal and self-sufficient qualities.

Surah Al-Ikhlas is a profound and concise chapter of the Quran that encapsulates the essence of monotheism in Islam.

Here are some reflections on the surah and the lessons it imparts:

1. Uncompromising Monotheism: Surah Al-Ikhlas is a powerful affirmation of Tawhid, the oneness of Allah. It emphasizes that Allah is unique and singular, with no partners, associates, or equals. This uncompromising monotheism is central to Islamic theology and serves as a foundation for the faith of believers.
2. Divine Attributes: The surah highlights key attributes of Allah, including His uniqueness (Ahad) and His role as the Eternal Refuge (As-Samad). These attributes remind believers of Allah's complete self-sufficiency and independence. He is the one upon whom all creation depends, yet He depends on none.
3. Rejection of Anthropomorphism: By stating that Allah "neither begets nor is born," the surah clearly refutes any anthropomorphic conceptions of the divine. It rejects the idea of Allah having offspring or a lineage, emphasizing His eternal and uncreated nature. This serves as a refutation of beliefs that attribute human-like qualities to Allah.
4. Incomparable Nature of Allah: The declaration that "there is none comparable to Him" reinforces the idea that Allah is beyond comparison and cannot be likened to anything or anyone. This invites believers to reflect on the transcendence and majesty of Allah, recognizing that His essence and attributes are beyond human comprehension.
5. Simplicity and Depth: Despite its brevity, Surah Al-Ikhlas conveys profound theological concepts in simple and clear language. This simplicity, coupled with its depth, makes the surah accessible to all believers, regardless of their level of understanding. It serves as a reminder that the core of Islamic belief is both profound and straightforward.
6. Spiritual Assurance: The surah offers spiritual assurance to believers by emphasizing Allah's all-encompassing nature. It provides comfort in knowing that the one they worship is the ultimate source of support and refuge. This assurance strengthens faith and encourages reliance on Allah in all aspects of life.

7. Encouragement for Reflection: Surah Al-Ikhlas invites believers to reflect on the nature of Allah and their relationship with Him. It encourages introspection about one's understanding of Tawhid and how it manifests in daily life. By internalizing the message of the surah, believers can deepen their connection with Allah and align their actions with the principles of Islamic monotheism.

Overall, Surah Al-Ikhlas serves as a timeless reminder of the core tenet of Islam: the oneness and uniqueness of Allah. It calls for unwavering devotion, reflection on divine attributes, and a rejection of any beliefs that compromise the purity of monotheism.

SUMMARY OF
SURAH AL-IKHLAS-SURAH 112

Surah Al-Ikhlas, the 112th chapter of the Quran, is a succinct and powerful declaration of Islamic monotheism. Comprising only four verses, it encapsulates the essence of Tawhid, the fundamental concept of the oneness and uniqueness of Allah. The surah is often recited for its profound meaning and is considered a cornerstone of Islamic theology, emphasizing the belief in Allah as the singular, incomparable, and eternal deity.

The surah begins by commanding the Prophet Muhammad to proclaim the oneness of Allah, using the term "Ahad" to denote His unique singularity. This term signifies not just numerical oneness, but also the absolute indivisibility and incomparability of Allah. The surah continues by describing Allah as "As-Samad," often translated as "The Eternal Refuge" or "The Self-Sufficient Master." This highlights Allah's role as the ultimate source of support and sustenance, upon whom all creation depends, while He Himself is independent and self-sufficient.

Further, Surah Al-Ikhlas negates any notion of Allah having offspring or being born, emphasizing His eternal existence without beginning or end. It refutes any anthropomorphic conceptions of Allah and underscores His transcendence above human attributes. The surah concludes by affirming that there is nothing and no one comparable to Allah, reinforcing the idea that He is beyond any likeness or equivalence.

Overall, Surah Al-Ikhlas serves as a clear refutation of polytheism and idolatry, reaffirming the core Islamic belief in the oneness of Allah. It is a testament to the purity and simplicity of faith in Islam, offering comfort and assurance to believers through its emphasis on Allah's unique and all-encompassing nature. The surah invites reflection on the divine attributes of Allah and encourages adherence to the principle of Tawhid as the foundation of Islamic belief.

SURAH IKHLAS (SURAH 111)

Questions

1. What is the primary theme of Surah Al-Ikhlas?
2. How many verses are there in Surah Al-Ikhlas?
3. What does the term "Ahad" in the first verse signify about Allah?
4. What does "As-Samad" mean, and what does it tell us about Allah's attributes?
5. How does Surah Al-Ikhlas address the concept of Allah having offspring or being born?
6. Why is it significant that there is "none comparable" to Allah, as stated in the surah?
7. How does Surah Al-Ikhlas refute polytheism and anthropomorphism?
8. In what way is Surah Al-Ikhlas considered equivalent to one-third of the Quran?
9. How can the teachings of Surah Al-Ikhlas be applied in a believer's daily life?
10. What comfort and assurance does Surah Al-Ikhlas provide to believers?

These questions are designed to engage students in thoughtful reflection on the key themes and theological concepts presented in Surah Al-Ikhlas. They encourage deeper understanding and personal application of the surah's message.

Answers

1. What is the primary theme of Surah Al-Ikhlas?
   - The primary theme of Surah Al-Ikhlas is the affirmation of Tawhid, the oneness and uniqueness of Allah. It emphasizes that Allah is singular, self-sufficient, and incomparable to anything else.

2. How many verses are there in Surah Al-Ikhlas?
   - Surah Al-Ikhlas consists of four verses.

3. What does the term "Ahad" in the first verse signify about Allah?
   - The term "Ahad" signifies that Allah is unique and singular in His essence and attributes. It emphasizes that there is nothing like Allah, and He is one without partners or equals.

4. What does "As-Samad" mean, and what does it tell us about Allah's attributes?
   - "As-Samad" means "The Eternal Refuge" or "The Self-Sufficient Master." It tells us that Allah is the ultimate source of support and sustenance, upon whom all creation depends, but He Himself is independent and needs nothing.

5. How does Surah Al-Ikhlas address the concept of Allah having offspring or being born?
   - Surah Al-Ikhlas explicitly states that Allah "neither begets nor is born," refuting any notion that Allah has offspring or a lineage. This emphasizes His eternal and uncreated nature, distinct from creation.

6. Why is it significant that there is "none comparable" to Allah, as stated in the surah?
   - The statement that there is "none comparable" to Allah underscores His transcendence and uniqueness. It affirms that no one and nothing can be likened to Allah, reinforcing the purity of monotheism and the futility of associating partners with Him.

7. How does Surah Al-Ikhlas refute polytheism and anthropomorphism?
   - Surah Al-Ikhlas refutes polytheism by affirming Allah's oneness and uniqueness, denying any partners or equals. It refutes anthropomorphism by stating that Allah does not beget or is born, rejecting any human-like attributes or relationships.

8. In what way is Surah Al-Ikhlas considered equivalent to one-third of the Quran?
   - Surah Al-Ikhlas is considered equivalent to one-third of the Quran in terms of its theological significance. It succinctly encapsulates the core principle of Tawhid, which is a foundational concept in Islam and permeates one-third of the Quran's teachings.

9. How can the teachings of Surah Al-Ikhlas be applied in a believer's daily life?
   - Believers can apply the teachings of Surah Al-Ikhlas by maintaining a clear and unwavering belief in Allah's oneness, relying on Him as the ultimate source of support, and rejecting any form of idolatry or associating partners with Him in their actions and worship.

10. What comfort and assurance does Surah Al-Ikhlas provide to believers?
    - Surah Al-Ikhlas provides comfort and assurance by reminding believers of Allah's unique and all-encompassing nature. It reassures them that the one they worship is the eternal refuge and source of all support, encouraging trust and reliance on Allah in all circumstances.

These answers aim to provide a comprehensive understanding of Surah Al-Ikhlas and its significance in Islamic theology and daily practice.

Multiple-Choice Questions

1. What is the primary theme of Surah Al-Ikhlas?

    - A) The importance of charity

    - B) The oneness and uniqueness of Allah

    - C) The rewards of patience

    - D) The beauty of creation

2. How many verses are there in Surah Al-Ikhlas?

    - A) Two

    - B) Three

    - C) Four

    - D) Five

3. What does the term "Al-Ikhlas" mean?

    - A) The generosity

    - B) The sincerity or purity

    - C) The patience

    - D) The charity

4. What does the surah say about Allah's nature?

    - A) Allah is one and has no partners

    - B) Allah is many and has different forms

    - C) Allah is dependent on others

    - D) Allah is created

5. According to Surah Al-Ikhlas, what is unique about Allah?

    - A) He is one of many gods

    - B) He begets and is begotten

    - C) He is eternal and has no equals

    - D) He has physical limitations

6. What is the significance of Surah Al-Ikhlas in Islamic teachings?

    - A) It is considered equivalent to one-third of the Quran in terms of its message

    - B) It is rarely recited in prayers

    - C) It is only applicable during Ramadan

    - D) It emphasizes the importance of wealth

7. How does Surah Al-Ikhlas describe Allah's dependence on creation?

    - A) He depends on all creation

    - B) He needs assistance from angels

    - C) He is self-sufficient and independent

    - D) He relies on human worship

Answers

1. *Answer:* B) The oneness and uniqueness of Allah
2. *Answer:* C) Four
3. *Answer:* B) The sincerity or purity
4. *Answer:* A) Allah is one and has no partners
5. *Answer:* C) He is eternal and has no equals
6. *Answer:* A) It is considered equivalent to one-third of the Quran in terms of its message
7. *Answer:* C) He is self-sufficient and independent

These questions and answers can be used for quizzes, educational discussions, or self-study to enhance understanding of Surah Al-Ikhlas.

SURAH FALAK

SURAH FALAK

Bismillahi ar-Rahmani ar-Raheem

Verse 1

Qul a'oozu bi rabbil-falaq

"Say, 'I seek refuge in the Lord of daybreak'"

- Tafseer: This verse instructs the Prophet Muhammad to declare seeking refuge in Allah, specifically as the "Lord of daybreak." The term "daybreak" symbolizes the emergence of light from darkness, representing hope and the dispelling of evil. By invoking Allah as the Lord of daybreak, the verse emphasizes His power to bring relief and protection from all forms of harm.

Verse 2

Min sharri maa khalaq

"From the evil of that which He created"

- Tafseer: This verse acknowledges that while Allah is the creator of everything, within creation there can exist elements of evil or harm. The verse seeks protection from any potential harm that may arise from any aspect of creation, whether it be natural phenomena, living beings, or other forces that could cause distress or injury.

Verse 3

Wa min sharri ghaasiqin izaa waqab

"And from the evil of darkness when it settles"

- Tafseer: Here, the verse seeks protection from the dangers associated with darkness. Darkness can be both literal, as in the fear and uncertainty of night, and metaphorical, representing ignorance, confusion, or malice. It highlights the vulnerabilities that people may experience when enveloped in darkness and the importance of seeking Allah's protection from these uncertainties.

Verse 4

Wa min sharrin-naffaa-saati fil 'uqad

"And from the evil of the blowers in knots"

- Tafseer: This verse addresses seeking protection from those who practice witchcraft or sorcery, specifically those who blow on knots as part of casting spells. Such practices are seen as attempts to manipulate or harm others through supernatural means. The verse underscores the need to rely on Allah for protection against such malevolent intentions and actions.

Verse 5

Wa min sharri haasidin izaa hasad

"And from the evil of an envier when he envies."

- Tafseer: The final verse seeks protection from the harm caused by envy and jealousy. Envy can lead to destructive behaviors and intentions, as an envier may wish harm upon others due to their jealousy. This verse reminds believers of the insidious nature of envy and the importance of seeking Allah's refuge to protect against its effects.

Overall Reflection:

Surah Al-Falak highlights the various forms of evil and harm that can affect individuals and emphasizes the necessity of seeking Allah's protection. It teaches believers to recognize the potential dangers in the world, both seen and unseen, and to place their trust in Allah's ability to safeguard them. The surah serves as a powerful reminder of the importance of divine reliance and the comprehensive protection that Allah provides against all forms of malevolence.

Surah Al-Falak offers profound reflections on the nature of seeking divine protection and the recognition of various forms of harm that can affect individuals. Here are some reflections on this surah:

1. Reliance on Divine Protection: The surah emphasizes the importance of seeking refuge in Allah, highlighting the need for divine protection against all forms of evil. This reliance underscores the belief that true security and safety come from Allah alone, encouraging believers to turn to Him in times of fear and uncertainty.
2. Symbolism of Daybreak: By referring to Allah as the "Lord of daybreak," the surah uses the imagery of dawn to symbolize hope and the overcoming of darkness. This reflects the belief that just as light dispels darkness, Allah's protection can dispel fear and harm, offering reassurance and comfort to believers.
3. Awareness of Potential Harms: The surah identifies specific sources of harm, including the general evil within creation, darkness, witchcraft, and envy. This encourages believers to be aware of the various threats in the world, both tangible and intangible, and to seek protection from them. It highlights the comprehensive nature of potential harms and the need for vigilance.
4. Condemnation of Malice and Envy: The mention of witchcraft and envy points to the destructive power of malicious intentions. Envy, in particular, is highlighted as a harmful emotion that can lead

to negative actions. This reflection serves as a warning against harboring such emotions and encourages believers to purify their hearts and intentions.
5. Interconnectedness of Physical and Spiritual Realms: The surah underscores the interplay between the physical and spiritual realms, where unseen forces can have tangible effects on individuals. This reminds believers of the complexity of creation and the importance of seeking protection beyond just the physical world.
6. Encouragement of Humility: By seeking refuge in Allah, believers acknowledge their own vulnerabilities and limitations. This act of turning to Allah for protection fosters humility and reinforces the understanding that human strength is limited without divine assistance.
7. Daily Practice of Seeking Refuge: Surah Al-Falak is often recited as part of daily prayers and supplications, reinforcing the habit of seeking Allah's protection regularly. This practice serves as a constant reminder of the need for divine guidance and support in navigating the challenges of life.

SUMMARY OF SURAH FALAK. SURAH 113

Surah Al-Falak, the 113th chapter of the Quran, is a short surah consisting of five verses. It is part of the "Mu'awwidhatayn," which, along with Surah An-Nas, is recited for seeking protection. The word "Al-Falak" translates to "The Daybreak" or "The Dawn," highlighting the theme of seeking refuge from evil as light overcomes darkness.

The surah begins with a command to the Prophet Muhammad to seek refuge in the Lord of the daybreak. This sets the tone for the rest of the surah, emphasizing reliance on Allah for protection. The imagery of daybreak signifies hope and the dispelling of darkness, both literal and metaphorical.

The subsequent verses specify various sources of evil from which protection is sought. These include the evil of what Allah has created, the darkness as it approaches, and the harm caused by practitioners of witchcraft who blow on knots to cast spells. Lastly, it seeks refuge from the envy of those who harbour jealousy.

Surah Al-Falak serves as a reminder of the various unseen and seen harms that can affect an individual and underscores the importance of seeking divine protection. It teaches believers the necessity of turning to Allah for safeguarding against all forms of malevolence, encouraging a sense of reliance and trust in divine power to overcome adversity.

SURAH FALAQ (SURAH 113)

Questions

1. What is the primary purpose of Surah Al-Falak?
2. How many verses are there in Surah Al-Falak?
3. What does the term "Lord of daybreak" signify in the context of the surah?
4. From what types of evil does Surah Al-Falak seek protection?
5. Why is seeking refuge from the evil of darkness significant?
6. How does the surah address the threat of witchcraft or sorcery?
7. What is the significance of seeking protection from envy in Surah Al-Falak?
8. How can Surah Al-Falak be applied in a believer's daily life?
9. What does Surah Al-Falak teach about the relationship between the physical and spiritual realms?
10. Why is it important to regularly seek refuge in Allah as taught in Surah Al-Falak?

Answers

1. The primary purpose of Surah Al-Falak is to seek refuge in Allah from various forms of evil and harm, both seen and unseen. It emphasizes the need for divine protection.

2. Surah Al-Falak consists of five verses.

3. The term "Lord of daybreak" signifies the power of Allah to bring light and dispel darkness, symbolizing hope and protection against evil.

4. Surah Al-Falak seeks protection from the evil of what Allah has created, the darkness as it settles, witchcraft or sorcery, and the envy of those who harbor jealousy.

5. Seeking refuge from the evil of darkness is significant because darkness can bring fear and uncertainty, both literally and metaphorically, representing ignorance or malice.

6. The surah addresses the threat of witchcraft by seeking protection from those who blow on knots, a practice associated with casting spells, emphasizing reliance on Allah for safeguarding against such harm.

7. Seeking protection from envy is significant because envy can lead to harmful intentions and actions. It highlights the destructive potential of jealousy and the need for divine protection.

8. Surah Al-Falak can be applied in a believer's daily life by reciting it regularly to seek Allah's protection against various harms and maintaining awareness of potential threats.

9. Surah Al-Falak teaches that the physical and spiritual realms are interconnected, with unseen forces potentially affecting individuals, emphasizing the need for protection beyond the physical world.

10. Regularly seeking refuge in Allah is important as it fosters humility, acknowledges human limitations, and reinforces reliance on divine support in facing life's challenges.

These questions and answers are designed to facilitate understanding and reflection on the key themes and messages of Surah Al-Falak.

Multiple Choice Questions

Multiple-choice questions on Surah Al-Falak, along with their options:

1. What is the primary theme of Surah Al-Falak?

    - A) The importance of charity

    - B) Seeking refuge from various forms of evil

    - C) The rewards of patience

    - D) The story of Prophet Ibrahim

2. How many verses are there in Surah Al-Falak?

    - A) Three

    - B) Four

    - C) Five

    - D) Six

3. What does "Lord of daybreak" symbolize in the surah?

    - A) The beginning of a new year

    - B) The power of Allah to bring light and dispel darkness

    - C) The significance of early morning prayers

    - D) The end of times

4. From what type of evil does Surah Al-Falak seek protection?

    - A) The evil of what Allah has created

    - B) The evil of darkness as it settles

    - C) The evil of those who blow on knots (witchcraft)

    - D) The evil of an envier when he envies

    - E) All of the above

5. Why is seeking refuge from the evil of darkness significant in the surah?

    - A) Darkness is always harmful

    - B) Darkness represents fear and uncertainty, both literally and metaphorically

    - C) Darkness is associated with wealth

    - D) Darkness is a time for prayer

6. What practice is associated with the "blowers in knots" mentioned in the surah?

   - A) Praying at dawn

   - B) Casting spells through witchcraft

   - C) Tying friendship bracelets

   - D) Writing poetry

7. What is highlighted by seeking protection from envy in Surah Al-Falak?

   - A) Envy is a minor issue

   - B) Envy has the potential to lead to harmful actions and intentions

   - C) Envy is beneficial for growth

   - D) Envy is only about material wealth

   These questions are designed to assess understanding of the key themes and messages of Surah Al-Falak.

Answers

1. *Answer:* B) Seeking refuge from various forms of evil
2. *Answer:* C) Five
3. *Answer:* B) The power of Allah to bring light and dispel darkness
4. *Answer:* E) All of the above
5. *Answer:* B) Darkness represents fear and uncertainty, both literally and metaphorically
6. *Answer:* B) Casting spells through witchcraft
7. *Answer:* B) Envy has the potential to lead to harmful actions and intentions

SURAH AN-NAS

SURAH AN-NAS

Bismillahi ar-Rahmani ar-Raheem

Verse 1

Qul a'oozu birabbin naas

"Say, 'I seek refuge in the Lord of mankind,'"

- This verse instructs the Prophet Muhammad, and by extension all believers, to seek protection in Allah, who is the Lord of all people. It emphasizes Allah's sovereignty and the importance of turning to Him for refuge.

Verse 2

Malikin naas

"The King of mankind,"

- Allah is described as the King, highlighting His supreme authority and control over all creation. This reinforces the idea that He is the ultimate protector and ruler.

Verse 3

Ilaahin naas

"The Allah of mankind,"

- This verse identifies Allah as the Allah to be worshipped, underscoring His divine nature and the duty of humans to direct their worship solely to Him. It also emphasizes that Allah alone is worthy of worship and devotion.

Verse 4

Min sharril waswaasil khannaas

"From the evil of the whisperer who withdraws,"

- The "whisperer" refers to Satan and other evil forces that attempt to lead humans astray with evil suggestions and doubts. These whispers are subtle and can cause harm if not protected against.

Verse 5

Allazee yuwaswisu fee sudoorin naas

"Who whispers in the hearts of mankind,"

- This verse explains that these whispers occur within the hearts, meaning they are internal and can influence thoughts and behaviors. It highlights the need for vigilance and spiritual awareness.

Verse 6

Minal jinnati wannaas *(End Juz 30, Juz Amma)*

"Of jinn and mankind."

- The source of these whispers can be both jinn and human beings, indicating that the influence can come from supernatural entities as well as other people. This serves as a reminder that believers must be cautious of both visible and invisible threats.

Overall, Surah An-Nas teaches the importance of seeking Allah's protection from all forms of evil, especially those that are not immediately apparent. It calls on believers to recognize Allah's ultimate authority and to rely on Him for safety and guidance. Reciting this surah is a practice to ward off evil influences and to reaffirm one's faith in Allah's power and mercy.

Reflecting on Surah An-Nas provides valuable insights into its spiritual and practical significance for Muslims. Here are some reflections on this profound chapter:

1. Acknowledgment of Human Vulnerability: Surah An-Nas highlights the inherent vulnerability of human beings to external and internal influences. By seeking refuge in Allah, believers acknowledge their need for divine protection against forces that can lead them astray. This recognition fosters humility and dependence on Allah.

Overall, Surah Al-Falak provides a powerful reminder of the importance of divine protection, the reality of various threats, and the necessity of maintaining spiritual awareness and humility. It encourages believers to place their trust in Allah and seek His refuge in all aspects of life.

SUMMARY OF SURAH AN-NAS. SURAH 114

Surah An-Nas is the 114th and final chapter (surah) of the Quran, consisting of six verses. It is a Meccan surah, meaning it was revealed in Mecca. The surah emphasizes seeking refuge in Allah from the evils whispered by Satan and other harmful entities. It calls upon Allah using three of His attributes: Lord, King, and Allah of mankind. The surah serves as a reminder of the importance of seeking divine protection against spiritual and worldly harm, particularly from the deceptive whispers that can lead people astray. It is often recited for protection and is paired with Surah Al-Falaq for this purpose.

SURAH NAS (SURAH 114)

Questions

1. What is the primary theme of Surah An-Nas?
2. How many verses are there in Surah An-Nas?
3. What does the term "An-Nas" mean, and why is the surah named after it?
4. Which three attributes of Allah are mentioned at the beginning of Surah An-Nas?
5. What type of protection does the surah seek from Allah?
6. From what specific evil does Surah An-Nas ask for protection?
7. Who is described as whispering into the hearts of people according to Surah An-Nas?
8. How does Surah An-Nas emphasize the concept of seeking refuge in Allah?
9. What is the significance of the surah being placed at the end of the Quran?
10. How can the teachings of Surah An-Nas be applied to contemporary life to promote spiritual resilience?

Answers

1. What is the primary theme of Surah An-Nas?
   - The primary theme is seeking protection in Allah from the evil of external and internal influences, particularly the whispering of the devils.

2. How many verses are there in Surah An-Nas?
   - Surah An-Nas consists of six verses.

3. What does the term "An-Nas" mean, and why is the surah named after it?
   - "An-Nas" means "mankind." The surah is named after it because it addresses the protection of mankind from evil influences.

4. Which three attributes of Allah are mentioned at the beginning of Surah An-Nas?
   - The three attributes are: Lord of mankind, King of mankind, and God of mankind.

5. What type of protection does the surah seek from Allah?
   - The surah seeks protection from the evil of whisperings, particularly from the devils and those who whisper evil into the hearts.

6. From what specific evil does Surah An-Nas ask for protection?
   - It asks for protection from the evil of the whisperer who withdraws after whispering.

7. Who is described as whispering into the hearts of people according to Surah An-Nas?
   - The whisperer is described as the devil, who whispers evil into the hearts of people.

8. How does Surah An-Nas emphasize the concept of seeking refuge in Allah?
   - The surah emphasizes seeking refuge in Allah by invoking His attributes as the ultimate protector and guardian of mankind.

9. What is the significance of the surah being placed at the end of the Quran?
   - Placing it at the end of the Quran highlights the importance of seeking Allah's protection and guidance as a continuous need for spiritual resilience.

10. How can the teachings of Surah An-Nas be applied to contemporary life to promote spiritual resilience?
    - The teachings encourage individuals to constantly seek Allah's protection against negative influences and to remain vigilant against internal and external temptations.

These questions and answers can be used for educational purposes, study sessions, or discussions to enhance understanding of Surah An-Nas.

Multiple Choice Questions

1. What is the primary theme of Surah An-Nas?

    - A) The rewards of charity

    - B) Seeking protection from the evil of external and internal influences

    - C) The importance of fasting

    - D) The creation of the universe

2. How many verses are there in Surah An-Nas?

    - A) Four

    - B) Five

    - C) Six

    - D) Seven

3. What does the term "An-Nas" mean?

    - A) The animals

    - B) The mountains

    - C) The heavens

    - D) Mankind

4. Which three attributes of Allah are mentioned at the beginning of Surah An-Nas?

    - A) Creator, Sustainer, Destroyer

    - B) Lord of mankind, King of mankind, God of mankind

    - C) Merciful, Compassionate, Just

    - D) Powerful, Wise, Eternal

5. From what specific evil does Surah An-Nas ask for protection?

    - A) Natural disasters

    - B) Poverty and hunger

    - C) The evil of the whisperer who withdraws

    - D) Illness and disease

6. Who is described as whispering into the hearts of people according to Surah An-Nas?

    - A) Angels

    - B) The whisperer, identified as the devil

    - C) Prophets

    - D) Scholars

7. How does Surah An-Nas emphasize the concept of seeking refuge in Allah?

    - A) By recounting stories of past prophets

    - B) By invoking Allah's attributes as the ultimate protector and guardian of mankind

    - C) By emphasizing the importance of wealth

    - D) By listing the benefits of charity

8. What is the significance of Surah An-Nas being placed at the end of the Quran?

    - A) It emphasizes the historical context of the revelation

    - B) It highlights the importance of seeking Allah's protection and guidance as a continuous need

    - C) It signifies the end of the Prophet's mission

    - D) It marks the completion of the Quran's narrative

Answers

1. *Answer:* B) Seeking protection from the evil of external and internal influences
2. *Answer:* C) Six
3. *Answer:* D) Mankind
4. *Answer:* B) Lord of mankind, King of mankind, God of mankind
5. *Answer:* C) The evil of the whisperer who withdraws
6. *Answer:* B) The whisperer, identified as the devil
7. *Answer:* B) By invoking Allah's attributes as the ultimate protector and guardian of mankind
8. *Answer:* B) It highlights the importance of seeking Allah's protection and guidance as a continuous need

These questions and answers can be used for quizzes, educational discussions, or self-study to enhance understanding of Surah An-Nas.

www.ingramcontent.com/pod-product-compliance
Lightning Source LLC
Chambersburg PA
CBHW081102070526
44584CB00021B/3169